D1199129

OAXACA AL GUSTO

 THE WILLIAM & BETTYE NOWLIN SERIES
in Art, History, and Culture of the Western Hemisphere

DIANA KENNEDY

Oaxaca al Gusto

AN INFINITE GASTRONOMY

University of Texas Press   Austin

< Oaxacan utensils/Michael Calderwood

Cover photo by Diana Kennedy

Copyright © 2010 by Diana Kennedy
All rights reserved
Printed in Malaysia
Fourth printing, 2018

Requests for permission to reproduce material from this work
should be sent to:
    Permissions
    University of Texas Press
    P.O. Box 7819
    Austin, TX 78713–7819
    utpress.utexas.edu/rp-form

∞ The paper used in this book meets the minimum requirements of
ANSI/NISO Z39.48–1992 (R1997) (Permanence of Paper).

Originally published in Spanish as *Oaxaca al gusto: el mundo infinito de su
gastronomía,* by la Universidad Metropolitana de Monterrey, Monterrey,
Nuevo León, Mexico, © 2008.

LIBRARY OF CONGRESS CATALOGING-IN-PUBLICATION DATA
Kennedy, Diana.
    [Oaxaca al gusto, el mundo infinito de su gastronomía. English]
    Oaxaca al gusto, an infinite gastronomy / by Diana Kennedy. — 1st ed.
    p.   cm. — (The William and Bettye Nowlin series in art, history, and
culture of the Western Hemisphere)
    Includes index.
    ISBN 978-0-292-72266-8 (cloth : alk. paper)
    1. Cookery, Mexican. 2. Cookery—Mexico—Oaxaca. 3. Oaxaca
(Mexico)—Social life and customs. I. Title.
    TX716.M4K46813   2010
    641.5972—dc22   2010000260

    doi:10.7560/722668

Contents

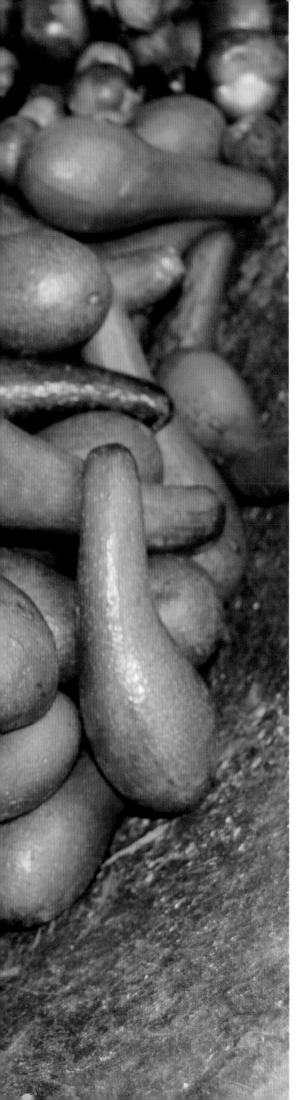

Acknowledgments

This book could never have been written without the generous help of so many people throughout the years 1994–2005. First, I would like to thank all the wonderful Oaxacan cooks who welcomed me into their kitchens and shared their knowledge so generously and patiently, and without whose cooperation this book would never have come to fruition. They have been named along with their recipes.

I would like to thank Señora Graciela Cervantes and Arquitecta Claudina López for their generous help, both moral and financial, at different stages of the research. I am so grateful to all those friends who have given me such generous hospitality, either in my constant journeys to and from Oaxaca, in the city itself, or elsewhere around the state, including Licenciado Carlos and the late Virginia Barrios in Metepec, Señores Alejandro and Renata Danon in Tepoztlán, Licenciado Frederic and Wendy Laffan in Cuernavaca. In the City of Oaxaca: Señora Pina Hamilton de Córdova, Señora Beatriz Hamilton de García, Licenciada Amelia Lara, Señores Rodolfo and Norma Ogarrio, Licenciadas María Teresa and Rosalba Vargas. In Cuicatlán: Licenciado Diódoro Carrasco Altamirano and *la* Maestra Gloria Odriozola Pacheco. In Huautla de Jiménez: Señora Blanca Vda. de García and the Señoritas Terán Carrera. In La Esperanza: Señor Eusebio López and his wife. In La Merced de Potrero: Señora Agustina Santiago Ramírez. In Tehuantepec: Arquitecto Gerardo García of the Hotel Calli. In Tezoatlán: Señores Josué and Aldegunda Andrade. In Tuxtepec: Señora Eva Sacré de Cué. In Zicatela: Señores Rodolfo and Norma Ogarrio and the late Señorita Josie Smith.

There were so many people that I would constantly telephone to confirm the details of an ingredient, a recipe, or a tradition, and I am especially grateful to Señora Blanca Vda. de Señor Renato García and Señores Valente and Aurora Paraguirre in Huautla de Jiménez; Señora Clementina Baños in Tamazulapan; Señor Alfonso García Villagómez from Yododeñe; Señor Manuel García Isidro and his sister Señora Irma García in Tuxtepec; and in the City of Oaxaca, Señora Kelly Bolaños and Señora Emilia Arroyo, among many, many others.

I would like to thank the staff of the University of Texas Press for publishing *Oaxaca al Gusto* in English translation, and following, but embellishing, the original design. I would particularly like to thank the former director, Joanna Hitchcock; editor Casey Kittrell, for understanding *Oaxaca al Gusto* in the first place and immediately agreeing to publish it; manuscript editor Victoria Davis; copy editor par excellence Nancy Warrington; designer Ellen McKie; and publicity director Colleen Devine.

I would also like to thank Dr. Marcus Winter and Fray Eugenio M. Torres for their invaluable contributions to the book. Botanists Bob Bye and his wife, Edelmira Linares, of the Universidad Nacional Autónoma de México (UNAM), Mexico's National University, have always been on hand to answer my queries; to them, and especially to ethnobotanist Gary Martin, who opened the door to what became my particular interest in the wild foods of the Sierra Juárez and La Chinantla Alta, my sincere thanks for their unfailing help and friendship. My thanks also to Pesach Lubinsky, of the University of California at Davis, who enlightened me on the vanilla of Usila, and a very special thank-you to Señora Pina Hamilton de Córdova for her constant help through the many years of research for this book.

Queso fresco (fresh cheese)/Diana Kennedy

Introduction

Diana Southwood Kennedy—August 26, 2008

It was about 1994 that I was first asked to write a book for the governor of Oaxaca on the traditional foods of that state, but for various reasons, politics among them, the project was never realized. Two more frustrating attempts were abandoned, and it did not get written until about 2003, when I received a definite commitment from a Mexican publisher for a joint project with a U.S. publisher. However, when it was apparent that the style and content of the book were being severely compromised, I broke off negotiations and retrieved my material. Another prolonged delay ensued before I was able to find a publisher that was willing to include the text and recipes from the indigenous areas and not just the more familiar material illustrated with the usual predictably glamorous photographs.

Trying to record the ethnic foods as well as the more sophisticated recipes from the urban centers presented an enormous challenge and responsibility. Oaxaca is the most mountainous and diverse state of Mexico, with many different cultural and linguistic groups, often living in areas difficult to access, and with an incredible biodiversity. Like many authors before me, I am sure that if I had known what it would entail to travel almost constantly through the year, and often uncomfortably, to research, record, photograph, and then cook and eat over three hundred recipes, I might never have had the courage to start the project in the first place.

I am not an academic, historian, anthropologist, or botanist, but just an adventurous cook and a lover of the natural world who delights in the experience of traveling to discover and taste foods, some of which I had only heard about, but many that I was yet to discover in this infinite world of Oaxacan gastronomy. It was an enormous challenge to try to record in words and images these little-known foods, both wild and cultivated, the way they were prepared, and the part they play in the daily or festive life of the communities I visited.

Of course, it would take various volumes and many years to do full justice to this fascinating subject, as well as contributions from anthropologists, archaeologists, botanists, and linguists (a pity that local gastronomy does not play a part in their professional training). Nevertheless, in these pages I have attempted to relate something of what I found in my many years of wandering throughout the state of Oaxaca. I realize that there are notable omissions of the specific foods of the Mixe, Zoque, and Amuzgo areas, for example. I only hope that the many wonderful cooks whose recipes I have not been able to include will forgive me. They may not agree with my choices (there are always disagreements and rivalries among cooks about ingredients, quantities, and methods), but I have tried to include the most representative recipes for the foods that I have eaten and cooked in Oaxaca since my first visit there in 1965.

Those who do not know Oaxaca outside the popular tourist areas may perhaps get a broader view of the enormous gastronomic wealth that plays a part in the daily, religious, and festive life of Oaxacans of different cultures and economic levels.

Apart from all the intense work and difficult travel over many years, I have been immensely enriched, not only by discovering the incredible natural beauty of the countryside but by getting to know Oaxacans from all walks of life. Even the most humble have invited me into their kitchens to share and demonstrate their culinary knowledge; they have fed me and given me shelter without a question asked and with a generosity and caring without limits. They are the soul of this book.

About This Book

This book evolved over many years of research traveling to the remote corners of the state of Oaxaca. Since there are pronounced contrasts, both cultural and physical, between the eleven areas into which the book is divided, I decided not to organize the book in conventional chapters—appetizers, soups, main courses, etc.—but to give each area its unique identity and place by first showing the landscapes that identify each geographical area, with the one notable exception of the coast.

A special chapter is devoted to three ingredients that are, without doubt, the mainstays of the Oaxacan regional cuisines: chocolate, corn, and chiles. Chocolate's importance is not because the state is a large producer of cacao—indeed the cacao of Chiapas is preferred—but because of the fascinating ways in which it is prepared. Chocolate is not only a comforting drink but plays an important part in social and religious customs, particularly expressed in the *espumas,* or foams, either served alone, as in *tejate,* or as a frothy topping for *atoles.* Fray Eugenio Torres Torres, an eminent historian of the Dominican Order in Mexico and Latin America, has given us a glimpse of how chocolate has played its part in the conventual history of Oaxaca.

Oaxaca is the birthplace of corn, and not only are the number and variety of races superior to those of any other region of Mexico but, not surprisingly, so also is the number of different ways in which it is prepared, as demonstrated in the following pages. Who better than Amado Leyva to write about corn? An agricultural engineer, he has devoted his recent years to the conservation of the endemic varieties of corn (maize) by sponsoring and encouraging their cultivation, finding markets for their harvests, and demonstrating their individual uses for tortillas, *antojitos,* tamales, and *atoles.*

The local chiles, which I myself have collected and cooked with over many years throughout all the regions of Oaxaca, are unique to each particular area and are, with minor exceptions, cultivated nowhere else. They lend their characteristics to the moles and sauces that define Oaxacan cuisine as one of the most outstanding and colorful in the world.

The photographs, many taken by me *in situ,* do not necessarily illustrate the adjacent recipe but are included to show the multiple ingredients and local cooking methods, respecting the components of each of the indigenous cuisines, many of which are unknown outside their own areas.

Except in the cases of a few well-known general recipes, the persons who shared their culinary wisdom with me are named at the head of each recipe.

The following pages offer a unique journey across this diverse and alluring state to discover, as its subtitle proposes, the "infinite world" of the traditional regional cuisines of Oaxaca. Prepare yourself to savor this fascinating journey.

All translations are my own unless otherwise noted.

Pillars of Oaxacan Cuisine

CHOCOLATE

CORN

CHILES

Chocolate

By Fray Eugenio Martín Torres Torres

In Oaxaca, chocolate is more than history. It signifies the binding of a pueblo to its roots and to the belief that the divine (sacred) purifies, gives new force to, and celebrates life.

Before their evangelization in the sixteenth century, the Zapotecs conceived a life force called *pee*, which translated into Spanish means "wind, breath, spirit." *Pee* created life and movement for man and the things surrounding him. The Zapotecs believe this force shook the earth during an earthquake, created lightning in the heavens, moved the clouds, caused the beating of the heart, and formed the foam on the chocolate served in a gourd.

Perhaps this explains why, during the pre-Hispanic period, chocolate was a drink reserved for nobles, who themselves only drank it on very special occasions. In contrast, the *macehuales*, or plebians, were not allowed to drink it. Their drinks were *atole* and water, and they were only allowed to drink chocolate when the nobles ordered them to do so on particular feast days.

After the Spanish Conquest, chocolate ceased to be a drink exclusive to the nobles, but it commanded a very high price. Nevertheless, over time, it became so popular that even the ancients saw in it one of the causes of an epidemic that decimated the population. It was said that chocolate made "*pesadas las carnes*" (the meat/flesh gross), took away the appetite and all desire to work, and caused the onset of incurable diseases.

The indigenous products most demanded by the Spaniards were gold, silver, cochineal, and cacao. The Spaniards readily embraced the use of the latter, accepting it as money, tribute, medicine, or food, perhaps because of their predilection for sweetmeats and drinks.

The principal markets for the commerce of cacao were in the City of Oaxaca and the town of Tehuantepec. In the former, it was sold or bartered in the large Saturday market, while in Tehuantepec, it was sold not only in the weekly market but by *tehuanas* traveling throughout the surrounding area.

Early in the evangelization of Oaxaca the Dominican friars desacralized the collection of cacao pods and accepted them as a source of energy and a remedy for kidney troubles, pleurisy, stomach problems, sores, and sunstroke.

By the middle of the sixteenth century, the drinking of chocolate was habitual among the clergy, but there were those who criticized this practice because they believed it should be used solely as a remedy. Among the latter was Fray Jordán de Santa Catarina, a missionary in the Sierra Norte, who was against this abuse of chocolate, maintaining that the devil had perverted this "medicine" by the sinful addition of sugar and by drinking it at all hours of the day. Other Dominicans defended chocolate, saying that it provided a source of energy and a consolation to the heart.

There was no lack of chocolate in the fiestas of Santo Domingo, Santa Rosa, and Santo Tomás de Aquino, during which the *frailes* accompanied it with *torteras de pasta*, *soletas* (ladyfingers), *bizcochos* (a type of yeast bread), *pastelones* (cakes), and flowers and figures made of pastry.

In life outside the convents, chocolate was not generally used until the early seventeenth century, when this slightly bitter drink of chocolate dissolved in hot water or milk and sweetened with raw sugar, vanilla, or cinnamon spread across the world. This hot chocolate, more suited to Spanish palates, was of course an adaptation of the indigenous Oaxacan pre-Hispanic drink that was drunk cold. The cacao was mixed with ground maize, or masa, diluted with water, and often sweetened with honey. It was also frequently flavored with chile, herbs, or seeds like those of *achiote*, which added different tones of purple, orange, black, and even white.

In the first decades of the seventeenth century, while hot chocolate was spread and praised throughout the world, the indigenous people of Oaxaca continued to prepare it in their unique ways. For instance, in the second half of the sixteenth century, in Atlatlauca and Malinaltepec, the cacao beans were ground with a maize dough, or masa, and drunk from *tecomates* (a type of gourd), whereas in La Chinantla, the ground pit of the mamey fruit (*Pouteria sapota*) was added to the masa.

Even today, in many indigenous communities of Oaxaca, drinking chocolate signifies the honoring of life, being at one with family, neighbors, the community, and, above all, with God, the patron saints of the church, and the dead. That is why, perhaps without being aware of this, Oaxacans always serve chocolate, prepared with water, at their celebrations, wakes, and novenas. The presence or absence of foam on the chocolate is important and signifies the type of occasion at which it is being served. For fiestas and reunions of the community, the thick and delicious foam on the chocolate *atole* signifies happiness, brotherhood, and hope. At wakes, sorrow is momentary, for in Oaxaca there is no life without a fiesta, and there is no fiesta without chocolate.

Corn

By Amado Ramírez Leyva

Man selected *teozintle* (the wild forerunner of maize); he domesticated it and sowed corn. The corn, in turn, chose man and cultivated him, teaching him about the patterns and harmony of nature. It established itself in his kitchen and in his culinary rituals.

Oaxaca plays a most important part in the history of corn, not only because it originated there but because it has spread from there in different forms to other areas of Mexico. Early macro remains (i.e., cob fragments) were found in the Guilá Naquitz cave near Mitla in the Valley of Oaxaca and date to about 4300 BC. No doubt corn will continue to spread because new varieties are constantly evolving.

In the kitchen—the intimate space dedicated to the creation and re-creation of dishes—we acknowledge each type of corn as a being with a separate identity, like every element in nature: human, vegetable, or animal.

Corn is the foundation of the Oaxacan kitchen, used in the preparation of tortillas, tostadas, *tlayudas*, and *totopos* that, despite their lowly status, accompany nearly every dish. Corn transformed into masa is indispensable not only for *atoles* and other traditional drinks but also as the mainstay for many *antojitos*, for tamales, and for *chochoyotes* that are added to soups, moles, and other main dishes.

Different types of corn can be transformed in different ways, depending on the creativity of the cook, but they can only reach their height of perfection when prepared in their traditional ways: "*maíces bolita*" from the Central Valleys for *tlayudas* and *tejates*, "*maíces zapalote*" from the Isthmus for *totopos*, and "*chalqueño*" from the Mixteca for pozoles and tortillas.

This book attempts to bring some of the knowledge and lore from past generations that has been safeguarded in their land and kitchen hearths; there are many varieties of indigenous corn and edible plants ready to be accepted and appreciated in their diversity.

The Chiles of Oaxaca

By Diana Kennedy

Oaxaca is famous for its multicolored moles but not so much for the array of chiles that lend their colors and tastes to those moles. A stand selling dried chiles in the market is an intriguing sight, and although they sell quantities of the better-known ones from other parts of Mexico, the chiles from around the state of Oaxaca stand out from the rest, identifiable by their unique colors and shapes: red and yellow costeños, from the coast, as their name implies, perhaps more difficult to distinguish from the red and yellow onzas from the Sierra Norte; the black, red, and yellow chilhuacles; and red chilcosles from La Cañada, to name but a few.

The unique pasilla de Oaxaca or chile Mixe can still be bought according to size: small for sauces, medium for pickling in vinegar, and the largest for stuffing, each with its price per hundred. Until very recent years, the Mixes themselves would be selling these chiles on strategic corners of the market, with their wares stowed in sacks made of henequen—now, alas, of plastic. These chiles are a deep reddish brown with a wrinkled skin. They are very picante and have a delicious fruity-smokey flavor from the process of smoke-drying the mature chiles—though, curiously, in their green state they do not have a pronounced flavor.

The chilhuacles from La Cañada, both colorful and flavorful either fresh or dried, are indispensable for the moles of Oaxaca. They are generally shaped like a squat triangle, with exceptions of course. A ripe field of these chiles is a spectacular sight, for instead of ripening from green through yellow to red (like many other—but not all—types of chiles), the fruits will start as a dark green, and each plant will ripen to *either* yellow, red, *or* a deep chocolate color. In this fresh state, they are used for local dishes, the most important of which is the very colorful *chilecaldo* given on p. 240. When dried, they are hollow with a thinnish skin and matte surface. While they are light in weight—you get a lot for one kilo—because of limited production, they command a very high price compared with more prosaic dried chiles.

In the same *chilares* (cultivated chile fields), there are also much narrower red chiles sometimes referred to as either chiles cuicatecos or chilcosles (the latter name is also sometimes given to the chilhuacle rojo, which is very confusing). There are also small bushes of what seem like miniature chilhuacles, which, when dried, turn a burnished orange color. These achilitos are used in uncooked sauces, notably that made from the seeds of the cardón cactus (p. 253).

Another smallish chile, about 2 inches (5 cm) long, used for table sauces (as opposed to cooked sauces) in the valleys and part of the Sierra Sur is the taviche. While it is mostly used dried, like many

Chiles soledad/Diana Kennedy

Red chiles costeños/Diana Kennedy

other chiles, it is only used fresh when in season, either after the rains or at other times of year where the fields are irrigated (see photo below).

The chile tusta is a small, squat, triangular chile cultivated along the Pacific coast of Oaxaca and the foothills of the Sierra Sur. When fresh, it is a light yellow with patches of mauve, but its colors change to orangey red as it ripens. This chile is mostly used, when fresh, for table sauces, although it is also dried in small quantities.

Chiles costeños, both red and yellow, are grown extensively around the Pinotepa area. When fresh and still green, they are sold in the markets for sauces, but most of the crop is dried in the sun around the patios of the local houses (see photo p. xix) to be used not only in table sauces but also in the local moles, broths, and stews as well as the local *chilecaldo*. There is a slightly larger, less picante variety that is added to the local black mole to lessen the concentrated heat of the smaller variety.

ACHILITOS FROM CUICATLÁN/DIANA KENNEDY

CHILES TAVICHE/DIANA KENNEDY

CUERUDO CHILES /DIANA KENNEDY

LOCAL CHILES FROM NOCHIXTLAN/DIANA KENNEDY

LOCAL CHILES FROM TEHUANTEPEC/DIANA KENNEDY

CHILES CHOCOLATES/DIANA KENNEDY

FRESH YELLOW CHILES COSTEÑOS/DIANA KENNEDY

TUSTA CHILES /DIANA KENNEDY

Chiles costeños are used extensively in local dishes such as sauces, *chilates,* and soups of the Mixteca area; in fact, they are grown, but on a smaller scale, in the Mixteca Baja and, I am told, in the neighboring coastal areas of the states of Guerrero and Michoacán.

The preeminent fresh chile used in the Central Valleys is the chile de agua. A typical one is about 4 inches (10 cm) long and about 1 inch (2.5 cm) across the top. The color varies from medium to light green, which changes as it ripens to an orangey red; however,

it is mostly used while still green. Charred and peeled, it is either stuffed, covered with beaten egg and fried, cut into strips and macerated in lime juice as a relish (p. 25), blended in a cooked sauce, or ground with other ingredients for a table sauce. I am told that until recently, it was also used dried for sauces, but that preparation is not commonplace these days.

The areas of Papaloapan and Usila in La Chinantla Baja have their own local chiles, confusingly referred to as paisanos, criollos secos, and tabaqueros. The latter, according to the experts, are also known as chiltepes. They are used dried not only in the dishes of the Sierra Mazateca but also in the area of La Cañada bordering on the state of Puebla, usually in stews, sauces, soups, and *piltes* (see Glossary). They have a bright red, shiny thin skin and are very picante. Flourishing bushes of small round or elongated chilpayas can be seen outside restaurants or in home gardens around Tuxtepec to be on hand fresh for their very hot sauces or to be bottled in vinegar.

During my stay in Yogopi in La Chinantla Baja, the chile soledad was being cultivated on small plots of land. It is a narrow, dark green chile about 2 inches (5 cm) long and tightly packed with seeds. I am told it is very much sought after in the markets of Mexico City but not so popular when dried. In Yogopi, a sauce was prepared with a small round chile called cuerudo, named for its characteristic tough skin when fresh.

On another occasion, when stopping on my way up to Huautla de Jiménez, I was given a taco of *pochicuiles* (see photo p. 354) and toasted chiles canarios. To my surprise, they were fruity and mild, whereas the same chile called perón or manzano in the states of Mexico and Michoacán—and even those I have tried in Jalapa, Veracruz—are searingly hot. In Huautla, they are cooked in *pilte* (see recipe and photo p. 339).

As in many parts of Mexico, there are a number of unclassified chiles criollos, or local chiles, and unless one arrives at the time they are harvested, it is difficult to distinguish them all. Such was the case with those sold in the Nochistlán market; some resembled chiles de agua, but I was told they were grown in Santa Inés, not far away, along with small, round deep red chiles called canica, or marble. They are both used in sauces and broths, and the larger ones are stuffed.

In other areas, there are small chiles growing wild or cultivated in pots on local patios. For instance, in San Pedro Huilotepec, en route to San Mateo del Mar in the Isthmus, I heard about—but it was not the season to see it growing—a chile called guiña shirunduu (its local Zapotec name, identified by botanist Porfirio López).

Tehuantepec also has its chile criollo (see photos pp. xxi and 200), used fresh when in season and dried in many local dishes. Returning to the city of Oaxaca, I stopped off in the mountain village of San Pedro Totolapa to see chiles xigoles growing, which I had bought dried in the central markets of Oaxaca. The great Zapotec cook Abigail Mendoza makes her table sauces either with fresh chiles paraditos— small, narrow chiles pointing upward, as their name implies—from plants growing in *macetas* (pots) in the patio of the family compound, or from dried chontales—which somewhat resemble taviches—which she says come from Yalalag in the Sierra Norte.

Athough I have heard mention of a chile loco (photo p. 304) in the area of Huajuapan de León, I have yet to come across a dish there in which it is used. I suspect it is an invasion from neighboring Puebla, where I have seen it in markets there on many occasions.

Oaxaca al Gusto

PUEBLA

Huautla

SIERRA
MAZATECA

Ojitlán

Usila

Tuxtepec

CHILTEPEC

LA
CHINANTLA

La Esperanza

Cuicatlán

LA CAÑADA

Huajuapan
de León

MIXTECA Tezoatlán
BAJA

Nochixtlán

MIXTECA
ALTA

Tlaxiaco

SIERRA JUÁREZ / REGIÓN MIXE

Ixtlán

Etla

Benito Juárez

Etla   o

CD. DE OAXACA

Tlacolula

GUERRERO

Putla

LOS VALLES

Teotitlán
del Valle

Sola de
Vega

Ejutla

San Pedro
Amuzgos

Juquila

SIERRA SUR

Ixte

Pinotepa
Nacional

Jamiltepec

LA COSTA

Tehuantepe

Sal

Puerto
Escondido

Pochutla

OCÉANO PACÍFICO

GOLFO DE MÉXICO

VERACRUZ

ISTMO

CHIAPAS

SPINAL

UCHITÁN

IXHUATÁN

AN MATEO DEL MAR
DRO HUILOTEPEC
RUZ

Regions of Oaxaca

BY MARCUS WINTER

O axaca's great cultural diversity, manifested by languages, dress, foods, and other customs of the many ethnic groups, has pre-Hispanic roots that continue into the present. Diversity has emerged through the interaction, over centuries, of humans with their natural and cultural environment.

At 17° north of the equator, Oaxaca has many physiographical-ecological zones, each with its own geological formations, climate, soils, and conditions, which, through the processes of adaptation and evolution, have given rise to a great variety of plants, mammals, birds, and insects. With the arrival at least 10,000 years ago of the first hunter-gatherers in Oaxaca, human groups began visiting and exploring the different areas of the state. Thousands of years later, about 1500 BC, permanent settled communities based on agriculture were established in areas with well-watered land apt for early cultivation. Populations grew, but the groups remained relatively isolated despite the fact that there was exchange of technical innovations and products like obsidian, highly valued for making cutting tools. Diversification flourished and in fact predominated. Although some areas were more suitable than others for agriculture, and were precocious in the growth and settlement complexity, towns and small cities were eventually established throughout what was to become the state of Oaxaca.

Ecological zones are sometimes classified based on their elevation above sea level: hot country below 500 m, a temperate zone between 500 and 1,500 m, and cold country above 1,500–2,000 m, each zone with its own resources. Interestingly, in Oaxaca, many regions, and even individual communities, often encompass a variety of physical and ecological zones. This phenomenon, called verticality by anthropologists, provided the inhabitants with direct access to a large variety of products. Some characteristics of Oaxaca's principal regions are mentioned in the pages that follow.

< MAP OF OAXACA/SERGIO AGUIRRE

UNDER THE DIRECTION OF ALEJANDRO DE ÁVILA BLOMBERG, THE JARDÍN ETNOBOTÁNICO IN
THE FORMER CONVENT OF SANTO DOMINGO COMPLEX IS THE MOST IMPORTANT CENTER FOR
CONSERVING THE BOTANICAL BIODIVERSITY OF THE STATE OF OAXACA./MARCELA TABOADA

City of Oaxaca
By Marcus Winter

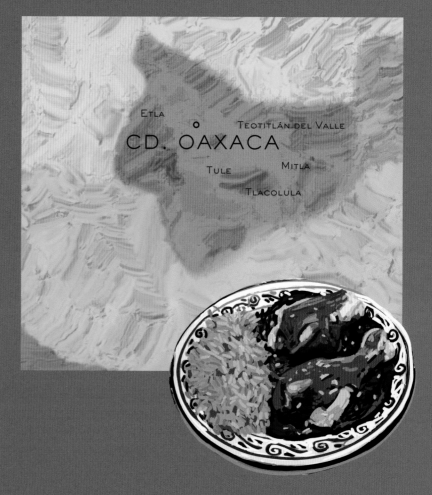

Oaxaca de Juárez, the capital of the state, situated in the center of the Valley of Oaxaca, was founded in the early Colonial period. The name Oaxaca, or Huayacac in Nahuatl, the language of the Aztecs, signifies "in the nose of the guajes," referring to the abundance of that tree. Just to the north is San Felipe del Agua, with a tributary stream that flows down from the mountains and supplied the city with water brought in by canals and an aqueduct. To the south are the wide extensions of fertile alluvial land, now nearly covered by shopping centers and housing developments, which provided corn and other foods. Outcrops of volcanic tuff at Ixcotel on the north edge of the city were quarried for the green "cantera" (or building stone) used in most of the Colonial building and lending the name "the verde Antequera." The city's central location, with respect both to the valley and the state, was and continues to be a strategic factor in its function as an administrative and commercial center.

CIUDAD OAXACA/SERGIO AGUIRRE

Albóndigas para fiestas
(Festive Meatballs)

SEÑORA JUSTINA ALTAMIRANO, CITY OF OAXACA

THE CHICKEN

1 small white onion, quartered
Leaves and stalks of 3 very large scallions, roughly chopped
7 small garlic cloves, unpeeled
2 pounds (900 g) chicken pieces, unskinned
Salt to taste

THE PORK

1 small white onion, quartered
Leaves and stalks of 3 very large scallions, roughly chopped
7 small garlic cloves, unpeeled
1¼ pounds (approximately 500 g) cubed pork with a little fat

MIXTURE FOR THE MEATBALLS

4 tablespoons of vegetable oil
1 medium white onion, finely chopped
5 small garlic cloves, peeled and finely chopped
1 pound (450 g) tomatoes, finely chopped
4 mild black peppercorns, crushed
1 tablespoon dried Oaxacan oregano leaves or 1 heaped teaspoon
    Mexican oregano
1 tablespoon fresh marjoram leaves, finely chopped, or 1 teaspoon
    dried
2 tablespoons fresh mint leaves, finely chopped
1 tablespoon sugar
Salt to taste
1 cup (250 ml) dried breadcrumbs
2–3 eggs, beaten

THE BROTH

2 tablespoons vegetable oil
1 small white onion, finely chopped
5 small garlic cloves, peeled and finely chopped
1 pound (450 g) tomatoes, finely chopped
4 cups (1 L) chicken and pork broth
4 sprigs flat-leaved parsley
2 large sprigs mint
Salt to taste

This rather elaborate, and very tasty, dish of meatballs is served traditionally for baptisms and birthdays. It is usually accompanied by white rice and fried plantain. The cooking method is unusual because Señora Justina cooks the meat first, shreds it, and then chops it.

8 PORTIONS

- Put enough water to cover the chicken into a pan with the onion, the scallions, and the garlic and simmer for 5 minutes. Add the meat and continue cooking over low heat until just tender, approximately 20 minutes. Set aside to cool in the broth. Strain, reserving the broth. Remove skin and bones, shred the meat, and then chop finely.

- Repeat the instructions above for cooking the pork, but it will take longer, about 35–40 minutes. Combine the two broths. You will need about 4 cups (1 L), so reduce or make up to that amount with water. Combine the meats.

- Heat 2 tablespoons of the oil in a large skillet. Add the onion and garlic and fry gently until translucent. Add the tomatoes and cook over fairly high heat until they have reduced and thickened. Add the chopped meats, peppercorns, herbs, sugar, and salt and continue cooking over fairly high heat, stirring and scraping the bottom of the pan to prevent sticking, until the mixture is well seasoned, still moist but not juicy, about 10 minutes. Add the breadcrumbs and eggs and mix well. Divide the mixture into 24 parts, rolling each one into a ball about 1½ inches (about 3.5 cm) in diameter.

- Heat the remaining oil in a skillet and fry the meatballs until golden, but not too dry. Drain on paper towels.

TO MAKE THE BROTH

Heat the oil in a casserole, add the onion and garlic, and fry without browning for about 1 minute. Add the tomatoes and cook over medium heat until reduced a little, about 5 minutes. Add the reserved 4 cups (1 L) broth, the parsley, and the mint and cook over low heat until well seasoned, about 20 minutes. Adjust salt. About 10 minutes before serving, add the meatballs and let them heat through gently in the broth.

MOLE AMARILLO WITH CHILE CHILCOSLE/MICHAEL CALDERWOOD

Amarillo
(Yellow Mole)

SEÑORA DAMIANA MARCIAL ÁNGELES, CITY OF OAXACA

The recipes for this mole, and the chiles used, vary not only in Oaxaca, the city, but in other parts of the state. This recipe calls for chilcosle (either the slender long chile, as named in the markets, or the fat triangular chilhuacle rojo, both of Cuicatlán), but many cooks nowadays use guajillos instead, which do not have such a complex flavor; in fact, this *amarillo* generally turns out to be an orangey red color.

It is customary for this mole to be flavored with *yerbasanta*, but if it is cooked with beef, *pitiona* (see Glossary) would be used.

8 PORTIONS

THE MEAT

1 large scallion, cut into 4 pieces with green leaves
½ small head of garlic, unpeeled
Salt to taste
1 pound (450 g) stewing pork, cut into small pieces
1 large chicken, about 4 pounds (1.8 kg), cut into serving portions, plus 1 large chicken breast, quartered (with skin and bone)

THE VEGETABLES

2 small chayotes, peeled and cut into ½-inch (1.25 cm) wedges
12 ounces (350 g) potatoes, peeled and cut into cubes
8 ounces (about 225 g) green beans, trimmed and halved crosswise

THE MOLE

16 chilcosles or guajillos, cleaned of seeds and veins
½ large white onion, cut into wedges and toasted
8 small garlic cloves, toasted and peeled
6 allspice, crushed
6 cloves, crushed
¼ teaspoon cumin seeds, crushed
1 tablespoon dried Oaxacan oregano leaves or ½ tablespoon Mexican oregano
5 *tomates verdes*, coarsely chopped
3 tablespoons melted pork lard or vegetable oil
1 cup (250 ml) tortilla masa
4 *yerbasanta* leaves, central rib removed, torn into large pieces
Salt to taste
Optional: chochoyotes (p. 29)

To serve: strips of chile de agua in lime juice (p. 25)

- Put water to boil in a large pot with the scallion, garlic, and salt; after 5 minutes, add the pork and cook over medium heat for 15 minutes. Add the chicken pieces and cook until the meats are just tender (do not overcook at this stage). Strain and reserve the broth; you will need about 6 cups (1.5 L) for the mole. If necessary, add water to make this amount.

- Cook the vegetables in salted water, separately, to avoid overcooking. Strain, reserving the cooking water; there should be about 2 cups (500 ml).

- Toast the chiles lightly on a comal, rinse, strain, and cover with fresh water. Leave to soak for 15 minutes. Strain again.

- Put ½ cup (125 ml) of the vegetable water in the jar of the blender; add the onion, garlic, spices, and oregano; and blend until smooth. Add the *tomates verdes* with another ½ cup (125 ml) of the vegetable water and blend again.

- Heat the lard or oil in the casserole in which you are going to cook the mole, add the blended ingredients, and fry over fairly high heat, stirring to prevent sticking, for 5 minutes.

- Put the remaining vegetable water in the blender jar and add the chiles a few at a time, blending well after each addition. Add the purée to the casserole, pressing it hard through a strainer to extract as much of the juice as possible. There will be some debris from the tough chile skins left in the strainer. Cook the mixture over fairly high heat, stirring and scraping the bottom of the casserole to prevent sticking, for about 8 minutes.

- Dilute the masa with 2 cups (500 ml) of the meat broth and add to the pan, cooking over medium heat until the sauce starts to thicken. Add the remaining meat broth, the meats, and the vegetables and cook for a further 15 minutes. Finally, add the *yerbasanta*, test for salt, and cook for about 15 minutes more. The mole should be of a medium consistency.

Optional *chochoyotes*: Add the *chochoyotes* at the same time as the *yerbasanta*.

Arroz con pollo
(Rice with Chicken)

SEÑORA ESPERANZA MORALES DE KATZ, CITY OF OAXACA

Arroz con pollo, as it is better known, is prepared in many parts of the world, varying in flavor, of course, with local ingredients and seasonings. This version of the dish reflects the Spanish influence in the more sophisticated cooking of the central valley of Oaxaca. It is generally served with bread rolls, called *bolillos*, rather than tortillas.

Although water is generally used, the flavor of the rice is enriched when cooked with a good chicken broth. And the chicken should not be skinned; you don't have to eat it!

8 SERVINGS

1 large chicken, cut into serving pieces (the breast should be quartered)
3 unpeeled garlic cloves, lightly crushed
½ medium white onion, roughly chopped
Chicken broth or water to cover
Sea salt to taste
1 heaped cup, about 8 ounces (225 g), long-grained unconverted rice
3 tablespoons vegetable oil
½ medium white onion, finely chopped
3 garlic cloves, peeled and finely chopped
2 *tomates verdes*, finely chopped
1¼ pounds (approximately 500 g) tomatoes, roughly chopped and blended
1 clove, lightly crushed
1 allspice, lightly crushed
1 large sprig flat-leaved parsley
About 20 saffron threads
Salt to taste

- Put the chicken, onion, and garlic into a large pot; cover well with chicken broth or water and add salt to taste. Cook over a moderate heat until the chicken is just tender, slightly undercooked, about 30 minutes (it will continue cooking in the rice). Strain the chicken and measure the broth. You will need about 5 cups (1.25 L), so add water or reduce to that amount.

- In the meantime, cover the rice with hot water and leave it to soak for 5 minutes.

- Strain rice, rinse in cold water, and strain again.

- Heat the oil in a casserole, add the rice, and fry over medium heat, stirring well so that the grains fry evenly. It should sound brittle but should not brown. Strain the rice of excess oil over the pan and set aside.

- Add the onion, garlic, and *tomate verde* to the pan and fry for a few seconds before adding the tomato purée. Continue the frying, stirring and scraping the bottom of the pan to prevent sticking, for 10 minutes. Stir in the rice and then place the chicken pieces over the surface.

- Lightly toast the saffron threads and crush or grind in a mortar. Dissolve in ¼ cup (65 ml) of the chicken broth and stir into the rice. Add the rest of the broth with the spices and parsley, test for salt, and cover and cook over a low flame until the liquid has been absorbed and the rice is tender, about 30 minutes. The rice should be very moist.

Note: This dish can be reheated in a slow oven for about 30 minutes. Do not freeze; the chicken will be horrible.

Arroz con leche (Rice Pudding)

Señora Esperanza Morales de Katz,
City of Oaxaca

A typical and favorite dessert of Oaxaca is rice cooked with milk. It is often served topped with chickpeas cooked in syrup (see recipe p. 44). A final delicious touch is to stir in some good thick cream, or *nata,* about 5 minutes before the end of the cooking time.

8 PORTIONS

1 scant cup (180 g) long-grained rice
1 allspice, lightly crushed
1½ inch (about 4 cm) cinnamon stick
Approximately 1–1½ cups (250–375 ml) water
2 cups (500 ml) whole milk
¾ cup (195 ml) evaporated milk
Pinch salt
2 strips lime rind (optional)

To serve: finely grated rind of 2 limes

• Rinse rice well in hot water and strain. Put the rice into a heavy pan with 1 cup (250 ml) of the water, add the allspice and cinnamon, and cook, covered, over slow heat until all the water has been absorbed and the rice is beginning to soften, about 10 minutes. (Only add more water if the rice is sticking to the pot; if you add too much, it will become soft and sticky.)

• Add the two types of milk, the salt, and the lime rind. Cover the pot and continue cooking over slow heat, stirring carefully from time to time to prevent sticking, for about 30 minutes. The rice should now be soft but still rather moist. Turn the rice out into a serving dish and sprinkle the top with the grated rind.

Bistec con pimienta (Peppered Beefsteak)

Señora Esperanza Morales de Katz,
City of Oaxaca

This recipe is a great favorite of the Katz family, one that has been handed down for several generations. Like all simple recipes, so much depends on the quality of the ingredients. It is served with tortillas and either a tomato sauce (from Chinantla p. 96, Isthmus p. 200) or one made with dried chiles (Valles p. 423).

6 PORTIONS

4 whole allspice
8 mild black peppercorns
1 tablespoon coarse sea salt
3 tablespoons mild fruity vinegar
⅓ cup (85 ml) water
6 shoulder steaks, ½ inch (about 1 cm) thick
2 tablespoons lard or vegetable oil
1 medium white onion, cut into thin crescents
12 ounces (340 g) potatoes, peeled and cut into thin slices
6 stems flat-leaved parsley

• Grind together the allspice, peppercorns, and salt and mix with the vinegar and water. Rub the mixture onto the surface of the steaks and set aside to season for about an hour.

• Heat the lard in a large, deep skillet and fry the onion, without browning, until translucent. Remove with a slotted spoon and reserve. In the same fat, sear the steaks quickly over high heat and remove.

• Layer the steaks with the potatoes, onions, and pan juices. Cover the pan and cook over very low heat until the juices have been absorbed, about 1¼ hours, basting the meat with the juices from time to time. (Don't try to speed up the cooking.) It is always best to let the dish sit for a short time before serving to allow the flavors to intensify.

Meat stand in the market, >
City of Oaxaca/Pedro Valtierra

Food stand with local dishes/Pedro Valtierra

Caldillo zapatero
(Quick Soup for Lent)

Señorita Soledad Díaz, Restaurante "El Topil," City of Oaxaca

"Quick and light, like the tapping of a shoe," *un zapateado*, is the explanation given by Soledad's mother for the name in Spanish for this soup. It is generally prepared during Lent, when meat is forbidden, and served with a picante sauce of onza or pasilla chiles.

MAKES 6–8 PORTIONS

7 cups (1.75 L) water
1 medium white onion, coarsely chopped
2 garlic cloves, peeled and smashed
Salt to taste
18 ounces (500 g) nopales, cleaned and cut into small squares
2 large sprigs epazote
14 ounces (400 g) unpeeled tomatoes, finely chopped
½ medium white onion, finely chopped
4 small garlic cloves, peeled and finely chopped
2 eggs, lightly beaten
Optional: ⅔ cup (190 ml or 50 g) small- or medium-sized dried shrimps

- Put the water into a large pot with the onion, garlic, and salt and simmer for 5 minutes. Add the nopales and 1 sprig of epazote and cook over medium heat for 6 minutes. Remove onion and garlic.

- Add the tomatoes, with the raw chopped onion and garlic, and cook over medium heat for 15 minutes. (If you are using the shrimps [see note below], add them and cook for 5 minutes.) Finally, add the second sprig of epazote, stir in the eggs, and continue stirring gently until they are set, about 5 minutes.

- *To prepare the shrimps:* Rinse twice in cold water to remove excess salt, then drain. Remove the heads and legs and grind with some of the cooking water until smooth. Add this with the shrimps to the broth.

Calabaza amarilla/Diana Kennedy

A CAZUELA OF MEAT AND VEGETABLES FOR *Chichilo negro*/Jorge López

Chichilo negro
(Black Chichilo)

SEÑORA DAMIANA MARCIAL ÁNGELES, CITY OF OAXACA

This black *chichilo* is considered one of the important moles of Oaxaca. As a cook, I am fascinated by the technique of making it, and as an eater, intrigued by the flavor; it is both rustic and sophisticated.

The most important and unique ingredient is the chilhuacle negro from Cuicatlán. This *chichilo* is served in large bowls, accompanied by chile de agua strips (p. 25); it is often enriched with *chochoyotes* (p. 29).

6–8 PORTIONS

THE MEAT

2¼ pounds (about 1 kg) stewing beef, half of which should be brisket and/or short ribs on the bone, cut into serving pieces
1 small head of garlic, halved horizontally
1 medium white onion, coarsely chopped
Salt to taste
1¼ pounds (550 g) stewing pork, with some fat, cut into serving pieces

THE VEGETABLES

2 small chayotes, about 1 pound (450 g), peeled and cut into strips
8 ounces (225 g) green beans, trimmed and cut into halves crosswise

THE MOLE

20 chilhuacles negros, seeds removed and saved
2 pasilla (Mexican, not Oaxacan) chiles, seeds removed and saved
2 medium-sized dried tortillas
½ small head garlic, toasted, cloves separated and peeled
1 medium white onion, cut into 4 pieces and toasted
2 cloves, crushed
4 mild black peppercorns, crushed
¼ teaspoon cumin seeds
1 tablespoon dried Oaxacan oregano leaves or 1 heaped teaspoon of Mexican oregano
¼ teaspoon dried thyme leaves
¼ teaspoon dried marjoram leaves
4 tablespoons melted pork lard
6 ounces (about 180 g or 5 medium) *tomates verdes*, toasted
8 ounces (225 g) tomatoes, toasted
1 cup (250 ml) tortilla masa
1 small spray avocado leaves (see Note on Toxicity, p. 426)

- Put the beef into a large pot with the garlic, onion, and salt. Cover well with water and cook over medium heat for 40 minutes; add the pork and continue cooking until both meats are tender but not soft, about 35 minutes, depending on the quality of the meat. Strain and reserve the broth.

- Return the broth to the pot, add the chayotes and green beans, and cook the vegetables until al dente. Strain. (They can also be cooked in water separately and the cooking water saved for the mole.) You will need about 7 cups (1.75 L) of broth for the mole; if necessary, add water to reach that amount.

- Toast the chiles on a comal over low heat, turning them so they do not burn, until they are crisp. Rinse in cold water and then soak in hot water for 15 minutes.

- Put the chile seeds and tortillas into a skillet and heat until they blacken and start to flame. Quickly throw them in a bowl of cold water and let them soak for 5 minutes.

- Strain. Put 1 cup (250 ml) of the meat broth into the blender jar; add the garlic, onion, spices, and herbs and blend well. Add another 1 cup (250 ml) of the broth along with the chiles, seeds, and tortillas and blend to a slightly textured, thick consistency.

- Heat the lard in a heavy casserole, add the blended ingredients, and cook over medium heat, stirring well to avoid sticking, about 8 minutes.

- Blend the *tomates verdes* and tomatoes together and add to the pan. Continue cooking for another 5 minutes.

- Blend the masa with another 1 cup (250 ml) of the broth, add to the pan, and cook, taking care that the mixture does not stick to the bottom of the pan, until it begins to thicken. Add the remaining broth, the meats, and the vegetables; salt as necessary and continue cooking over medium heat until the flavors are well combined, about 15 minutes. Finally, char the avocado leaves over a flame, add them to the mole, and cook for 5 minutes more. The mole should be slightly thickened.

Optional: Chochoyotes can be added about 15 minutes before the end of the cooking time.

Chichilo rojo
(Red Chichilo)

In the early seventies, one of my first informal teachers in Oaxaca was Señora Domitila Santiago, with whom I cooked many traditional dishes, including a red *chichilo* (my notes are now almost illegible). I had never made it since, until I came across this recipe.

The unique flavors come from the red chilhuacle (called chilcosle in Cuicatlán) and the musky *hierba de conejo*.

Hierba de conejo (*Tridax coronapiifolia*) is rarely found growing wild outside the Central Valley area. The only other wild herb, or *quelite*, with a similar flavor and with a much wider growing range is *piojito* (*Galinsoga paviflora*), which would be the best substitute. But failing that, I suggest using—although the flavor will not be the same—5 toasted avocado leaves (see Note on Toxicity, p. 426).

This *chichilo rojo* may be thickened to taste with some tortilla masa.

6–8 PORTIONS

THE MEAT

3½ pounds (about 1½ kg) stewing beef: shin, brisket, short ribs with bone, and some fat
½ medium white onion, coarsely chopped
½ small head garlic, unpeeled
Salt to taste

THE VEGETABLES

1 chayote, about 12 ounces (340 g), peeled and cut into strips
8 ounces (225 g) green beans, trimmed and cut into halves crosswise

THE SAUCE

18 chilhuacles, or 8 guajillos and 3 anchos, seeds and veins removed, but seeds reserved
1 medium white onion, cut into 6 pieces and toasted
8 garlic cloves, toasted and peeled
¼ teaspoon cumin seeds, crushed
4 allspice, crushed
6 cloves, crushed
4 tablespoons lard
12 ounces (350 g) tomatoes, toasted
12 ounces (350 g) *tomates verdes*, toasted
½ cup (125 ml) tortilla masa
1 roll of *hierba de conejo*, finely chopped and blended with a little water
Salt to taste

- Put the meat into a large pot with the onion, garlic, salt, and enough water to cover well. Cook over medium heat until tender but not too soft, about 1½ hours. Strain, reserving the broth. You will need 5 cups (1.25 L); add water if necessary to make that amount. Bring to a boil, add the vegetables, and cook until still a little al dente. Strain.

- Heat a comal or skillet over low heat and toast the chiles, turning them so they cook evenly but taking care not to let them burn. Rinse chiles in cold water and set aside to soak in warm water until soft, about 20 minutes. Strain.

- In a small skillet, toast the chile seeds, stirring them constantly, until they turn a dark brown.

- Put ½ cup (125 ml) of the meat broth in the blender and blend the onion, garlic, and spices. Then add another 1 cup (250 ml) of the broth with the chile seeds, and after blending until almost smooth, add the chiles, a few at a time, blending well after each addition. The mixture should be slightly textured.

- Heat the lard in a heavy casserole, add the blended ingredients, and cook over medium heat, stirring and scraping the bottom of the pan to prevent sticking, until the fat floats to the surface, about 10 minutes.

- Dilute the masa with a little of the meat broth and stir into the sauce. Continue cooking and stirring until the sauce begins to thicken slightly.

- Blend the tomatoes and *tomates verdes* until smooth, add to the pan, and continue cooking for another 10 minutes.

- Cook until the sauce begins to thicken a little, then add the remaining broth, the vegetables, the meat, and the *hierba de conejo*, strained. Continue cooking for 15 minutes more, adjusting the salt as necessary.

Torteando (patting out) a tortilla/Pedro Valtierra

Chileajo de legumbres
(Vegetables in Chileajo Sauce)

This preparation of vegetables in *chileajo* is not to be confused with the Mixteca dish of *chileajo* cooked with meat. It is really like a relish, which, though it may be served the year round, is particularly popular during Lent. It is served cold, either stuffed into a bread roll or, more tasty still, as a topping on a tostada that has been spread with a paste of black beans and topped with onion rings, *queso fresco,* and a dusting of dried oregano. The pungent sauce is rarely cooked.

MAKES ABOUT 7 CUPS (1.75 L)

6 cups (1.5 L) water (for the vegetables)
Salt to taste
8 ounces (225 g) green beans, cleaned and halved crosswise
8 ounces (225 g) carrots, scraped and cut into thin rounds
8 ounces (225 g) cauliflower, flowerlets separated
8 ounces (225 g) shelled peas
8 ounces (225 g) potatoes, cut into 1-inch (2.5 cm) cubes
5½ ounces (150 g) guajillo chiles, about 24 chiles
Approximately 1 cup (250 ml) water
8 garlic cloves, peeled and finely chopped
2 whole cloves, crushed
2 whole allspice, crushed
1 tablespoon dried Oaxacan oregano leaves or 1 heaped teaspoon Mexican oregano
Approximately 1¾ cups (440 ml) pineapple or other fruity vinegar
Salt to taste

- Put the 6 cups water into a pan with salt to taste, bring to a boil, and cook each of the vegetables separately; they should be al dente, so take care not to overcook them.

- Approximate times: green beans and carrots, 10 minutes; cauliflower and peas, 5 minutes; and potatoes, 10 minutes (much will depend on the quality of the vegetables). Strain and put into a nonreactive bowl.

- Rinse the chiles, cover with hot water, and set aside to soak until soft, about 20 minutes. Strain. Put the 1 cup (250 ml) of water into the blender jar and add the chiles a few at a time, blending well after each addition. Add only a little more water if necessary to release the blender blades. Pass the purée through a strainer into a bowl, pressing hard to extract all the flesh and juice; there will be quite a bit of debris left in the strainer.

- Put ¼ cup (65 ml) of the vinegar into the blender jar, add the garlic, spices, and oregano and blend until smooth. Add to the chile purée with the rest of the vinegar and salt. Pour over the vegetables, mix well, and set aside to season for at least 2 days before using.

Top: Prepared *Chile de agua en rajas con limón y orégano*; bottom: Ingredients for this dish/Pedro Valtierra

Chile de agua en rajas con limón y orégano
(Chile de Agua in Lime Juice)

The chile de agua may look inoffensive, but it is very picante. It is cultivated year-round in the Valley of Oaxaca, especially in the Zimatlán area. This "relish" is one of the many ways in which it is used, and it is a delicious accompaniment to many of the Oaxacan dishes: mole *amarillo, chichilo, enfrijoladas,* among others. Because of the acid content, it is absolutely necessary to keep, or serve, these chiles in a nonreactive bowl.

MAKES ABOUT 2 CUPS (500 ML)

12 chiles de agua, or substitute a very picante, light-colored medium-sized chile
1 large white onion, thinly sliced into half moons or crescents
Approximately ⅓ cup (85 ml) lime juice
Salt to taste
½ tablespoon dried Oaxacan oregano leaves or ¼ tablespoon Mexican oregano

- Toast the chiles directly over a flame if possible. Set aside for 5 minutes in a paper bag. Skin, remove seeds, and cut into strips about ¼ inch (less than 1 cm) wide.

- Put into a bowl with the rest of the ingredients and allow to macerate for an hour or so before serving.

Chiles rellenos oaxaqueños
(Oaxacan Chiles Rellenos)

Fresh chiles de agua are the most commonly used for this recipe, with the dried chiles pasillas in second place. The former look innocent enough but can be very picante; therefore, some cooks recommend, after charring and peeling the chiles, letting them soak in lightly salted water, with a little vinegar added, for about ½ hour.

If you prefer to stuff the pasillas, choose the largest ones. If they are very dry and brittle, warm them on a comal, and they will soften in a few seconds.

Although generally very picante, some are much milder nowadays, probably because they are grown commercially in areas other than the Sierra Mixe.

In preparing any chile for filling, make sure the top holding the stem is intact.

Makes 12 chiles for 6 portions

Have ready:
3 cups (750 ml) tomato broth (see following page)
3 cups (750 ml) *picadillo* (see following page)
12 chiles de agua or 12 large dried pasillas from Oaxaca
Flour for coating
4 large eggs, whites and yolks separated
Salt to taste
Vegetable oil for frying

- To prepare the chiles de agua: char, peel, and make a slit down one side of the chile, leaving top intact, and carefully remove seeds and veins. If the pasillas are dry and brittle, heat for a few seconds on a comal over medium heat to soften. Make a slit down one side, leaving the top intact. Remove seeds and veins. Cover with warm water and leave to soak until soft, about 15 minutes. Do not leave them too long in the water; strain.

- Fill the chiles with enough of the *picadillo* to make them fat, but making sure that the cut edges meet and cover the stuffing.

- Heat the oil in a skillet; it should be about 1¼ inches (3 cm) deep.

- Beat the egg whites until they hold their shape; they should not slip around the bowl, but neither should they become too firm and dry. Add salt to taste and the yolks, one by one, beating well after each addition. Pat the flour around one of the chiles, coat with the beaten egg, and carefully lower it into the hot oil. Turn the chile after a minute or so and continue frying until the coating acquires an even gold color. Drain and continue with the rest.

- Serve the chiles bathed in the warm tomato broth.

CALDILLO DE TOMATE ROJO

(TOMATO BROTH FOR CHILES RELLENOS)

MAKES ABOUT 3 CUPS (750 ML)

1¼ pounds (about 500 g) tomatoes, toasted
1 thick slice medium white onion, roughly chopped
2 garlic cloves, peeled and roughly chopped
1 tablespoon melted lard or vegetable oil
Approximately 1 cup (250 ml) broth from the stuffing meat
Salt to taste

- Put a few of the tomatoes into the blender with the onion and garlic and blend well. Gradually add the rest of the tomatoes and blend again to a fairly smooth mixture.

- Heat the lard in a wide pan, add the tomato mixture, and cook over medium heat until well seasoned and reduced and thickened slightly, about 5 minutes. Add the broth with salt as necessary and continue cooking for a further 5 minutes.

PICADILLO

(STUFFING FOR CHILES)

Apart from chiles, this stuffing can be used for enchiladas and tamales. Some cooks prefer to use a variety of meats or one or the other of pork, beef, or chicken. Any leftover stuffing can be frozen.

MAKES ABOUT 4½ CUPS (1.125 ML)

3 tablespoons melted lard or vegetable oil
1 medium white onion, finely chopped
4 garlic cloves, peeled and finely chopped
1¼ pounds (550 g) tomatoes, finely chopped
3 black peppercorns, crushed
3 cloves, crushed
½ teaspoon dried thyme or 1 teaspoon fresh leaves
½ teaspoon dried marjoram or 1 teaspoon fresh leaves
1 tablespoon dried Oaxacan oregano leaves or ½ tablespoon Mexican oregano
2 Mexican bay leaves or 1 bay laurel, finely crumbled
½ cup (125 ml) raisins, roughly chopped
20 almonds, skinned and roughly chopped
1 tablespoon large capers, roughly chopped
10 green pitted olives, roughly chopped
3 cups (750 ml) meat (see notes above: one or a mixture of the above), cooked, shredded, and chopped
Approximately ½ cup (125 ml) reserved meat broth
Optional: 1 tablespoon pineapple or other fruity vinegar
Salt to taste
2 tablespoons sugar, or to taste

- Heat the lard in a wide pan or deep skillet and fry the onion and garlic until translucent. Add the tomatoes and fry over fairly high heat until reduced and thickened.

- Stir in the herbs, spices, raisins, almonds, capers, and olives and cook over medium heat for about 5 minutes. The mixture should be fairly dry. Add the meat and the rest of the ingredients and continue cooking until all the ingredients are well combined. The mixture should be moist, not juicy, and shiny.

Chochoyotes
(Masa Dumplings)

Chochoyotes are small balls of masa, enriched with *asiento*—or lard if not available—to give more substance to certain moles, soups, or bean dishes. They have a deep indentation in the center so that they cook more evenly.

MAKES 12 CHOCHOYOTES

½ cup (125 ml) tortilla masa
1 heaped tablespoon *asiento* or pork lard
Salt to taste

- Mix the ingredients together and divide the dough into 12 pieces. Roll each piece into a smooth ball about 1 inch (2.5 cm) in diameter. Take a ball of the masa in the palm of your hand and rotate, making a depression in the center with the index finger of the other hand.

- The broth or sauce in which they are to be cooked should be simmering, not boiling fast, or they will disintegrate. The *chochoyotes* will float when done, in about 15 minutes.

SWEET EMPANADAS/DIANA KENNEDY

Empanadas de Corpus Christi
(Empanadas for Corpus Christi)

Señor Marcelino Barragán, City of Oaxaca

Señor Marcelino and his wife, Señora Soledad, prepare these empanadas (although, strictly speaking, a specialty for Corpus Christi) and other traditional sweets and pastries to sell in the Sánchez Pascua market every Sunday. They both inherited the knowledge and recipes from their families, which included bakers going back several generations, and through the years these empanadas have won many accolades.

Although many cooks now use vegetable fat, this couple insists on using the original *manteca criolla*, pork lard, which makes all the difference to the flavor and texture of the pastry. Interestingly, no salt is used. Traditionally, these empanadas are filled with one of three fillings: *lechecilla*, a custard (recipe p. 32); pineapple (recipe p. 32); or coconut.

MAKES ABOUT 30 EMPANADAS

2¼ pounds (about 1 kg) all-purpose flour
10 egg yolks
18 ounces (500 g) pork lard

- On a board or in a bowl, mix together the flour, yolks, and half the lard. When all the ingredients are well incorporated, divide the dough in two parts. Cover with plastic wrap and refrigerate in a cool place, but not in the refrigerator, overnight.

- Heat the rest of the lard a little. On a floured pastry cloth, roll out one of the balls of dough into a very thin square. Using your hands, spread half the lard lightly over the surface of the dough, then coax the dough into a rather tight roll, lifting up the cloth as you go. Repeat the process with the second ball of dough. Put the rolls, covered with the cloth, in the refrigerator for 2 hours.

- Heat oven to 425°F (220°C)

- To form the empanadas, cut the roll of dough into slices, a little more than ½ inch (1.5 cm) thick. Roll one of the pieces out to a circle about 4 inches (10 cm) in diameter.

- Turn it over, put a tablespoon of the filling on one half of the circle, and cover with the other half. Pinch the sides together to seal in the filling. Place on an ungreased baking sheet and proceed with the rest.

- Bake until the dough is crisp and golden, about 30 minutes.

RELLENO DE PIÑA

(PINEAPPLE FILLING)

1 large, slightly underripe pineapple
Approximately 2 cups (500 ml) water
1 cup (250 ml) cornstarch
1 pound (450 g) sugar

- Trim and peel the pineapple. Cut in half and remove the core; cut the flesh into small cubes. Blend the cubes with 1 cup (250 ml) of the water and transfer to pan. Cook over medium heat, stirring from time to time, until the juice has evaporated, about 15 minutes.

- In the meantime, put the cornstarch into a bowl and stir in the remaining water gradually; continue stirring until the mixture is completely smooth. Add this gradually to the pineapple and cook over low heat, stirring continuously to avoid lumping, until the mixture thickens; it should barely plop off a wooden spoon. Set aside to cool before filling the empanadas.

LECHECILLA

(CUSTARD FILLING)

SEÑOR MARCELINO BARRAGÁN, CITY OF OAXACA

This *lechecilla* can be eaten as a dessert or used as a filling for empanadas and other confections. The number of yolks, Señor Marcelino tells me, can vary, depending on how rich you can afford, or want, to make the custard.

MAKES 5 CUPS (1.25 L)

1 quart (1 L) whole milk
4 inches (10 cm) cinnamon stick, broken up
1 scant cup (about 240 ml) or just over 5 ounces (150 g) sugar
Rounded ¾ cup (190 ml) or 3½ ounces (100 g) cornstarch
1 cup (250 ml) water
6 egg yolks, lightly beaten

- Put the milk, cinnamon, and sugar into a pan and cook over low heat, stirring from time to time until the sugar has melted.

- Put the cornstarch into a bowl, add the water, and stir until smooth. Gradually stir in the egg yolks and mix until totally combined. Add ½ cup (125 ml) of the hot milk mixture and stir well. Add the egg mixture, a little at a time, to the hot milk in the pan, stirring well after each addition, and cook over low heat, stirring continuously and scraping the bottom of the pan to avoid sticking and lumping. When the custard thickens, in about 3–4 minutes, and no longer tastes of raw egg, remove from flame but keep stirring until it cools a little. Cover to prevent a skin forming on the surface, and set aside to cool.

Traditional sweet pastries/Diana Kennedy

Cuitlacoche/Diana Kennedy

Empanadas de cuitlacoche
(Empanadas of Cuitlacoche)

SEÑORA JOSEFINA CUEVAS, CITY OF OAXACA

These large and delicious empanadas are practically a meal in themselves. Made with uncooked masa pressed out as for a 10-inch (25 cm) tortilla, they can be stuffed with other fillings, but these of *cuitlacoche*, or corn fungus, are one of the most popular during the rainy season.

The empanadas are usually cooked on an ungreased griddle, or comal, but in one of the popular markets, the final touch of flavor is given by a brief toasting in a wire rack over the hot charcoal ashes of the brazier.

It is worthwhile making this amount of filling while you are at it; leftovers can be frozen to use in the next batch of empanadas or quesadillas or even crêpes.

> **MAKES ABOUT 6 CUPS (1.5 L), SUFFICIENT FILLING FOR 24 LARGE EMPANADAS**

4 tablespoons vegetable oil

1 medium white onion, finely chopped

5 garlic cloves, peeled and finely chopped

3 fresh jalapeño chiles (or to taste), finely chopped

3 cups (750 ml) fresh corn kernels (should not be sweet)

3 cups coarsely chopped *cuitlacoche*

Salt to taste

3 tightly packed cups squash flowers

⅓ cup (85 ml) coarsely chopped epazote leaves

2¾ pounds (about 1.3 kg) tortilla masa

Approximately 1 pound (450 g) *quesillo*, shredded not too finely, or substitute string cheese

- Heat the oil in a large skillet. Add the onion, garlic, chiles, and corn kernels and fry over medium heat for 5 minutes. Add the *cuitlacoche*, with salt to taste, and cook, covered, over medium heat for 10 minutes. Add the flowers and epazote and continue cooking for 10 minutes more.

- Heat a comal or griddle over medium heat.

- Divide the masa into 24 pieces and roll each one into a ball about 1¾ inches (about 4.5 cm) in diameter. Using a tortilla press lined with plastic, press the ball of masa out to a circle 6 inches (15 cm) in diameter. Lift off the top piece of plastic (only to loosen it from the dough) and replace. Turn the whole thing over and remove the top plastic. Put ¼ cup (65 ml) of the filling and a few strands of the cheese over one half of the dough. Lifting up the plastic, double the other half of the dough over so that it covers the filling completely. Press the edges together to seal. Put the empanada onto the comal and cook, turning it over twice, until the masa is cooked through and slightly browned, about 12 minutes. Serve and eat immediately.

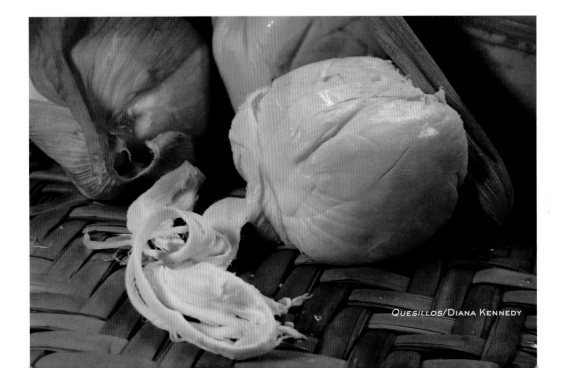

QUESILLOS/DIANA KENNEDY

Entomatadas

Entomatadas, literally tortillas bathed in a tomato sauce, are a very popular breakfast dish in Oaxaca. They are either served alone, with eggs, or with a piece of *tasajo*.

Makes 6 portions

THE SAUCE

2 tablespoons vegetable oil
½ medium white onion, thinly sliced
2 small garlic cloves, peeled
2 chiles de agua, toasted, skinned, and seeded, or substitute jalapeños, toasted only
1¾ pounds (about 700 g) tomatoes, quartered and cooked in very little water
2 large sprigs epazote
Salt to taste

• Heat the oil in a skillet and fry the onion and garlic until golden. Transfer to the blender jar with ½ cup (125 ml) of the tomato cooking liquid and the chiles. Blend until smooth.

• Add the tomatoes with the rest of their cooking liquid and blend to a smooth purée. Return mixture to the skillet and fry over medium heat until reduced a little, about 5 minutes. Add the epazote and salt to taste and keep hot.

PREPARING THE *ENTOMATADAS*

Approximately ¼ cup (65 ml) vegetable oil
12 tortillas about 6 inches (15 cm) in diameter
1 medium white onion, cut in thin half-moons
Approximately ¾ cup (190 ml) crumbled *queso fresco* or shredded *quesillo*
1 small bunch flat-leaved parsley, torn into small pieces

• Heat a little of the oil in a skillet and fry the tortillas, one by one, lightly on both sides; they should not become crisp around the edge. Drain on paper towels and proceed with frying the rest, adding more oil as necessary.

• Dip the tortillas, one by one, into the hot tomato sauce, fold into four and place on a warm serving dish or on individual plates. Pour the remaining sauce over them and garnish with the onion, cheese, and parsley.

Estofado

SEÑORA TOMASA BOURGUET DE ESPINOZA, CITY OF OAXACA

This *estofado,* or stew (though stew is an inadequate word to describe this dish), is considered one of the moles of Oaxaca. It is usually prepared for a festive meal starting with a *sopa de pasta* (p. 65) and accompanied by white rice.

10 PORTIONS

2¼ pounds (about 1 kg) chicken, cut into serving pieces
½ medium white onion, coarsely chopped
½ small head of garlic, unpeeled
Salt to taste
Melted pork lard for frying
2¼ pounds (about 1 kg) rib pork chops, slightly flattened
4 small chorizos
¼ cup (65 ml) water
½ cup (125 ml) sesame seeds
2 Mexican bay leaves or 1 bay laurel
½ tablespoon dried Oaxacan oregano leaves or ¼ tablespoon
    Mexican oregano
6 cloves, crushed
6 allspice, crushed
1 inch (2.5 cm) cinnamon stick
½ large white onion, cut into pieces and toasted
2¼ pounds (about 1 kg) tomatoes
1 tablespoon raisins
20 almonds, peeled and cut into strips
15 green pitted olives
15 large capers
Strips of pickled jalapeños to taste
1 tablespoon sugar, or to taste
Salt to taste
Optional: olives and raisins to decorate

- Put the chicken pieces into a pan with the onion, garlic, salt, and water to cover.

- Cook over medium heat until it is just becoming tender, about 25 minutes.

- Strain and reserve the broth; you will need 2–3 cups (500–750 ml).

- Heat 2 tablespoons of the lard in a skillet and fry the pork lightly on both sides; remove and set aside.

- Skin and crumble the chorizos and add to the pan with the water; cook over medium heat until the water has evaporated and the meat has browned a little. Set aside.

- Toast the sesame seeds lightly in an ungreased pan and put into the blender jar with 1 cup (250 ml) of the broth; blend until smooth. Add a little more lard to the skillet and lightly fry the herbs and spices, strain off excess fat, add to the blender with the onion and garlic, and blend to a slightly textured consistency (you may need a little more of the broth).

- Heat 2 tablespoons of lard in the casserole in which you are going to cook the *estofado,* add the blended ingredients, and fry over medium heat for about 2 minutes.

- Blend the tomatoes until smooth and add to the casserole, stirring to mix well, and cook for about 10 minutes over medium heat. Add the raisins, almonds, olives, and capers and continue cooking for 5 minutes before adding 2 cups (500 ml) of the broth, the meats, the chile strips and their liquid, the sugar, and salt to taste. Continue cooking for about 15 minutes or until all the flavors have been enhanced and combined. If desired, decorate with olives and raisins before serving.

Frijoles negros quisados (Seasoned Black Beans)

FRIJOLES NEGROS CON HUEVO

(BLACK BEANS WITH EGG)

This fried bean paste is used for filling tamales, for *tetelas* (p. 307), or to accompany *tasajo* or eggs for *almuerzo*.

MAKES ABOUT 2½ CUPS (625 ML) BEAN PASTE

3 tablespoons lard

1 small white onion, thickly sliced

½ small head garlic, toasted, cloves separated and peeled

5 large avocado leaves, fresh or dried, lightly toasted and crumbled (see Note on Toxicity, p. 426)

2 chiles pasillas de Oaxaca, lightly toasted and crumbled

4 cups black beans and their broth

Salt to taste

• Heat the lard in a large skillet, add the onion, and fry until golden. Transfer with a slotted spoon to the blender. Add the garlic cloves, avocado leaves, and chiles and blend well with ½ cup (125 ml) of the bean broth. Gradually add the remaining beans and their broth, blending well after each addition, until the purée is almost smooth.

• Add to the lard in the skillet, with salt to taste, and cook over fairly high heat until reduced to a soft, fairly thick paste.

This is a very simple but nutritious way of preparing eggs for *almuerzo*. It is usually served with a tomato sauce with chile de agua (see p. 25).

MAKES 4 PORTIONS

2 tablespoons lard

2 tablespoons finely chopped white onion

2½ cups (625 ml) cooked (salted) black beans with their broth

1½ tablespoons vegetable oil

4 large eggs, beaten with salt

• Heat the lard in a skillet and fry the onion until translucent. Add the beans and their broth and mash them down a little. Cook over medium heat until the broth has reduced a little, about 8 minutes.

• Heat the oil in a second skillet, add the eggs, swirling them around, and cook over medium heat until the underside is set and just beginning to color. Turn the "omelet" over and cook for about 2 minutes on the second side. Remove from pan carefully and cut into 8 pieces. Heat the beans, add the eggs, and serve immediately with tortillas, with the sauce passed separately.

ENFRIJOLADAS

Enchiladas are tortillas dipped in a chile sauce, so *enfrijoladas* are tortillas immersed in a purée of beans. There are some other regional versions of *enfrijoladas*, but to my mind, the best are those prepared in Oaxaca, where the main elements—corn tortillas and little black beans—are so delicious. Because this is such a simple dish, it relies on the very freshest of tortillas and well-seasoned beans. Some cooks just immerse warmed tortillas into a sauce of cooked and puréed beans, but if you season that purée by reducing it in a little lard (or oil), you will have much more tasty *enfrijoladas*. Ideally, tortillas should be from 5½ to 6 inches (14 to 15 cm) in diameter. If they are not of the best quality or have been frozen, heat them well before using or go one step further and heat them through in very little melted lard or oil before immersing them in the sauce.

For cooking and seasoning the beans, follow the recipe on p. 43 for bean tamales, but reduce for about 8 minutes.

You will need about 3½ cups sauce for the 12 tortillas. I suggest you reduce the beans to a very loose paste and then dilute with bean broth or water to reach that amount; when the tortilla is immersed, it should emerge well coated, neither too thick nor too thin.

In Oaxaca, black beans are flavored with any one of a variety of herbs: *poleo* (*Satureja oaxacana*), *hierba de conejo* (*Tridax coronopiifolia*), *yerbasanta* (*Piper auritum*), epazote (*Teloxys ambrosioides*). It is more usual to flavor them with avocado leaves (see Note on Toxicity, p. 426) for this recipe.

Enfrijoladas are served most frequently for *almuerzo* or midmorning breakfast or to accompany eggs, *tasajo* (dried beef), or chicken coated with oregano and garlic and topped with sliced white onion and crumbled *queso fresco*. They should be eaten as soon as they are prepared. Of course, the black bean purée can be prepared well ahead, and any left over can be frozen and will keep well for about 3 months.

3½ to 4 cups (875 ml to 1 L) bean purée (see above)

12 corn tortillas about 5½ to 6–7 inches (14 to 15 cm) in diameter

1 medium white onion, cut into half-moons

¾ cup (188 ml) crumbled *queso fresco*

⅓ cup (83 ml) flat-leaved parsley leaves

Optional: chile de agua strips with lime juice

• Heat the bean purée and the tortillas.

• Immerse the tortillas one by one into the bean purée (they should be well coated) and fold them into four. Sprinkle with the onion, cheese, and parsley leaves.

• *Optional:* Pass separately the strips of chile de agua (p. 25).

PASTA DE FRIJOL

(BEAN ROLL)
Señora Esperanza Morales de Katz, City of Oaxaca

This bean roll, or *brazo*, is decorated or topped with *totopos* (crisp tortilla triangles) and crumbled fresh cheese. To serve, the roll is cut into thick slices.

Warning: You will need patience and a strong arm.

12–14 PORTIONS

1¼ pounds (about 500 g) black beans, picked over, rinsed, and drained
2 garlic cloves, peeled
1 large sprig epazote
Salt to taste
½ cup (125 ml) water
4 avocado leaves, toasted and crumbled (see Note on Toxicity, p. 426)
2 medium Oaxacan pasilla chiles or chipotles mora, lightly toasted
2 garlic cloves, toasted and peeled
Approximately 6 tablespoons melted pork lard or vegetable oil
1 small white onion, finely chopped

To serve:
totopos
⅓ cup (85 ml) crumbled *queso fresco*

- Put the beans to cook in a large pot with the garlic, epazote, and salt. Cover with plenty of water and cook, covered, over medium heat until the beans are quite soft, about 3 hours, depending on age of beans.

- Put the water into the blender jar, add the crumbled avocado leaves, discarding stalks and tough central vein; the chiles torn into pieces; and the garlic. Blend to a fairly smooth consistency.

- Add the beans and their broth a little at a time, blending well after each addition, to a smooth purée. (If using a standard-sized blender, you will probably have to blend the beans in several batches.)

- Heat the lard or oil and fry the onion until golden. Add the bean purée and cook over medium heat until the mixture has reduced to a thick paste. (Have handy a metal spatula to keep scraping the bottom and sides of the pan where the bean paste sticks.)

- When the mixture begins to shrink from the surface of the pan, you can begin to roll it like an omelet onto a warmed serving dish. Add a little more fat if necessary to make the process easier; it should take about 35–40 minutes.

TAMALES DE FRIJOL

(BEAN TAMALES)

There are many regional varieties of tamales filled with beans in Oaxaca, but these, made in and around the city of Oaxaca, are especially delicious. They are served either alone with a sauce of chiles pasilla (p. 56) or to accompany *tasajo* or a mole. The local way of reheating them is to remove the wrapping, spread the surface with a paste of garlic ground together with oregano and salt, and heat through on a comal with a little melted lard.

They can be wrapped either in a dried cornhusk or a fresh or dried *hoja de milpa*, the long corn leaf.

MAKES 30 TAMALES ABOUT 3½ x 2 INCHES (9 x 5 CM)

Have ready:
A tamale steamer, the top section lined with the cornhusks or leaves
30 cornhusks or long fresh or dried corn leaves
5 cups (1.25 L) seasoned black bean paste (p. 40)
30 large pieces of *yerbasanta*
A tortilla press, both plates lined with a plastic bag

THE MASA

2¼ pounds (1 kg) tortilla masa
5 ounces (about 150 g)
Salt to taste

- Work the lard into the masa with your hands until smooth, adding salt to taste. Divide the dough into 30 even pieces and roll each into a smooth ball.

- Put steamer on to heat.

- Press one of the balls out to form a circle about 5½ inches (14 cm) in diameter. Lift up the top, just to loosen it from the masa, and turn the bags over. Remove the (now) top bag. Spread a heaped tablespoon of the bean paste over the surface, leaving a border of about ½ inch (1.25 cm) around the edge.

- With the aid of the plastic bag, fold the dough two-thirds of the way over the bean filling; repeat on the other side to completely cover the filling and then fold the masa over about ½ inch at each end to form a rectangular shape about 3½ x 2 inches (9 x 5 cm).

- Place the tamal flat into a cornhusk, put a piece of the *yerbasanta* on the masa, then turn the point of the husk over the masa. Finally, fold the sides over to cover the masa completely. (Wrapping the tamale in the long leaf is a bit more complicated and can be seen in the photograph on p. 248.)

- Place the tamales flat in overlapping layers in the steamer, cover with more husks, and steam over high heat for about 45 minutes. Test to see if the masa is cooked through at that time; the masa should separate cleanly from the husk. If it doesn't, steam for a further 15–20 minutes.

Garbanzos en miel (Chickpeas in Syrup)

SEÑORA ESPERANZA MORALES DE KATZ, CITY OF OAXACA

This is a typical dessert of Oaxaca often served over rice pudding. But a word of warning: You must use the normal chickpeas, *garbanzos,* and not the large ones, *garbanzas,* which are softer in texture.

In order to peel chickpeas more easily, it is better to let them soak overnight or even for 24 hours. But if you don't have the time, cover them with hot water and let them soak for 2 hours, then cook over slow heat for 15 minutes. That should do it, unless they are very stale.

6 PORTIONS

Approximately 4 cups water (1 L)

1½ cups (250 g) dried chickpeas

1 teaspoon baking soda

1 pound (450 g) *piloncillo,* broken up, or dark brown sugar

1 scant cup (240 ml) water

3 2-inch pieces (about 15 cm) cinnamon stick

2 thick slices fresh pineapple, cut into small triangles

• Put the chickpeas to soak as noted above, strain, and remove the papery skins. Put the chickpeas into a pan with the water, add the baking soda, and cook over medium heat until tender but not too soft, about 45 minutes.

• In the meantime, prepare the syrup. Put the *piloncillo* or sugar with the 1 cup (240 ml) of water and cinnamon and cook over low heat until the sugar has dissolved. Increase the heat so that the mixture boils and thickens slightly, about 15 minutes. Add the cooked, and still hot, chickpeas with the pineapple and cook over medium heat, stirring gently so as not to break them up, until the chickpeas are well impregnated with the syrup, about 15 minutes. Set aside to cool before serving.

Gollorías (Nut Candies)

SEÑOR JAIME KATZ, CITY OF OAXACA

This is a favorite candy, reminiscent of the nut-based candies of the southern United States. In Oaxaca, the best are traditionally made with *nuez criolla,* a type of small pecan, the trees of which abound especially in the Zaachila area.

The word *gollorĩa* appears in *Clave Dictionary of Modern Spanish* as: "*Comida exquisita y delicada*" (Exquisite and delicate food) but also, amusingly, as "*Lo que es innecesario . . . un exceso de delicadeza o de refinamiento*" (That which is unnecessary . . . an excess of delicacy or refinement).

To prevent the sugar from "seizing up," it is best to use a candy thermometer.

MAKES ABOUT 20 GOLLORÍAS ABOUT 1½ INCHES (3.75 CM) IN DIAMETER

Have ready:

A tray lined with lightly oiled wax paper

18 ounces (500 g), or 3 cups (750 ml), sugar

1 cup (250 ml) water

4½ ounces (125 g) whole pecan halves

• Put the sugar and water into a heavy pan and dissolve the sugar over low heat.

• Turn heat to high and cook, stirring continuously, until the syrup begins to thicken and the thermometer reads 225°F (110°C). Immediately add the nuts and mix well. Place spoonfuls of the mixture onto the greased paper. As it cools, the sugar will turn opaque.

Mole verde oaxaqueño
(Green Oaxacan Mole)

SEÑORA VIRGINIA MURCIO JIMÉNEZ, CITY OF OAXACA

This mole is simply referred to as *"verde"* in Oaxaca, and as with all the traditional moles, there are variations in the ingredients. The vegetables or white beans, for example, are not always included. Every cook's recipe differs slightly.

6 PORTIONS

2¼ pounds (about 1 kg) half boneless stewing pork and half meaty ribs or 1 large chicken, cut into serving pieces

1 large scallion with leaves, quartered

4 garlic cloves, unpeeled

Salt to taste

1 large scallion with leaves, coarsely chopped

6 small garlic cloves, peeled and coarsely chopped

3 small chiles de agua, coarsely chopped

10 ounces (about 300 g) *tomates verdes*, coarsely chopped

3 tablespoons melted pork lard

Salt to taste

½ cup (125 ml) tortilla masa

1 cup (250 ml) cooked white beans

1 chayote about 12 ounces (340 g), peeled, cut into wedges, and cooked in lightly salted water, strained, water reserved

12 ounces (340 g) squash, cut into cubes and cooked in the chayote water, strained, water reserved

⅓ cup (85 ml) coarsely chopped epazote leaves

⅓ cup (85 ml) coarsely chopped flat-leaved parsley leaves

⅓ cup (85 ml) coarsely chopped *yerbasanta* leaves

• Put the meat into a pan with the scallion, garlic, and salt; cover with water and cook over medium heat until just tender, about 45 minutes. Strain, reserving the broth. You will need about 5 cups (1.25 L). If necessary, add water to make that amount.

• Put ½ cup (125 ml) of the broth into the blender jar; add the scallion, garlic, and chiles and blend well. Gradually add the *tomates verdes* with a little more of the broth and blend until smooth.

• Heat the lard in a casserole, add the sauce, and cook over medium heat until reduced, about 8 minutes.

• Blend the masa with 1 cup (250 ml) of the broth and stir gradually into the sauce to avoid lumps forming, and continue cooking, stirring to prevent sticking, for about 3 minutes. Add the 3 cups (750 ml) more of the broth with the meat, vegetables, and cooked white beans and cook over medium heat for 10 minutes more.

• 10 minutes before serving, put the reserved vegetable water into the blender with the herbs and blend as smoothly as possible; add to the casserole through a strainer. Add salt as necessary and cook until all the flavors have combined, about 10 minutes. The mole should be of a medium consistency.

Menudo
(Tripe)

REPORTED BY SEÑORA EMILIA ARROYO, CITY OF OAXACA

The traditional cantinas in the City of Oaxaca serve certain dishes on certain days and have done so for generations. The week begins with tripe; on Tuesdays, it is *sopa de guías*; Wednesdays, *viuces*, pork entrails fried crispy; Thursdays, *chicharrón*, pork skin fried to a crisp; on Fridays, a dried shrimp soup; and Saturdays, *barbacoa* of either goat or lamb.

A spicy tripe soup has always been touted as a cure for a hangover and what better day than "San Lunes" to help one recover from the weekend spree. In the cantinas, the cooks prepare a hearty and very picante soup/stew of the entrails of a goat, plus the head and feet and lots of vegetables: cabbage, chayote, green beans, and carrots, flavored with mint and cilantro. However, to serve *menudo* at home, the housewife or family cook will usually buy beef tripe and a calf's foot in the market that is already cooked and cut into small pieces. This is then served either reheated in a tomato sauce or fried with garlic and oregano.

For a really good *menudo*, you should buy all parts of the tripe, and though the regional names vary a little, they can be recognized as: *libro, corazón, callo,* and *pichancha*. These parts and the foot take a long time to cook, and I suggest you use the pressure cooker on the lowest pressure. Only buy tripe that has been very well scrubbed—even then, I like to rub it with limes or bitter oranges and soak it again.

½ calf's foot, about 2¼ pounds (about 1 kg), cut into 6 pieces
1¾ pounds (about 750 g) cleaned tripe (see note above), cut into large pieces
1 large white onion, roughly chopped
1 small head garlic, unpeeled and cut horizontally
Salt to taste

- Put the foot and tripe into a large pot with the onion and garlic. Cover well with water, add salt to taste, and cook over medium heat until tender but not too soft, about 4 hours.

- Strain, reserving the broth. Remove the bones from the foot and cut into small pieces. Cut the tripe into small pieces.

FOR 4 CUPS (1 L) COOKED AND DICED TRIPE AND FOOT

Menudo en salsa de tomate rojo (Tripe in Tomato Sauce)

1 pound (450 g) tomatoes, quartered
1 cup (250 ml) water
½ medium white onion, cut into thick slices and toasted
6 garlic cloves, toasted and peeled
4 chiles de árbol, toasted crisp
1 tablespoon melted pork lard or vegetable oil
2 cups cooked and diced tripe and foot (see recipe p. 46)
Salt to taste

- Put the tomatoes into a pan with the water and cook over medium heat until soft. Drain and transfer to the blender, reserving the liquid. Add the onion, garlic, and chiles and blend to a slightly textured purée.

- Heat the lard in a casserole, add the sauce, and fry over fairly high heat until slightly reduced, about 3 minutes. Add 1 cup (250 ml) of the cooking water and salt to taste and continue cooking for 5 minutes more. Add the meats and heat through a few minutes more.

Menudo frito con ajo y orégano (Tripe Fried with Garlic and Oregano)

In the country, this fried *menudo*, with chopped onion and green chiles, is eaten in a *tlayuda* doubled over like an empanada. Or it is served on a plate in the center of the table, with onion and chile on the side so everyone can make his own taco.

3–4 PORTIONS

The amount and proportion of garlic and oregano will vary to taste.

8 garlic cloves, peeled and finely chopped
2 tablespoons dried Oaxacan oregano leaves or 1 tablespoon Mexican oregano
Salt to taste
2–3 tablespoons water
2 tablespoons melted pork lard or vegetable oil
3 cups cooked and diced tripe

- Crush the garlic, oregano, and salt together. Gradually add the water and mix to a paste.

- Heat the lard in a skillet, add the meats, stir in the paste, and mix well. Cook over low heat, scraping the bottom of the pan from time to time because the gelatinous tripe tends to stick to the pan, about 4 minutes.

Chilmolera with red chilhuacle/Diana Kennedy

Molotes oaxaqueños (Oaxacan Molotes)

These *molotes* (there are similar ones in the Sierra de Puebla), shaped like small weaving shuttles, are generally included in the very substantial *botana oaxaqueña* (see photo p. 55). More simply, these *molotes* are served with guacamole, black beans, and a chile pasilla sauce. A favorite filling is that of chorizo and potato (recipe follows).

MAKES 24 MOLOTES

THE MASA

1 pound (450 g) tortilla masa
2 ounces (about 60 g) pork lard
Salt to taste
Approximately 2 cups (500 ml) chorizo and potato filling
Pork lard or vegetable oil for frying

- Mix together the masa, lard, and salt until smooth. Divide the dough into 24 pieces and roll each one into a ball just over 1 inch (about 3 cm) in diameter. Cover with a cloth while you form the *molotes*.

- Take one of the balls and flatten it between your palms, or in a tortilla press, to a disk about 3 inches (about 8 cm) in diameter. Put some of the filling in the center and roll the dough to cover the filling and to form like a small shuttle. Proceed with shaping the rest of the balls.

- Heat the lard or oil in a medium-sized skillet—it should be about ½ inch (1.25 cm) deep—and fry the *molotes* over medium heat until golden and the masa is cooked, about 5 minutes. Drain on paper towels and serve immediately.

RELLENO DE CHORIZO Y PAPA

(CHORIZO AND POTATO FILLING)

MAKES ABOUT 2 CUPS (500 ML)

6 ounces (about 165 g) Oaxacan chorizo (recipe p. 173)
2 tablespoons pork lard
12 ounces (350 g) waxy potatoes, cooked and cut into small cubes
Salt to taste

- Remove skin and crumble the chorizo. Heat the lard in a medium-sized skillet and fry the chorizo over low heat until the fat exudes, about 3 minutes. Add the potatoes, salt as necessary, and fry gently, stirring to avoid sticking, until the potatoes have absorbed the flavor of the chorizo, about 5 minutes more. Set aside to cool.

Mole negro oaxaqueño
(Black Oaxacan Mole)

SEÑORA LUZ ALLEC DE CALDERÓN[†]

This black Oaxacan mole and that of Puebla are the most famous of all the moles in Mexico—and addictive! The recipe was given to me by Maestro Luis Zárate, who considers it to have no equal, but one must follow his very precise instructions to the letter. It was given to him some years ago by a primary school teacher, the late Señora Luz, who won fame by winning first place in many gastronomic events with her mole. It is served with tortillas and platters of white rice.

The shape of the earthenware *cazuela* in which it is to be cooked is important; it has to have a round base and a "collar" around the top to hold in the heat. The mole has to be stirred constantly with a long-handled wooden paddle, so you need at least four helpers to take it in turns. It should also be cooked on a charcoal brazier.

The toasting of the chiles is very important too. They should be toasted very briefly, but carefully, on a clay comal over a lively heat, but on no account should they be allowd to char; this mole is not as black and stringent as many that are prepared not with the traditional black chilhuacles but with charred guajillos.

It is best to make this amount while you are at it, because the paste keeps for a very long time in the freezer without any ill effects; it also makes a welcome present! When needed, the mole paste is diluted and cooked with tomatoes and chicken or turkey broth.

Start to prepare the chiles the day before.

MAKES ABOUT 5 POUNDS (2¼ KG)

9 ounces (250 g) chilhuacles negros, about 40
9 ounces (250 g) mulato chiles, about 7
9 ounces (250 g) (Mexican not Oaxacan) pasilla chiles
15 chipotle mora chiles
Approximately 9 ounces (250 g) melted pork lard
9 ounces (250 g) sesame seeds, about 1¾ cups (440 ml)
9 ounces (250 g) shelled peanuts, about 1¾ cups (440 ml)
9 ounces (250 g) almonds, about 1½ cups (375 ml)
4½ ounces (125 g) walnuts
4½ ounces (125 g) pecans (*nuez criolla* there)
9 ounces (250 g) raisins, about 2 cups (500 ml)
9 ounces (250 g) plantain, peeled
1½ small semisweet rolls (*pan de yema*), sliced and dried
9 ounces (250 g) white onion, cut into wedges and toasted
1½ heads garlic, toasted, cloves separated and peeled
3 inches (7.5 cm) cinnamon stick
½ tablespoon mild black peppercorns
¼ teaspoon cloves, about 10
½ tablespoon cumin seeds
1½ tablespoons dried Oaxacan oregano leaves or ¾ tablespoon Mexican oregano
½ tablespoon dried thyme leaves or 1 tablespoon fresh
½ tablespoon dried marjoram leaves or 1 tablespoon fresh
4 Mexican bay leaves or 2 bay laurel
9 ounces (250 g) Oaxacan drinking chocolate
9 ounces (250 g) sugar
Salt to taste

- Remove seeds and veins from the chiles, reserving the seeds, except leave the chipotles whole.

- Toast the chiles carefully (see note above). Cover with warm water and leave to soak for about 1 hour, no longer. Strain.

- Toast the chile seeds in an ungreased pan until very dark brown but not charred. Rinse in two changes of water and strain.

- Heat a small quantity of the lard in a skillet and fry the following ingredients separately, adding more lard as necessary and straining to remove excess oil: sesame seeds, peanuts, almonds, walnuts, pecans, raisins, plantain, bread. Mix these ingredients with the chiles, chile seeds, onion, garlic, spices, and herbs and grind—or have them ground at the mill—almost dry, to a paste. Very little water should be used.

- Heat the remaining lard in a heavy casserole, add the paste, and fry, adding a little boiling water from to time to prevent sticking. Stir continuously (see note above) over medium heat for about 30 minutes (adjust time in proportion to quantity cooked).

- Add the chocolate, sugar, and salt and continue cooking for about 1 hour more.

- The consistency should be that of a thick paste, and you should be able to see the bottom of the pan as you stir.

FOR 24 PORTIONS

TO USE THE PASTE

2 tablespoons lard
18 ounces (500 g) tomatoes, toasted
18 ounces (500 g) mole paste
Approximately 5 cups (1.25 L) chicken or meat broth (see below)
Salt to taste

- Heat the lard in a casserole. Blend the tomatoes until smooth and fry until reduced, about 10 minutes. Add the mole paste with 3 cups (750 ml) of the broth and cook over medium heat, stirring and scraping the bottom of the pan to prevent sticking, for about 20 minutes. Add salt to taste and more broth if necessary for the mole to be of medium consistency.

THE MEAT

- Cook the turkey, hen, or chicken of choice with onion, garlic, and salt, well covered with water, until almost tender (the cooking will continue in the mole). Strain, reserving the broth.

Pico de Gallo

I have never seen so many or such tall grapefruit trees in a city as I have in Oaxaca. You can see them, laden with fruit, totally neglected, in parking areas, in empty lots, and in a few gardens, of course. The fruit is very large, misshapen, and delicious with its large, juicy segments. But a few people do take notice and make this refreshing, crisp *pico de gallo* as a *botana*, like the one I first tried in Fonda Santo Domingo.

ABOUT 6 PORTIONS

2 large grapefruits
4 medium-sized Oaxacan pasilla chiles
3 garlic cloves, peeled and finely chopped
Salt to taste

- Peel the grapefruit and separate the segments. Carefully pry the flesh from the tough membranes and spread out on a serving dish.

- Toast the whole chiles over low heat until, when cooled, they become crisp, but be careful not to let them burn. Grind the chiles to a powder. Mash the garlic with the salt and add the chile powder. Just before serving, sprinkle over the grapefruit.

Pipián de camarones para Vigilia (Shrimp Pipián for Lent)

SEÑORA DOMITILA SANTIAGO DE MORALES,[†] CITY OF OAXACA

I have given this recipe without shrimp (vegetables only) in another book, but it has its place here, with the dried shrimps, to remember a great, unheralded cook of the 1960s and 1970s who was my first, unofficial, teacher of Oaxacan cuisine.

This *pipián* is served with tortillas only.

6 PORTIONS

4 ounces small dried shrimps, with heads, about 1 heaped cup (265 ml)

9 ounces (250 g) unhulled pumpkin seeds, about 2½ cups (625 ml)

¼ teaspoon cumin seeds

1 ancho chile, seeds and veins removed

2 chilcosles or guajillos, whole

1 garlic clove, peeled and coarsely chopped

Approximately 4 cups (1 L) water

3 tablespoons vegetable oil

1 pound (450 g) nopales (diced fresh makes 3½ cups; cooked and strained makes 2 cups)

2 large sprigs epazote or 2 toasted avocado leaves (see Note on Toxicity, p. 426)

Salt to taste

- Clean the shrimps, removing head and legs. Rinse to remove excess salt, cover with cold water, leave to soak for 5 minutes, and drain.

- Toast the pumpkin seeds in a skillet over low heat, stirring to toast evenly. Set aside to cool, then grind with the cumin seeds to a fine texture.

- Put the chiles into a saucepan, cover with water, and cook over low heat for 5 minutes.

- Set aside to soak for 10 minutes and strain.

- Put 1 cup (of the 4 cups) of water in the blender jar, add the garlic and chiles, and blend to a smooth consistency. Heat the oil in a casserole; add the purée through a strainer, pressing the contents well to extract as much of the chiles as possible—there will be skin debris left in the strainer. Cook over low heat, stirring to prevent sticking, for 5 minutes.

- Put the ground seeds into a bowl, add the remaining water, and stir to a smooth consistency. Add to the chiles in the casserole through a (not-too-fine) strainer, pressing down hard to extract all the substance, leaving quite a lot of husk debris in the strainer. Cook over medium heat, making sure to scrape the bottom of the pan to prevent sticking, for about 10 minutes. By this time, the sauce should have thickened a little and pools of oil formed on the surface. Add the shrimps, nopales, and epazote or avocado leaf and cook for another 15 minutes, adding salt as necessary. The *pipián* should have a medium consistency; add more water if it thickens too much.

Puerco frito en tomate rojo (Pork Fried in Tomato Sauce)

SEÑORA ESPERANZA MORALES DE KATZ, CITY OF OAXACA

This is a simple but delicious everyday dish, but because of its simplicity, the flavor depends very much on the quality of the pork and tomatoes. It is served with a black bean paste.

The chile de agua, toasted and peeled, lends a special flavor, but where not available, any hot light green chile should be used as a substitute.

6 PORTIONS

2¼ pounds (about 1 kg) of pork, loin chops and ribs, with some fat, cut into 1-inch (2.5 cm) pieces
3 garlic cloves, unpeeled
3 sprigs Oaxacan oregano or ¼ teaspoon Mexican oregano
Salt to taste
2 tablespoons melted pork lard, if necessary
1¾ pounds (800 g) tomatoes, toasted
2 chiles de agua, toasted and peeled

- Put the pork into a pot with the garlic, oregano, and salt. Cover with water, bring to a boil, and simmer, covered, until the meat is almost cooked, about 40 minutes. Strain and reserve the broth. You will need about 6 cups (1.5 L) for the recipe, so reduce over high heat or add water up to that amount.

- Return the meat to the pan with 1½ cups (375 ml) of the broth and continue cooking, uncovered, over medium-high heat until the broth has been absorbed, the meat is tender, and the fat has been exuded. Lightly brown the meat, adding the extra lard if necessary.

- Blend the tomatoes and the chiles to a fairly smooth consistency and add to the pan.

- Cook over high heat, stirring to prevent sticking, until the sauce has been absorbed, about 15 minutes. Add the remaining broth, with more salt if necessary, and cook over fairly high heat until the sauce has been reduced to a medium consistency, about 20 minutes.

Salsa de chapulines (Chapulín Sauce)

SEÑORA EMILIA ARROYO, CITY OF OAXACA

The average visitor to Oaxaca would never dream of eating insects, but after seeing *chapulines* sold on small plates in the markets, or presented with them as part of a *botana oaxaqueña* in a restaurant, curiosity usually overcomes prejudices.

This crunchy sauce is delicious and, what's more, very nutritious. Of course, it is much better made in a *molcajete* or Oaxacan *chilmolera* (photo, p. 48), but if you do use a blender, don't overblend.

MAKES ABOUT 1¾ CUPS (ABOUT 440 ML) SAUCE

6 garlic cloves, toasted and peeled
6 dried taviche or de onza chiles, or substitute chiles de árbol, lightly toasted and crumbled with seeds
Sea salt to taste
1 cup (250 ml) *chapulines*
9 ounces (250 g) *tomates verdes*, cooked in very little water and strained
Approximately ¼ cup (65 ml) water

- Grind the garlic, chiles, and salt to a paste. Add the *chapulines* a few at a time, grinding well after each addition. Add the *tomates verdes* and blend thoroughly.

- Add the water to dilute the sauce a little. It should be of medium consistency.

< THE BOTANA SERVED IN THE CITY OF OAXACA IS A VERY SUBSTANTIAL ONE, CONSISTING OF, WITH SLIGHT VARIATIONS, CHILES DE AGUA RELLENOS, CHICHARRÓN CHAPULINES, GUACAMOLE, MOLOTE, TORTILLAS CON ASIENTO, SALSA DE CHILE PASILLA, QUESILLO, CHORIZO, AND TASAJO./MICHAEL CALDERWOOD

Salsa de chile de árbol (Chile de Árbol Sauce)

SEÑORA OLIVIA CRUZ, CITY OF OAXACA

You can make this sauce with either boiled or toasted *tomates verdes*. In Oaxaca, very small *tomates criollos* are used. It can be made in either a *molcajete* or a blender.

MAKES 1¼ CUPS

8 ounces (about 250 g) *tomates verdes*
8 chiles de árbol, or to taste
1 garlic clove, peeled
Salt to taste

- Cut the *tomates* into small pieces and put them into a saucepan. Half cover with water and simmer until soft, about 5 minutes. Strain, reserving the water.

- Toast the chiles whole on an ungreased comal over very low heat, turning them so they toast evenly and taking care not to let them burn. Crumble the chiles into the blender and blend well. Add the garlic and a few of the *tomates* and blend. Add the rest of the *tomates,* with salt to taste, and blend to a textured consistency, adding a little of the cooking water as necessary.

Salsa de chile pasilla de Oaxaca (Oaxacan Pasilla Chile Sauce)

The chiles pasillas de Oaxaca or, more properly named, chiles mixes, are unique to the Sierra Mixe. Unlike other chiles, they are often sold—by the Mixes themselves out of sacks—divided by size and price; they are priced by the hundred. Generally speaking, the largest ones are usually used for stuffing, the medium for pickling, and the small for sauces. In their raw, green stage, they do not have a distinguishing flavor, but once ripened and smoke-dried, they are one of if not the most delicious chiles in existence.

When preparing this sauce, the famous Zapotec cook Señorita Abigail Mendoza heats them in hot, but not red, ashes, only "*re-calentando*," not toasting, she insists.

Sometimes dried and toasted grubs from the mezcal agave are added to this sauce, which always appears on the table to eat with rice, on tortillas *con asiento*, or with bean tamales, among many other foods.

MAKES 2 CUPS (500 ML)

10 ounces (about 300 g) *tomates verdes*
4 small pasilla chiles
4 small garlic cloves, toasted and peeled
Salt to taste
¼ cup (65 ml) water

- Cut the *tomates* into small pieces, add a very little water, and cook until soft.

- Put the chiles on a comal over low heat or in warm ashes; they should first soften, then heat through, and often inflate.

- In a *molcajete*, crush the garlic with the salt. Add the chiles (with seeds) and grind with the water to a slightly textured consistency. Gradually add the *tomates*, with a little of the water in which they were cooked, and grind or blend to a slightly textured sauce of medium consistency.

INGREDIENTS FOR *Salsa de chile pasilla de Oaxaca*/JORGE LÓPEZ

Salsa de huevo y Salsa de queso
(Eggs in Tomato Sauce and Cheese in Tomato Sauce)

These salsas are undoubtedly the most popular breakfast dishes in the City and Valley of Oaxaca; they are both served with black beans and *blandas,* or soft tortillas. The traditional drink to accompany this breakfast is *atole de granillo,* described briefly as an *atole* textured with cooked, dried corn, roughly ground.

SALSA DE HUEVO

MAKES 4 PORTIONS

5 large eggs
Salt to taste
2 tablespoons vegetable oil
1 pound (450 g) tomatoes, broiled or simmered in very little water
3 garlic cloves, toasted and peeled
2 chiles de agua, broiled, skinned, and deseeded, or substitute either chiles güeros or jalapeños
Approximately ⅔ cup (170 ml) water
Salt to taste
2 large sprigs epazote

To serve: queso fresco, crumbled
¼ cup coarsely chopped flat-leaved parsley

- Beat the eggs well with salt to taste.
- Heat the oil in a large skillet, add the eggs in a fairly thin layer, and cook, lifting up the edge and tilting the pan so that the eggs cook evenly. When the "omelet" is set and the bottom slightly browned, remove from heat and cut into 8 pieces. Leave the residue of oil in the pan.
- Blend together the tomatoes, garlic, and chiles to a slightly textured sauce.
- Add to the pan and cook over fairly high heat until the sauce is reduced a little, about 5 minutes. Dilute the sauce with the water, add the salt and epazote, and continue cooking over medium heat for another 5 minutes. Add the omelet pieces and reheat for just a few minutes. Serve with plenty of the sauce and sprinkle with the cheese and parsley.
- *As a variation:* With or without the eggs, add 2 ounces (about 50 g) of thin *chicharrón,* broken into small pieces, and cook until it softens.

SALSA DE QUESO

MAKES 4 PORTIONS

12–14 ounces (350–400 g) *quesillo de Oaxaca,* or substitute string cheese
Tomato sauce (see instructions above)
¼ cup coarsely chopped flat-leaved parsley

- Unwind the skeins of the cheese and cut into pieces. Heat the tomato sauce and when it comes up to a simmer, add the pieces of cheese. Serve as soon as it melts so it will not be overcooked and rubbery. Sprinkle with the parsley.

Sopa de guías
(Squash Vine Soup)

SEÑORITA IRENE GARCÍA, CITY OF OAXACA

This rustic soup is both healthy and delicious, with many intriguing flavors and textures contributed by the vegetables, *quelites*, and fragrant herbs. It is often served with a sauce of Oaxacan pasilla chiles with *gusanos*, grubs from the mezcal agave.

To make a more substantial dish, *chochoyotes*, or small masa dumplings enriched with *asiento*, are added (p. 29).

This important recipe had to be recorded because of its use of these wild plants, many of which are now cultivated. Although it is impossible to duplicate the soup exactly outside of this area, at least it might inspire aficionados to use what they have on hand or can gather locally. (See photo on p. 62 of the herbs used.)

8–10 PORTIONS

3 ears tender corn
12 ounces (350 g) zucchini or green squash (substitute for *calabacita criolla* used there)
16 vines (about 12 inches, or 30 cm) of zucchini or other squash or chayote
1 bunch *piojitos*
2 bunches *chepil*
1 bunch *chepiche*
1 bunch squash flowers
12 cups (3 L) water
1 medium white onion, coarsely chopped
1 head garlic, halved horizontally
Salt to taste
Optional: chochoyotes (see p. 29)

- To prepare the vegetables and herbs, after rinsing and drying: Shave the kernels off one of the ears of corn, and cut the other two into 1-inch (2.5 cm) slices. Trim and cut the squash into small cubes. Remove the tendrils from the squash vines, strip off the fibrous exterior, and cut into 2-inch (5 cm) pieces.

- Use the leaves and only the tender stalks of the three herbs. Remove the tough sepals only of the squash flowers and chop coarsely.

- Put the water into a large pot; add the onion, garlic, and salt and simmer for 5 minutes.

- Put 1 cup (250 ml) of the water into the blender jar, add the corn kernels, and blend until almost smooth. Add to the pot with the rest of the corn and cook until almost tender, about 10 minutes. Add the vines and cook for 5 minutes more before adding the *calabacitas*, herbs, and flowers. Continue cooking the soup over moderate heat until all the ingredients are tender and the herbs have flavored the broth, about 15 minutes. Adjust salt.

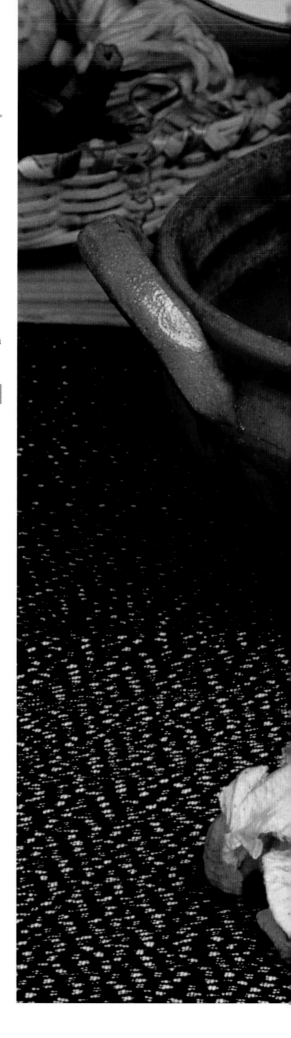

Ingredients for *Sopa de guías*/Jorge López

Piojito/Jorge López

Chepil/Jorge López

Guía de calabaza/Jorge López

Sopa de acelgas y pasta
(Swiss Chard and Pasta Soup)

FAMILIA HAMILTON, CITY OF OAXACA

This hearty soup is traditionally served at weddings or special family festivals. It is served in deep soup bowls and garnished with bread croutons.

In Oaxaca, a small, feather-shaped pasta called *pasta de pluma* is used, but I suggest using medium penne pasta as a substitute.

MAKES 6–8 PORTIONS

3 tablespoons vegetable oil
7 ounces (200 g) *pasta de pluma*, or substitute medium penne
1 small white onion, finely chopped
2 garlic cloves, peeled and finely chopped
12 ounces (350 g) tomatoes, finely chopped
8 cups (2 L) hot, lightly salted chicken broth
4 large chicken livers, cleaned and coarsely chopped
4 cups (1 L) tightly packed, coarsely chopped Swiss chard
1 small bunch flat-leaved parsley
Salt to taste
Crisp-fried croutons

- Heat the oil in a medium-sized skillet and fry the pasta over medium heat, stirring it constantly so that it browns lightly and evenly, about 5 minutes. Remove pasta from oil and set aside in a strainer. Remove all but 1 tablespoon of the oil and fry the onion and garlic until translucent. Add the tomatoes and cook over medium heat until reduced a little, about 10 minutes.

- Put 1 cup of the chicken broth in a small pan, add the chicken livers, and cook over low heat until they are just tender but still slightly pink inside, about 10 minutes. Set aside.

- Add the tomato mixture to the rest of the broth in a soup pot and when it comes to a boil, add the chard, the parsley, and the pasta, with salt to taste, and cook over medium heat until the ingredients are cooked, about 20 minutes. Add the livers and cook for about 5 minutes more. Remove the parsley and serve the soup topped with the croutons.

Tamales de mole negro
(Chicken Tamales in Black Mole)

SEÑORA JUDITH GÓMEZ, CITY OF OAXACA

These tamales are the best known of all the Oaxacan tamales. They are in some way unique in that the masa is extended in such a thin layer that when cooked, one has to scrape the masa off the folds of the very tender banana leaf in which it is wrapped.

It is worth making this quantity while you are at it, as Señora Judith does, because they freeze very well.

In Oaxaca, this black mole is first made into a paste (and that is how most people buy it), which keeps very well for months, or it can be frozen for a year or so.

To prepare the mole, it is diluted with a cooked tomato purée and broth from the cooked meat. The tomatoes may be either toasted or simmered in water.

THE MOLE

Approximately 2 cups (500 ml) chicken or turkey broth
1 large white onion, cut into about 8 segments and toasted
2 small heads garlic, toasted, cloves separated and peeled
3¼ pounds (1.5 kg) tomatoes, toasted until soft and skinned (optional)
2¼ pounds (about 1 kg) black mole paste (p. 50)
Optional: **additional 4 ounces (115 g), or to taste, Oaxacan drinking chocolate, broken into small pieces**
Salt to taste

- Put 1 cup (250 ml) of the broth into the blender jar, add the onion and garlic, and blend well. Gradually add the tomatoes and blend until smooth. Pour the purée into a casserole (without oil) and cook over medium heat, stirring well to prevent sticking, about 10 minutes.

- Stir in the mole paste and continue cooking until the mixture begins to boil, about 10 minutes. Add the optional chocolate, the remaining broth, and salt as necessary. Cook over medium heat until all the flavors are well incorporated and the mole is reduced to a medium consistency, about 15–20 minutes. Set aside to cool before using.

THE CHICKEN

3 quarts (3 L) chicken broth or water
1 large white onion, coarsely chopped
1 small head garlic, unpeeled and halved horizontally
Salt to taste
1 large chicken, cut into large serving pieces, plus 2 whole chicken breasts with bone and skin, each quartered

- Put the broth or water to heat with the onion, garlic, and salt. Simmer for 5 minutes, add the chicken, and cook over medium heat until barely cooked, about 30 minutes.

- Strain. Remove bones and some of the skin and tear into medium strips (do not shred finely).

2¼ cups (565 g) softened pork lard
4¼ pounds (2 kg) textured masa for tamales
Salt to taste
Approximately 2 cups (500 ml) chicken broth

- Put the lard into a bowl and beat, either by hand or with an electric mixer, until white and well aerated. Beat in the masa a little at a time, alternating with the broth and reserving a little of the broth until you see how much the masa will absorb. Add salt to taste.

The masa should be neither runny nor dry and should spread easily.

FORMING THE TAMALES

- Have a tamale steamer, the top section lined with banana leaves, heating over low heat.

- You will need 50 pieces of banana leaf, the thinnest possible, about 12 × 8 inches (30 × 20 cm), softened in hot water or wilted over heat.

- Take one very heaped tablespoon of the masa and with a spatula smear it smoothly over almost all of one of the leaves. Put a few pieces of the chicken and about ⅓ cup (85 ml) of the mole in the center of the masa and fold the leaves, covered with the masa, over the filling. Fold back the end of the leaf to form a rectangular package. Tie each with a strip of the banana leaf or string, place the tamales horizontally in overlapping layers in the steamer, and cook over high heat until the masa separates easily from the leaf, about 1¼ hours.

Sopa de pasta
(Pasta Soup)

SEÑORA TOMASA BOURGUET DE ESPINOZA,
CITY OF OAXACA

This very homey and delicious soup is often served before a dish of *almendrado* or *estofado* (p. 39), prepared for special occasions. Although this soup is generally served with the giblets, in deference to the delicate eaters who don't like them, they can be presented on a separate plate for those who do. *Queso fresco* is often crumbled on top of the soup at the time of serving.

MAKES 6–7 PORTIONS

6 cups (1.5 L) salted chicken broth
5 chicken gizzards, rinsed and cleaned
5 chicken hearts, rinsed and cleaned
5 chicken livers, rinsed and cleaned
6 ounces (165 g) macaroni or bowtie pasta
10 ounces (about 300 g) tomatoes, coarsely chopped
¼ medium white onion, coarsely chopped
2 garlic cloves, peeled and chopped
1 tablespoon melted chicken fat or vegetable oil
¼ cup roughly chopped flat-leaved parsley
Salt to taste

To serve: approximately 1½ cups (375 ml) crumbled *queso fresco*

- Heat the chicken broth in a large pot, add the gizzards and hearts, and cook over medium heat for 20 minutes; add the livers and cook for 10 minutes more. Strain, chop into small pieces, and set aside.

- In a second pan, heat sufficient water to cover the pasta and when it comes to a boil, add the pasta and salt to taste, and cook for 7 minutes only—it should be only half cooked. Strain.

- Put the tomatoes, onion, and garlic into the blender jar and blend to a smooth purée.

- Heat the fat or oil in a skillet, add the purée, and cook over fairly high heat until reduced a little, about 3 minutes. Add to the broth with the pasta and parsley and cook over low heat until the pasta is cooked, about 10 minutes. Add the giblets and salt to taste and cook for 5 minutes more.

La Chinantla

View of Chinantla Alta area, Sierra Juárez/Diana Kennedy

La Chinantla

By Marcus Winter

The Chinantla region in northern Oaxaca includes a mountainous area bordering on the Zapotec Sierra, and even farther north, an area of piedmont and lowlands. The region is drained by tributaries of the Papaloapan that flow across the coastal plain toward the Gulf of Mexico. The mountains of the northern Chinantla include limestone outcrops with horizontal caves used in pre-Hispanic times for burying the dead. The higher areas include cloud forests with abundant vegetation.

OJITLÁN TUXTEPEC
USILA CHILTEPEC
LA CHINANTLA
LA ESPERANZA

MAP OF CHINANTLA/SERGIO AGUIRRE

Exploring the Papaloapan Basin

I was first introduced to this area of La Chinantla Alta by ethnobotanist Gary Martin, who did his doctoral thesis on the plants of the area around La Esperanza, a small dependency of Santiago de Comaltepec. That was in the early 1980s; since then, I have returned many times to record some of the recipes and lore of this area of exuberant cloud forest, which provides so many of the wild foodstuffs that sustain the people living there.

On that first occasion, I visited Eusebio López Hernández, who not only was a great source of information about the native plants but had also collected local recipes using those plants. I remember we ate a type of watercress, gathered that morning, tossed in oil with tomatoes and chiles; grilled *tepejilotes* (*Chamaedorea tepejilote*; see photo p. 328), the buds of a palm; an extraordinary *amarillo de cherimole* (*Renealmia* sp.; see recipe p. 73); and frijoles with *cilantro de monte* (a *Peperomia*, probably *pseudo-alpino*; see photo below).

I have also many times taken the sinuous highway from Huautla de Jiménez, in the Sierra Mazateca, that winds down to Jalapa de Díaz to visit Usila and Ojitlán in La Chinantla Baja. It is one of the most spectacular drives in Mexico, with towering cliffs covered with dense green vegetation and numerous horsetail waterfalls. I shall never forget driving the road, or, more precisely, track, that leads down into the valley of the Usila River, which requires great expertise and steady nerves to negotiate as your tires slip and the car bounces over loose rocks along an unguarded edge above a drop of several hundred feet. But you are rewarded with a spectacular view of the valley and surrounding mountains—alas, always hazy. There is a much more gentle approach to Yogope, a *municipio* of San Juan Lalana. For the most part, it runs along tracks with thick undergrowth on either side, some 25 kilometers from the highway, until a sudden, looping unguarded drop of a few more miles into the village.

The people living in these isolated places have unique dishes made with locally grown corn, chiles, fruits, herbs, and wild greens. Thus, it presents a challenge to do full justice to their food-ways, which depend so heavily on conserving their local environment.

CILANTRO DE MONTE/DIANA KENNEDY

La Esperanza Area

Searching for cherimole with local law official/Diana Kennedy

Amarillo de cherimole
(Cherimole in Amarillo)

SEÑOR EUSEBIO LÓPEZ, LA ESPERANZA

This dish made out of a wild fruit is one of the most extraordinary, not only in Oaxaca and Mexico but perhaps in the world. (I was introduced to it by ethnobotanist Gary Martin.) The color of the sauce, a brilliant yellow, is not from the chiles used, as one would think, but from the color of the fruit's flesh. The *cherimole* plant, which grows in the tropical cloud forests of the northern slopes of the Sierra Juárez, is a species of *Renealmia*; its leaf, which is long and narrow, has a fruity flavor and is used as a wrapping for tamales, especially the bean tamales of La Chinantla.

The fruiting flower spike is crowded with red berries, which turn a deep purple as they mature and develop a shell-like skin. Inside, the yellow flesh is dotted with small, very hard brownish/black seeds.

A similar dish is made from the *Renealmia* in the Sierra Mazateca, in Usila, and in the Sierra Norte of Puebla. It may never be made outside those areas but has to be recorded as an important and intriguing dish in the gastronomy of Oaxaca. It is served in bowls, accompanied by tortillas.

MAKES 4–6 PORTIONS

6½ pounds (3 kg) *cherimole*
4 guajillo chiles, seeds and veins removed and lightly toasted
½ medium white onion, coarsely chopped
4 garlic cloves, peeled
1 cup (250 ml) tortilla masa
4 *yerbasanta* leaves, torn up roughly
Salt to taste

- Cut the fruits in halves, scoop out the flesh into a bowl of water, and separate it with your hands to release the seeds. Then strain and patiently remove the seeds. Cover the chiles with water and soak for about 10 minutes. Strain and transfer to the blender jar with 1 cup (250 ml) water, the onion, and the garlic and blend well.

- In a bowl, dilute the masa with 2 cups (500 ml) of water and add blended ingredients. Put the *cherimole* flesh into a casserole and cook over medium heat until it begins to boil; add the masa mixture and continue cooking, making sure to stir and scrape the bottom of the casserole to prevent sticking, about 10 minutes. Add the leaves with salt to taste and cook for a further 10 minutes.

Bolitas de yuca en frijoles negros/
Diana Kennedy

Bolitas de yuca en frijoles negros (Black Bean and Yuca-Ball Soup)

MAESTRA CLEOFAS FELICIANO BAUTISTA, TUXTEPEC AND USILA

This rustic dish is not just a soup, but a main meal for many in and around the Tuxtepec area. When cooked, the beans should have plenty of broth. The dish is served in bowls, accompanied by tostadas.

THE SOUP

ABOUT 6 PORTIONS

18 ounces (500 g) black beans cooked with salt only, about 8 cups (2 L) in their broth

15 regional dried chiles, tabaqueros or serranitos, or substitute dried serranos, toasted whole

2 garlic cloves, peeled and roughly chopped

5 *aguacatillos*, or avocado leaves (see Note on Toxicity, p. 426), fresh or dried

30–32 *yuca* balls (see preparation below)

• Put 1 cup (250 ml) of the bean broth into the blender, add the chiles and garlic, and blend well. Add to the beans and cook over medium heat for 5 minutes. Add the whole avocado leaves and the *yuca* balls and continue cooking until the balls are cooked; they will be almost transparent and float to the surface, about 5 minutes.

THE YUCA BALLS

MAKES 30–32 *YUCA* BALLS

2¼ pounds (about 1 kg) *yuca*, peeled and cut into small pieces (see p. 101)

A little salt

• Grind the *yuca* as finely as possible, squeeze out the liquid, add a little salt, and form into small balls of about ½ inch (about 1.5 cm) in diameter.

Cabeza de res
(Barbecued Beef Head)

Señor José Solís Palma, Tuxtepec

I happen to think, and I am not alone, that the head of a steer or cow has the most delicious meat, especially the tongue (although it is not for the squeamish eater). I was introduced to the expert in barbecuing the head, Señor José Solís, by the Sacre Cué family in Tuxtepec, whose menfolk often order it for a hearty *botana*, or *comida*, of tacos *de cabeza* served with a picante green sauce and black beans. In the past, the head was cooked in a pit in the ground, wrapped, or rather packaged, in a straw mat called *tenatón*. Now, more often it is cooked in a large container with a rack over several inches of water and left to steam overnight over a very low wood fire.

To prepare the head, it is first skinned and the brains removed to be cooked separately. It is then washed in several changes of water, after which it is rubbed well with a mixture of lime juice, vinegar, salt, and (yes) sweet sherry and left to macerate for about 30 minutes. The juice is then drained and discarded and the head seasoned with the chile paste given below.

FOR A HEAD WEIGHING ABOUT 22 POUNDS (10 KG)

Have ready:

A quantity of banana leaves sufficient to cover the head in a double layer

Several sprays of *aguacatillo*, or avocado leaves (see Note on Toxicity, p. 426), and 20 bay leaves to put under and on top of the seasoned head

2 cups (500 ml) water

2 tablespoons dried Oaxacan oregano leaves or 1 tablespoon Mexican oregano

10 allspice, crushed

10 mild black peppercorns, crushed

10 cloves, crushed

2 large white onions, roughly chopped

20 garlic cloves, peeled and roughly chopped

1¼ pounds (565 g) tomatoes, roughly chopped

9 ounces (250 g) ancho chiles, seeds and veins removed, lightly toasted and soaked for 15 minutes and drained

9 ounces (250 g) guajillo chiles, seeds and veins removed, lightly toasted and soaked for 15 minutes and drained

1 cup (250 ml) softened lard or vegetable oil

Salt to taste

- Put 1 cup (250 ml) of the water in the blender jar and blend the oregano and spices with the onion and garlic. Gradually add the tomatoes, blending well after each addition. Add the remaining water and the chiles and blend to a fairly smooth sauce. Strain.

- Heat the lard in a deep skillet, add the sauce, and cook over medium heat, stirring and scraping the bottom of the pan to avoid sticking, until the sauce has reduced and thickened to a loose paste. Stir in more salt than usual, and set aside to cool a little.

- Spread the paste over the surface of the head.

- Spread out the banana leaves in two layers. Put half of the avocado and bay leaves over the center. Lay the head on this, with the rest of the avocado and bay leaves spread over the top, and wrap in the banana leaves, making sure that no juice can escape.

- See cooking instructions above.

GUISO DE SESOS DE RES

(BEEF BRAINS)

SEÑOR JOSÉ SOLÍS PALMA, TUXTEPEC

After preparing the head, the brains are cooked separately, and for those who don't cringe at the thought, they are delicious. Señor Solís cooks them in the traditional local way, to be eaten in tacos as a *botana*. They are wrapped first in a *pozole* leaf (photo p. 115), which is tough, and then in banana leaves (since the former is not available to most, three layers of banana will suffice) and cooked either on a clay comal or in a wood-fired oven. Since these are not options for many people, a griddle or a metal comal set on a rack over a very low fire can be used. In the latter case, Señor Solís advises putting a thick layer of ashes on the griddle to prevent the leaves from scorching on the hot metal.

Typically, a narrow green chile called soledad is used, but since it is rarely available (they are seasonal), he substitutes fresh jalapeños.

> ONE SET OF BEEF BRAINS IS SUFFICIENT FOR 15–20 TACOS.

Have ready:
4 large banana leaves and 4 *yerbasanta* leaves

1 set of beef brains
8 chiles soledad or 4 jalapeños, finely chopped
5 garlic cloves, peeled and finely chopped
4 tomatoes, finely chopped
1 medium white onion, finely chopped
Salt to taste

- Put the brains to soak in salted water for 15 minutes. Rinse well, removing any traces of blood. Drain, cut into small pieces, and mix with the rest of the ingredients.

- Spread the banana leaves out in 3 layers, with 2 of the *yerbasanta* leaves on top.

- Place the brains onto the *yerbasanta* leaves, cover with the remaining 2 leaves, and then fold the banana leaves over, tying down firmly into a flattish package. Cook as suggested above, turning the package over every ½ hour for about 1½ hours. It should be firm to the touch when the brains are cooked.

Caldo de paisano
(Paisano Soup)

SEÑORA VICTORIA ROQUE ORTEGA, TUXTEPEC

This *caldo*, or broth, seasoned with fragrant herbs, is often served at a wedding before the main dish of perhaps a mole or barbecued beef. But it is always served on the eve of the wedding, when the bride's family visits the bridegroom's home. It is served with tostadas and quartered limes.

IO PORTIONS

4¼ pounds (2 kg) pork ribs, cut into small pieces
10 cups (2.5 L) water
Salt to taste
⅓ cup (85 ml) dried chiles serranitos, or substitute costeños, lightly toasted
¼ teaspoon pure *achiote* or ½ teaspoon prepared *achiote* paste
½ small onion, sliced
2 garlic cloves, peeled and coarsely chopped
18 ounces (500 g) tomatoes, coarsely chopped
2 tablespoons fat from the broth
2 bunches regional potherbs
    4 sprigs mint
    8 culantro leaves
    4 fresh oregano (*oreganón*) leaves
    4 *cebollines*, or substitute 4 small scallions, chopped with leaves

- Put the meat into a large pot with the water and salt. Bring to a simmer and cook over medium heat until the meat is just tender, about 40 minutes. Do not overcook.

- Strain and skim the fat off the broth. Return the meat and all but 1 cup (250 ml) of the broth to the pan. Put the 1 cup (250 ml) of broth in the blender. First, add the whole chiles and *achiote* and blend until smooth; then add the onion and garlic and blend well. Finally, add the tomatoes and blend to a purée.

- Heat the 2 tablespoons of the skimmed fat in a skillet and fry the purée until reduced a little, about 5 minutes. Add this to the pot with the herbs and salt as necessary, and cook over medium heat until the meat is tender and the broth well seasoned, about 20 minutes more.

Casamiento
(Beans and Rice)

Señora Silvia Castillo de García, Tuxtepec

This "marriage" of beans and rice reflects a Caribbean influence, that of *Cristianos y moros*, for instance, and the Yucatecan beans and rice in the dish *Frijol con puerco. Casamiento* is served for *almuerzo* or *comida*, either just with fried plantain or to accompany eggs or broiled meats.

THE RICE WILL MAKE ABOUT 4 CUPS (1 L).

THE WHITE RICE

1 cup (250 ml) long-grained unconverted rice
¼ cup (65 ml) vegetable oil
¼ medium white onion, finely chopped
2 garlic cloves, peeled and finely chopped
Approximately 2½ cups (625 ml) water
Salt to taste

- Cover the rice with hot water and let soak for 10 minutes. Strain, rinse with cold water, and strain again.

- Heat the oil in a casserole and fry the rice over medium heat, stirring most of the time, until it sounds brittle, adding the onion and garlic toward the end so that they do not burn, about 5 minutes. Add the water and salt to taste, cover the pan, and cook over fairly low heat until all the water has been absorbed and the grains are tender. Remove from flame and set aside, still covered, so that the rice will absorb the steam.

THE BLACK BEANS, WHICH MAKE ABOUT 4 CUPS (1 L) WITH THEIR BROTH

9 ounces (250 g) black beans, picked over and rinsed
½ medium white onion, coarsely chopped
½ small head garlic, unpeeled and cut horizontally
Salt to taste
1 large sprig epazote
⅓ cup (85 ml) dried regional chiles: uña de picho, serranitos, or tabaqueros, or substitute 5 chiles de árbol
3 garlic cloves, peeled
Approximately ½ cup (125 ml) bean broth
4–6 tablespoons melted lard or vegetable oil

- Put the beans to cook in plenty of water with the onion and garlic over medium heat until they are just beginning to soften. Add the salt and epazote and continue cooking until the beans are soft but not falling apart, about 3½ hours, depending on the age of the beans. Strain.

- Lightly toast the whole chiles on a comal or skillet, taking care not to let them burn. Put them into the blender jar with the garlic and the ½ cup (125 ml) of bean broth and blend until smooth.

- Heat 3 tablespoons of the lard in a wide casserole or heavy skillet, add the strained beans and the blended chiles, and cook over medium heat, mashing them down until they form a somewhat textured loose paste, about 10 minutes. Add the remaining lard and the rice, with salt as necessary, mixing well together and scraping the bottom of the pan to prevent sticking, about 10 minutes. The mixture should not be too dry; add more bean broth if necessary.

Chileatole de elote
(Chileatole of Fresh Corn)

MAESTRA CLEOFAS FELICIANO BAUTISTA, TUXTEPEC AND USILA

This *chileatole* is always prepared in Usila when the fresh corn is harvested in both Holy Week and later in the rainy season. It is a meal in itself and served alone. The *chileatole* is best cooked in a clay pot, or *olla*.

6 PORTIONS

8 cups (2 L) water
6 small, tender ears of corn, each cut into 4 pieces
1½ cups (375 ml) fresh corn kernels
12 chiles tabaqueros or dried serranos or 10 red costeños
2 large sprigs epazote
Sugar to taste
Salt to taste

- Heat the water in an earthenware pot (if available), and when it comes to a boil, add the pieces of corn. Cook over medium heat until just tender, about 15 minutes.

- In the meantime, toast the whole chiles lightly in an ungreased pan, taking care not to let them burn. Transfer to the blender jar with ½ cup (125 ml) of the cooking water and blend until smooth. Add to the pan and cook for about 3 minutes. Blend the corn kernels with 2 cups (500 ml) of the cooking water to a slightly textured purée; add to the pot with the epazote, sugar, and salt if necessary. Cook, stirring and scraping the bottom of the pot to prevent sticking, until the *atole* begins to thicken, about 15 minutes. Add more water— up to 2 cups (500 ml)—if necessary to obtain a medium consistency.

- Serve the *chileatole* in deep plates with 4 pieces of corn per portion.

Chiles jalapeños rellenos de Tuxtepec
(Stuffed Jalapeños from Tuxtepec)

SEÑORA EVA MARÍA SACRE DE CUÉ, TUXTEPEC

These stuffed jalapeños from Tuxtepec are served either as a very picante *botana* or with white rice as a first course. The *picadillo* is also used for stuffing onions.

MAKES STUFFING FOR 16 JALAPEÑO CHILES

9 ounces (250 g) ground beef

Salt to taste

3 cups (750 ml) water

1 thick slice white onion

1 garlic clove, peeled

2 tablespoons vegetable oil

1 garlic clove, peeled and finely chopped

¼ cup (65 ml) finely chopped white onion

7 ounces (200 g) tomatoes, about 1¼ cups (315 ml), finely chopped

10 almonds, peeled and finely chopped

4 pitted green olives, finely chopped

½ tablespoon large capers, roughly chopped

2 cloves, crushed

2 allspice, crushed

1 Mexican bay leaf or 1 small bay laurel

½ teaspoon dried Oaxacan oregano leaves or ¼ teaspoon Mexican oregano

1 tablespoon vinegar

1 tablespoon sugar

⅓ cup (85 ml) raisins

Salt to taste

¼ cup (65 ml) finely chopped flat-leaved parsley

12 jalapeño chiles

Approximately ⅓ cup (85 ml) vegetable oil

THE PICKLING MIXTURE

3–4 tablespoons olive oil

1 large garlic clove, peeled and sliced

1-inch (2.5 cm) piece cinnamon stick

4 cloves

4 allspice

1 teaspoon dried Oaxacan oregano leaves or ½ teaspoon Mexican oregano

1 Mexican bay leaf or 1 small bay laurel

3 sprigs fresh thyme

1 large white onion, cut into ¼-inch (6 mm) slices

Approximately ½ cup (125 ml) white vinegar

Salt to taste

- Mix the ground beef with the salt and divide into 2 equal balls. Put the 3 cups (750 ml) of water into a pan with salt, the onion, and the garlic and bring to a boil. Add the meatballs and cook over low heat for 45 minutes. Cool in the broth, strain, and crumble the meat like textured breadcrumbs.

- Heat the oil in a skillet and fry the garlic for a few seconds, then add the onion for two minutes more. Add the tomatoes and cook over medium heat until reduced a little, about 3–5 minutes. Add the almonds, olives, capers, and after 2 minutes, the spices, herbs, vinegar, and sugar. Cook the mixture over medium heat, mashing it down, for 5 minutes. Add the raisins and the crumbled meat with the salt to taste and continue cooking over medium heat for 10 minutes. Stir in the parsley just before the end of the cooking time. Set aside to cool.

- Prepare the chiles by making a cut halfway around the top (where the stalk joins) and another down the length of the chile. Carefully remove the seeds and veins (it is easier if you use an apple corer). (See photo p. 82.)

- Heat the oil in a skillet, add the chiles, and cook over low heat until the skin begins to blister. Remove from heat, cover, and set aside to steam for about 5 minutes. When cooled, the skin should be easily peeled off. A bit messy!

THE PICKLING MIXTURE, OR ESCABECHE

- Heat the olive oil in a skillet and fry the garlic till golden. Add the whole spices and herbs and fry for a few minutes more. Add the onion and fry for 3 minutes. Add the vinegar and salt and cook over medium heat for 5 minutes more. Add the peeled chiles, cover the pan, and let them soak and absorb the *escabeche* for 20 minutes.

- Remove the chiles and stuff them well; you should be able to see the *picadillo*.

- Place the chiles on a serving dish and pour the *escabeche* over them. It is best to let them season for at least one hour before serving.

Cochinito a la cubana
(Cuban Roast Pig)

SEÑOR JOSÉ DOMINGO CRUZ COBOS, CHILTEPEC

In the Papaloapan area of Oaxaca, this Cuban roast pig is a very popular dish, especially for Sunday's *día de campo* or for special family occasions. Señor José Domingo, whose grandfather was Cuban, and who is considered one of *the* experts in preparing it, has operated his business in Chiltepec for fifteen years in a large *palapa* by the side of the highway where you can watch the roasting process as you sit and eat. He told me that when the Cuban Revolution started in 1953, his grandfather, like many others, emigrated to southern Veracruz to work in the tobacco industry there and in the neighboring Papaloapan area of Oaxaca. Then tobacco prices dropped and the fields were converted to the growing of sugarcane. Since then, the Cuban influence persists in some of the local food.

It is customary to serve pieces of solid meat with a few pork ribs to chew on in *mojo de ajo*, a portion of *vísceras* (see recipe p. 86), fried black beans, with avocado and lime to complete this substantial repast. And for those who ask for it, there is always extra *mojo de ajo* to season the meat.

Three pigs, about three months old and weighing between 65 and 85 pounds (30 and 40 kilos), are killed daily, and more are killed on weekends or for special orders. They are gutted and, without skinning, cut in halves lengthwise, the head included, then spiked onto long metal spits and left to drain and dry all night. The next morning a fire is started, preferably of guava or oak wood. The skin of the pigs is rubbed with lard, and the laborious process of cooking starts; laborious, because the spits have to be turned constantly for four hours until the skin, or rind, is crisp and golden and the meat tender. When served, the hot meat is submerged in a *mojo de ajo*.

Recipes for the *mojo* vary between cooks, but they all are based on garlic, lime juice or vinegar, and salt, with varying amounts of spices: principally peppercorns, allspice, and cloves to suit individual tastes. Señora Socorro Pulido, Señor Cruz's wife, makes 5 gallons (20 L) of *mojo* twice a week by blending 1½ gallons (5 L) of white vinegar, 9 pounds (4 kg) of onion, and 2½ pounds (1 kg) of garlic. She first fries in oil 5 sliced onions, and when they are just beginning to color, she adds the blended ingredients. This cooks for 10 minutes before adding salt.

LAS VÍSCERAS

(PORK OFFAL)

Señora Socorro Pulido de Cruz, Chiltepec

The *vísceras* are served with the *cochinito* but in a separate bowl. The offal from a 44-pound (20-kilo) pig will weigh about 2¼ pounds (2 kg), including the liver, heart, and lungs.

1 large white onion, cut into 6 pieces
1 head garlic, halved horizontally
Salt to taste
Approximately 1 cup (250 ml) vegetable oil
1 large white onion, finely chopped
2 large garlic cloves, peeled and finely chopped
3 heaped tablespoons pitted green olives, drained and finely
  chopped
3 heaped tablespoons large capers, drained and finely chopped
10 pickled jalapeño chiles, finely chopped
2 Mexican bay leaves or 1 bay laurel, torn into pieces
2½ pounds (about 1.25 kg) tomatoes, finely chopped
20 raisins, finely chopped
Approximately 6 cups (1.5 L) of the broth
Salt to taste

- Cut the offal into large pieces and put into a large pot with the onion, garlic, salt, and water to cover. Cook, covered, over moderate heat until the liver is tender, about 30 minutes. Take out the liver, cool, and cut into 1-inch (2.5 cm) cubes. Continue cooking until the lungs are tender, about 30 minutes. Take out, cool, and cut into 1-inch cubes.

- Continue cooking until the heart is tender, about 40 minutes more. Remove, cool, and cut into small cubes. Strain and reserve the broth.

- Heat the oil in a wide casserole and fry the onion and garlic until translucent. Add the meat and fry until just beginning to brown. Add the olives, capers, chiles, and bay leaves and continue cooking over high flame for 5 minutes. Add the tomatoes and continue cooking until the mixture is almost dry. Add the raisins and the broth and cook until well seasoned for 10 minutes more. Adjust the salt. The mixture should be rather brothy.

A SERVING OF *COCHINITO*/DIANA KENNEDY

Quelites guisados
(Seasoned Wild Greens)

SEÑORA NELVA MARTÍNEZ GRAHAM, TUXTEPEC

This is such a simple and healthy way of cooking wild greens or, in fact, any type of tender greens.

MAKES 3 PORTIONS

3 cups (750 ml) water
Salt to taste
3 cups well-packed wild greens, stalks removed and rinsed
1 tablespoon lard
1 tablespoon finely chopped white onion
3 tablespoons tomato sauce (p. 96)

- Put the water and salt into a pan and bring to a boil. Add the greens and cook until tender, about 10 minutes. Strain, pressing down to extract all excess water, and chop roughly.

- Heat the lard in a skillet, add the onion, and fry for a few seconds. Add the greens and cook for 2 minutes more. Finally, stir in the sauce, mix well, and cook for a further 6 minutes, adding salt as necessary.

Local squash/Diana Kennedy

Machuco
(Plantain Mashed and Fried)

SEÑORA CHATA JORDÁN, JACATEPEC

Machuco is eaten for *almuerzo* or *comida,* accompanied by soupy or fried beans and served with fresh cheese, *nata,* and fried dried chiles.

8 PORTIONS

2¼ pounds (about 1 kg or about 4 medium-sized) green (unripe) plantains
Approximately 3 tablespoons melted pork lard
2 peeled garlic cloves
Salt to taste
1 tablespoon sugar, or to taste

- Peel the plantains and cut each one into three pieces. Put into a pan, cover with hot water, and cook over medium heat until they are soft, about 30 minutes. Strain, reserving 1½ cups (375 ml) of the cooking water.

- Mash the plantains on the metate (traditional) or in the food processor and add the reserved cooking water and salt. It should resemble a slightly textured paste.

- Heat the lard in a 10-inch (about 26 cm) skillet. Add the garlic and fry until golden, then add the plantain with salt and sugar and cook over medium heat until the mixture begins to bubble and slides about in the pan. Turn the *machuco* out onto a serving dish so that it forms a smooth roll. To serve, cut into slices and serve with the *nata,* cheese, and chiles.

PEELING A PLANTAIN/DIANA KENNEDY

Pescado en moste
(Fish in Moste Sauce)

Señora Eva María Sacre de Cué, Tuxtepec

I had come across the use of *moste* leaves burned black for a sauce in Tlacotalpan in the 1970s. It seemed that nearly everyone had a bush growing outside their front doors (alas, no longer). But here in Señora Eva's garden, it had grown into a large tree (probably *Clerodendron ligustrinum*) and, what's more, was a mass of white blossoms. In preparing this dish, the leaves were only lightly toasted.

4 PORTIONS

5 allspice, crushed

Salt to taste

¼ cup (65 ml) lime juice

4 fish steaks about ½ inch (1.25 cm) thick—about 1½ pounds (about 700 g)

1½ heaped cups (about 390 ml) *moste* leaves

Approximately 2 cups (500 ml) water

2 thickish rings of white onion

2 garlic cloves, peeled

¼ cup (65 ml) olive oil

1 medium plantain, peeled and cut into thin rounds

1 fresh jalapeño chile, halved lengthwise

• Grind the allspice and salt with the lime juice and spread over the fish.

• On a comal or skillet, toast the *moste* leaves until dry and they develop light brown spots.

• Put 1 cup (250 ml) of the water in the blender jar, add one of the onion rings and the garlic, and blend well. Add the second cup of water and the toasted leaves, a few at a time, blending well after each addition until the mixture is as smooth as possible.

• Heat the oil in a skillet and fry the plantain slices until they are lightly browned on both sides. Remove from oil. Add the second onion ring to the oil and fry for a few seconds. Add the purée and the chile and cook over high heat, stirring to prevent sticking, until slightly reduced, about 3 minutes. Add the plantain and a little salt and cook for 5 minutes more.

• Dry the fish with paper towels, add to the sauce, and cook over low heat for 5 minutes. It should be slightly underdone because it will finish cooking in the heat of the sauce.

• Serve the fish with plenty of the sauce, accompanied by white rice.

Moste in flower/Diana Kennedy

Quelite Blanco en huevo (Egg with Wild Greens)

SEÑORA NELVA MARTÍNEZ GRAHAM, TUXTEPEC

Knowing my predilection for wild greens, Señora Nelva prepared these *quelites* (*Amaranthus* sp.) with eggs for that much-mentioned hearty breakfast, or brunch. Any tender greens can be substituted. A very special flavor is lent to this, and other dishes, by the little green balls of cilantro formed when the plant runs to seed. In and around Tuxtepec, they refer to their small, stringy plants of cilantro as *criollo*. (In fact, in my climate in Michoacán, the same seeds produce a plant no different from the usual one.)

The greens reduce by about half in the cooking.

MAKES 3 PORTIONS

3 cups (750 ml) water
Salt to taste
4 cups (1 L) tightly packed greens, cleaned of stalks, etc.
1½ tablespoons lard
2 heaped tablespoons finely chopped white onion
2 (or to taste) green soledad or serrano chiles, finely chopped
8 ounces (about 250 g) tomatoes, finely chopped
3 large eggs, lightly beaten with salt
1 teaspoon green cilantro seeds or tender shoots, chopped

- Heat the water in a pot with the salt, and when it comes to a boil, add the greens. Cook until *just* tender, about 5 minutes.

- Strain, pressing the greens down well to extract excess liquid, and chop roughly.

- Heat the lard in a skillet and fry 1 tablespoon of the onion and chiles for 1 minute. Add the tomatoes and cook for 3 minutes more. The mixture should not be too juicy. Add the *quelites* and cook until well seasoned, about 5 minutes. Stir in the eggs, mixing all the ingredients together well. Just before the eggs reach setting point, add the remaining onion and the cilantro seeds. Serve the moment the eggs are set.

Salsa de camarón fresco (Fresh Shrimp Sauce)

SEÑORA MARÍA ISABEL GARCÍA JORDÁN, JACATEPEC

Although this is called a sauce, it is much more like a soft paste to spread on a tortilla or serve on top of beans. Fresh chiles are used, either soledad or jalapeños, both grown in the region. Although vegetable oil is used, olive oil makes the dish extra flavorful.

MAKES ABOUT 1 CUP (250 ML)

8 ounces (about 250 g) peeled, deveined shrimps
About ½ cup (125 ml) water
3 (or to taste) green chiles (see above), roughly chopped
2 garlic cloves, roughly chopped
¼ medium white onion, roughly chopped
6 ounces (180 g) tomatoes, roughly chopped
3–4 tablespoons vegetable or olive oil
Salt to taste

- Heat an ungreased comal and toast the shrimps until the flesh is opaque. Remove and chop roughly.

- Put ¼ cup of the water in the blender; add the chiles, garlic, and onion and blend well.

- Add the tomatoes and blend again. Add the shrimps with the remaining water and blend a few at a time, blending well after each addition to a textured paste, adding a little more water only if necessary to release the blender blades.

- Heat the oil in a small skillet, add the mixture, and fry over low heat, stirring to avoid sticking, adding salt as necessary, until well seasoned, about 8 minutes.

Salsa de camarón seco (Dried Shrimp Sauce)

SEÑORA CHATA JORDÁN, JACATEPEC

Despite its name, this is a delicious concentrated paste rather than a sauce, eaten spread on a tortilla.

MAKES 1 CUP (250 ML)

1⅓ cups (100 g) small dried shrimps, without heads
4 dried paisano (or substitute costeño) chiles, lightly toasted whole
3 garlic cloves, toasted, peeled, and chopped
4 tomatoes, toasted
Approximately ½ cup (125 ml) water
2 tablespoons melted pork lard or vegetable oil

- Briefly rinse the dried shrimps to eliminate excess salt. Dry and then toast lightly until golden. Crumble shrimps and chiles into a blender jar and grind to a slightly textured consistency. Add the garlic and tomatoes with the water and blend.

- Heat the lard or oil in a small skillet and fry the mixture over medium heat until reduced to a loose paste, about 5 minutes.

Salsa de tomate rojo I (Tomato Sauce I)

SEÑORA CHATA JORDÁN, JACATEPEC

The local ingredients used for this sauce are interesting and certainly worth recording. The *cilantro de rancho* is in fact normal cilantro that soon runs to seed (because it doesn't like the damp heat) and forms tiny round green seeds, which are used in sauces in this area. The chile soledad (see photo p. xix) is produced on a very small scale and mostly used fresh. It is narrow and very full of seeds and therefore does not dry so successfully as other chiles grown in the Chinantla-Papaloapan area.

Although the sauce is much better made in a *molcajete*, most cooks use the blender.

MAKES 1 CUP (250 ML) SAUCE

1 garlic clove, peeled
1 tablespoon finely chopped white onion
4 (or to taste) chiles soledad, or any small hot green chile, toasted
7 ounces (200 g) tomatoes, toasted
Salt to taste
Approximately ¼ cup (65 ml) water
2 heaped tablespoons cilantro, with stems and seeds, roughly chopped

- Grind together the garlic, onion, and chiles. Add the tomatoes little by little, grinding well after each addition. Add salt to taste and the water to form a slightly textured, loose sauce. When ready to serve, stir in the cilantro.

Salsa de tomate rojo II (Tomato Sauce II)

SEÑORA NELVA MARTÍNEZ GRAHAM, TUXTEPEC

This is a rustic, textured sauce, predominantly flavored by the fresh green seeds of cilantro. It is served with rice, *antojitos*, eggs, or grilled fish.

The *chilpayas* are small bird chiles that grow wild in the region, although now they are also cultivated on a small scale in the patios of local homes.

MAKES 1 CUP (250 ML)

7 ounces (200 g) tomatoes, quartered
7 fresh chilpayas, or substitute chiltepines
½ cup (125 ml) water
Salt to taste
1 garlic clove, peeled
1 small slice white onion
1 teaspoon fresh, green cilantro seeds

- Put the tomatoes and chiles into a pan, barely covered with water; add salt and cook over medium heat until soft, about 5 minutes. Put the drained chiles, garlic, onion, and cilantro seeds in a *molcajete* or blender and grind smooth. Gradually add the tomatoes, with the water in which they were cooked, and blend to a textured sauce.

Sopa de pollo tuxtepequeña
(Chicken Soup Tuxtepec)

SEÑORA LORENA MOLINO LÓPEZ, TUXTEPEC

This is the most fragrant of chicken soups, owing to the *hierbas de guisar*, the potherbs, typical of the area: *cebollines, orégano extranjero, cilantro de Habana* or *culantro*, and mint. It is served as the main dish in deep soup bowls with tortillas. It is easier to serve and eat this substantial soup if the chicken is cut into small pieces.

To intensify flavor, I have presumptuously changed the recipe a little: instead of adding the tomato raw, I have suggested frying it in melted chicken fat first. If time permits, let the soup sit for about ½ hour before serving for all the flavors to combine and intensify.

6 PORTIONS

7 cups (1.75 L) chicken broth or water

1 chicken, about 3 pounds (about 1.5 kg), cut into 12 pieces with skin and bone

Salt to taste

Optional: 3 tablespoons melted chicken fat or vegetable oil

7 ounces (200 g) bow-tie or elbow pasta, or substitute farfalle or *chifferi lisci* Italian pasta

10 ounces (about 300 g) tomatoes, finely chopped

½ medium white onion, finely chopped

3 garlic cloves, peeled and finely chopped

Herbs: 4 leaves of *orégano extranjero* (or substitute normal oregano)

    8 leaves *culantro* (or substitute cilantro)

    4 large sprigs mint

    4 small *cebollines* or very small scallions

Put the broth or water in a large pot, add the chicken pieces with salt to taste, and cook, covered, over low heat until the meat is half cooked, approximately 30 minutes.

Meanwhile, heat the fat in a skillet and fry the pasta until golden. Drain and add to the broth. In the remaining oil, fry the tomatoes, onion, and garlic for 5 minutes and add to the soup; cook over low heat until the pasta and the chicken are cooked, about 30 minutes, adding the herbs about 10 minutes before the end of the cooking time. Adjust salt and set aside to season as suggested above.

Tortillas de plátano
(Plantain Tortillas)

MAESTRA CLEOFAS FELICIANO BAUTISTA, TUXTEPEC AND USILA

A very unusual tortilla is made of plantains mixed with tortilla masa in this area, and despite their rather unappetizing greenish brown color and chewy texture, they are very tasty. They are served with meals in place of corn tortillas. Maestra Cleofas says they were invented to eke out the corn when it became scarce. When she and her friends made them for me, I was amazed at their dexterity in handling the dough and transferring such a large tortilla from the plastic to the clay comal set over a very hot wood fire.

The plantains they used were still green; 4¼ pounds (2 kg), peeled and ground twice to a smooth texture, then mixed with half that quantity of tortilla masa (the proportion varies slightly from one cook to another).

To make these tortillas, first cut a circle of plastic 12 inches (30 cm) in diameter, and have ready a much larger piece of plastic or a banana leaf (originally a *pozole* leaf).

Take a ball of the dough and press it out with the hands onto the larger piece of plastic, guided by the circle of plastic on top. Turn the whole thing over, remove the big piece that is now on top, and place the dough, still with the circle of plastic on it, onto the comal. (An unglazed clay comal is used there, coated with a wash of lime.)

Then carefully peel off the plastic circle. Cook the tortilla briefly on the first side, flip it over, and cook a little longer on the second side, then back to the first side. The tortilla should, ideally, inflate to ensure that the masa was thoroughly cooked. Maestra Cleofas keeps the tortillas hot in a large gourd, or *chical*.

Yucas on roadside stand, Tuxtepec/Diana Kennedy

Yuca

Ground *yuca* flesh/Diana Kennedy

Patting out *yuca* tortilla/Diana Kennedy

Cooking *yuca* tortilla/Diana Kennedy

There is a Chinantec saying in San Juan Lalana: "It is not good to walk over a piece of *yuca* peel, because when it grows, it will be hard, and when there are more *yucas*, you will not be able to peel them."

The *yuca* (*Manihot esculenta*) is a native of southern Mexico and other countries to the south. It is a long, fat tuber—not to be confused with *guacamote*, which has a sweetish flavor and is sometimes also called *yuca*—and its white, starchy flesh is covered with an almost scaly light brown skin (see photo p. 100).

The *yuca* is a popular staple food in the Papaloapan area of Oaxaca, where it is often grown in small family plots of land. It is prepared in many different ways: for tortillas and tamales, in *mojo de ajo*, and for balls cooked with black beans, among other uses.

Once dug out of the ground, to retain its optimum flavor and texture, it should be used within four to five days (I have noticed that in Latin markets in the United States, it is often waxed).

To prepare *yuca*, it has to be peeled and the center tough core, when it exists, cut out. 2¼ pounds (about 1 kg) whole, unpeeled *yuca* should yield about 2–2½ cups (500–625 ml) pulp. As a guide for making tortillas or tamales: 2¼ pounds (about 1 kg) of whole *yuca* will produce 1¾ pounds (about 800 g) of flesh.

To use it for tortillas and tamales, the flesh should be cut into small cubes and then crushed (as they do in Usila with a large, flat stone) or ground in a metal hand-grinder to a smooth, loose consistency. (I have seen this done in a metal hand-grinder for corn or in a juicer.) The pulp is then squeezed well to extract as much liquid as possible—the water will be full of natural starch.

To make these white, slightly chewy tortillas, take a ball of the prepared *yuca* flesh, press it out, and smooth it with your hands (not in a tortilla press) into a circle onto a piece of plastic. Transfer to a hot comal and peel off the plastic. Cook for a few minutes on each side; the surface will be speckled with brown. As you remove it from the comal, hang it on the side of a pot (see photo p. 99) to cool off. If you pile the tortillas one on top of the other, as you do for corn tortillas, they will stick to each other and be impossible to separate without breaking.

Tortillas of *yuca* are served to accompany a meal in place of corn tortillas. However, during Holy Week and on special occasions, it is traditional to serve very large *yuca* tortillas, 14–16 inches (about 35–40 cm) in diameter, spread with a bean paste (see recipe p. 116), doubled over into four, and left to season overnight. The next day, they are opened up and reheated on a hot comal. Typically, they accompany a chicken in mole *amarillo*.

Usila Area

Asadura de puerco usileña (Pork Offal from Usila)

Maestra Cleofas Feliciano Bautista, Usila

In the Papaloapan area of Oaxaca, when a pig is killed for a fiesta or special family occasion, the offal, or *asadura*, are prepared in this hearty dish.

In Usila, it is prepared in this way but with some different flavors to those used in neighboring Chiltepec and Tuxtepec. The *asadura* is served in deep bowls, only accompanied by corn tortillas.

Serves about 15

Approximately 1 cup (250 ml) melted lard
2¼ pounds (about 1 kg) pork ribs, cut into small pieces
2¼ pounds (about 1 kg) pork liver, heart, and spleen, cut into small cubes
Salt to taste
3 ancho chiles, seeds and veins removed
½ cup (125 ml) paisano or piquín chiles, left whole
9 ounces (about 250 g) tomatoes, roughly chopped
3 garlic cloves, peeled
Approximately 3 cups (750 ml) water
2 bunches large chives (see note p. 430 about regional herbs), roughly chopped
1 small bunch mint
1 small bunch *culantro*

- In a large, wide casserole, heat the lard and fry the pork ribs until golden, about 15 minutes. Add the liver, etc., and salt and continue frying over high heat, stirring and scraping the bottom of the casserole to avoid sticking, until the mixture is almost dry, about 30 minutes.

- Meanwhile, prepare the chiles: lightly toast the anchos, cover them with warm water, and leave to soak for about 10 minutes. Strain. Lightly toast the small dried chiles and put them, crumbled, into the blender jar with the tomatoes and garlic. Blend as smoothly as possible. Add 1 cup (250 ml) of the water with the anchos and blend again to a slightly textured purée. Add this to the meat and cook the mixture over fairly high heat for about 15 minutes. Add the herbs and the rest of the water, cover the pan, and cook over low heat, adding more salt as necessary, for about 30 minutes. The *asadura* should be rather soupy.

Barbacoa de res
(Barbecued Beef)

Señor Norberto Juárez Gallegos, Ojitlán

Señor Norberto gave me a "package" of his barbecued meat as part of an improvised and sumptuous breakfast in his mother-in-law's house. There is no better way of passing the time while waiting for tamales to cook than eating—and with such a variety of new tastes and textures to boot.

Barbecued beef is always prepared for special festivals or family occasions in the area, accompanied by a green sauce and black beans. The pieces of meat, usually on the bone, are seasoned with a chile sauce, wrapped in either a *pozole* (see p. 429) or a banana leaf, and steamed for many hours over a wood fire (or, more practically, although not as tasty, 1½ hours in a pressure cooker). Señor Beto prepares up to 220 pounds (100 kg) at a time, but this recipe is for 8 portions.

The best meat for this type of dish is brisket with bone or short ribs, both with some fat, cut into 3-inch (7.5 cm) pieces. Since the exotic leaves are rarely available, use a double layer of banana leaves. If time permits, the meat is best if prepared and seasoned for several hours or overnight.

3 ancho chiles, cleaned of seeds and veins
3 guajillo chiles, cleaned of seeds and veins
2 chipotle moras (if not available, use canned chipotles en adobo), whole
Approximately 2 cups (500 ml) water
2 cloves, crushed
2 mild black peppercorns, crushed
5 garlic cloves, peeled and roughly chopped
1 tomato, roughly chopped
1 thick slice of white onion, roughly chopped
1 tablespoon pork lard
1 teaspoon pineapple or other fruit vinegar
Salt to taste (use more than usual)
4¼ pounds (2 kg) beef (see note above) with bone, cut into 3-inch (7.5 cm) pieces
(If available: 16 *pozole* or *platanillo* leaves, softened over heat, or) 8 large banana leaves (if possible, whole with tough center vein), halved and softened over heat
16 Mexican or 8 bay laurel leaves
16 *aguacatillo* or avocado leaves (see Note on Toxicity, p. 426)
16 ties, 2 for each package

- Have ready a steamer with rack, set above 3 inches (7.5 cm) of water, or a pressure cooker with about 1 inch (2.5 cm) of water.

- Cover the dried chiles with water and leave to soak for about 20 minutes. Drain.

- Put ½ cup (125 ml) water in the blender jar, add the spices, garlic, tomato, and onion and blend until smooth. Add the rest of the water and the chiles, a few at a time, and blend as smoothly as possible.

- Heat the lard in a skillet and fry the sauce until slightly reduced, about 5 minutes.

- Add the vinegar and plenty of salt, mix well, and spread the meat with the sauce—best done with your hands. If time permits, leave to season overnight. Spread out the banana leaves for the 8 portions. Place a piece of the meat, with the sauce, on each one, top with 2 *aguacatillo* or 1 avocado leaf and 2 bay leaves. Then fold the banana leaves over to form tightly sealed packages so that none of the sauce oozes out. Tie each one firmly, place in the steamer or cooking pot, and cook until the meat is tender, about 4 hours and 1½ hours, respectively.

Caldo de piedra

One of the most extraordinary foods in the Chinantla region is *caldo de piedra*, literally "broth of stone," referring to the heated stones that cook the ingredients. I had heard of this *caldo* from friends in Oaxaca many years before I actually paid my first visit to Usila to see its preparation firsthand.

There must have been much earlier references to this *caldo*, but from a study done by anthropologist Roberto Weitlaner in 1973, it was called *caldo de playa*, or "beach broth," since it was prepared on the sandy borders of the river by the men who fished there. They made a pit in the sand and lined it with leaves of *pozole* (probably *Calathea lutea* or *Heliconia bihai*), then added water with the chiles and vegetables.

Stones a little larger in size than a large hen's egg were heated until almost red hot and added to the water; when it was boiling, the fish was added. The *caldo* was served in the *pozole* leaves with tortillas. Meanwhile, the young boys caught shrimp (a type of crayfish), which they spiked onto a stick and cooked in a gourd—no doubt the same type of gourd, which is still used today, for serving the *caldo*.

In those days, apparently, the river abounded in aquatic life, but today it has been greatly diminished because the closed breeding season has not been observed and, no doubt, because of the growing demand from the expanding city of Tuxtepec, the nearest commercial center.

On one of my visits to Usila the *caldo* was prepared for me in a home that housed a small informal restaurant (see photo below). The gourds were lined up, each containing a small quantity of chopped tomato, onion, green chiles, and epazote. Small gutted fish and shrimps were added with salt and covered with water. The stones had been heated ahead of time, and when they were almost red, were picked out of the wood fire with two strong sticks—the same twigs that would be used to heat the large tortillas by dangling them over the fire—and put into the gourds. As the water bubbled furiously, a column of steam hissed upward like a geyser. When the bubbling died down, the stones were removed, and, believe it or not, the ingredients were cooked. I am told that the delicacy for the dedicated gourmet to accompany the *caldo* is a taco filled with the fish entrails.

Another cook in the area told me that traditionally the small wild tomatoes, wild "cilantro," and local green chiles would be used, the latter being tabaqueros, which I saw planted among the boulders rising above the rocky track that descends precipitously into the valley of the Usila River (see photo p. 78).

Caldo de res usileño
(Beef Soup from Usila)

MAESTRA CLEOFAS FELICIANO BAUTISTA, USILA

In Usila, the most important celebrations of the year are for La Natividad de María on September 8; for the patron saint, San Felipe, on May 3; and for All Saints and All Souls on November 1 and 2. This fragrant *caldo de res* is prepared for all those occasions.

Preparations start three days ahead: for instance, on September 5, about thirty animals are slaughtered to provide enough meat for this festive dish, with extra to sell to visitors who go there from the neighboring villages and *rancherías*. Until a few years ago, the preparation of this dish was a communal effort, but now most families prepare their own. A family of some rank in the village, and who has the resources, is in charge of buying and slaughtering the cattle, employing four men who specialize in preparing the meat. Nothing is wasted; *chicharrón* is made of the beef fat and trimmings, and the blood is cooked in water and fried with the local fragrant herbs and chiles for tacos.

The *caldo* is served in bowls, with tortillas only.

8 PORTIONS

3½ pounds (about 1.5 kg) beef on the bone: shin, brisket, and short ribs, cut into large serving pieces

Salt to taste

9 guajillo chiles, seeds and veins removed

¼ cup (65 ml) small regional dried chiles: tabaqueros or serranitos (or substitute costeños)

4 garlic cloves, peeled and coarsely chopped

2 large chayotes, about 1 pound (450 g) each, peeled and sliced

20 chayote leaves, coarsely chopped

20 chayote vines (see preparation note below)

1 large bunch of *cebollines blancos* (or substitute small scallions and chives, coarsely chopped with leaves)

2 large sprigs *oreganón* (see Glossary), left whole

1 small bunch *culantro* (see Glossary), coarsely chopped

1 small bunch mint

- Put the meat into a large pot with plenty of water to cover and salt to taste. Cook over medium heat until tender but not too soft, 2 to 3 hours, depending on the quality of the meat.

- Meanwhile, prepare the chiles: lightly toast the guajillos, flattening them out with a spatula but taking care to not let them burn. Cover them with water and let them soak 15 minutes. Strain. Toast the tabaqueros whole.

- Put 1 cup (250 g) of the meat broth in the blender, add the garlic and the tabaquero chiles, and blend well.

- Add a second cup of the broth and the guajillos, a few at a time, blending well after each addition. Add this purée to the pot with the meat through a strainer, pressing down well to extract as much of the juice and flesh as possible; there will be debris of chile skins left in the strainer. Add the chayotes, the leaves, and the vines and cook over medium heat for 20 minutes. Then, finally, add the herbs, with salt if necessary, and continue cooking for a further 15 minutes.

PREPARATION OF THE CHAYOTE VINES

- First break off the tough ends of the vines; then remove the tendrils and strip off the tough, stringy fibers around the stems. Cut the cleaned stems into pieces about 1½ inches (3.75 cm) long. You can also use the tips of the vines with their corolla (if any) of flower buds and small leaves.

Empanadas de cocolmécatl (Empanadas of Cocolmécatl)

SEÑORA ALTAGRACIA ISIDRO, USILA

One morning in Usila, Señora Altagracia prepared one of the most memorable breakfasts I have ever seen or eaten. Among other foods was this extraordinary empanada filled with *yerbasanta* and *cocolmécatl* (*Smilax* sp.; see Glossary). She pressed out tortilla masa to a large circle about 9 inches (23 cm) in diameter. On one half, she put a leaf of *yerbasanta* and on top of that a mashed stalk of *cocolmécatl*. This was covered with another *yerbasanta* leaf and the dough folded over to make a large turnover, which was then cooked on an ungreased comal. It was eaten just like that, without any sauce.

Pato frito en chile seco (Duck Fried in Dried Chile)

SEÑORA GUADALUPE JUÁREZ GALLEGO, OJITLÁN

This dish is usually prepared in Ojitlán for the Days of the Dead, November 1 and 2, and served with white rice. It is cooked with a duck that has been running around the patio and is therefore rather tough. Another way they prepare duck locally is in a simple *pipián* made with sesame seeds, ancho chiles, and small dried regional chiles paisanos.

4–6 PORTIONS

1 large duck about 4 pounds (about 2 kg), with giblets
⅓ cup (85 ml) lime juice
1 small head of garlic, halved horizontally
1 medium white onion, roughly chopped
Salt to taste
3 tomatoes, quartered
⅓ cup (85 ml) dried regional chiles (see p. 426) or piquín chiles
4 garlic cloves, peeled and roughly chopped
½ medium white onion, roughly chopped
Salt to taste
Approximately 1 cup (250 ml) melted pork lard
3 Mexican bay leaves or 2 bay laurel

- Cut the duck and the giblets into small pieces, about 1 inch (2.5 cm), and wash with the lime juice in cold water. Put the meat in a pot with the garlic, onion, and salt.

- Cover well with water and cook, covered, over medium heat until the meat is just tender, approximately 50 minutes. Do not overcook, or it will fall apart at the next stage.

- Meanwhile, barely cover the tomatoes and chiles with water and cook over medium heat for about 5 minutes. Transfer them to the blender jar, add the garlic and onion, and blend to a slightly textured sauce. Add salt to taste.

- Heat the lard in a large skillet and fry the duck and giblets until they are golden brown—don't crowd the pan; it is better to do it in several batches. Pour on the sauce, add the bay leaves, and mix to cover the meat as evenly as possible. Then fry, stirring and scraping the bottom of the skillet to prevent sticking, until the sauce has dried and caked around the duck pieces.

Popo

Popo is the name given to the foam that is served on top of a bowl of *atole* in Usila. It is served after a special or festive meal and no *posada* at Christmastime would be complete without it. The foam, or *espuma*, is also sold daily along the sidewalks in the center of Tuxtepec by the women of Ojitlán, who also specialize in making it.

Like many other similar preparations, the base is made with cacao and corn, but here the foam is created by toasting and crushing the petiole of a vine called *cocolmécatl* (*Smilax*, probably *lanceolata*). The vine grows wild in the surrounding mountains, and the people who collect it keep the exact whereabouts of their source of supply a secret.

An anthropological study of the area by Robert Weitlaner in the 1970s describes the method of preparing the ingredients for the foam: the cacao beans were washed in warm water, wrapped in a *pozole* (*Calathea lutea*) leaf, and left for eight days to ferment until they looked putrid, with a white feathery growth. After drying in the sun for one or two days, the cacao was toasted and ground. It was then diluted with water to which were added the toasted tender leaves of *cocolmécatl,* which had been ground with raw sugar. It is not clear when the corn was added. This paste was beaten for the foam.

Through the years, the method of preparation has become much simpler: the ingredients are toasted and ground to a powder, which can easily be stored. It is then moistened when required. There is even a difference now between the ingredients of two cooks in Usila today: Señora Altagracia mixes a gourd of toasted and pulverized cacao with the same amount of corn treated in the same way. Maestra Cleofas says that her mother sometimes toasted rice instead of corn because she preferred the lighter color it gives the foam, and added a little cinnamon.

When preparing the foam, the powdered ingredients are mixed with a little water and ground on the metate with a stalk of toasted and peeled *cocolmécatl.*

The mixture is diluted with water, sugar added, and beaten until foam collects on top of the liquid.

Cocolmécatl plant/Diana Kennedy

Salsa de camarón fresco usileña (Fresh Shrimp Sauce from Usila)

MAESTRA CLEOFAS FELICIANO BAUTISTA, USILA

This fresh shrimp sauce is delicious spread thickly on a freshly made tortilla or tostada, but more delicious still when used in a taco with cooked *hierbamora*. Maestra Cleofas says that, of course, this sauce is more tasty made with shrimps caught in the Usila River, which runs very close to the village, and also when using the miniature wild red tomatoes and the local chiles tabaqueros when in season.

MAKES ABOUT 1 CUP (250 ML)

8 fresh medium-sized shrimps, or 5 large ones, unshelled and head intact
10 (or to taste) green tabaqueros, or substitute 6 serrano chiles
2 garlic cloves, peeled and finely chopped
10 green (fresh) cilantro seeds, or 1 tablespoon cilantro, finely chopped
3 tomatoes, cooked in water, strained, and water reserved
Salt to taste

- Toast the whole shrimps on a comal over medium heat, or over a wood-fired grill, until the heads are crisp and slightly charred. Chop finely.

- Preferably using a *molcajete*, crush together the chiles, garlic, and cilantro seeds. Add the tomatoes and blend with about 1/3 cup (85 ml) of the cooking water. Add the chopped shrimps and mash briefly. Add salt to taste. The sauce should be juicy; if not, add a little more of the water.

Salsa de chile frito (Fried Chile Sauce)

SEÑORA GLORIA PATRÓN, OJITLÁN

Although this is called a sauce, it is more of a very picante condiment used on top of fried beans and tostadas, among other things. Señora Nelva, in her restaurant in Tuxtepec, uses it in fish broth, with fish and other seafood.

Small dried local chiles are used, particularly moritas, the smoke-dried last picking of the serrano chiles.

MAKES ¾ CUP (185 ML)

½ cup (125 ml) vegetable oil
2 cups (500 ml) small dried chiles
2 garlic cloves, peeled
Salt to taste

- Heat the oil in a skillet, add the chiles and garlic, and fry until the chiles are very crisp and the garlic browned. Grind, without water, to a textured paste. Add salt to taste.

Tamales de elote
(Fresh-Corn Tamales from Ojitlán)

SEÑORA FRANCISCA PADRÓN, OJITLÁN

It is customary to wrap these tamales in fresh or dried cornhusks but to line them with a leaf that is called *molinillo*; which is, in fact, the leaf of a tree (*Quararibea funebris*) known in the Valley of Oaxaca as *rosita de cacao*.

It is necessary to choose mature corn, starchy but still juicy.

Once assembled, the tamales should go immediately into a very hot steamer so that the rather loose mixture sets quickly and doesn't exude from the husk.

> **MAKES APPROXIMATELY 36 TAMALES ABOUT 4 INCHES (10 CM) LONG**

Have ready:

A tamale steamer with the top section lined with (preferably) fresh or dried cornhusks

36 fresh or dried cornhusks

36 *molinillo* leaves (omit if not available)

3 cups (750 ml) black bean paste (p. 116)

THE MASA

10 cups (2.5 L) fresh corn kernels (see note above)

1 cup (250 ml) melted pork lard

2 tablespoons sugar, or to taste

1½ tablespoons salt, or to taste

- Grind the corn in a metal hand-cranked grinder or a food processor to a finely textured purée. Mix in a large bowl with the rest of the ingredients.

- Put the steamer to heat over high heat.

- Spread one of the husks with a heaped tablespoon of the corn mixture in a thick layer.

- Put a tablespoon of the bean paste down the middle, cover with a *molinillo* leaf, then fold the husk firmly to cover the contents, bending up the pointed end. Put each tamale immediately into the steamer, horizontally in overlapping layers. When all have been assembled, cover the steamer and cook over high heat until the masa has set well and separates easily from the husk, about 1¼ hours.

Tamales de yuca rellenos de frijol (Yuca Tamales Filled with Beans)

SEÑORA FRANCISCA PADRÓN, OJITLÁN

Señora Francisca, helped by members of the family, every week makes hundreds of tamales of *yuca*, filled either with a black bean paste or pork, to sell principally in Tuxtepec. To clean, grind, and squeeze the liquid out of the *yuca* flesh is a lengthy business, and many hands are needed until the tamales are finally boiling (yes, in water) in an enormous copper *cazo* over a wood-burning fire.

There are various leaves used in that area for wrapping the tamales: *molinillo* (*Quararibea funebris*), and *huilimole* (*Renealmia* sp.), the same as *cherimole* in other parts of La Chinantla, which has a pronounced fruity flavor. For other types of tamales, *hojas de pozole* (*Calathea lutea*), canna lily leaves: *frutilla* (*Canna indica*), and, of course, banana leaves are used.

These truly delicious tamales were wrapped, first in ½ leaf of *huilimole* and then in a piece of banana leaf.

Makes 26 tamales

Have ready:
26 pieces of banana leaf about 11 × 9 inches (28 × 23 cm), wilted over heat, and 13 *Canna indica* leaves (instead of *huilimole*), cut across in half.
A prepared steamer, and heat over very low heat while you form the tamales.

8 cups (2 L) prepared *yuca* pulp (p. 101)
3 cups (750 ml) melted pork lard
Salt to taste
4 cups (1 L) black bean paste

- Put the *yuca* in a large bowl with the lard and salt and beat with the hand to mix well. The mixture will be like a loose paste.
- Put a piece of the *Canna* leaf in the center of a piece of banana leaf. Spread a scant ⅓ cup (85 ml) of the masa over the center of the leaves—it should be about ⅜ inch (1 cm) thick. Put about ¼ cup (65 ml) of the bean paste on one side of the dough. Double the half leaf over the mixture, then fold the banana leaf over to form a rectangular package that covers the contents completely and securely.
- When the water in the steamer is boiling, place the tamales horizontally in overlapping layers in the steamer and cook over high heat for about 1½ hours. The tamales should be firm to the touch when cooked. They are eaten alone.

FRIJOLES NEGROS PARA TAMALES

(BLACK BEANS FOR TAMALES)

SEÑORA GLORIA PADRÓN DE JUÁREZ, OJITLÁN

THE BEAN PASTE

MAKES 5 CUPS (1.250 L); ANY LEFTOVERS CAN BE USED FOR TAMALES, ETC.

1 pound (450 g) black beans, picked over, rinsed, and strained
Salt to taste
3 garlic cloves, toasted and peeled
12 *aguacatillo* or avocado leaves (see Note on Toxicity, p. 426), toasted and crumbled
½ cup (125 ml) small dried local chiles: tabaqueros or serranitos, lightly toasted whole

- Put the beans into a large pot with water to well cover and salt. Cook, covered, over medium heat for approximately 2½ hours; they should be slightly undercooked.
- Strain the beans, reserving the broth.
- Put garlic with the crumbled leaves and chiles into the blender jar with ½ cup (125 ml) of the bean broth and blend until smooth. Add to the beans and grind them to a fairly dry but spreadable paste, either in a metate or a food processor, only adding a little more bean broth if necessary.

Making a *yuca* tamale with black bean paste/Diana Kennedy

Tamales de yuca de puerco
(Yuca Tamales Filled with Pork)

SEÑORA FRANCISCA PADRÓN, OJITLÁN

MAKES 28–30 TAMALES

Have ready:

A tamale steamer, the top portion lined with banana leaves

30 *pozole* leaves, or pieces of banana leaf about 11 × 13 inches (28 × 33 cm)

30 *yerbasanta* leaves

THE MEAT

3¼ pounds (1.5 kg) meaty ribs or boneless stewing pork, cut into small pieces

½ medium white onion

½ small head garlic, halved horizontally

Salt to taste

THE *MOLITO*

1 scant cup (225 ml) regional dried chiles, tabaqueros or serranitos, toasted

4 garlic cloves, peeled and coarsely chopped

⅓ medium white onion, coarsely chopped

2 cups (500 ml) pork broth

1 tablespoon pork lard

Salt to taste

THE MASA

10 cups (2.5 L) prepared *yuca* pulp (p. 101)

4 cups (1 L) melted pork lard

2 cups pork broth

Salt to taste

TO PREPARE THE MEAT

- Put the pork, onion, garlic, and salt into a pan; cover with water; and cook over medium heat until almost tender. Strain and reserve the broth. You will need about 5 cups (1.25 L).

TO PREPARE THE *MOLITO*

- Cover the toasted whole chiles with water and leave to soak for 10 minutes. Strain, transfer to the blender jar, and blend with the garlic, onion, and 2 cups (500 ml) of the pork broth until smooth.

- Heat the 1 tablespoon of lard in a skillet, add the chile purée, and cook over medium heat, stirring to prevent sticking. Add salt to taste. There should be about 3 cups (750 ml) of sauce of medium consistency.

TO PREPARE THE MASA

- Mix the *yuca* with the lard and broth, add salt to taste, and mix well. It should be of a loose consistency.

- Place a *yerbasanta* leaf on each piece of banana leaf. Put ½ cup (125 ml) of the *yuca* masa in the center and spread it out until about ½ inch (1.25 cm) from the edge. Put a piece or two of the meat on the masa and cover with 1½ tablespoons of the *molito* (take care; it will be runny). Double the *yerbasanta* leaf over to cover the filling and then fold the banana leaf over to form a rectangular package, taking care that the contents do not leak out.

- Make sure that the water in the steamer is boiling, then place the tamales horizontally in overlapping layers and cook over high heat until the *yuca* masa is firm to the touch, about 1¾ hours.

Yogope Area

A TYPICAL HOUSE IN YOGOPE/DIANA KENNEDY

Caldo de guajolote ahumado
(Caldo of Smoked Turkey)

SEÑORA MACLOVIA DOLORES DE MARTÍNEZ, YOGOPE

I had been hearing for many years of this *caldo* of smoked turkey, which is prepared for special occasions in this part of La Chinantla, from ethnobotanist Alejandro de Ávila. So when I finally met members of a family who lived in Yogope, I decided to go and seek it out.

The day before the meal was to be prepared, a turkey was killed, plucked, and gutted. It was then cut down the back and flattened out.

While this was happening, other members of the family had started a fire over which they constructed a rack of crisscrossing branches of a tree called *cocuite* (*Gliricidia sepium*), which does not burn easily. When the fire had died down to hot ashes, the turkey was placed on the rack and smoked very slowly. It was turned at regular intervals during the 6 hours of smoking until it acquired a deep brown shiny surface.

The next day, the turkey was cut into pieces, rinsed thoroughly to remove the traces of smoke, and put to cook in a large pot filled with water, but without salt. While it was cooking, ½ cup (125 ml) of small dried chiles cuerudos (the name means "leathery," describing their tough skin) were toasted, with 5 *aguacatillo* leaves, and then ground on the metate with 6 cloves of garlic and about ½ teaspoon of paste of pure *achiote* (made from the seeds of the *Bixa orellana* bushes that grow wild in the area).

When the meat was just tender, Señora Maclovia added salt and 6 fresh *aguacatillo* leaves to the broth and let it cook for another 15 minutes. She then added the ground ingredients to the pot and let the contents cook for another 10 minutes. By that time, the meat was soft, and a small bunch of coarsely chopped *cebollines* (the local equivalent of chives) was added. After another 10 minutes of slow cooking, the *caldo* was proclaimed ready to serve with the very large yellow corn tortillas typical of that area, *tortillas chinantecas*.

Tortillas chinantecas
(Tortillas from La Chinantla Baja)

The tortillas made in San José Yogope in La Chinantla Baja are perhaps the largest and thinnest of all: almost 24 inches (about 60 cm) in diameter. They are cooked until almost crisp (if they were completely crisp, they couldn't be transported without breaking into pieces).

I was invited by the Martínez family to San José to see how they were made. Local corn, either white or yellow, is used, and it is cooked with lime a bit longer than is usual for *nixtamal* in other areas. To make these tortillas, the masa is spread in a very thin layer onto a piece of plastic that has been cut to the size of the tortilla; the surface of the masa is then smoothed with a flat stone. (It is astonishing to think that before plastics arrived on the scene, the women making those tortillas were actually able to pat them out to that size—now that dexterity has mostly been lost.)

What caught my attention immediately was the comal on which they were cooked; it was totally different from any I had seen before, made of special stones ground and mixed with clay. It was about ¾ inch (about 2 cm) thick in the center, tapering off to ⅜ inch (1 cm) around the perimeter. The clay is pressed out to the size required onto a henequen sack so that the surface is imprinted with the rather irregular squared pattern of the sack. This, and the thickness of the comal, ensures that the tortilla can be dried out without scorching. As the masa dries out, a pebble is placed on one side of the tortilla to keep it tilted and ensure that it dries out evenly.

A neighbor of the Martínez family, Señora Elia Pacheco, one of the very few women who still make these comales, made a small one for me. Once the clay was shaped, it was dried in the sun and then, with the surface completely covered with dried corncobs, and supported by two sturdy sticks, it was placed into the hot embers of the (cooking) fire below a heated comal. It took about one hour to "cook."

When it was time for me and one of the daughters to leave, a huge pile of these tortillas was wrapped and tied securely in a cloth for delivery to the family members in the city. This bulky package first accompanied us in my truck for about 33 kilometers over a dirt road to the bus stop on the main highway. As I said good-bye, I saw the unwieldy bulk being tied securely onto the rack on top of the bus bound for the City of Oaxaca.

A LOCAL COMAL AND BASKET/DIANA KENNEDY

OPPOSITE PAGE, CLOCKWISE FROM TOP LEFT: "BAKING" THE COMAL/DIANA KENNEDY; THE MATERIALS USED IN MAKING THIS TYPE OF COMAL/ DIANA KENNEDY; *TORTILLAS CHINANTECAS* READY TO BE TRANSPORTED/DIANA KENNEDY; PRESSING OUT THE MASA FOR A TORTILLA/DIANA KENNEDY

Frijoles picosos (Picante Beans)

SEÑOR MAURO MARTÍNEZ, AYAUTLA

Ayautla is a small tropical town on the northern slopes of the Sierra Mazateca. It is in an area that produces chiles, coffee, *achiote*, beans, corn, and a variety of fruits and edible plants, much of which is sold in the markets of Huautla and Tuxtepec.

This recipe for black beans utilizes locally grown ingredients and is served as a main meal with corn tortillas.

4 PORTIONS

8 ounces (225 g) black beans, picked over, rinsed, and boiled in water with salt only—about 5 cups (1.25 L), broth reserved

20 chiltepes or chiles paisanos, or 10 chiles de árbol, lightly toasted whole

¼ teaspoon pure *achiote* paste

4 garlic cloves, peeled

4 tablespoons melted lard

8 *cebollines* (see Glossary) or 1 small bunch chives with 2 small scallions, roughly chopped with leaves

3 sprigs epazote

Salt to taste

- Put 1 cup (250 ml) of the bean broth in a blender jar, add the chiles, *achiote*, and garlic and blend until smooth. Heat the lard in a casserole, add the beans and blended ingredients and cook over medium heat for 10 minutes. Add the *cebollines*, epazote, and salt if necessary and continue cooking for another 10 minutes.

Huevos en hoja de pozol (Eggs in Pozol Leaf)

SEÑORA LUGARDA JARQUÍN LÓPEZ, YOGOPE

In this remote village of the lower Chinantla, Señora Lugarda prepared these eggs as a snack, although they are usually served as a meal with a tomato sauce and black beans. They are cooked there on a clay comal.

The *cebollines* used are cultivated from the wild and resemble chives but with flatter leaves. Pieces of banana leaf can be substituted for the *Calathea lutea*.

2 PORTIONS

Have ready:

2 large pieces of banana leaf with 2 large *yerbasanta* leaves in the center

A heated comal or large heavy skillet

3 large eggs

6 *cebollines*, finely chopped with leaves, or 2 small scallions, finely chopped, and 2 tablespoons of finely chopped chives

Salt to taste

- Beat the eggs lightly with the salt, stir in the scallions and chives, and pour onto the *yerbasanta* leaves.

- Quickly fold the leaves over firmly so that the beaten egg does not run out, and form into a package. Cook on the comal over moderate heat for 10 minutes. Turn the package over and cook for about another 10 minutes or until the eggs have set. (The cooking time may seem long, but the protecting leaves are rather tough.)

Pozol de Chinantla Alta
(Chinantla Alta's Pozol)

San José Yogope

In Yogope, *pozol* is a refreshing and nutritive cold drink made of a soured corn masa. It is made with the local white or yellow corn and flavored with the bark of a tree that they call *cáscara de pozol* or *canelilla*; it has a curious flavor similar to that of fenugreek. I gathered that the tree, which grows in the surrounding *selva*, is not prolific, and each family jealously guards the whereabouts of its source of supply. I was discouraged from seeking it out.

The corn is cooked in water, without lime, until it is almost tender. It is strained, rinsed, and then cooked again in water until it opens up. It is then left overnight in the cooking water with a piece of the *canelilla* bark that has been dried in the sun. The bark is discarded and the corn rinsed again before being sent to the local mill, where it is ground into a very roughly textured masa. This is divided into large balls, which are left to ferment for 3 days, wrapped in *hojas de pozol*, until it acquires an acidic flavor. Diluted in cold water, like a thin gruel, it is drunk throughout the day.

The leaves and masa for *Pozol*/Diana Kennedy

Three types of chiles are cultivated in Yogope: chile cuerudo, triangular in form with a tough skin, as its name implies. It is used either fresh or dried in sauces. Chile boludo, small and round, that grows wild but is planted in *macetas* (pots); it is used fresh in sauces. The much-appreciated chile soledad, long, slender, and dark green, is used mostly fresh.

Some are dried in the sun, but if not dried within three days, they spoil.

In so many isolated places in the world, let alone rural Mexico, it is fascinating to see how people sustain themselves with what is available, cultivated or wild, and Yogope is no exception. For example, in October, the fruits of a tree called *cacao de tigre* are ripe. The name was given locally because the fruits resemble those of the real cacao (which they call *cacao agrio*). The seed is toasted, peeled, and ground with fresh chiles for a sauce. (Unfortunately, it was not in season when I was there.)

When I was there, the large, thick pods of *cuajinicuil* (*Inga* sp.; see photo p. 126) were ripe, and their fleshy beanlike seeds were cooked and eaten with salt—in the Tuxtepec area, they are preserved in vinegar.

The rains had barely started, and with their arrival the season for eating dragonflies (*libélulas*) had ended. The local people explained to me that with the first rains the dragonflies "*agusanan*" (untranslatable in this sense) and are inedible. The way in which the local children catch this source of free protein is both intriguing and laborious, and one cannot help but wonder how on earth this method was evolved.

The children crush the large, oily mamey (*Pouteria sapota*) seeds with a large pebble and then make a type of "glue" by mixing this with the sap of a rubber tree, which they have chewed for about 15 minutes; the mixture is then covered with leaves and left to season for two or three days. At the end of that time, they smear the "glue" onto one end of a twig, and as the dragonflies settle on rocks in the river, they can easily catch them as they stick to the glue.

The dragonflies are strung on lengths of twine and sold around the village. To prepare them for eating, the local women first soak them in salted water, then toast them on a comal so that the wings fall off. They are then eaten alone or ground to a paste with dried chiles, salt, and a little water. The mixture is then eaten spread onto tortillas.

FISH VENDOR, JAMILTEPEC/DIANA KENNEDY

The Coast

By Marcus Winter

The coast of Oaxaca is a narrow strip of land bordering the Pacific Ocean to the south. It extends from the border with Guerrero, on the west, to the port of Salina Cruz, on the east. It is a hot, dry region crossed by one main river, the Atoyac-Verde, with a large catchment area in the Mixteca Alta and the Valley of Oaxaca and numerous smaller rivers that rise in the mountains sloping down to the Pacific. There is a great difference between Oaxaca's Pacific coast and the wide, flat plains of Veracruz and Tabasco along the Gulf of Mexico, with their navigable rivers, tropical forests, and floodplains. The coastal strip of Oaxaca is narrow and broken in places by mountains that reach down to the sea. The rivers are fast-flowing—especially in the rainy season—steep, rocky, and navigable only near the ocean. The most important products of the region include salt, shrimp, fish from the lagoons, a purple mollusk valuable for its dye, and native cotton used to weave the local traditional textiles.

Today the main crops are peanuts, limes, papayas, and other fruits, while cattle-raising and fishing are also important activities of the area. No evidence has been found of deep-sea fishing during pre-Hispanic times. The inhabitants of the area were Chatinos until Late Postclassic times, approximately AD 1250, when the Mixtecs from the highlands arrived and established their center at Tututepec. Around the same time, the Chontals established settlements in the eastern coastal area around Huamelula and Astata and in the mountains to the north.

SAN PEDRO AMUZGOS

PINOTEPA NACIONAL

JAMILTEPEC

LA COSTA

PUERTO ESCONDIDO

POCHUTLA

OCÉANO PACÍFICO

MAP OF THE COAST/SERGIO AGUIRRE

Pinotepa Nacional

The dry, narrow coastal strip of Oaxaca stretches for 568 kilometers along the Pacific Ocean. It is separated from the central part of the state by the Sierra Sur that towers above it. The rivers that cross the land are dry for most of the year, but where there is more permanent water, there are cattle ranches and areas of cultivation: corn and papayas, but more frequently, coconut palms sheltering lime trees. While the main highway is dotted with small settlements and villages, the principal towns—Pochutla, Puerto Escondido, and Pinotepa Nacional—are far enough apart to have separate identities.

One could never describe these areas as important centers of gastronomy, but each has its distinctive ingredients—which may be gathered wild, cultivated, fished from the rivers and sea, or brought down from the Sierra—that are used in their simple (with few exceptions) but tasty dishes.

Without doubt, the most varied and colorful regional market is that of Pinotepa Nacional, for not only does it have its local products but those arriving via one of the principal trade routes as well. (There are three such routes: the convergence of the highways from Huajuapan de León in the Mixteca Baja and Tlaxiaco in the Mixteca Alta, that from Sola de Vega to Puerto Escondido, and that from Miahuatlán to Pochutla.)

The *mercado* is colorful, whatever the season, not only because of the produce but because of the (dwindling) number of women from Pinotepa Don Luis and the Amuzgo area who still wear their colorful native attire. There are always boxes of tomatoes, different varieties of squash, an array of multicolored corn, *camotes*, small yellow

cucumbers, 18-inch-long green beans, orange-fleshed mamey, large bunches of *chepil*, fresh cheese in green leaf wrappers, and *yucucata*, among many other seasonal ingredients. But most colorful of all are the piles and piles of dried costeño chiles, mostly red, along with a much lesser quantity of yellow. Although there are two harvests a year, the main one is in September, and for a very short period you can buy the fresh green, with some yellow, chiles; but they do not last long in the heat of Pinotepa. When driving to Pinotepa Don Luis and along the highway north to San Pedro Amuzgos and Putla, it is a colorful sight to see the brilliant chiles drying on *petates* in the sun.

Of course, there are varieties of fish available, but the most unusual is a small, flattish, almost round fish called *salmiche* or *sacamiche,* which are *horneados,* or partially dried, in a rustic wood-fired oven. They are cooked in a simple broth with tomato, onion, epazote, and fresh costeños, when in season, or with dried chile and garlic, but the most popular use for them is in a sauce (see photo p. 146). The heads are toasted on a comal and ground in a *molcajete* with garlic and fresh chiles costeños.

One local and extraordinary use of sea salt, one I had never come across before, is *sal quemada,* or "burnt salt," to be taken to eat in the fields. It is crumbled onto a tortilla, preferably one made of *maíz nuevo,* or new, not-quite-dried corn. The method of making it probably dates from pre-Columbian times. Grainy sea salt is ground with a little water and some dried leaves of *candó.* It is molded into a dried cornhusk, like a tamale, and cooked in hot ashes for about 2 hours.

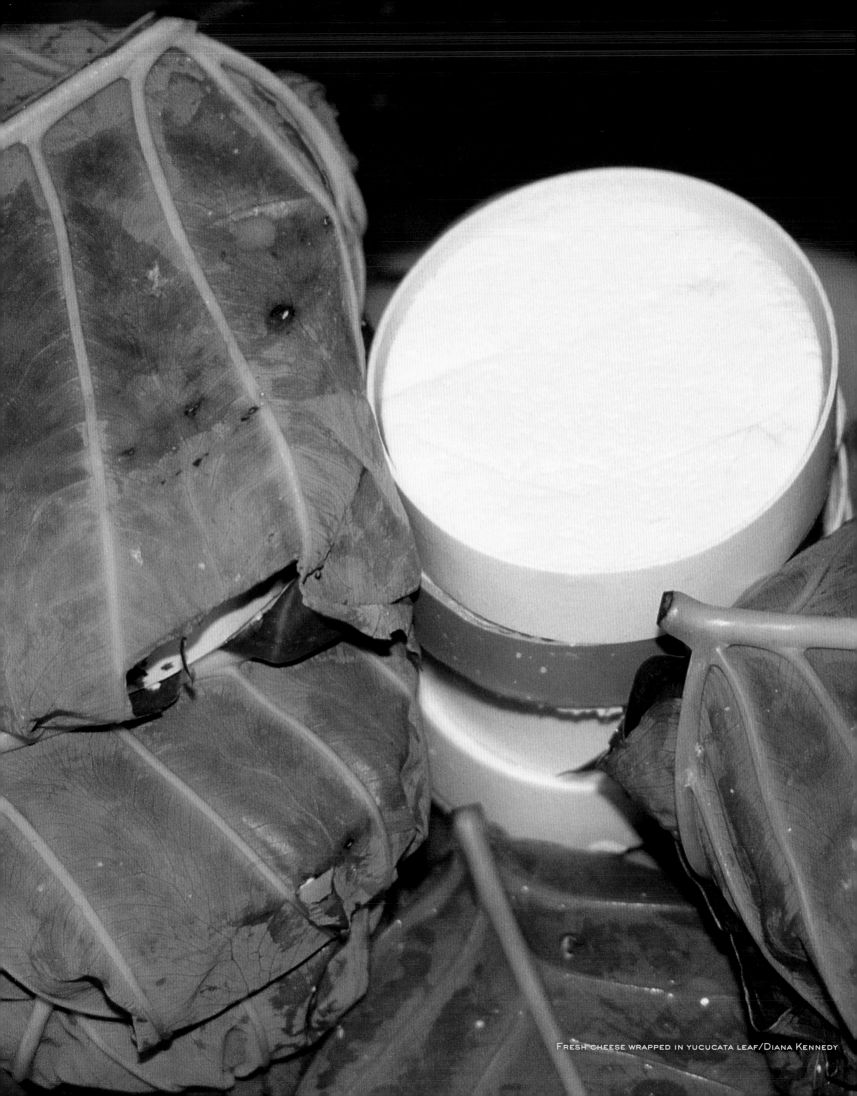

Fresh cheese wrapped in yucucata leaf/Diana Kennedy

Los Amuzgos

The Amuzgos are an indigenous group centered around San Pedro Amuzgos in the foothills of the Sierra Madre Occidental, between the eastern coast of Oaxaca and the Mixteca. Thanks to the indefatigable work of Maestro Fermín Tapia García, a native of San Pedro (who, although he is called a *técnico bilingüe,* is, without doubt, a most knowledgeable and wise person), we have a record of the traditional foods, wild and cultivated, of that region.

His research has culminated in a publication by the Centro de Investigaciones y Estudios Superiores en Antropología Social titled *Recetas de platillos vegetarianos de los amuzgos* (*Recipes of Vegetarian Dishes of the Amuzgos*). Three of those recipes are given here.

Unfortunately, bad weather (including a hurricane) on several occasions made the narrow highway impassable and hindered me from going to see some of the lesser-known plants that he mentions. However, I was able to try some of the simple local foods, which Señor Fermin's wife cooked for me. Although she spoke no Spanish, we understood each other as cooks. I was impressed by the fresh, natural tastes of the ingredients that were on hand, either gathered from the countryside or grown in their plot of land: corn, beans, pumpkins, sweet potatoes, and plantains, along with wild greens and roots, plus mushrooms and palm buds when in season. Only when there is a little extra money do they buy chicken, beef, pork, or goat, but even then they consider it much healthier to consume wild meats of deer, armadillo, raccoon, and badger, among others.

They use chiles costeños both fresh and dried, as well as small chiles that they grow in pots in the patio. For their moles, they use guajillo chiles seasoned with cumin, cloves, peppercorns, and dried oregano; other dishes use aromatic plants: epazote, *yerbasanta, candó,* and wild avocado leaves.

In his publications, Maestro Fermín explains the different preparations of corn for a variety of tortillas mixed with the flower of amaranth, beans, a wild root, and the Samaritan fruit (*Brosimum alicastrum*). They make *memelas* (see Glossary) with salt, *tetelas* (p. 307) filled with black beans, and empanadas filled with mushrooms. A gift taken to godparents would include a *totopo dulce*—sweetened masa pressed out on the *metate.*

There are many types of pozoles prepared specially for *mayordomías,* as well as *atoles* of pineapple, banana, coconut, or *piñole* (toasted and ground corn).

Tamales, too, play an important part in their diet. They are filled with iguana, armadillo, goat, shrimp, mushrooms, beans, pumpkin, and even the black grubs known as *cuetlas.* These tamales are wrapped in either banana leaves or those of *zapote borracho* (a *sapotacea*) or *belijan,* a plant of the ginger family.

It was almost the end of the rainy season when I last visited the Tapia family, but there were still some of the little grayish mushrooms around, called *oreja de ardilla,* "squirrel's ear," which were prepared as a filling for the large empanadas typical of the area, cooked on the comal. The local green bananas, not plantains, Señora Tapia also used in two ways: cooked and mashed and fried in lard and served in black beans. And this was after a broth of *chipile* or *chepile,* as they call *chepil* (see photo p. 62) there. On the table as snack were a fresh, salty cheese and toasted pumpkin seeds.

Mole de hongos de cuernito de venado
(Clavaria Mushrooms in Mole)

In several regions of Oaxaca, notably the coast and the Mixteca Alta, mushrooms are ground to a paste similar to the method in this recipe. Traditionally this is done on a metate, but a food processor, rather than a blender, is best for this.

This dish is served just with tortillas as a meal in itself.

MAKES 5 PORTIONS

¾ pounds (about 800 g) *Clavaria* mushrooms
Salt to taste
6 dried chiles costeños, lightly toasted whole
½ teaspoon cumin seeds, crushed
12 ounces (340 g) tomatoes
1 clove garlic, peeled
3 thick slices of medium white onion, roughly chopped
3 tablespoons lard
⅓ cup tortilla masa
Salt to taste

- Rinse and strain the mushrooms. Put into a pan, barely cover with water, add salt, and cook over medium heat until almost tender, about 15 minutes.

- Strain and press down to extract as much liquid as possible. Reserve cooking water, which should measure just over 2 cups (500 ml).

- Using a food processor, blend to a textured paste.

- Toast the chiles on a comal, turning them from time to time and taking care not to let them burn—they should be crisp when cool. Crumble the chiles into the blender, add the cumin, and blend well (dry). Add 1 cup (250 ml) of the cooking water, the tomatoes, garlic, and onion, and blend to a smooth consistency.

- In a large skillet, heat the lard; add the mushroom paste, the tomato mixture, and salt; and fry over fairly high heat until reduced and seasoned, about 10 minutes.

- Put the masa with 1 cup (250 ml) of the cooking water and blend until smooth. Add to the pan with salt to taste and continue cooking over medium heat, stirring and scraping the bottom of the pan to avoid sticking, for about 8 minutes. The mole should be of medium consistency. If it is too thick, dilute with a little more of the cooking water.

Guisada de nopalito en frito (Nopales with Eggs)

1 pound (450 g) nopales, cleaned of spines
4 chiles costeños
½ teaspoon crushed cumin seeds
1 garlic clove, peeled
2 tablespoons lard
3 thick slices medium white onion, finely chopped
Salt to taste
2 large eggs, lightly beaten with salt

- On an ungreased comal (preferably clay) or griddle, toast the nopales on both sides until tender, about 8 minutes on each side. Cut them into small squares.

- Toast the whole chiles lightly on a comal, turning them from time to time to prevent them from burning—they should be brittle when cool. Crumble into the blender. Add the cumin and garlic and blend with ½ cup (125 ml) water until smooth. Heat the lard in a skillet and fry the onion until translucent. Add the blended ingredients and fry for a few minutes. Add the nopales with salt to taste and cook over medium heat for about 5 minutes.

- Stir in the eggs and cook until they are set.

Sopa de arroz (Savory Rice)

This is a simple rice dish usually served alone and often as the main meal in these communities. It has a predominant flavor of cumin and chile. As in the City of Oaxaca, the Amuzgos eat rice topped with slices of an uncooked banana *de seda*—not plantain—a delicious banana with a soft flesh and a very fruity taste.

MAKES ABOUT 5 PORTIONS

½ pound (225 g) long-grained unconverted rice, rinsed and strained
2–3 tablespoons lard
2 thick slices medium white onion, finely chopped
Approximately 2½ cups (625 ml) water
1 large tomato, roughly chopped
2–3 chiles costeños, toasted whole and crumbled
¼ teaspoon cumin seeds, crushed
Salt to taste

- Shake the rice well in the strainer. Heat the lard in a fairly wide pot. Add the onion and fry until translucent; stir in the rice and fry, stirring from time to time, until it turns a light golden color.

- Put ½ cup (125 ml) water into the blender with the tomato, chiles, and cumin and blend until smooth. Stir into the rice and cook for about 3 minutes.

- Add salt to taste and the remaining water, cover the pan, and cook over a fairly low heat until the liquid has been absorbed and the rice is tender.

El cabió

El cabió is the ceremonial dish in this part of the coast and the Mixteca Baja that is believed to date from pre-Hispanic times. Until a few years ago it was prepared exclusively for *mayordomías*, but nowadays it is also prepared for weddings and other special occasions.

El cabió is basically a beef broth, presumably first made with venison or other wild meats. It is cooked by indigenous men and women, Mixtecs from that area, who are specialists in its preparation. As is the custom, enough food is prepared not only for the family of the *mayordomo* and their guests but also for the neighbors, who bring a *cooperación,* which varies according to what they can afford. They take their food away in earthenware bowls called *borcelanas,* the sizes appropriate to their cash contribution.

Preparations start the day before. A "canopy" made of *guarumbo* (*Cecropia peltata*) branches, which do not burn, is erected over a wood fire. The pieces of meat, as many as will fit, are spread over this and are in effect grilled, though constantly turned, for about 40 minutes. They are then wrapped in *biliján* leaves and stored in natural fiber sacks.

Meanwhile, the next batches of meat are cooked.

The cooking starts again very early the following day because the meat has to cook for 3 or 4 hours and be ready to serve at midday. After washing the meat well, it is cooked in water seasoned with salt, a purée of red costeño chiles, and whole *yerbasanta* leaves.

The village authorities arrive at the *mayordomo's* house accompanied by the old and respected men of the village, *los tatamandones*; a band; and a troupe of official dancers. A bottle of *mezcal* is passed around among them for each to take a swig until it is finished.

The meal is then served, the meat in its broth accompanied only by tortillas and *jícaras* of water, while the guests are entertained by dancers known as *coyantes.*

Caldillo de huevo
(Eggs in Chile Costeño Sauce)

SEÑORA AMANDA GONZÁLEZ AYONA, PINOTEPA NACIONAL

This egg dish is very picante, but to diminish the heat a little, without losing flavor, you could either add some chiles costeños, a bit larger and less hot but very difficult to come by outside the immediate area, or substitute 3 guajillos for 10 costeños.

MAKES 4 PORTIONS

20 costeños, seeds and veins removed

2½ cups (625 ml) water

2 garlic cloves, peeled

1 tablespoon melted lard

⅓ cup (85 ml) tortilla masa

Salt to taste

1 large sprig epazote

5 large eggs, lightly beaten with salt

- Rinse and strain chiles. Put 1 cup (250 ml) of the water into the blender, add the garlic and chiles, and blend well.

- Heat the lard in a shallow pan, add the purée through a strainer, pressing down well to extract as much liquid as possible, and cook over medium heat for about 3 minutes.

- Blend the masa with a second cup of the water and add to the chile, stirring constantly to avoid sticking, until the mixture begins to thicken, about 3 minutes, adding salt to taste. Then add the epazote with the remaining water and, after another 3 minutes, stir the eggs in gradually and cook gently until they are set. Serve immediately with tortillas.

LONG BEANS, PINOTEPA MARKET/DIANA KENNEDY

Cangrejos en frijol molido
(Crabs in Black Beans)

Aficionados of wild seasonal foods wait anxiously in May for signs of the first large crabs making their way down the streams gushing from the mountains of the Sierra Sur to the sea. But it takes dexterity to catch them, and only those who have practice and strong, gloved hands can do so.

The indigenous people include those of African ancestry, originally brought from Cuba to work in the sugarcane fields. Not only are the crabs cooked with this sauce of black beans, but nothing is wasted—the main shells are supported on sticks and dried in the sun. They are then ground and made into a sauce with chiles costeños and garlic.

Most local cooks buy the crabs live in the market and cook them either with salt alone or with garlic and onion. Some buy black beans already toasted and ground to a powder, while others prefer to prepare the beans themselves. The toasting of the beans is done on a clay comal over a very low heat, moving them around constantly until they sound brittle and the skins are shiny, as if they were cooked in oil; this takes about 15–20 minutes, depending on the quantity. But this process requires practice, since they can scorch so easily.

This recipe is also prepared with the small local mussels called *tichindas* or dried shrimps.

Two crabs are served in each portion.

MAKES 5 PORTIONS

9 ounces (250 g) powdered black beans
Approximately 6–7 cups (1.5–1.75 L) water
Salt to taste
2 avocado leaves (see Note on Toxicity, p. 426)
10 crabs, cleaned but left whole

- Mix the bean powder with 1½ cups (375 ml) of the water. Heat the remaining water in a large pot, add the bean paste, and stir to make sure that no lumps form. Add salt and cook over medium heat until the sauce begins to thicken. Add the leaves with the crabs and cook over medium heat until they are cooked through. Serve in deep bowls with tortillas.

Empanadas de hongos
(Mushroom Empanadas Costeños)

SEÑORA VERÓNICA REYES, JAMILTEPEC

One morning, driving along the coast of Oaxaca, an unusual breakfast awaited me. It was the rainy season, and in the little market of Jamiltepec I came across very small, mouse-colored mushrooms; in fact, they were called *orejitas de ratoncitos,* "little mouse ears." I bought some at three times the original price: the cost of taking a photograph of them.

Luckily, Señora Verónica, who was preparing food at a makeshift stand outside the market, said she would cook them for my breakfast. I was surprised when she mixed all the raw ingredients together in the blender (traditionally they would have been ground on the metate) and stuffed them, as juicy as they were, with spoonfuls of a finely grated dry cheese, into a large uncooked tortilla. The masa was then doubled over to cover the filling and the empanada cooked on an ungreased clay comal. Served alone, it made an unusual and delicious breakfast.

Any soft, juicy mushroom could be substituted.

> MAKES 1½ CUPS (375 ML) FILLING,
> SUFFICIENT FOR 6 LARGE OR 12 SMALL EMPANADAS

Approximately ½ cup (125 ml) water

1¼ cups (315 ml) cleaned, rinsed, strained, and coarsely chopped wild mushrooms

5 (or to taste) dried costeño chiles, rinsed, seeds removed, and torn up into small pieces

3 garlic cloves, peeled and coarsely chopped

1 large *yerbasanta* leaf, center rib removed and roughly torn up

Salt to taste

- Put the water into the blender. Add the ingredients a few at a time and blend to a textured, loose consistency.

- Make the empanadas as indicated above.

Orejita de venado mushrooms, Jamiltepec market/Diana Kennedy

Enchiladas costeñas and El relleno de pollo

SEÑORA ANA AGUIRRE FLORES, PINOTEPA NACIONAL

These enchiladas are prepared for special occasions. They are served as a main dish, accompanied by white or red rice or spaghetti and refried black beans.

The tortillas are covered with the local black mole and filled with a *picadillo*—the recipe follows—made with either chicken or pork. The enchiladas are served topped with chopped white onion and finely ground dry cheese.

> **MAKES ABOUT 6 CUPS (1.5 L) FILLING, SUFFICIENT FOR 12 LARGE OR 18 SMALLER TORTILLAS**

½ medium white onion, thickly sliced

4 garlic cloves, peeled

Salt to taste

1 large or 2 small chicken breasts—about 1½ pounds (675 g)—or 1 pound stewing pork cut into 1-inch (2.5 cm) cubes

12 ounces (340 g) potatoes, peeled and cut into small cubes

4 tablespoons vegetable oil or melted chicken fat

¾ cup (about 190 ml) finely chopped white onion

3 garlic cloves, peeled and finely chopped

1¼ pounds (about 500 g) tomatoes, unskinned and finely chopped

Salt to taste

25 almonds, skinned and cut into strips

4 ounces (115 g) raisins

3 chiles jalapeños in *escabeche*, cut into thin rounds

• Put sufficient water into a pot to cover the meat. Add the onion and garlic with salt to taste; bring to a boil and simmer for 5 minutes. Add the meat and cook over low heat (pork over medium heat) until tender, about 25 minutes for the chicken and 40 minutes for the pork. Strain, reserving the broth, and set aside to cool. Remove the bones and half of the skin from the breasts; shred the meat and skin but not too finely; shred the pork but again not too finely.

• Reheat the broth, add the potatoes, and cook until almost tender. Strain. (Use the broth for diluting the mole, a soup, or another dish.)

• In a large skillet, heat the oil. Add the shredded meat, the onion, and the garlic and fry over medium heat, stirring until they begin to brown lightly. Add the tomatoes, with salt as necessary, and cook until the juice has been reduced, about 8 minutes. Add the almonds, raisins, chiles, and potatoes and cook until all the flavors have combined, about 8 minutes.

TO ASSEMBLE THE ENCHILADAS

5–6 cups (1.25–1.5 ml) prepared *Mole costeño* (see p. 153)

Approximately 1 cup (250 ml) meat broth or water

Oil for frying

12 large or 18 smaller tortillas

4–6 cups (1–1.5 L) meat filling (depending on the size of the tortillas)

To serve:

1½ cups (375 ml) finely chopped white onion

1 cup finely grated dry cheese

• Heat the mole, diluted with enough broth to a consistency that will cover the tortillas well. Keep hot.

• Heat a little of the oil in a skillet and fry the tortillas lightly, one by one, adding more oil as necessary. Blot off the excess oil and dip the tortillas into the hot mole—it should cover them well. Put a generous amount of the filling in each of the tortillas, roll up loosely, and serve sprinkled liberally with the onion and cheese.

Escabeche de pescado horneado
(Escabeche of Fish)

SEÑORA ANA LUZ TOLEDO DE GARCÍA, POCHUTLA

In the mornings along the streets of central Pochutla, the sale of *pescado asado* is predominant. It is the women who prepare the fish to sell. They buy it from the fishermen, clean and grill it, liberally brushed with oil, over a slow wood fire of huisache or *cacahuanano.* It acquires a burnished mahogany color.

The local fish used for this *escabeche* is *barrilete,* a dark-fleshed skipjack. It is generally served on *tostaditas,* along with ceviche and shrimp and oyster cocktails, as part of the popular local *botana* with drinks.

18 ounces *barrilete asado* or a lightly smoked fish
½ cup (125 ml) olive oil
6 garlic cloves, peeled and finely chopped
2 medium white onions, finely chopped
10 medium-sized tomatoes, finely chopped
5 fresh chiles, tuxtas or costeños (or substitute serranos), finely chopped
3 tablespoons commercial white vinegar
Approximately ½ cup (125 ml) water
2 Mexican bay leaves or 1 bay laurel
Salt and pepper to taste
½ cup (125 ml) pitted green olives
1 cup (250 g) fresh or frozen peas, cooked
½ cup (125 ml) strips sweet red peppers

• Remove skin and bones from fish and shred, not too finely.

• Heat the olive oil in a deep skillet or casserole. Add the garlic and onion and fry gently until translucent. Add the tomatoes and cook until reduced, about 10 minutes.

• Add the fish, chiles, vinegar, water, and bay leaves and cook over medium heat until the mixture is well seasoned and the fish cooked, about 20 minutes. Add the rest of the ingredients and cook another 10 minutes. Serve at room temperature.

Farangoyo de huevo de tortuga
(Turtle Eggs in Broth)

SEÑORA AMANDA GONZÁLEZ AYONA, PINOTEPA NACIONAL

Turtle eggs are part of the natural diet along the Oaxaca coast despite their prohibition. They are eaten fresh when in season or even dried. Hen's eggs can be substituted, although they are not as flavorful.

This recipe is in fact a broth that is served in bowls for *almuerzo*, a late breakfast. When in season, fresh costeños are used, but serranos can be substituted.

2 PORTIONS

2 cups (500 ml) water

Salt to taste

3 (or to taste) fresh costeño chiles or serranos

2 tablespoons finely chopped white onion

1 garlic clove, peeled and finely chopped

1 large sprig of epazote

4–5 turtle or 3 hen's eggs, lightly beaten

• Put the water to boil with salt in a small shallow casserole or skillet. Add the chiles, onion, garlic, and epazote and boil for 3 minutes. Lower the heat, stir in the beaten eggs, and cook until set, about 3 minutes more.

Achiote husks with seeds/Diana Kennedy

Local *quelite*, Merced del Potrero/Diana Kennedy

Merced del Potrero

Señora Agustina Santiago Ramírez and family

Another chance meeting and conversation with Arquitecto Rigoberto Chávez and his wife, Ana Berta (who introduced me to the unusual steamed tortilla *guetabache*), and I was off again, this time toward the Pacific coast. After driving east from Pochutla along the narrow coastal highway for about 30 kilometers, I turned onto a dirt road toward the foothills of the Sierra Sur and, after about 15 kilometers, entered a village called Merced del Potrero (see below). I had been enticed there by the description of a most unusual ceremonial dish called *shobe de frijol,* prepared for the initiation of a new mayor or for funerals. Arquitecto Rigoberto had spent his early years there and intrigued me with his description of the simple foods his mother, Señora Agustina, cooked, what they collected in the countryside to eat, and how they played in the thermal springs before leaving it all behind to further his education in the City of Oaxaca.

It was February, the dry season, and the countryside was parched brown except for scant fields of cultivation along the sides of the river and the waters gushing out from thermal springs above the village. The village is picturesque, with the mountains of the Sierra Sur towering above, but strewn with plastic bags and all the detritus of our modern age. There was nobody around, and it was quiet except for the dogs barking around my truck. I was struggling to put up my camp bed on the veranda of Señora Agustina's house when a drunk came swaying up the road and deftly assembled it for me.

The next day my lesson on *shobe* began, given by the two daughters, Felicita and Oliva. It was so simple, relying solely on ingredients—black beans and white corn—grown right there and cooked with care in clay pots over a wood fire.

The corn had been cooked, without lime, until just softened. It was rinsed, rubbed to remove any loosened skins, strained, and sent to the mill to be ground to a very smooth masa. It was diluted with water to a gruel-like consistency. Black beans were cooked with onion and salt, strained, but saving the broth. The broth was heated, chopped onion was added, followed by the diluted and strained masa. The mixture was cooked gently and stirred until it began to thicken. It was as simple as that. The *shobe* was served in gourds with the cooked beans on top. Raw torn-up tusta chiles were served separately. When they are available and affordable, dried shrimps are added. It is served with tortillas and accompanied by beer or preferably *mezcal.*

Caldo de pescado horneado (Soup of Dried Fish)

Another local dish that is prepared throughout the year but especially for Semana Santa, Holy Week, is *Caldo de pescado horneado* (Soup of Dried Fish).

For 4 portions, they used 1 medium oven-dried *lisa*, bought in the streets of Pochutla or Jamiltepec (photo pp. 128–129). About 2 cups water were put into a clay pot to heat. A tomato, ½ onion with its green stalk, and 1 clove garlic were chopped and added with several aromatic leaves (unidentified) called *hojas* or *hierbas de pescado*, "fish leaves or herbs," that give a unique musky flavor to the broth. When the soup, or broth, was well seasoned, the fish was cut into pieces, added with salt, and cooked gently until the fish was soft, about 15 minutes. Sometimes they add whole eggs to poach in the broth.

Caldo de res o chivo (Beef or Goat Broth)

The most important celebration of the year in Merced is that of their patron saint on September 24, when a *caldo* of beef or goat is prepared. Once the animal has been butchered, the meat is soaked in water for about an hour. It is dried and then covered with a paste of chiles:

1¼ pounds (about 500 g) guajillos, seeds removed
2 large onions, toasted
1 small head garlic, toasted whole and cleaned
1¼ pounds (about 500 g) tomatoes, toasted
Small quantity each of dried herbs: thyme, marjoram, *almoraduz* (see Glossary), and oregano
4 whole allspice, crushed
Salt to taste
Water to blend
4 tablespoons lard for frying

• All the ingredients are blended together well with water to a paste. The paste is fried briefly to season it and spread over the meat. It is then steamed on a rack in a sealed earthenware pot, the water below seasoned with ground *achiote* and *cilantro extranjero*.

Selling *soyamiche*, Puerto Escondido market/ >
Diana Kennedy

Plantas comestibles (Edible Plants)

There are several different palms in the coastal areas that provide food. The oleaginous fruit, or nut, of the *Bactris baculifera* is toasted and ground for tostadas and to grind in the local mole. A typical sweetmeat during Holy Week is this *coyol* cooked in raw sugar.

There are two other types of palms, one that grows nearer the coast and another in the foothills, whose tender young trunks are cooked in water or toasted. They are split open, and the tender flesh inside (see photo p. 329) is eaten with salt or with a tortilla; it has a slightly bitter quality but somewhat resembles very tender coconut flesh with its unctuous, sweetish flavor.

I had often bought the palm flower buds called *soyamiche* from a vendor in the Puerto Escondido market, but here I was able to see how it was cut from the palm *Cryosophila nana* by expert hands that delved into the thick, spiny covering of the trunk. Locally, the buds from palms in their area are preferred over those from palms nearer the coast, whose buds are thinner and have a bitter taste. These inflorescences, toasted or baked in the ashes of the fire under the comal, are peeled and eaten with salt. They are crisp in texture and have a hint of bitterness.

Another wild plant that is collected and eaten in Merced is called *quelite de hoja larga* (see photo p. 144), literally translated as "wild green with long leaf." It grows mainly in the nearby coffee plantations. It has a long leaf, as its name implies. Usually the new, tender sprouts are eaten either raw or cooked, covered with a tortilla, and "sweated" on the comal. They are wrapped in the tortilla and eaten with salt and a sauce of chile tusta (see recipe p. xix). Since it was the dry season and the leaves were rather tough, Felicita cooked them for me in water with salt—they were bitter but not unpleasantly so.

Every household has an *achiote* bush planted nearby. When the fruits are ripe, the abrasive brown husks are broken open and the red seeds removed (see photo p. 143) and saved for future use. When preparing a dish that requires the color and flavor of *achiote*, the seeds are crushed and soaked in water; the latter is strained and added to the *caldo*, sauce, or stew.

A succulent climbing plant called *cocolmécatl* (*Smilax* sp.) grows wild in the countryside and is also used in many ways, as it is in Usila in La Chinantla Baja. The young shoots are peeled and eaten raw; the petioles, or leaf stalks, are toasted, peeled, and put into an *amarillo* (far simpler than the mole of that name prepared in the Central Valley) or *shobetá*, as it is called there. Another local way of preparing the *cocolmécatl* is to cut the juicy stems into small lengths, which are then cooked in water until tender. Raw tomatoes, onion, and garlic are crushed together on the metate and added to the broth, which is then thickened with masa. Then, when the dish is almost ready, mint and *cilantro extranjero* are added.

There is another climbing plant of the *Peperomia* genus used in different parts of the Sierra Sur called *oreja de león* (see photo p. 367). It has a dark green heart-shaped fleshy leaf and a polished, waxy appearance striated with pale yellow. It has a taste very similar to coriander. The leaf is eaten either raw or cooked with black beans.

Among the many culinary surprises, here is another climbing plant with woody, dark brown stems (see photo p. 373) called *palo de chile* (*Drimys granadensis*). Here and in parts of the Sierra Sur, the stems are peeled and eaten raw with a meal. Campesinos carry it to the fields to chew on to dispel their hunger. It has a bite to it like a chile and gives the tongue a sleepy sensation. It is said to disinfect the mouth. In Merced, this *palo de chile* is also cooked in water for about an hour, peeled, and chewed during or after a meal. And then there is the little-known rarity of *tortitas*: the inside flesh (called *ixtle*) is taken out, ground, and formed into flat cakes about 2 inches in diameter. They are dried overnight and eaten the next day with beans or tortillas.

Green plantains are also cooked with *cando* and added to the bean pot. When corn is scarce, they are made into tortillas and tostadas.

One of the staple, indispensable foodstuffs is, of course, black beans; here they are cooked with many types of wild greens and herbs, including those I have mentioned along with *chepil* (*Crotolaria* spp.) and the small yellow flowers called *guachepil* (*Diphysa robinioides*; see p. 365).

Mole de iguana negra
(Coastal Mole with Black Iguana)

SEÑORA CLARA GALVÁN, PUERTO ESCONDIDO

A favorite dish in this part of the coast of Oaxaca is black iguana cooked in this simple mole typical of this part of the coast.

6 PORTIONS

A black iguana, skinned, entrails removed, and cut in serving pieces
Salt to taste
4 ounces (115 g) red costeño chiles—about 40
3 garlic cloves, toasted and peeled
¼ medium white onion, cut into wedges and toasted
½ teaspoon dried Oaxacan oregano leaves or ¼ teaspoon Mexican oregano
3 *yerbasanta* leaves, toasted
2 mild black peppercorns, crushed
2 cloves, crushed
3 tablespoons melted pork lard or vegetable oil
8 ounces (225 g) tomatoes, each cut into 6 pieces, cooked in a little water
⅔ cup (170 ml) tortilla masa

- Put the iguana in a large pot, cover well with water, with salt to taste, and cook over medium heat until the meat is tender (time varies considerably, depending on the age of the iguana), about 1 hour. Strain, reserving the broth.

- Toast the whole chiles lightly, moving them around so as not to let them burn. Cover with water and leave to soak for 15 minutes. Strain.

- Put 1 cup (250 ml) of the iguana broth into the blender jar; add garlic, onion, herbs, and spices; and blend well.

- Heat the lard in a casserole and fry the blended ingredients for 1 minute.

- Put 2 cups (500 ml) of the iguana broth into the blender jar, add the chiles, and blend as smoothly as possible. Add to the pan through a strainer, pressing hard to extract all the juice possible—there will be some debris of chile skins left in the strainer. Cook over medium heat for about 5 minutes.

- Add the tomatoes in their cooking water to the blender jar with the masa and blend until smooth. Add to the pan and cook over medium heat, stirring to avoid sticking, until the mixture begins to thicken. Add the pieces of iguana and salt to taste and continue cooking for 15 minutes more. The mole should be of a medium consistency; add more of the broth if it is too thick.

THE FINAL GRINDING OF ALL INGREDIENTS
TOGETHER/DIANA KENNEDY

Mole negro costeño
(Black Mole from the Coast)

SEÑORA ANA AGUIRRE FLORES, PINOTEPA NACIONAL

Señora Ana has a modest restaurant in Pinotepa, but she is more famous for her mole, which she prepares in large quantities in the form of a paste. In that form, it will last for some months and can be sent to fill orders that come from many parts of the country.

To use the mole paste, as in other parts of Oaxaca, it is diluted with blended cooked tomatoes and chicken broth. It has a flavor that is quite different from that of other black moles. It is delicious! It is worth making this large quantity at a time because it can be divided into 1-pound bags and frozen.

Señora Ana sends all her prepared ingredients to the nearby market where there is a special mill for this sort of grinding—usually without any water or just a small amount. Although not as efficient, a hand-cranked mill or food processor could be used.

> THIS QUANTITY WILL MAKE ABOUT 6½ POUNDS (3 KG) PASTE, WHICH FREEZES WELL, SUFFICIENT FOR 12 PORTIONS.

2¼ ounces (65 g) whole red costeño chiles
9 ounces (250 g) whole pasilla chiles
9 ounces (250 g) ancho chiles, seeds and veins removed, seeds reserved
4½ ounces (125 g) guajillos, with seeds
1¼ (approximately) pounds (500 g) pork lard
1¼ pounds (about 500 g) thickly sliced white onion
11 small heads garlic, unpeeled
4½ ounces (125 g) raisins—1 cup (250 ml)
4½ ounces (125 g) shelled peanuts—about 1 cup (250 ml)
4½ ounces (125 g) unskinned almonds—about ¾ cup (190 ml)
4½ ounces (125 g) sesame seeds—1 scant cup (240 ml)
2 inches (5 cm) cinnamon stick, crushed
12 cloves, crushed
14 allspice, crushed
2 tablespoons dried Oaxacan oregano leaves or 1 tablespoon Mexican oregano
3½ ounces (100 g) dried breadcrumbs—1 heaped cup
4½ ounces (125 g) Oaxacan drinking chocolate, broken into small pieces
4½ ounces (125 g) sugar
Approximately 10 cups (2.5 L) water

- In separate batches, toast the chiles well: they should be crisp when cool. The whole guajillo chiles and the ancho seeds should be toasted until black. Grind to a powder.

- Heat 3 tablespoons of the lard in a skillet and brown the onions and garlic, then add the raisins and fry lightly. Set aside.

- In a dry pan, toast the nuts separately until crisp and the sesame until golden. Add them to the spices and oregano with the onion and garlic and grind, only adding water if absolutely necessary, to a slightly textured paste.

- Heat about 8 tablespoons of the lard in a heavy casserole and fry the breadcrumbs until golden; add the paste and fry over low heat, scraping the bottom of the pan to prevent sticking, for 5 minutes. Add the ground chiles, the chocolate, and the sugar with 2 quarts of the water, adding more lard as necessary to prevent sticking, and continue the cooking over medium heat, stirring continually. When the mixture starts to boil, lower the heat and cook, stirring, for 1 hour. The paste should be very dry but shiny.

- To prepare and serve the mole paste, see p. 154.

TO SERVE THE MOLE

2 large chickens, about 7–8 pounds (about 3–3.5 kg) total, cut into serving pieces
1 small white onion, coarsely chopped
1 small head garlic, unpeeled
Salt to taste

• Put water to boil, sufficient to cover the chicken pieces; add the onion, garlic, and salt and cook for 5 minutes. Add the chicken and cook over medium heat until it is just tender, not completely cooked through. Strain, reserving the broth. You will need about 10 cups (2.5 L). Add water if necessary to complete this amount.

1 tablespoon melted pork lard
1½ pounds (675 g) tomatoes, toasted and blended until smooth
1¼ pounds (500 g) mole paste
Salt to taste

• Heat the lard in a casserole, add the tomato purée, and cook over high heat until reduced, about 5 minutes. Add the mole paste and mix well. Add the broth, and when it comes to a boil, lower the heat, add salt to taste, and cook another 10 minutes. Add the chicken and heat through in the mole for about 10 minutes more.

Salsa de ajonjolí o de cacahuate (Sesame Seed or Peanut Sauce)

SEÑORA BERTA ORTIZ, PUERTO ESCONDIDO

MAKES 1 CUP (250 ML)

½ cup (125 ml) toasted sesame seeds or ½ cup (125 ml) skinned, toasted, and crushed peanuts
4 chiles costeños, toasted whole and torn into pieces
2 garlic cloves, toasted and peeled
⅔–1 cup (165–250 ml) water
Salt to taste

• Grind the sesame seeds, or the peanuts, together with the chiles, dry. Add the garlic and the water a little at a time to make a slightly textured sauce of medium consistency.

• Add salt to taste and set aside to season for about 1 hour before serving. It will thicken as it stands, so you may need to dilute with a little more water.

Pollo enchilado costeño
(Chicken in Chile Paste from the Coast)

SEÑORA AMANDA GONZÁLEZ AYONA, PINOTEPA NACIONAL

In Pinotepa Nacional, on the coast of Oaxaca, it is customary, eight days before a wedding, for the future bridegroom to send to the bride's parents one or two chickens, depending on what he can afford, for an evening meal. With each chicken there are three oval balls of refried beans and rice cooked with tomatoes. Three balls of chocolate with a large *pan de vida*, a local semisweet bread, complete the gift.

The chicken can be prepared in two different ways. The first, *en blanco*, has the chicken seasoned with a paste of spices ground with garlic and onion (no chile) and fried in a lot of lard. The second, preferred way covers the chicken with a seasoning paste of spices with herbs and a lot of costeño chiles. It is then wrapped (now, alas, in aluminum foil rather than with banana leaves, as in the past) and baked in a wood-fired oven. When resources permit, the chickens will be stuffed with a savory meat stuffing, a *picadillo* (recipe p. 28).

CHILE PASTE FOR 1 CHICKEN ABOUT 3½ POUNDS (1.5 KG)

30 costeño chiles, seeds removed
Approximately ½ cup (125 ml) of the chicken broth (see below)
10 garlic cloves, peeled and roughly chopped
1 medium white onion, roughly chopped
6 cloves, crushed
6 mild black peppercorns, crushed
1 tablespoon dried Oaxacan oregano leaves or 1 heaped teaspoon Mexican oregano
Salt to taste
2 tablespoons pineapple or other fruity vinegar
1 tablespoon pork lard

- Put the whole chicken into a large pot with water to cover and salt to taste and cook over medium heat until barely tender, about 25 minutes. Leave to cool off in the broth. Strain, reserving the broth.

- Meanwhile, put the chiles to soak in warm water for about 20 minutes and then strain.

- Put ½ cup (125 ml) of the broth into the blender, add the garlic, onion, spices, oregano, and salt and blend well. Add the vinegar and chiles and blend as smoothly as possible.

- Heat the lard in a skillet, add the purée, and fry over medium heat, scraping the bottom of the pan to prevent sticking, for about 8 minutes. It should then be reduced to a paste. Set aside to cool.

- Spread the paste liberally over the surface and cavity of the chicken and set aside to season for at least ½ hour.

- Heat the oven to 350°F (180°C).

- Wrap the chicken in foil or banana leaves (see note above) and bake until it is well browned but not too dry, about 1 hour.

FRIED CHICKEN

- After cooking the chicken as given above, prepare the following paste and rub over the surface and cavity of the cooled chicken.

⅓ cup (85 ml) of the chicken broth
2 tablespoons of pineapple or other fruity vinegar
10 garlic cloves, peeled and roughly chopped
2 medium white onions, roughly chopped
1 tablespoon dried Oaxacan oregano leaves or 1 heaped teaspoon Mexican oregano
6 cloves, crushed
6 mild black peppercorns, crushed
Salt to taste
Lard or vegetable oil for frying

- Put the broth and vinegar into the blender jar, add all the ingredients except the oil, and blend to a smooth paste.

- Spread the paste over the surface and cavity of the chicken and leave it to season for at least ½ hour.

- Heat the lard or oil in a deep pot, add the whole chicken, and fry until it is golden.

- Serve with the rice and balls of refried beans.

Salsa de chicatanas
(Chicatana Sauce)

SEÑORA ARMANDINA PEÑA,
PINOTEPA NACIONAL

Toward the end of May or beginning of June, with the arrival of the rains, comes a much-anticipated gastronomic delight. The flying ants, or *chicatanas* (*Atta mexicana*), begin their nuptial flight. Everyone in the family is prepared with nets to capture them as they fly from the sandy soil toward the lights of the house, which are left on for that purpose.

The ants are immediately put into salted water for one hour and then toasted on the comal so that the wings and legs fall off. They are now ready to eat or to prepare in a sauce as a filling for tamales or cooked in a *molito* for chicken.

Apart from being full of protein, they are delicious, and at first taste, I thought they resembled hazelnuts.

The sauce is usually ground on the metate, crushing out and releasing the flavors of the ingredients. However, many cooks nowadays use the blender.

FOR 2 CUPS (500 ML) TOASTED *CHICATANAS*

10 red costeño chiles, toasted whole
2 large garlic cloves, toasted unpeeled
Approximately ½ cup (125 ml) water
2 tablespoons vegetable oil
1 tablespoon finely chopped white onion
Salt to taste

- Grind or blend the *chicatanas* with the chiles, garlic, and water.

- Heat the oil in a skillet and fry the onion until translucent. Add the sauce with salt to taste and fry over medium heat for about 5 minutes. The sauce should be of a medium consistency.

GRINDING *CHICATANAS* FOR SAUCE/DIANA KENNEDY >

Wasp's nest for sauce, Puerto Escondido/Diana Kennedy

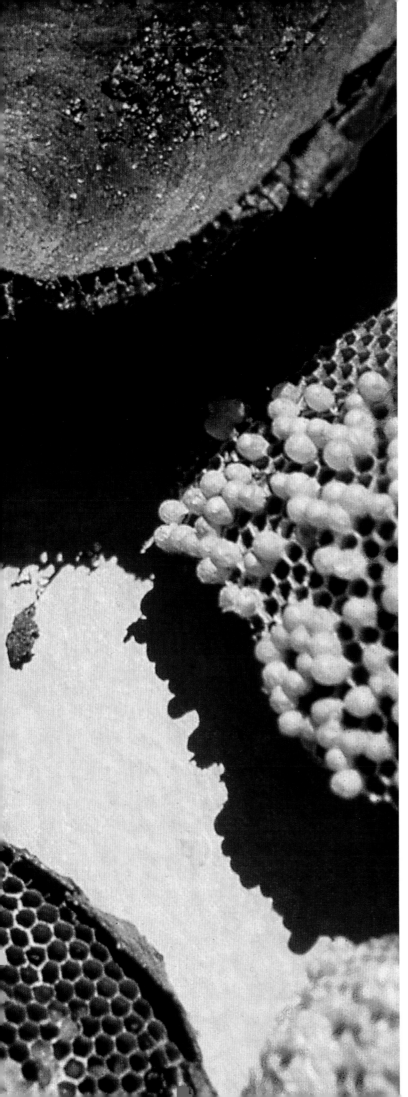

Salsa de panal (Wasp-Nest Sauce)

Señora Berta Ortiz, Puerto Escondido

This interesting and delicious sauce made of a wasp's nest on the coast of Oaxaca is probably the most unusual sauce by any world standard.

I was taken to see the large, cone-shaped nests of a *rayada* wasp (*Polybia occidentalis bohemani*) hanging in a low tree near the restaurant kitchen where Señora Berta worked. The comb was dotted with white eggs, and the time was ripe to harvest them because it was precisely five days after the new moon.

Not all the comb was used for the sauce, only the parts that contained eggs. This was broken into pieces and toasted on a comal until lightly browned. Twenty costeño chiles, half of them seeded, were toasted until crisp. These were ground together in a *molcajete*, garlic and salt added, and all blended with a little water to make a juicy, textured sauce to eat wrapped in a tortilla.

MAKING WASP-NEST SAUCE IN A *MOLCAJETE*/DIANA KENNEDY

Tamales costeños de carne cruda
(Coastal Pork Tamales)

SEÑORA ARMANDINA PEÑA, PINOTEPA NACIONAL

The meat in these tamales is put in raw, hence the name and the longer cooking time. They are served alone for breakfast or supper. Local cooks beat the masa by hand.

MAKES ABOUT 30 TAMALES

2 pounds (900 g) meaty pork ribs, cut into 30 small pieces
⅓ cup (85 ml) vinegar
Salt to taste
30 costeño chiles, stalks and seeds removed
5 guajillo chiles, veins and seeds removed
18 ounces (500 g) tomatoes, coarsely chopped
½ medium white onion, coarsely chopped
8 peeled garlic cloves, coarsely chopped
10 cloves, crushed
5 mild black peppercorns, crushed
1 tablespoon dried Oaxacan oregano leaves or ½ tablespoon Mexican oregano
12 ounces (350 g) softened pork lard
2¼ pounds (about 1 kg) textured masa as for tamales
Salt to taste

Have ready:
30–32 (just in case) pieces of banana leaf 9 × 8 inches (23 × 20 cm.), wilted over a flame
A tamale steamer with the top part lined with banana leaves

- Put the pork, vinegar, and salt into a glass or nonreactive bowl and set aside for ½ hour.

- Rinse chiles in cold water, strain, and soak in hot water for 15 minutes until soft; strain.

- Put some of the chopped tomatoes into the blender jar with the onion, garlic, spices, and oregano and blend until smooth. Add the remaining tomatoes and the chiles and blend again until very smooth. Pour the sauce over the meat through a strainer and mix well.

- Beat the lard until white and fluffy. Gradually beat in the masa with the salt and continue beating until the masa is spongy, about 15 minutes.

- Heat the tamale steamer.

- Spread the center of the banana leaves with a thin layer of the masa. Put a piece of the pork with sauce on one side of the masa. Double over the leaf with the other half of the masa so that it covers the filling. Fold back the sides firmly to form a rectangular package so that the juices will not exude. Place the tamales horizontally in overlapping layers and steam until the meat is thoroughly cooked and the masa separates cleanly from the wrapping, about 2–2½ hours.

Tamales de tichindas (Tichinda Tamales)

SEÑORA JOSEFINA CUEVAS, PINOTEPA AND CITY OF OAXACA

Tichindas are very small mussels, about 1 inch (2.5 ml) long, that proliferate in the mangroves of the eastern part of the Oaxacan coast. For these tamales, they are cooked in the masa, shells and all, so it is always a surprise for the uninitiated to bite into them for the first time, but they are usually delighted anyway by the blend of flavors.

There should be about 12 *tichindas* in each tamale.

The traditional cooks there still beat the masa by hand.

MAKES 24 LARGE TAMALES

2 cups (500 ml) costeño chiles, seeds removed
18 ounces (500 g) tomatoes
1 small head garlic, cloves separated and peeled
½ cup (125 ml) water
2¼ cups (565 ml) pork lard—18 ounces (500 g)
4¼ pounds tamale masa (textured), the drier the better
Salt to taste
Approximately 290 *tichindas*, cleaned and left whole
6 large *yerbasanta* leaves, stalk and central vein removed, and torn into small pieces
Approximately 48 dried cornhusks, soaked to soften and drained

Have ready:
A tamale steamer, the top part lined with extra cornhusks

- Put the chiles, tomatoes, and garlic into a pot; cover with water; and cook over medium heat for 5 minutes.

- Strain, transfer to the blender jar with about ½ cup (125 ml) water, and blend well.

- Beat the lard with salt until it turns very white and fluffy. Gradually beat in the masa and continue beating until it is spongy, about 20 minutes. Add the chile purée and mix thoroughly before stirring in the *tichindas* and *yerbasanta* leaves.

- It is best to use a double layer of cornhusks for each tamale. Put 2 large tablespoons of the mixture into the cornhusks, fold the edges over, and turn up the tip (as for any tamale). Stack them horizontally in a hot steamer and cook until the masa separates cleanly from the husk, about 2 hours. These tamales are served alone.

Torta de tingüiches
("Torta" of Tingüiches)

RECIPE: SEÑORA GLORIA HERNÁNDEZ, POCHUTLA
INFORMATION: SEÑORA ANA LUZ TOLEDO, POCHUTLA

Tingüiches are minute fish, about ¾ inch (2 cm) long and very narrow, that arrive in swarms once a year, in August and September, against the current of the Xonene River.

They are caught at the narrowest part of the river, aptly named *el tingüichero*, where many are stranded on the huge flat rocks. The inhabitants of the two nearby *rancherías* capture them, salt them, and dry them in the sun before they are ready to be sold in the Pochutla market.

Tingüiches are used in various ways: in a fish broth, with rice, in fritters, or in a large *torta* that is cut into portions and served hot in a tomato sauce with white rice, soupy black beans, and tortillas or tostadas to accompany it.

> **MAKES 3 CUPS (750 ML) TOMATO SAUCE, ENOUGH FOR 4 PORTIONS**

12 ounces (350 g) tomatoes, each cut into 6 pieces
3 (or to taste) fresh chiles costeños, or substitute serranos
Approximately ½ cup (125 ml) water
3 garlic cloves, peeled and coarsely chopped
2 tablespoons vegetable oil
2 slices medium white onion
1 cup (250 ml) water
Salt to taste

- Put the tomatoes and chiles in a pan with the ½ cup (125 ml) of water and cook until soft, about 10 minutes. Transfer to the blender jar, add the garlic, and blend smooth.

- Heat the oil in a casserole in which you are going to serve the dish, and fry the onion until golden. Add the tomato purée and cook over medium heat until reduced, about 5 minutes. Add the 1 cup (250 ml) water with salt to taste and cook 5 minutes more.

THE TORTA

½ cup (125 ml) *tingüiches*
¼ cup (65 ml) vegetable oil
3 eggs
Salt to taste

- Rinse, strain, and shake dry the *tingüiches*. Toast them in an ungreased heavy skillet until they begin to brown.

- Heat the oil in a medium-sized skillet. Beat the eggs well with the salt and stir in the *tingüiches*. Pour the mixture into the skillet and cook over medium heat until the eggs are set and the underside is lightly browned. Turn the *torta* over and cook on the second side. Turn out onto paper towels to absorb the excess oil. Cut into 8 pieces, add to the sauce, and heat through gently for about 5–10 minutes.

Tortitas de camaroncitos
(Fritters of Miniature Shrimps)

SEÑORA ANA LUZ TOLEDO, POCHUTLA

These extraordinary miniature shrimps, measuring about ⅜ inch (1 cm) long, occur in September and October in the mouth of the River Copalita. They are caught at night or very early in the morning with *chacalmates*, bags of very fine netting held at the top by flexible lianas. To preserve the shrimps, they are cooked until they absorb the salted water in which they are immersed, and then dried in the sun for 3 days.

These *camaroncitos* can be used in a fish soup, with white rice, or in these fritters.

Have ready:
The same tomato sauce as for the *Torta de tingüiches* (see recipe preceding page)

THE FRITTERS

½ cup (125 ml) *camaroncitos*
3 eggs
Salt to taste
Vegetable oil for frying

- Rinse the *camaroncitos*, shake dry, and toast briefly in an ungreased skillet.

- Beat the eggs well and stir in the *camaroncitos*; add salt if necessary

- Heat the oil in a medium-sized skillet, add a few spoonfuls of the mixture (but do not crowd the pan), and fry until golden underneath. Turn them over and fry on the other side, about 2 minutes or less on each side. Drain on paper towels and then reheat for 5 minutes over low heat in the hot sauce.

Camaroncitos and *tingüiches*, Pochutla/Pedro Valtierra

The Isthmus

Early morning on Mar Muerto, near San Mateo del Mar/Diana Kennedy

The Isthmus

By Marcus Winter

The Isthmus of Tehuantepec is the narrowest part of Mexico where 220 kilometers of land separates the Atlantic and Pacific Oceans. Ancient groups that settled Central and South America from the north had to pass through the Isthmus area, as did merchants in much later times who moved goods between Central Mexico and the Maya area. The Isthmus can be divided into north and south portions. The northern Isthmus, in the states of Veracruz and Tabasco, includes the extensive Gulf coastal plain with a hot, damp climate and the great rivers that compose the Coatzacoalcos-Uxpanapa system. In contrast, the southern Isthmus, in Oaxaca, has a dry climate with a dry sandy coastal plain crossed by several rivers, principally the Tehuantepec, Los Perros, Santo Domingo, and Ostuta, which flow into the Gulf of Tehuantepec or adjacent lagoons. The dry climate dictates that settlements be situated along the rivers, both today as in the past. Agriculture, supplemented by cattle-raising, is practiced today on the coastal plains, using water from canals that originate in the Benito Juárez dam in Jalapa del Marqués. Pre-Hispanic settlements are mainly along the rivers, where the low alluvium was cultivated, perhaps using small canal irrigation systems. Violent floods were common, as reflected in deposits found in the sites near the rivers. Springs at Laollaga and Tlacotepec, today converted into bathing areas, also provided water that was channeled to the settlements.

Several subareas occur in the southern Isthmus: the extensive coastal plain, the large lagoons of the Gulf of Tehuantepec, the low mountain range between Oaxaca and Veracruz, and the Valley of Jalapa del Marqués. This last area, in Colonial times, was considered the granary of the Isthmus, due to the extensive fertile plains, abundantly watered by the confluence of the Tehuantepec and Tequisistlán Rivers. The mountainous Chimalapas area, in the extreme east of Oaxaca, is also considered part of the southern Isthmus. With the exception of the Zapotec fortified site of Guiengola, next to the Tehuantepec River, archaeological sites in the southern Isthmus are not open to the public.

Ethnographically, the region is complicated, with Mixes to the west, Zoques to the east, Chontales in the mountains to the southeast, and Huaves along the coastal lagoon area. Exactly how the panorama looked in pre-Hispanic times is debated. In the late Postclassic period, probably after AD 1250, Zapotecs from the Central Valleys colonized the southern Isthmus; their culture dominates the area today. It is interesting to note that the comal, or tortilla griddle, does not appear in the area until the Late Postclassic, possibly introduced by the Zapotecs, though certainly known before then. Until that time, in the Isthmus area, maize (corn) was probably consumed as pozol (ground corn and water) or tamales. The suquí, a special subsurface oven used to make the totopos typical of the Isthmus, has not been documented archaeologically and was perhaps introduced by Middle Eastern immigrants after the Spanish Conquest.

ISTMO

IXTEPEC
ESPINAL
JUCHITÁN
TEHUANTEPEC
IXHUATÁN
SAN MATEO DEL MAR

OCÉANO PACÍFICO

Kaleidoscopes of Color

After a journey of several hours driving the sinuous highway across the Sierra Madre from the Central Valley of Oaxaca, you descend into the immense, hot, and windy valley of the Isthmus.

It is like entering another world, mainly inhabited by Zapotecs, but with a different culture and even language to those of the Central Valleys.

The untidy main streets of Tehuantepec and Juchitán are crowded with people, traffic, and motorized bicycles with their simple, sheltered benches that serve to carry people and their merchandise to and from the market.

The streets around the markets are a kaleidoscope of color as women go about their business dressed in colorfully embroidered *huipiles* and long skirts. There is a certain arrogance in their gait, probably because this is a matriarchal society where women are in charge of finances and organization of business, social obligations, and *mayordomías*.

I dare to give here only a few personal observations about this fascinating and complex culture, given how many writers before me have described it in much more authoritative terms. The late Andrés Hinojosa, for example, eloquently painted in words and poetry the customs and beliefs of his native Isthmus.

I have been constantly amazed, during my numerous visits to the area over many years, at the faithful dedication, mostly by the women, to maintaining their traditions, especially those of the *mayordomías*, and at the enormous effort and expense implied to provide the ritual foods for all who participate.

Note: I have attempted to give the recipes included here their place in the local rituals, but for a more detailed account of the ceremonies and foods of the Velas—el Lavado de Cera, el Lavado de Maíz, el Lavado de Olla—there is a charming account in a little book called *Colores, olores y sabores festivos de Juchitán, Oaxaca*. No doubt there are also anthropological theses on the subject but without recipes.

Given the complexity of the Isthmus area, this section is divided into four zones: Ixtepec-Espinal, Juchitán, San Mateo–San Pedro, and Tehuantepec.

Local *cazuelas*, Espinal/Diana Kennedy

The Velas

The most important religious festivals in the Isthmus are the Velas, usually to celebrate saints' days of the local (Catholic) churches. The Velas have their roots, however, in the pantheistic celebrations of the pre-Columbian Zapotecs who came south from the Valley of Oaxaca to the Isthmus. At that time, the Velas were invocations to the gods for flowers, corn, fruit trees, fish, and alligators—all of which were important to Zapotec life. During the centuries that followed, these fiestas were modified by the Church—a perfect example of syncretism—so that the spring celebrations came to honor San Clemente, the celebrations of rain and abundance now honor San Juan, and the corn Vela honors San Isidro Labrador.

Today's Velas include a mass, followed by festivities with food in the house of the *mayordomo* and a parade of allegoric floats and horse-drawn carts with *capitanas*, women dressed in their splendid *huipiles* distributing fruit and other presents to the onlookers. At night, there is an open *baile* for the public at which *botanas* and beers are passed around among family or groups of friends. The next day, there is a smaller celebration called Lavado de Olla, or, more prosaically, "washing the pot." After the mass, people can go to the house of the *mayordoma* and, for a contribution of a stipulated amount of money, can be served, or take away, a portion of mole, a *marquesote* (a type of sponge cake), and a bread roll called *bollo de agua* (see photo p. 182). Again there is a *baile* to which

everyone contributes a carton of beer and *botanas*: beef empanadas, tacos filled with beef or chicken, potato purée, and seafood salads.

Relleno de puerco is served not only for breakfast or *comida* during these festive days, but also for Sunday breakfasts throughout the year. One of the great experts in preparing it is Señora Julia Romero, who has done so for about forty years.

Every Saturday afternoon, she and the family members (who all live next door to each other) cut up and prepare the pork and entrails, which have to cook all night. Early on Sunday morning people begin to arrive from all parts of Juchitán with their pots and plastic containers to buy the pork and the offal, along with *chicharrón* and a sauce.

By eight o'clock in the morning, there is nothing left.

Another way of serving the *relleno* is with some of the broth from the offal with potato, tomato, and onion.

The meat is washed first in water and then with the juice of either lime or bitter orange and salt. Four large pieces of pork, with rind, are put into each oval clay *cazuela* (see photo p. 170) with a portion of the offal, a quart of vinegar, and plenty of salt.

The evening I was there, two large pigs were slaughtered to fill eight *cazuelas*, which were put into a wood-fired oven and left to cook eight hours. At the end of that time, the meat was tender but rather dry. The excess salt was rinsed off and the meat fried in hot lard until crisp.

Caldo de res oreada
(Salted Beef Broth)

SEÑORA SONIA FUENTES TOLEDO, ESPINAL

The salted, partially air-dried beef in this substantial dish gives it a very special and delicious flavor. This *caldo* is prepared midday in large quantities to feed the women who have attended the ceremony of Lavado de Olla, the day after a Vela (see p. 171). It is a dish typical of Espinal and Ixtaltepec.

The beef prepared is from grass-fed cattle whose natural flavor is enhanced by salting and hanging the meat for one or two days.

This type of broth is always better when cooked in a traditional clay pot, but that takes time and fuel, so at home it could be hurried along in a pressure cooker, then transferred to a clay pot when the vegetables are about to be cooked.

The *caldo* is generally served just with tortillas, but when prepared at home, it could be served with white rice.

START ONE DAY AHEAD

APPROXIMATELY 10–12 PORTIONS

3½ pounds (about 1.5 kg) beef ribs, cut into 2 large pieces
Approximately ½ cup (125 ml) sea salt
Water to cover
1 medium white onion, quartered
1 head of garlic, halved horizontally and lightly crushed
4 large sprigs mint
6 large sprigs cilantro
2 cups (500 ml) chickpeas, partially cooked and skinned
Vegetables to taste:
12 ounces (350 g) zucchini, trimmed and each cut into 6 pieces
12 ounces (350 g) carrots, trimmed, scraped, and each cut into several pieces
1 large chayote, trimmed, peeled, and cut into slices
12 ounces (340 g) potatoes, peeled and cut into small pieces
1 pound (450 g) cabbage cut into 8 pieces
1 ripe but firm plantain—about 1 pound (450 g)—peeled and cut into 15 pieces
Salt to taste

- Rub the salt into the meat and hang it for about 24 hours in a dry, airy place.

- Wash the meat well to remove the salt; cut it into serving pieces, with the bone; and put it into a large pot. Cover well with water; add the onion, garlic, and herbs and cook over medium heat until it is just tender, about 2 hours. Add the chickpeas and vegetables, except the cabbage and plantain, with salt if necessary, and continue cooking over medium heat until all the ingredients are tender, about ½ hour. Add the plantain and cabbage and cook for about 10 minutes more.

Chorizo istmeño
(Chorizo from the Isthmus)

Señora Cecilia Alvarado Vda. de Matús, Espinal

Every day in the Juchitán market the meat vendors, mostly women, tie strings and strings of chorizo into small balls. They are used freshly made.

But this recipe from Señora Cecilia, renowned for decades for her chorizos, is the most delicious I have ever come across there. She thinks nothing of making them with up to 50 kilos of meat.

> **MAKES APPROXIMATELY 40 SMALL CHORIZOS**

Have ready:

3 pieces of small pork casings, each one approximately 28 inches (about 70 cm). Wash each piece with lemon or lime juice or vinegar in several changes of water and drain well.

2¼ pounds (about 1 kg) pork with some fat, cut into sheets about ¼ inch (65 mm) thick
Approximately 2 tablespoons medium-grind sea salt
3 ancho chiles, cleaned of seeds and veins
3 guajillo chiles, cleaned of seeds and veins
½ cup (125 ml) water
¼ to ½ cup (85–125ml) pineapple or other fruity vinegar
2 allspice, crushed
2 mild black peppercorns, crushed
½ inch (about 1 cm) cinnamon stick, broken up
3 garlic cloves, peeled and roughly chopped
¼ teaspoon dried thyme leaves or ½ teaspoon fresh thyme
½ teaspoon pure *achiote* or 1 teaspoon prepared *achiote* paste

- Salt the pork liberally, roll it up, and set aside to season for at least 3 hours.

- Cover the chiles with warm water and leave to soak for 20 minutes. Drain.

- Put the water and vinegar in the blender jar; add the spices, garlic, thyme, and *achiote* and blend as thoroughly as possible. Add the chiles a few at a time, blending well after each addition. Add a little more water, if necessary, to blend to a paste, not a sauce.

- Chop the meat roughly and grind to a medium texture and transfer to a glass or nonreactive bowl. You can fill the casings right away, but it is always better to let the meat season in the sauce for a few hours or overnight.

- You can either hand-fill the casings using a funnel or use the attachment on your mixer and tie the chorizo into small balls with string or, more rustically, with strips of dried cornhusk.

COOKING *ESTOFADO DE BODAS*, ESPINAL/DIANA KENNEDY

Estofado de bodas
(Ritual Dish for a Wedding)

Señora Sonia Fuentes Toledo, Espinal

Estofado de bodas, or beef stew, which is a total understatement, is the most important celebratory food in the part of the Isthmus that includes Espinal, Ixtepec, and Ixtaltepec. It is said that it was first concocted in Ixtaltepec, where the huge *palanganas*, or clay cooking pots (see photo p. 177), as well as the oval-shaped *cazuelas* (see photo p. 170) were, and still are, made.

It would be unthinkable to celebrate the patron saint of Ixtepec, or the Virgen Patrona of Ixtaltepec and Espinal, or a wedding, without what is considered to be the ritual meal for those occasions.

The celebrations commence with the Lavado del Maíz—before the river was contaminated, the women designated to do so would go there to wash the corn—and finish with the Lavado de Olla, the washing of the pots. All these celebrations mean days and nights of work. To quote Señora Patricia Ortega, a native of the region and a specialist in the study of the local traditions, "Men and women participate as a moral obligation, as an act of reciprocity, of mutual help, of giving alms, and service."

A bull or steer, or two, is skinned and butchered; the flesh and bones, with many other ingredients, are cooked for many hours in a huge clay *palangana* made especially for the occasion. Until fairly recent years, the animals, their horns decorated with colored ribbons, were led down to the river to drink, accompanied by a band of local musicians.

Good fortune had it that on one of my visits to Espinal a fiesta celebrated with an *estofado* was just finishing and the renowned specialist in preparing it,

Señora Elvia Pineda, and her daughter were in full swing preparing one on the next-door-neighbor's land to celebrate a fifteenth birthday the following day.

Preparations had begun early in the morning as about twenty women—friends, neighbors, and relatives—began to cut up ingredients for the *estofado* and the *ensalada* to accompany it. This "salad" seems to be a newcomer, because *chiles en vinagre*, pickled chiles, were served until fairly recent years.

Beneath a roofed but open area and in front of a large oven, there were piles of earth and dried wood. The men whose job it was to tend the cooking of the *estofado* were heaping and tamping down the earth with their feet around the base of the still-empty *palangana*, in order to hold it securely in place during the long cooking period. (It was surprising to learn that a *palangana* is rarely used a second time; after the contents have been served, it will often break, which means good business for those who make them.)

The *palangana* was then filled to the brim with the meat, bones, and other ingredients. So full in fact that I asked if it would spill over when boiling. The answer was "No, and it never has." *Milagros*!!!

As the mixture was heating up, it was stirred with a wooden paddle for the last time and left to cook from between 10 to 12 hours as the men designated to do so kept feeding the fire during their night-long vigil. If you have no desire to kill an ox but wish to re-create in kind this extraordinary dish, the recipe that follows is for a much more modest amount of meat.

4¼ pounds (about 2 kg) stewing beef on
    the bone with some fat, cut into serving
    pieces

1 pound (450 g) lard

1 cup (250 ml) water or more, as necessary

½ teaspoon whole cloves, crushed

½ teaspoon whole allspice, crushed

¾ inch (about 2 cm) cinnamon stick,
    crushed

2 Mexican bay leaves or 1 bay laurel, broken
    up

½ teaspoon pure *achiote* or 1 teaspoon
    prepared *achiote* paste

1 large white onion, roughly chopped

6 garlic cloves, peeled and roughly chopped

2¼ pounds (about 1 kg) tomatoes, roughly
    chopped

8 ancho chiles, veins and seeds removed,
    soaked in hot water for 15 minutes and
    strained

8 guajillo chiles, veins and seeds removed,
    soaked for 15 minutes and strained

1 underripe plantain, peeled and cut into
    small cubes

4 apples, peeled and cut into small cubes

½ pineapple, peeled and cut into small cubes

⅓ cup (about 100 ml) fruity vinegar

1 tablespoon sugar

2 tablespoons mustard

Salt to taste

4 semisweet rolls, crumbled

- Put the meat and lard into a casserole, preferably earthenware.

- Put the water into the blender; add the spices, bay leaves, *achiote*, onion, and garlic and blend well.

- Gradually add the tomatoes and blend well, then add the chiles, a few at a time, blending well after each addition. Add a little more water, if necessary, to loosen the blades of the blender. The mixture should be slightly textured.

- Stir the purée into the meat and lard, making sure the meat is well covered.

- Add the rest of the ingredients, minus the bread. Cover the casserole tightly and cook very slowly, either on top of the stove or, better still, in a 300-degree oven until the meat is so soft it is falling apart, about 6 hours. Stir in the breadcrumbs to thicken, and serve with tortillas and the salad.

The salad is composed of a mixture of cooked vegetables cut into different shapes, the quantities varying according to taste: chayote, cauliflower, broccoli, carrots, tender squash, green beans, onions, and small potatoes. The vegetables are seasoned with a dressing of white vinegar, olive oil, dried thyme, pickled jalapeños, and salt.

On the festive day, apart from preparing the salad, the women were cooking an *adobo de res*, beef in a pungent chile sauce, in oval-shaped *cazuelas* (photo p. 170). It was primarily for the men helpers, and if anything was left over, for themselves. A *caldo de res* (beef broth) was prepared for the women, accompanied by a fresh chile sauce, or *chile pastor*, made with chiles bolitas cut from a bush (see photo p. 216) outside the kitchen door of the neighboring house mixed with raw garlic, onion, and salt—all bathed in lime juice.

When the serving began, neighbors would also come by with their food containers, earthenware, or mostly plastic to receive a serving of the food in proportion to the amount of their monetary "cooperation."

Palanga for cooking Estofado de bodas, Espinal/Diana Kennedy

Huevos revueltos con camarones oreados (Scrambled Eggs with Dried Shrimps)

Señora Sonia Fuentes Toledo, Espinal

This is a delicious way of cooking eggs for breakfast, or supper, accompanied by black beans. It can also be served as a *botana* with *totopos*.

In the Isthmus, the recipe would be prepared with *camarones oreados*, the locally caught shrimps cooked and only half dried. But elsewhere, completely dried shrimps can be used.

Small quantities of this mixture can also be fried to make *tortitas* to be served in a tomato broth as a main meal.

Señora Sonia blends the ingredients, but I am presumptuous enough to say, chop them very finely to preserve more texture. The butter used there is very soft, more like a very thick cream; but if you can't bear to use this amount, use half or all olive oil.

4–5 PORTIONS

¾ cup (190 ml) small dried shrimps, measured with heads removed
¼ cup (65 ml) water
⅓ cup (85 ml) finely chopped epazote
2 (or to taste) fresh jalapeños, finely chopped (do not deseed)
5 large eggs
½ cup (125 ml) melted unsalted butter or oil (see note above)

- Rinse the dried shrimps to remove excess salt. Strain, soak in fresh water for 5 minutes, and strain well again. (Omit this step if using the *oreados*.)

- Put the water into the blender jar; add the shrimps, epazote, and chile and blend to a rough consistency.

- Beat the eggs and stir in the shrimp mixture, with salt if necessary. Or beat the eggs and stir in the finely chopped ingredients.

- Heat the butter in a heavy skillet, pour in the mixture, and cook over low heat, stirring constantly until the eggs set to taste.

Mole rojo ixtepecano
(Red Mole from Ixtepec)

SEÑORA FRANCISCA OSORIO, IXTEPEC

This mole can be used in the usual way with meat, or without, to accompany another type of meat, *puerco* or *pollo relleno,* or as a sauce for enchiladas. (Every cook I interviewed had a slightly different way of preparing it.)

ABOUT 15 PORTIONS

Melted pork lard for frying

9 ounces (250 g)—or about 14—ancho chiles, seeds and veins removed

2 ounces (about 65 g)—or about 10—guajillo chiles, seeds and veins removed

1 ounce (30 g)—or about 6—chipotles

Approximately 8 cups (2 L) chicken broth

1 medium white onion, thickly sliced and toasted

8 small garlic cloves, toasted and peeled

3 Mexican bay leaves or 1½ bay laurels

3 mild black peppercorns, crushed

1 inch (2.5 cm) cinnamon stick, crushed

2 avocado leaves (see Note on Toxicity, p. 426), toasted and broken up

¼ teaspoon dried thyme leaves

1 pound 12 ounces (about 750 g) tomatoes, toasted or cooked in 2 cups (500 ml) chicken broth

Salt to taste

2 cups (500 ml) crumbled semisweet bread

3½ ounces (100 g), or to taste, Oaxacan drinking chocolate

- Heat a little of the lard in a small skillet and fry the chiles, no more than two at a time, flattening them out so that they fry evenly, taking care not to let them burn. They should be crisp when cool.

- Put 2½ cups (625 ml) broth into the blender jar and add the chiles, a few at a time, blending well after each addition. Add more broth if necessary. Transfer to a bowl.

- Put another 1 cup (250 ml) of the broth into the blender jar; add the onion, garlic, herbs, and spices and blend smooth.

- Heat 3 tablespoons of lard in the casserole in which you are going to cook the mole and fry the mixture for about 5 minutes. Add the chiles and continue cooking over medium heat for another 5 minutes.

- Blend the tomatoes (peeled optional) with the broth in which they were cooked and add to the pan. Blend the breadcrumbs with 2 cups (500 ml) of the broth until smooth, add to the pan with the chocolate, and cook, stirring to prevent sticking, for about 20 minutes. Add salt as necessary. The mole should be thick like a paste. When ready to serve, dilute with the necessary broth.

Molito de camarón oreado
(Molito of Semidried Shrimps)

SEÑORA SONIA FUENTES TOLEDO, ESPINAL

This dish is traditionally prepared for Holy Week. Some cooks add nopales to the *molito*, while others prefer to serve a salad of nopales on the side. Tortillas cooked in a *comizcal* are served with it.

While in the Isthmus, *camarones oreados*, or semidried shrimps, are available, but dried shrimps can be substituted, though slightly less will be needed.

4–6 PORTIONS

9 ounces (about 250 g) semidried shrimps or 7 ounces (about 200 g) dried
4-plus ounces (125 g) unhulled pumpkin seeds
Approximately 8 cups (2 L) water
¼ medium white onion, roughly chopped
3 garlic cloves, peeled and roughly chopped
12 ounces (300 g) tomatoes, roughly chopped
1 tablespoon lard
Scant 4 ounces (about 100 g) tortilla masa
2 stalks epazote
2 large eggs, lightly beaten with salt
Salt to taste

- Briefly rinse the dried shrimps, strain, and peel; remove heads and legs. Reserve the heads, but remove the very hard black eyes. Toast the heads until crisp.

- Toast the whole pumpkin seeds, preferably on a comal (clay is preferred so they will not burn so easily), moving them around so that they toast evenly. The husks should turn a light brown color. Set aside to cool. Grind to a powder with the shrimp heads. Mix with 2 cups of the water.

- Meanwhile, put ½ cup of the water into the blender with the onion and garlic and blend well.

- Add the tomatoes and continue blending to obtain a smooth sauce. Heat the lard in a skillet and fry the sauce until it is well seasoned and reduced a little.

- Put the sauce into a pot in which you are going to cook the *molito*. Add the seed mixture, passing it through a strainer and pressing it hard to extract as much as possible. Cook over low heat, stirring and scraping the bottom of the pot to avoid sticking. Blend the masa with another 1 cup of the water and add to the pan. Add the remaining water and cook over medium heat until the sauce begins to thicken and pools of oil appear on the surface, about 10 minutes. Add the epazote and shrimps and cook for another 10 minutes.

- A few minutes before serving, stir in the beaten eggs, adjust salt, and cook until the eggs are set, about 5 minutes. Serve immediately.

Molito de garbanzo (Chickpea Soup)

SEÑORA ALICIA BUSTAMENTE GUZMÁN, CHIQUIHUITÁN

For this *molito* or soup, the majority of cooks buy the chickpeas, or black beans for that matter, in powdered form, rather than doing the toasting and grinding at home.

This *molito* can be prepared *en blanco*, white, or *rojo*, red. When prepared *en blanco*, often small masa dumplings, or *chochoyotes* (p. 29), are added to enrich it.

MAKES 6 PORTIONS

Have ready:
18 masa dumplings (see p. 29)

4-plus ounces (125 g) powdered chickpeas
Approximately 7 cups (1.75 L) water
½ medium white onion, roughly chopped (optional)
Salt to taste

- Mix the powder in a bowl with 2 cups of the water until completely smooth. Put the rest of the water into a pan with the onion and bring to a simmer. Gradually add the chickpea mixture, stirring continuously to prevent lumps forming.

- Add salt and continue cooking over low heat, stirring constantly, until it begins to thicken. While it is still simmering, add the dumplings and continue cooking until they rise to the surface, about 20 minutes. Test to see if the masa is cooked throughout.

- If the soup is too thick, add water, or even a light broth, to dilute to taste.

Molito de garbanzo rojo (Red Chickpea Soup)

4-plus ounces (125 g) powdered chickpeas
Approximately 7 cups (1.750 L) water
Salt to taste
½ cup (125 ml) water
¼ medium white onion
2 garlic cloves, peeled and roughly chopped
6 ounces tomatoes, roughly chopped
1 tablespoon lard

- In a bowl, mix the chickpea powder with 2 cups of the water until smooth.

- Put the rest of the water into a pan with salt, and when it begins to boil, lower the heat and gradually stir in the chickpeas. Keep stirring to make sure it does not form lumps.

- Put the ½ cup water into the blender with the onion and garlic and blend smooth; add the tomatoes and blend again.

- Heat the lard in a small skillet, add the blended ingredients, and fry until slightly reduced, for about 2 minutes. Add to the pan and continue cooking over low heat until the soup has thickened and is well seasoned. Add more water or broth to desired thickness.

Pasta o picle
(Vegetables in "Custard")

One can only describe this "pasta" as a solid vegetable custard served along with mole (sauce without meat) to accompany some of the local dishes in the Isthmus of Tehuantepec. Every family seems to have a slightly different recipe, but all seem to include commercially prepared mustard.

8 SERVINGS

Have ready:
A well-greased 2-quart (2 L) ovenproof or Pyrex dish.
   An ideal, and standard, size is 9 × 9 × 2 inches (22 × 22 × 5 cm)

1 tablespoon vegetable oil
1 medium white onion, finely chopped
4 garlic cloves, peeled and finely chopped
2 pounds + 2 ounces (1 kg) potatoes, peeled and cooked with salt
9 ounces (250 g) carrots, cooked with salt and finely chopped
1 cup (250 ml) loosely packed flat-leaved parsley, finely chopped
1 cup (250 ml) cooked peas
Canned pickled jalapeños to taste, finely chopped
3 tablespoons mustard
2 tablespoons thick cream
3 egg yolks, lightly beaten
Salt to taste

• Heat the oven to 375°F (190°C)

• Heat the oil in a small skillet and wilt the onion and garlic. Set aside.

• Mash the potatoes roughly; add the carrot and the fried onion and garlic with the rest of the ingredients and mix well together. Transfer to the prepared dish, cover, and bake until the surface is firm to the touch, about 1 hour.

Pollo adobado relleno y su pasta
(Stuffed Chicken with Adobo Seasoning and "Pasta")

SEÑORA CECILIA PINEDA, "CENADURÍA CECI," IXTEPEC

This chicken is prepared for festive occasions, particularly weddings. It is traditionally accompanied by a black mole sauce (without meat). It is advisable to start the day before.

1 large chicken, about 4½ to 5 pounds (2 kg)
1 cup (250 ml) adobo (see recipe that follows)
2 cups (500 ml) of "*pasta*" stuffing (see recipe that follows)

- Spread the adobo over the skin of the chicken and set aside to season for a minimum of 6 hours or preferably overnight.

- The next day heat the oven to 350°F (180°C).

- Stuff the cavity of the chicken with the "*pasta*." Sew up the cavity. Place in a roasting pan, cover with greased paper, and cook, basting the chicken from time to time with the pan juices, until it is tender, about 2½ hours. Let the chicken rest for about 20 minutes before attempting to carve and serve it.

ADOBO PARA POLLO RELLENO U HORNEADO DE PUERCO

(ADOBO FOR STUFFED CHICKEN OR ROASTED PORK)

It is hardly worth making a smaller quantity of this adobo, because it will keep well and be ready to use for another time. It is advisable to prepare the adobo at least one day ahead for it to mature in flavor before using.

5½ ounces (150 g) guajillo chiles, cleaned of seeds and veins
Approximately 1–1½ cups (250–375 ml) of pineapple or other fruity vinegar
4 mild black peppercorns, crushed
4 cloves, crushed
¼ teaspoon cumin seeds, crushed
¼ teaspoon dried thyme leaves or ½ teaspoon fresh thyme
½ tablespoon Oaxacan oregano leaves or 1 teaspoon Mexican oregano
6 garlic cloves, peeled and roughly chopped
½ medium white onion, roughly chopped
6 Mexican bay leaves or 3 ordinary bay leaves
Salt to taste

- Cover the chiles with warm water and leave to soak for 2 hours (Señora Cecilia's instructions) then drain.

- Put ¼ cup (65 ml) of the vinegar into the blender jar; add the spices, the herbs, and the garlic and onion and blend to a smooth consistency. Add another ½ cup (125 ml) of the vinegar and add the chiles a few at a time, blending well after each addition. Add more of the vinegar as necessary to blend to a smooth paste. If small pieces of the tough chile skin still remain, pass the adobo through a strainer. Add the whole bay leaves and salt and set aside to season for several hours or overnight.

PASTA PARA POLLO RELLENO

("PASTA" FOR STUFFING CHICKEN)
SEÑORA CECILIA PINEDA, "CENADURÍA CECI," IXTEPEC

THIS QUANTITY IS SUFFICIENT TO STUFF TWO CHICKENS.

8 ounces (225 g) potatoes, half cooked and finely chopped
4 ounces (115 g) carrots, half cooked and finely chopped
½ medium white onion, finely chopped
2 tablespoons capers, roughly chopped
12 pitted green olives, roughly chopped
3 (or to taste) jalapeños *en escabeche*, roughly chopped
2 tablespoons soft butter or thick cream
2 chicken gizzards, cooked and roughly chopped
2 chicken livers, cooked and roughly chopped
Salt to taste

- Mix all the ingredients together in a bowl until they are well combined.

Quelite and Tomate Nanachepa

Many years ago I had made note of an unusual *quelite*, or wild green, in the Isthmus, known as *lagu* or *guanaguini* in Espinal and *guishicuana* in Tehuantepec.

The much-anticipated young plant grows, and the established climbing plant sprouts, in the rainy season.

But the interesting thing about this plant is that sprouts are used when young and tender, including the flower buds later on and the fruits when they appear a little later in the year. The latter resemble small, round green tomatoes, just less than 1 inch (2.5 cm) in diameter, with a dull grayish green skin.

The flesh is rather dry, compact, and full of tiny soft seeds. The fruits are mild in flavor and not acidy; they are cooked and ground to make a sauce. When they ripen to a bright red, they are no longer edible.

In Espinal, the young shoots and tender leaves are cooked just in water with garlic and salt, the broth fortified with little masa dumplings enriched with *zorrapa*, and seasoned with chile and epazote.

These little "tomatoes" are also known as *tomates arrieros,* and in El Camarón, on the highway to the City of Oaxaca where I stopped to photograph the mature plant, they are called *tomatito de nanachepa* and made into a sauce. The *tomatitos* are cooked in water, skinned, and ground with garlic, chiles, and salt.

Farther along the highway, in San Pedro Totolapa, they are also referred to as *tomates silvestres*. There, a renowned local cook told me how her family improvised by cooking, skinning, and mashing the tomatoes to a paste, then layering it in a *cazuela* with *queso fresco*. It was cooked, covered, over a wood fire, and then cut into wedges and served like a savory pie, with tortillas and a sauce of the small local chiles, xigoles.

Juchitán Area

Street scene, Juchitán, 1999/Diana Kennedy

Arroz con camarón oreado
(Rice with Dried Shrimps)

In the Isthmus, semidried shrimps that have been cooked and partially dried in the sun in the homes of the local fishermen are used in this dish. But I am giving here the quantity for completely dried shrimps.

6 SERVINGS

1 heaped cup (about 265 ml)—or 8 ounces (225 g)—long-grained unconverted rice
1¼ cups (315 ml)—or 1¾ ounces (50 g)—small dried shrimps
2 to 3 tablespoons vegetable oil
Approximately 3½ cups (about 825 ml) water
½ small white onion, finely chopped
3 garlic cloves, peeled and finely chopped
5 mild black peppercorns, crushed
¼ teaspoon pure *achiote* or ½ teaspoon prepared *achiote* paste
1 heaped cup (about 265 ml) roughly chopped tomatoes
4 fresh jalapeño chiles
Salt to taste

· Soak the rice in warm water for about 5 minutes. Drain, rinse in cold water, and drain again.

· Remove the heads, tails, and legs from the shrimps. Reserve the heads, removing the hard black eyes. Rinse the bodies and heads separately in cold water to remove some of the salt and set aside.

· Heat the oil in a casserole, add the rice, and fry over medium heat, stirring until it sounds brittle but does not brown, about 5 minutes. Add the shrimps and continue frying until the rice begins to color, about 5 minutes.

· Meanwhile, add 1 cup (250 ml) of the water to the blender jar and blend first the onion, garlic, peppercorns, *achiote,* and shrimp heads, gradually adding the tomatoes, until reduced to a slightly textured purée. Add to the pan and continue frying, stirring constantly to avoid sticking, until the mixture is almost dry. Put the whole chiles over the top, add the rest of the water, and salt if necessary. Cover the pot and cook over low heat until all the liquid has been absorbed and the rice tender, about 15 minutes.

· This rice can be prepared well ahead but is best reheated in a moderate oven for about 20 minutes. It does not freeze successfully.

*Bu'pu foam/*Diana Kennedy

Bu'pu

Every afternoon around six o'clock, a few people begin to congregate on the benches on one side of the central *jardín* of Juchitán, eagerly awaiting the arrival of the two women who prepare and sell the traditional drink, an *atole* served hot and topped with a fragrant foam, or *bu'pu*.

I went to visit one of the women, Señora María de Lourdes, to see exactly how *bu'pu* is made. She was just finishing the *atole* when I arrived. She had cooked a local variety of corn, *zapalote*, without lime, for about 1 hour, then, after rinsing and straining, it was sent to the mill to be ground into a soft, smooth masa; there was no overnight soaking.

Hanging behind her work area, where a metal hand-cranked grinder was set up, were strands of fresh *cacalazuchil*, pink plumeria or frangipani, flowers and some that had been dried for about 5 days. Señora María always prepares the mixture for the *bu'pu* one day before using.

She began by toasting the cacao beans: 2¼ pounds (1 kg) of the best "red" cacao from Chiapas. Once cooled, their brittle coating can easily be removed. She then proceeded to grind the beans three times until they had been reduced to a smooth, cohesive paste. But with the third grinding, she added a handful of the dried flowers that had been reduced to a powder, then, surprisingly, 2 quarts of the fresh flowers. This homogeneous paste was then stored away to be used the following day.

The next day at the appointed hour, Señora María added grated raw sugar, *panela*, to the cacao paste with a small quantity of water. To complete the final preparation of the *bu'pu*, she put half a liter (about 2 cups) of water into a clay pot, a type of *cazuela*, to which she added two large spoonfuls of the paste. She then began beating the mixture with a *molinillo*, and within 3 minutes, a beige-colored foam began to form on the surface. She then scooped some up to add a foamy crown to the hot *atole*. Delicious!

PLUMARIA FLOWERS AND CACAO BEANS
FOR PREPARING *BU'PU*/DIANA KENNEDY

Chiles pasillas de Oaxaca rellenos (Stuffed Pasilla Chiles)

In the Isthmus, these delicious stuffed and fried chiles are often served just as they are as a *botana*. As the main dish in a meal, they are served topped with a tomato sauce, not in a broth, and thick cream and accompanied by white rice and black beans. Sometimes onions are stuffed with the same filling. This filling, or *picadillo*, is also used to fill enchiladas or to stuff a turkey at Christmastime.

It is worth making this amount because the chiles, without the egg covering of course, can be frozen and ready for an unexpected occasion.

28 (Oaxacan) pasilla chiles
5 eggs, separated
Salt to taste
Approximately 1 cup (250 ml) flour
Vegetable oil for frying

THE FILLING

Makes 3 cups (750 ml)

1¼ pounds (about 500 g) stewing boneless
    beef, cut into 1-inch (2.5 cm) cubes
1 small head garlic, crushed unpeeled
Salt to taste
½ pound (about 250 g) stewing boneless
    pork, cut into 1-inch (2.5 cm) cubes
3 tablespoons softened lard or vegetable oil
5 garlic cloves, peeled and finely chopped
1 small white onion, finely chopped
5 mild black peppercorns, crushed
1 tablespoon dried Oaxacan oregano leaves
    or 1 heaped teaspoon Mexican oregano
12 ounces (350 g) tomatoes, finely chopped
½ cup (125 ml) raisins
1 small plantain—about ½ pound (about
    200 g)—peeled and cut into small cubes
20 green pitted olives, finely chopped
1 heaped tablespoon large capers, finely
    chopped
1 tablespoon vinegar
1½ cups (375 ml) of the meat broth
1 tablespoon sugar
Salt to taste

- Make a cut down the length of each chile, leaving intact the base of the stalk, and remove as many of the seeds as possible. Cover them with warm water and leave to soak for about 30 minutes, strain, then carefully remove any remaining seeds.

- If they are very picante, change the water in which they were soaking and leave for a further 10 minutes. Drain them well before filling.

- Put the beef into a pot with the garlic and salt, cover with water, and cook over medium heat for about 30 minutes after it comes to a boil—the meat should be half cooked. Add the pork and continue cooking until both meats are tender, about 40 minutes more. Strain, reserving the broth. Shred and chop the meats finely.

- Heat the lard in a deep skillet; add the chopped meats with the garlic, onion, peppercorns, and oregano and fry the mixture, scraping the bottom of the pan occasionally to prevent sticking, until the mixture is well seasoned, about 15 minutes.

- Add the tomatoes and the rest of the ingredients (except the broth, sugar, and salt) and cook over medium heat until dry, about 10 minutes. Add the broth, sugar, and salt and continue cooking until the mixture is moist but not juicy, about 10 minutes.

- Set aside to cool before filling the chiles.

- Coat with egg batter and fry as for chiles rellenos (p. 210).

Frijoles de olla istmeños (Isthmus Black Beans)

For this recipe, it is more usual to use a local black bean called *anadalón*, which is larger and rounder than the small black bean called *chima*, grown in the Chimalapas. They are prepared in various ways: *de olla*, served in bowls to accompany *tasajo* or *carne asada*, enriched with balls of masa, or reduced to a paste as a filling for tamales or to spread on *totopos* as a *botana*.

When served, these frijoles are topped with chopped green chile and onion, cubes of a fresh cheese, and finally sprinkled with dried oregano.

MAKES APPROXIMATELY 10 CUPS (2.5 L)
CON TODO Y CALDO (BEANS WITH BROTH)

1¼ pounds (about 500 g) black beans
1 medium white onion, roughly chopped
1 small head of garlic, cut in half horizontally
Salt to taste
1 small bunch epazote

• Pick through the beans, rinse, drain, and put into a large pot. Cover with water; add the onion, garlic, and salt and cook until they begin so soften. Add the epazote and continue cooking until soft, 2–3 hours, depending on the age of the beans.

Garnachas istmeñas
(Garnachas from the Isthmus)

These *garnachas* are a favorite evening snack in the Isthmus, both in the food stands in the center of Tehuantepec or under the *portales* of Juchitán. They provide a delicious combination of textures and flavors, the same as used for a chicken dish, *pollo garnachero* (p. 199).

MAKES 12 *GARNACHAS* ABOUT 3 INCHES (ABOUT 8 CM) IN DIAMETER

1 cup (250 ml or 260 g) tortilla masa
Pork lard or vegetable oil for frying
Approximately 1½ cups (375 ml) cooked and shredded beef (recipe follows)
½ cup (125 ml) sauce (recipe follows)
½ cup (125 ml) very finely grated *queso seco*: *de* Chiapas or *cotija*

TO SERVE WITH:
THE *CHILITO* (RECIPE FOLLOWS)

- Divide the masa into 12 pieces and roll into balls about 1¼ inches (about 3 cm) in diameter. Either using a plastic-lined tortilla press or your hands, press out to a circle about 3 inches (8 cm) in diameter. Cook on an ungreased comal for about 2 minutes on each side. It will be thicker than a normal tortilla.

- Heat some of the lard (preferably) or oil in a skillet. Put some of the shredded meat on the *garnachas* with a tablespoon of the sauce and fry, sprinkling hot lard over the top, until the bottom of the masa is slightly browned, but not too crisp.

- Sprinkle liberally with the cheese and serve immediately with the *chilito* on the side to add to taste.

THE SHREDDED BEEF

MAKES ABOUT 1½ CUPS (375 ML)

12 ounces (about 350 g) skirt or beef for shredding, cut into 1-inch (2.5 cm) cubes
½ medium white onion, sliced
2 unpeeled garlic cloves
Salt to taste
⅓ cup (85 ml) finely chopped white onion

- Put the meat, with the onion, garlic, and salt, into a pan; barely cover with cold water; and cook, covered, over medium heat until tender, about 40 minutes. Leave to cool in the broth. Strain, reserving the broth for the sauce that follows. You will need 1¼ cups (315 ml). Shred the meat and mix with the chopped onion.

FRYING *GARNACHAS* ISTMEÑAS/DIANA KENNEDY

THE SAUCE

6 ounces (170 g) tomatoes
1¼ cups (315 ml) of the beef broth
7 medium-sized Oaxacan pasilla chiles, seeded
1 Mexican pasilla (long black) chile, seeded
1 tablespoon pork lard or vegetable oil
2 peeled garlic cloves

- Put the whole tomatoes into the broth and cook for 10 minutes to soften. Strain, reserving the broth.

- Rinse the chiles and shake dry. Tear into pieces and put into the blender jar with ¾ cup (195 ml) of the broth and soak for 15 minutes. Add the cooked tomatoes to the blender jar and blend until smooth.

- Heat the lard in a medium skillet. Add the garlic and fry for a few seconds, then remove and discard. Add the sauce and fry over medium heat, stirring to prevent sticking, until reduced a little and well seasoned, about 5 minutes. Dilute with the rest of the broth. Add salt as necessary and cook for 3 minutes more. The sauce should be rather thin.

THE *CHILITO*

It is worth making this amount, which can season not only the *garnachas* but *pollo garnachero* (p. 199) or any *antojito* for that matter. It lasts and, in fact, improves in flavor as it sits in the refrigerator for 1 week or more.

2 medium-sized Oaxacan pasilla chiles, seeded
3 fresh jalapeño chiles
1 large carrot, trimmed and scraped
3 cups (750 ml) finely shredded cabbage
3 peeled garlic cloves, cut into strips
½ small white onion, thinly sliced
½ tablespoon dried Oaxacan oregano leaves or 1 teaspoon Mexican oregano
⅓ cup (85 ml) pineapple or other fruity vinegar (see p. 386)
Salt to taste

- Rinse the pasilla chiles briefly and tear into small pieces. Slice the jalapeños thinly slantwise, with the seeds. With a potato peeler, shred the carrot into thin, broad ribbons.

- Put all the ingredients into a nonreactive bowl and mix well with salt. (The vinegar should just moisten the ingredients.) Set aside to season for at least one hour before serving.

Gueta binguis

These intriguing little tortillas (*gueta* signifies "tortilla") are sold at the entrance of the Juchitán market every morning. They are not tortillas as one usually thinks of them, but more like small oval cakes of tortilla masa filled with dried shrimps and topped with a *molito* of pumpkin seeds and dried shrimps. They are baked in a wood-fired oven.

One of the principal families making them for sale lives on the outskirts of Juchitán, and it was to their home that I went to see exactly how they were made.

Preparations begin the day before with cooking the corn with lime, *nixtamal*. The next day, two large containers of the prepared ingredients were taken to the mill: one with the cooked, washed corn; epazote; and *zorrapa* (see note p. 426) and the other with the *molito* ingredients: the pumpkin seeds, tomatoes, chiles, and dried shrimp heads. A tricycle had been adapted for this daily event. Several members of the family then took part in forming and baking the *gueta binguis*, which were taken to be sold in the market.

The recipe given below is for a more manageable amount:

> **MAKES 30 SMALL**
> *GUETA BINGUIS*

FIRST PREPARE THE SHRIMPS

4 cups (1 L) small whole dried shrimps

- Rinse the shrimps to remove excess salt; strain. Cover with fresh water, soak for 5 minutes, and strain. Clean by removing heads, tails, and feet, reserving the heads (without the eyes) for the *molito*.

THE MASA

2¼ pounds (about 1 kg) coarsely ground tamale masa
Approximately ¾ cup (190 ml) water
1 cup (250 ml) coarsely chopped epazote leaves
1 cup (250 ml) *zorrapa* or *asiento*
1 cup (250 ml) melted lard
Salt to taste

- Put the masa into a large bowl. Put the water into the blender jar with the epazote and *zorrapa* and blend until smooth. Add with the lard to the masa, add salt to taste, and mix until all the ingredients are well integrated.

< INGREDIENTS TO BE GROUND FOR
GUETA BINGUIS/DIANA KENNEDY

TAKING INGREDIENTS FOR *GUETA BINGUIS*
TO THE MILL/DIANA KENNEDY

MAKES 2 CUPS (500 ML)

1 cup (250 ml) unhulled pumpkin seeds
Approximately ½ cup (125 ml) water
7 ounces (200 g) tomatoes, coarsely chopped
2 fresh jalapeño chiles, coarsely chopped
¼ teaspoon pure *achiote* or ½ teaspoon commercial *achiote* paste
The shrimp heads
½ cup (125 ml) tortilla masa

- Toast the pumpkin seeds in a skillet over low heat, moving them around so they toast evenly but do not become too dark in color. Set aside to cool and then grind in the blender or electric spice grinder to a fine but textured consistency.

- Put the water into the blender jar; add the tomatoes, chiles, and *achiote* and blend, adding the shrimp heads little by little, to a textured sauce. Mix in the masa, diluted with a little water.

FORMING AND BAKING THE *GUETA BINGUIS*

- Heat the oven to 375°F (190°C). Have ready 3 ungreased baking sheets.

- To make the small *gueta binguis*: Take ¼ cup (65 ml) of the prepared masa. Press out to form a well in the middle; put 4 shrimps and a spoonful of the *molito* in the well and fold the masa over to cover the filling. Shape into an oval about ½ inch (1.25 cm) thick.

- Place on a baking sheet, flatten a little, put another spoonful of the *molito* over the top, and bake for about 30 minutes, or until the masa is firm to the touch and browned.

GUETA BINGUIS READY FOR THE OVEN/DIANA KENNEDY

Mole de res
(Beef in Mole)

SEÑORA AMELIA ROMERO, JUCHITÁN

This mole was originally made with venison. It is served in deep plates, accompanied by fried black beans and boiled plantain.

MAKES 6 PORTIONS

½ medium white onion, roughly chopped
1 small head of garlic, unpeeled
Salt to taste
8 cups (2 L) water
2¾ pounds (about 1.300 kg) beef on the bone, brisket and shin, cut into serving pieces
1¼ pounds (about 500 g) tomatoes
1 small ball pure *achiote* or 2 tablespoons prepared Yucatecan *achiote* paste
1 cup (250 ml) tortilla masa
4 fresh jalapeño chiles, left whole
Small bunch epazote

- Put the onion, garlic, salt, and water into a pan; bring to a boil and simmer for 5 minutes. Add the meat and cook over medium heat for about 40 minutes.

- Add the whole tomatoes and cook until soft, about 10 minutes. Remove tomatoes and garlic; add tomatoes and peeled garlic to blender with the *achiote* and blend to a smooth purée.

- Strain the meat and set aside. Degrease the broth; you will need about 6–7 cups (1.5 to 1.75 L) for the mole. Put the grease into the pan in which you are going to cook the mole.

- Add the tomato mixture to the pan through a strainer and fry over medium heat until reduced a little, about 5 minutes.

- Put 1 cup (250 ml) of the meat broth into the blender, add the masa, and blend smooth.

- Add to the pan through a strainer and stir constantly for a few minutes to avoid sticking until the sauce thickens, about 5 minutes. Add the remaining broth, the meat, the whole chiles, and epazote, with salt as necessary, and continue cooking until the meat is tender.

- Serve the meat with plenty of the mole.

Pollo garnachero

SEÑORA AMALIA ROMERO, JUCHITÁN

6 PORTIONS

1 large chicken, cut into 6 portions
½ medium onion, coarsely chopped
3 garlic cloves, unpeeled
Water or chicken broth
Salt to taste
3 large potatoes, peeled and thinly sliced
Approximately ⅓ cup (85 ml) melted lard
Approximately 1⅓ cups (333 ml) *garnacha* sauce (p. 193)
Approximately 3 cups (750 ml) *chilito* (p. 193)

- Put the chicken into a pot with the onion and garlic, barely cover with water, add salt, and cook over medium heat until almost tender, about 30 minutes.

- Add the potato slices and continue cooking another 10 minutes. Drain, reserving the broth for the *garnacha* sauce.

- Heat half of the lard in a skillet. Add the chicken pieces in one layer (you may have to do this in two lots); add the sauce and fry, basting the chicken until it begins to brown. Remove and keep warm. Add more lard as necessary and fry the potato slices in the remaining sauce. Serve the chicken topped with the potato and liberally doused with the *chilito*.

Salsa de tomate rojo istmeña (Tomato Sauce from the Isthmus)

This sauce has a distinct flavor when made with the local tomatoes, *criollos* or *tomates rojos tecas* (see photo opposite). In appearance, they are like a very small beefsteak tomato with their undulating surface; they are thin skinned, very juicy, and more acidic than the normal Roma-type more commonly used.

Another distinction is that, when in season, the small green chiles criollos are used in and around Tehuantepec, but not in Juchitán, where they would use either the chile chocolate or the jalapeño.

MAKES ABOUT 2 CUPS (500 ML)

18 ounces (500 g) tomatoes
Hot green chiles to taste
1 garlic clove, peeled
Salt to taste

To serve: finely chopped white onion

• Put the tomatoes and chiles into a small pan, barely cover with water, and cook over medium heat until soft, 10 minutes. Strain, reserving the cooking water, and put into the blender jar with the garlic and salt to taste. Blend to a textured sauce, adding a little of the cooking water if too thick.

• *To serve:* Sprinkle the top with the chopped onion.

LOCAL TOMATOES/DIANA KENNEDY

Tamales de cambray
(Cambray Tamales)

MAESTRA DEYANIRA AQUINO, IXHUATÁN

La Teca restaurant in the city of Oaxaca is well known for their delicious *tamales de cambray,* each one formed into a small cylinder shape and covered with a banana leaf.

La maestra Deyanira likes to wilt her banana leaves in the sun!

**MAKES ABOUT 36 TAMALES
ABOUT 4 INCHES (10 CM) LONG**

Have ready:

A tamale steamer with the top section lined with banana leaves

36 pieces of banana leaf 8½ inches (22 cm) square, wilted in hot water or over heat

THE FILLING

14 ounces (400 g) skirt steak

14 ounces (400 g) boneless pork with some fat

1 medium white onion, coarsely chopped

1 small head garlic, halved horizontally

Salt to taste

7 guajillo chiles, cleaned of veins and seeds

2 ancho chiles, cleaned of veins and seeds

Pork lard for frying

½ cup (125 ml) breadcrumbs

6 ounces (165 g) tomatoes, coarsely chopped

½ medium white onion, coarsely chopped

2 peeled garlic cloves, coarsely chopped

½ teaspoon each: dried thyme and marjoram leaves

½ tablespoon dried Oaxacan oregano leaves or 1 teaspoon Mexican oregano

1 plantain—about 12 ounces (340 g)—peeled and cut into small cubes

⅓ cup (85 ml) raisins

⅓ cup (85 ml) capers

15 peeled almonds, finely chopped

15 pitted green olives, finely chopped

Optional: **1 small apple, peeled and cut into small cubes**

9 ounces (250 g) potatoes, cooked and cut into small cubes

3 large eggs, cooked and chopped

Salt to taste

- Cut the meats into 1-inch (2.5 cm) cubes. Put into a pan with the onion, garlic, and salt and cook over medium heat until tender, about 35 minutes, but the beef will probably need another 15 minutes. Let the meats cool off in the broth. Strain, reserving the broth; shred roughly; and chop finely.

- Meanwhile, put the chiles into a pan, cover with water, and cook for about 5 minutes. Set aside to soak for about 15 minutes. Strain. Put 1 cup (250 ml) of the broth into the blender jar, add the chiles a few at a time, and blend to a smooth purée.

- Heat 1 tablespoon of lard in a skillet and add the chile purée through a strainer, pressing down hard to extract as much juice and flesh as possible. Fry over fairly high heat, stirring to prevent sticking, until reduced a little, about 5 minutes. Add the breadcrumbs to thicken the sauce and cook for about 3 minutes more.

- Put the tomatoes, onion, garlic, and herbs into the blender and blend smooth, adding a little of the meat broth if necessary. Add this purée to the pan and cook for about 5 minutes over high heat.

- Heat a little more lard in a skillet and fry separately: plantain, raisins, capers, almonds, olives, and apple (if using).

- Add to the pan with the meats; add the rest of the ingredients with 1 cup (250 ml) of the broth. Add salt as necessary and continue cooking the mixture for about 10 minutes.

- Set aside to cool.

2¼ pounds (about 1.5 kg) textured tamale masa

2½ cups (625 ml)—1¼ pounds (570 g)—pork lard

Salt to taste

Approximately 1 cup (250 ml) meat broth

- Beat the masa with the lard and salt, adding the broth by degrees, or, using an electric mixer, beat the lard with the salt until aerated and then add the masa by degrees, alternating with the broth. The mixture should be of medium consistency and spreadable.

- Start the steamer over low heat.

- Spread a heaped tablespoon of the masa in an oval shape 4 inches (10 cm) long and about ¼ inch thick (about 1 cm) on one side of a banana leaf, leaving the extremities free.

- Put 1 scant tablespoon of the filling along the center of the masa and start rolling the leaf so that the masa covers the filling. Twist the ends to prevent the filling from oozing out; the tamale should now resemble a small cylinder.

- When the water in the steamer is boiling, place the tamales horizontally in the top section and cook over high heat until the masa is firm to the touch, about 1¼ hours.

Tamales de elote juchitecos (Fresh Corn Tamales Juchitecos)

SEÑORA AMELIA ROMERO, JUCHITÁN

These fresh corn tamales are generally eaten for breakfast, topped with cream and a simple curd cheese called *cuajado*, literally "clabbered." And sometimes, to make them even richer, with *chicharrón*.

The corn, of course, is mature, starchy but still juicy. Field corn would have to be substituted for best results.

In Juchitán, the corn would be ground in a hand-cranked metal corn grinder (before, on the metate), but a food processor or even a blender will do an adequate job. With that in mind, I have modified the mixing method.

The fresh husks should be cut off as near the base as possible, and much care should be taken in unfurling the leaves.

MAKES ABOUT 25 TAMALES 3 INCHES (ABOUT 8 CM) LONG

Have ready:
A tamale steamer with the top part lined with the fresh cornhusks
25 (or more, just in case) fresh cornhusks

4½ ounces (125 g)—about ½ cup (125 ml) plus 2 tablespoons—*zorrapa* (see note p. 426)
⅓ cup (85 ml) water
6 cups (1.5 L) fresh corn kernels
4½ ounces (125 g)—about ½ cup (125 ml) plus 2 tablespoons—softened pork lard
1 tablespoon sugar
Salt to taste

- Start heating the steamer over low heat.

- Put the *zorrapa* with the water into a food processor and blend smooth. Gradually add the corn and blend to a slightly textured consistency. Add the rest of the ingredients and blend well.

- Put one very heaped tablespoon of the mixture into one of the fresh leaves and fold to cover the filling completely and securely. Immediately place horizontally in steamer and continue with the rest, placing them in overlapping layers. Cover the top with more leaves, cover the steamer with a tightly fitting lid, and cook over medium heat until the dough separates easily from the leaf, about 1 hour.

Warning note: Any mixture with raw, fresh corn will sour quickly, so once ground, it should be cooked as soon as possible.

San Mateo–San Pedro Area

Fishing boats in Mar Muerto/Diana Kennedy

San Mateo del Mar

San Mateo is situated halfway along a low-lying strip of land that juts out from the mainland into the Gulf of Tehuantepec. It is one of the three Huave villages: San Mateo, San Dionisio, and San Francisco del Mar. The last two exist in both the original and the new settlements because some years ago, San Francisco was completely covered with sand, and as a result, San Dionisio was isolated; both were relocated.

The Huaves, whose origins have always been disputed, were never conquered by the Spaniards and have retained their native tongue. While every village has different customs, ways of living, and dialect, they all can make themselves understood.

Bumping along a washboard road en route to San Mateo, you pass through a landscape completely different from that of the rest of the Isthmus, lined with scrubby plants and cacti, occasionally opening out to flat, sandy plains dotted with palm trees that are converted into lakes as the rains come.

Although the large majority of Huave men are dedicated to fishing, a few still plant the native corn, distinguished by its short stalks that withstand the strong winds on the small remaining areas of cultivable land.

Most of the fishermen work at night or in the early hours of the morning, and as anthropologist Paola García has told me, it is a magical scene to see the little boats riding the waves with the reflection of their lamps dancing on the water.

As dawn breaks, the fishermen return to their homes to cook the shrimps in salted water and dry-smoke their fish for the market. About midday, the women, balancing wide baskets on their heads, make their way to the marketplace; it is such a pleasure to watch them stride along with such a dignified air in their long, colorful skirts swaying in the constant breeze.

Under a covered area outside the small market, the women sit on low benches, selling their wares or bargaining with the *rega-tonas zapotecas*, the Zapotec women traders who buy and then sell the shrimps and fish in the markets of Tehuantepec, Juchitán, and even farther afield.

Entering the dim market, you first come across several food stands that cater to the Zapotec buyers or the occasional visitor; there are others selling small amounts of locally grown chiles and fruits, tortillas freshly baked in *comizcales*, and *salpicón de tollo* (see recipe p. 211).

The daily diet of the Huaves is a very simple one based on shrimps, either cooked in water or *oreado*, half dried, and tortillas: *bolitas* and *totopos*, *gueta binguis* (see p. 195), or tamales baked in *comizcales*. The tortillas made there of locally grown white corn are thick and a little chewy; they are dotted with small holes like *totopos*.

Totopos are also made in various ways by the local women: the masa mixed with a paste of black beans, or pumpkin seeds, or sweetened with *panela* and cinnamon—all the ingredients ground with the masa on metates. One of the common daily foods is a stew made of fish heads and toasted corn. But because their frugal diet is so lacking in other proteins and vitamins, there exists a large degree of malnutrition.

I was introduced to Señora Isabel Ampudia by anthropologist Paola García, who has studied the Huaves over many years, and Doña Isabel became my principal guide and teacher on the subject of Huave food. She told me about *tortillas de camarón fresco*, tortillas encrusted with fresh shrimp. I went to find them in the market, but, as is often my bad luck, the woman who usually sells them was not there. To console me, Doña Isabel offered to make them for me the following day. She also offered to contact the specialist in making the local celebratory *atole* with its foam of cacao, *chaw popox*; Señora Zenaida Rangel lives alone on a *ranchería* some distance from San Mateo.

Cooking fish in *comizcal*, San Mateo del Mar/Diana Kennedy

Arroz blanco con caldo de res (White Rice with Beef Broth)

SEÑORA JUVENTINA VELÁZQUEZ, SAN PEDRO HUILOTEPEC

This is a very simple but tasty variation of white rice if you have a good beef broth made or left over; but it is not to be cooked with the canned stuff.

8–10 SERVINGS

2 cups (500 ml)—or 14 ounces (400 g)—long-grained unconverted rice
3 cloves garlic, peeled and roughly chopped
3 mild black peppercorns, crushed
2 whole cloves, crushed
¼ cup (65 ml) water
4 tablespoons vegetable oil
½ medium white onion, finely chopped
Approximately 4 cups (1 L) beef broth (see note above)
Salt to taste

- Rinse the rice, strain, and set aside to drain for a few minutes. Crush together the garlic and spices with the water.

- Heat the oil in a heavy casserole, add the rice, and fry, stirring it from time to time, until it sounds brittle but not browned. Add the spice mixture and onion and continue frying for about 2 minutes, taking care it does not stick to the pan.

- Add the broth with salt to taste and cook the rice, uncovered, over moderate heat until all the liquid has been absorbed, about 15 minutes. Cover the pan and set aside to season for about 10 minutes before serving.

- This rice can be prepared ahead of time. It is best to reheat it in the same pan in a moderate oven for about 20 minutes. This rice also freezes well.

TYPICAL HOUSE, SAN MATEO/DIANA KENNEDY

Chaw popox

The foam on top of this *atole*, which is prepared for weddings and other important occasions, is called *popox*—*chaw* means *atole*. The main ingredient needed to create the foam for the cacao is the bark of a climbing plant known there as *ncheed*. We had to go to the house of Doña Isabel's niece, where it was growing over the wall of the house. It is, in fact, an ornamental plant with a small white flower that grows prolifically over the walls and patios in San Mateo.

Veronica, her niece, cut from the thickest part of the plant a length of the woody stem about ½ inch (about 1.5 cm) thick and 20 inches (about 50 cm) long.

All the ingredients had been bought and prepared by the time we returned to the house, and Señora Zenaida was toasting 80 cacao beans so as to be able to remove the outer brittle layer. She then stripped the brown covering off the stem and proceeded to crush it on the metate with a flat stone, adding 10 pieces of cinnamon stick. When she was satisfied that all the ingredients had been ground sufficiently, she added the cacao beans, a few at a time, repeating the grinding process for *ocho pasados* (eight times) until it formed a smooth, cohesive paste.

Diluting the paste in 1 liter (4 cups) of water, she began to beat the mixture; in a few seconds, the foam began to form and float to the top of the liquid; it was immediately scooped up and served on top of a small bowl of hot *atole*.

Chiles jalapeños rellenos
(Jalapeño Chiles Stuffed with Beef)

SEÑORA JUSTINA VELÁZQUEZ, SAN PEDRO HUILOTEPEC

Fresh jalapeño chiles are used for this recipe. Only if they are small are they left whole, but it is more customary to use halved larger ones. The chiles are stuffed with a beef filling (recipe follows), covered with the beaten egg, and fried as is usual; but they are served just like that, dry and not in a sauce, accompanied by red or white rice.

For those who like their food very spicy, it is not necessary to soak the chiles first in salted water with vinegar; nor is it customary there to dust the chiles with flour before covering with the beaten egg. If it makes it easier for the egg to adhere, do so.

9 large fresh jalapeño chiles, toasted and
    peeled
2 tablespoons salt (optional)
¼ cup (65 ml) commercial vinegar
    (optional)
2 cups (500 ml) beef filling
3–4 large eggs, separated
Salt to taste
Flour for dusting (optional)
Vegetable oil for frying

- Cut the chiles in half and remove seeds and veins (see note above). Press the stuffing into each half chile; they should be very fat.

- Have ready a tray lined with absorbent paper. Heat the oil in a skillet; it should be about ½ inch (1.5 cm) deep. Beat the egg whites until the peaks hold their shape, but they should not be too stiff and dry. Beat in the yolks with salt to taste.

- Dust the chiles with the optional flour or, if not, just dip the stuffed half chile into the beaten egg and fry, turning to fry evenly to a deep gold color. Drain and serve with the rice.

CARNE MOLIDA PARA CHILES JALAPEÑOS

(BEEF FILLING FOR JALAPEÑO CHILES)

SEÑORA JUVENTINA VELÁZQUEZ, SAN PEDRO HUILOTEPEC

MAKES 4 CUPS (1 L), SUFFICIENT FOR ABOUT 18 JALAPEÑO CHILES

1½ pounds (680 g) ground beef
½ medium white onion, roughly sliced
6 garlic cloves, unpeeled
3 cups (750 ml) water
Salt to taste
4 guajillo chiles, seeds and veins removed
1 clove, crushed
4 mild black peppercorns, crushed
½ teaspoon dried thyme leaves or 1 teaspoon fresh thyme
1 teaspoon dried Oaxacan oregano leaves or ½ teaspoon Mexican oregano
2 small garlic cloves, peeled
1 tablespoon vegetable oil
8 ounces (about 200 g) tomatoes, finely chopped
½ medium white onion, finely chopped
Salt to taste

- Put the meat, together with the onion and garlic, into a pan, add the water and salt to taste, and cook, uncovered, over low heat for 30 minutes. Strain and reserve the broth. There should be about 2½ cups (625 ml) of the broth.

- Cover the guajillo chiles with cold water and leave to soak for 20 minutes. Strain.

- Put ¼ cup (65 ml) of the meat broth in the blender jar; add the clove, peppercorns, thyme, oregano, and garlic and blend well. Add ½ cup (125 ml) of the broth and the chiles, a few at a time, blending well after each addition. Add more broth only if necessary to release the blade of the blender. The mixture should be very smooth.

- Heat the oil in a deep skillet, add the sauce, and fry over fairly high heat, stirring and scraping the bottom of the pan to prevent sticking, for 3 minutes.

- Add the tomato and onion and cook for 2 minutes more. Add the meat, with salt as necessary, and cook over fairly medium heat for 5 minutes more.

- The meat should be fairly dry. Use the remaining broth to cook the tasty white rice recipe (see p. 207).

Salpicón o Ceviche de cazón (Ceviche of Shredded Dogfish or Shark)

SEÑORA ISABEL AMPUDIO,
SAN MATEO DEL MAR

The market in San Mateo del Mar does not come alive until midday, when the local women come to sell the morning's catch of shrimps, which they have cooked with a lot of salt. Earlier, a few fruit and vegetable stands are open, and there are a few young women selling tamales, small fish in *escabeche*, and large *cazuelas* of what they call *ceviche* but is quite unlike any other that goes by that name. I was told that the correct name was *salpicón* made with dogfish, *cazón*, or a Pacific shark, *tollo*. It made a delicious breakfast with the small, typically thick tortilla, almost crisp from the *comizcal*.

Although not authentic, I like to make this *salpicón* with olive oil and serve it on tostadas.

MAKES ABOUT 2 CUPS (500 ML)

3 garlic cloves, crushed without peeling
Salt to taste
1 pound (450 g) skinless, boneless dogfish or shark
2–3 tablespoons vegetable or olive oil
1 small white onion, finely chopped
2 fresh chiles criollos or 1 jalapeño, finely chopped
½ cup (125 ml) finely chopped epazote
Salt to taste

- Put sufficient water in a pan to barely cover the fish, add the garlic and salt, and cook for about 5 minutes. Lower the heat to a simmer, add the fish, and cook over low heat until just cooked, about 10 minutes, depending on the thickness of the fish.

- Strain, shred, and squeeze in cheesecloth until almost dry.

- Put the oil into a skillet and fry the onion and chiles for one minute. Add the fish, the epazote, and salt and fry over medium heat, stirring to prevent sticking, for 10 minutes.

Tortillas de camarón fresco (Tortillas with Fresh Shrimps)

SEÑORA ISABEL AND SEÑORITA VALERIA
AMPUDIO, SAN MATEO DEL MAR

These tortillas, like all the traditional tortillas in San Mateo, are cooked on the heated surface of a *comizcal* (see Glossary). They can be cooked until either almost or totally crisp, according to taste. The masa is mixed with epazote and chiles and encrusted with whole, fresh shrimps.

Señora Isabel and her niece prepared the tortillas for me in San Mateo. They started the day before with the *nixtamal*, cooking 3 quarts (3 L) of corn with lime. It was ground the following morning at the local mill to a very smooth masa.

To make the tortillas, they first ground on the metate the leaves of 5 large sprigs of epazote, then 2 fresh whole jalapeño chiles, and finally 2 guajillo chiles that had been deseeded and soaked in water for 20 minutes, with the heads of the fresh shrimps. Very little water was added, just sufficient to produce a loose, not watery, paste. This mixture was added to the masa through a strainer and mixed until all had been thoroughly combined. A little salt was added.

The two women began making the tortillas by taking a handful of the dough and forming it into a thickish circle about 5½ inches (11 cm) in diameter. They then encrusted 4, sometimes 5, cleaned and peeled raw shrimps into the dough. When all the tortillas had been formed, after dampening their hands with water, they made a hole in the center with their little finger and pressed the tortillas to the curved surface of the heated *comizcal*. When the *comizcal* was full, the opening was covered with a lid.

After 30 minutes, the tortillas were pronounced cooked; they had acquired a slightly crisp surface and a light golden appearance. They are eaten just like that.

Biaxigui

SEÑORA CALLI LÓPEZ RAMÍREZ, TEHUANTEPEC

Señora Calli says that this dish is prepared especially for rainy or cooler days. The name is derived from the plain tamale that is served as part of the dish. It is made of finely ground masa, without salt or fat, and is formed and wrapped in a long corn leaf, not a husk.

The tamales are eaten in place of a tortilla. *Biaxigui* is served with, apart from two tamales, a *plátano criollo*, a local banana—which has been cooked unpeeled—seasoned with salt and sugar.

Some cooks prefer to substitute the more tasty pork offal instead of the ribs and to use dried instead of fresh chiles.

6 PORTIONS

2¼ pounds (about 1 kg) pork ribs, with fat
Salt to taste
1 small head garlic, cut into half horizontally and lightly smashed
1¼ pounds (about 550 g) tomatoes
2 fresh chiles criollos del Istmo or 2 jalapeños
Approximately 2 cups (500 ml) water or broth

To serve:
12 tamales (see above)
6 cooked bananas

- Put the meat into a pan and barely cover with water, add salt and the garlic, and cook over medium heat until the meat is just tender and almost dry, about 35 minutes. Squeeze the flesh from the garlic, return to the pan, and continue cooking until the meat is lightly browned with the fat that has exuded, adding extra lard if necessary.

- Meanwhile, cover the tomatoes and chiles with water and cook until soft. Strain and blend briefly—the purée should not be smooth. Stir into the meat in the pan and cook over fairly high heat for 8 minutes, stirring to avoid sticking. Add the 2 cups of water or broth and continue cooking for about 15 minutes more.

< *QUELITE*/DIANA KENNEDY

THE ISTHMUS (213

Calabaza tierna guisada
(Stewed Tender Pumpkin)

Señora Piedad Cortez de Ruiz, El Camarón

On the drive from Oaxaca to the Isthmus, I often stop at the modest little restaurant of Señora Piedad for *almuerzo*. She and her husband had mentioned a certain wild plant that produced a small green tomato-like edible fruit that they called *tomatito de nanachapa* (see p. 185). Once, the plant was in flower (also eaten), so we went off for me to photograph it. In Señor Martín Ruiz's cornfields nearby, the pumpkins were still tender; they were *calabazas indias*, also known as *huichis* (see photo p. 323). He cut two of them for our meal, and we went back for his wife to cook them. The dish was so simple but delicious.

Any mature squash or tender pumpkin can be used, but preferably not the usual dark green zucchini, which to me is pretty tasteless.

MAKES 4 PORTIONS

1 tablespoon vegetable oil (or substitute a light olive oil)
½ cup (125 ml) finely chopped white onion
3 small garlic cloves, peeled and finely chopped
2 serrano chiles, finely chopped (always with seeds)
2¼ pounds (about 1 kg) tender pumpkin, cut into cubes, unpeeled
½ cup (125 ml) water
Salt to taste
1 cup (250 ml) tightly packed, roughly chopped cilantro
1 cup (250 ml) tightly packed, roughly chopped fresh mint

- In a wide pan, heat the oil and cook the onion, garlic, and chiles until translucent.

- Add the pumpkin, water, and salt; cover the pan and cook over medium heat until the pumpkin is just tender, not soft, about 8 minutes. It should be moist but not too juicy.

- Stir in the herbs and cook, uncovered, until the pumpkin is tender. Serve with a dried chile, taviche or de árbol, sauce.

Molotes de plátano
(Plantain Molotes)

MAESTRA CARMEN LÓPEZ TOLEDO, TEHUANTEPEC

According to Maestra Carmen, this is the simple, classic way of preparing *molotes*, although some cooks in Juchitán cover them with an egg batter before frying.

These *molotes*, like those made of corn masa, are shaped like a weaving bobbin or shuttle. They can be served alone as an appetizer, or with white rice as a main dish, or even to accompany a chile relleno.

These *molotes* may be filled with a black bean paste, cheese, or a *picadillo* and served topped with cream and finely grated dry cheese.

Choosing the plantains is important: the skin should be yellow but the flesh inside should be firm and slightly underripe.

MAKES 12 MOLOTES APPROXIMATELY 3 INCHES (ABOUT 7 CM) IN LENGTH

3 medium-sized plantains—about 1¾ pounds (800 g)—each cut into 3 pieces unpeeled
6 ounces (165 g) *queso fresco,* cut into 12 strips
OR
⅔ cup (165 ml) black bean paste (p. 116)
Vegetable oil for frying

Topping: cream and finely grated Chiapas cheese (or substitute Romano)

- Put the plantains into a pan with water to cover and cook over medium heat until soft, about 15 minutes. Strain, set aside to cool a little, then peel. (If the flesh gets cold, it cannot be worked. If this happens, reheat over steam.) Mash the flesh to a cohesive but not completely smooth consistency. Divide into 12 parts and roll each one into a ball about 1½ inches (about 4 cm). Form into a cylinder about 3 inches (7.5 cm) long. Make a depression along it and fill with the bean paste or cheese. Reform into a bobbin shape, covering the filling completely.

- Heat the oil in a small skillet—it should be about ½ inch (about 1.25 cm) deep—and fry a few of the *molotes* at a time (they should be kept separate in the pan) until they are a deep gold color, about 8 minutes. Drain on paper towels. Serve portions of 2 *molotes*, pressing them down a little before topping with the cream and cheese.

Guisado de pollo o caldo guisado
(Tehuantepec Chicken Stew)

MAESTRA CARMEN LÓPEZ TOLEDO, TEHUANTEPEC

Despite its prosaic name, this is a rather sophisticated dish that is usually prepared for special occasions. But for an important fiesta, when it is customary to kill a bullock, the dish is cooked with beef. It is brothy and therefore served in deep plates, accompanied by *totopos* (see p. 231) or tortillas.

For those who like something spicy, the local green chiles criollos (see photo p. 200) are served separately: they are called *chiles de amor*, "love chiles," or more prosaically *chiles de a mordidas*, "chiles for biting."

6–8 PORTIONS

THE CHICKEN

Water to cover the chicken pieces

1 medium white onion, cut into 8 pieces

4 garlic cloves, peeled

3 large sprigs of cilantro

3 large sprigs of mint

2 large stalks of epazote

1 large chicken—about 4½ pounds (2 kg)— cut into serving pieces and the breast quartered

Salt to taste

• Put the water into a large pot with the onion, garlic, and herbs; bring to a simmer and continue cooking over low heat for 10 minutes. Add the chicken pieces with salt to taste and cook over medium heat for about 20 minutes—the chicken should be half cooked.

• Strain the meat and measure the broth; you will need about 6 cups (1.5 L). Reduce over high heat or add water to make that amount.

THE SAUCE

Approximately 4 tablespoons of lard or vegetable oil

1 plantain—about 1 pound (450 g)—peeled and cut into thick slices

⅓ cup (85 ml) chicken broth

10 cloves, crushed

2 mild black peppercorns, crushed

¼ teaspoon cumin seeds, crushed

2 tablespoons Oaxacan oregano leaves or 1 tablespoon Mexican oregano

1 teaspoon of fresh thyme leaves or ½ teaspoon dried thyme

2 garlic cloves, lightly toasted and peeled

8 large scallions, roughly chopped with leaves

1¾ pounds (800 g) tomatoes, finely chopped

2 thick slices white onion

12 ounces (340 g) potatoes, peeled, cubed, and half cooked

2 thick slices fresh pineapple, cut into medium cubes

12 green pitted olives, left whole

2 tablespoons capers, left whole

2 tablespoons raisins

2 (or to taste) pickled jalapeño chiles

2 tablespoons of chile liquid

1 tablespoon sugar, or to taste

Salt to taste

1 thick slice bread, roughly crumbled

• In a large casserole, heat 2 tablespoons of the lard and fry the plantain slices until lightly browned. Drain and set aside. Add the remaining lard to the casserole.

• Put ⅓ cup (85 ml) of the chicken broth into the blender jar; add the spices, herbs, and peeled garlic and blend until almost smooth. Add this mixture to the pan and fry for about 5 minutes or until almost dry. Add the scallions and continue frying until they are beginning to change color. Stir in the tomatoes and onion slices and continue cooking over high heat, stirring to avoid sticking, until the sauce is reduced, about 8 minutes. Add the potatoes, pineapple, olives, capers, raisins, and chiles and cook for a further 10 minutes. Finally, add the chicken pieces with the broth, plantain, vinegar, and sugar, with salt to taste. Cover the casserole and cook over low heat for about 30 minutes. Add the bread to thicken the juices a little, but the dish should be rather soupy.

• This chicken dish can be prepared several hours ahead—in fact, it improves in flavor. It is best reheated in the oven for about 20 minutes. This type of dish does not freeze.

GUAJILLO CHILES/PEDRO VALTIERRA

Pato en guajillo
(Duck in Guajillo Sauce)

SEÑORA JUANITA "CALABAZA," TEHUANTEPEC

Señora Juanita, like many of her neighbors, has a few ducks wandering around her patio; they tend to be rather tough, but tasty.

This dish is served in deep bowls, with tortillas, for the main meal in the afternoon.

5–6 SERVINGS

1 large duck—about 4½–5 pounds (2-plus kg)—cleaned and gutted, plus giblets
Juice of 3–4 limes
1 tablespoon salt
2 dried avocado leaves (see Note on Toxicity, p. 426)
Salt to taste
5 guajillo chiles, cleaned of seeds and veins
Approximately 1½ cups (375 ml) water
4 peeled garlic cloves, roughly chopped
5 mild black peppercorns, crushed
½ tablespoon Oaxacan oregano leaves or ¼ tablespoon Mexican oregano
½ teaspoon thyme leaves

- Cut the duck and giblets into smallish pieces (i.e., breast into 6, legs and wings halved).

- Wash in water to which the lime juice and salt have been added. Rinse again and drain.

- Put the meat into a large pot, cover with water, add the avocado leaves and salt, and start the cooking over medium heat.

- Cover the chiles with hot water and leave to soak for 10 minutes. Strain. Put ½ cup (125 ml) of the water into the blender jar; add the garlic, peppercorns, oregano, and thyme; blend well and add to the pot. Blend the chiles well with another ½ cup (125 ml) water and add to the pot through a strainer, pressing hard to extract as much as possible of the chile; but there will always be pieces of tough skin left in the strainer.

- Cover and continue the cooking over medium heat until the meat is tender and the broth reduced and well seasoned, about 1½ hours, depending on the quality of the duck. If the sauce is too thick, add the remaining water.

Pimbos
(Traditional Ring Cookies)

SEÑORA GLORIA RITO LÓPEZ AND HER FAMILY, SAN BLAS

These delectable little ring cookies, unique to the Isthmus, are now hard to find, but Señora Gloria and members of her family are keeping alive the tradition of making them as handed down from her great-grandfather.

She was very specific about the ingredients used: local white corn; *panela roja*, a type of raw sugar, as opposed to *panela negra*, a much darker type; and melted marrow bone fat, although some cooks use the fat from around the beef kidneys (suet). Alas, for health and expense reasons, a vegetable lard mixed with butter is now used by the family.

Preparations begin the day before with the toasting and grinding of the corn. The next day, the *panela* is melted and the ingredients are worked together while the wood-fired oven is heating. The baking time is short, and once they have cooled, they are packed into baskets ready to be taken to the markets in Tehuantepec and Juchitán.

MAKES 30 *PIMBOS*

7 ounces (200 g) *panela*, *piloncillo*, **or dark brown sugar**
⅓ cup (85 ml) water
18 ounces (500 g) toasted and ground corn
8 ounces (225 g) marrow fat, melted
1 tablespoon ground cinnamon
Pinch salt

- Put the sugar and water into a pan and heat until the sugar has melted. Increase heat and cook until the syrup begins to thicken a little. Set aside to cool.

- Mix the corn with the fat, adding the cinnamon and salt. Add the cooled syrup a little at time, and when it has been absorbed, work the dough until cohesive and smooth.

- Heat the oven to 350°F (180°C) and have ready 2 ungreased baking sheets.

- To form the *pimbos*, roll the dough into a cylinder ⅜ inch (1 cm) thick and cut into lengths of about 6½ inches (about 16 cm). Form into a circle and press the ends firmly together. Place on a baking tray and repeat with the rest of the dough.

- Bake the *pimbos* until firm to the touch and browned, about 20–25 minutes.

- Cool completely before attempting to remove from the baking sheet.

NOTES

- You will need 3 pounds of dried corn to obtain 18 ounces of toasted and ground corn.

- The fat: If using the beef kidney fat, buy 2¼ pounds (1 kg), cut into pieces, and melt over slow heat. Strain, cool, and weigh.

- For the marrow fat, you will need 16 inches (about 40 cm) marrow bones. Put into a skillet with ⅓ cup (85 ml) water, cover the pan, and heat gently until the marrow slips easily out of the bones (about 10 minutes). Discard the bones and melt the marrow fat over low heat. Strain before using.

Tamales de elote estilo Jalapa del Marqués
(Fresh Corn Tamales Jalapa de Marqués Style)

MAESTRA CARMEN LÓPEZ TOLEDO, TEHUANTEPEC.

The corn for these extraordinarily delicious tamales must be starchy but still juicy. Traditionally, it was ground on the metate, but now a hand-cranked metal grinder is used. A food processor, rather than a blender, does the job efficiently.

Take care when removing the leaves of the fresh cobs and cut as near to the base as possible to keep the cupped end intact.

The meat called for is pork ribs cut into small parts and flattened a little; but for those who don't want to find bones in their tamales, buy the fleshy end of the loin and cut into 1-inch (2.5 cm) cubes.

Have ready:

A tamale steamer, the top lined with fresh cornhusks

36 medium-sized *yerbasanta* leaves

36 fresh cornhusks

THE MEAT

1½ pounds (about 750 g) meaty pork ribs, cut into 1-inch (2.5 cm) pieces and flattened

Salt to taste

THE *MOLITO*

4 guajillo chiles, veins and seeds removed

1 thick slice white onion

2 peeled garlic cloves, coarsely chopped

12 ounces (350 g) tomatoes, coarsely chopped

Salt to taste

THE MASA

9 cups (2.25 L) fresh corn kernels

1 scant cup (about 235 ml)—7 ounces (200 g)—*zorrapa*, blended with ⅓ cup (85 ml) water

1 scant cup (about 235 ml)—7 ounces (200 g)—melted pork lard

1 tablespoon sugar

Salt to taste

- Put the meat into a pan with water to cover and salt. Cook over medium heat until just tender, not soft (it will continue cooking inside the tamale), about 35 minutes.

- Strain and reserve the broth. At least 1 cup (250 ml) will be needed.

- Cover the chiles with warm water and soak until soft, about 15 minutes. Drain.

- Put ½ cup (125 ml) of the meat broth in the blender jar, add the onion and garlic, and blend; then add the tomatoes and blend until smooth. Finally, add the chiles and blend as smooth as possible. Strain into a bowl, pressing down firmly to extract all the juices and flesh possible. Stir in salt to taste. There should be about 2 cups (500 ml) of raw sauce of medium consistency.

- Put the steamer over medium heat.

- Grind or process the corn as fine as possible. Gradually blend in the lard, sugar, and salt.

- Place half of the *yerbasanta* leaf inside a cornhusk, with the second half left outside, ready to cover the top of the masa. Spread a heaped tablespoon of the masa over the lined inside of the husk. It should not be too thick. Place a piece of the meat and a tablespoon of the sauce down the middle. Fold first the *yerbasanta* over the surface and then the corn leaf, doubling up the point to retain the juices.

- As soon as the tamale is assembled, place it horizontally in the top part of the steamer and continue with the rest, putting them in overlapping layers. Cover and cook over high heat until the masa is firm and spongy to the touch, about 1¼ hours.

Tamales de frijol del Istmo (Bean Tamales from the Isthmus)

Unfortunately, I don't have the name of the person who showed me how to make these delicious tamales. I lost the notebook with the name and never recovered it.

I looked for her in vain. But I did have the recipe.

These tamales are served with a tomato sauce (p. 200).

MAKES 24 TAMALES ABOUT 2½ X 4 INCHES (6½ X 10 CM)

Have ready:

A tamale steamer, the top section lined with cornhusks

About 30 (just in case) dried cornhusks, soaked and shaken dry

THE MASA

¾ **cup (about 190 ml) water**

⅓ **cup (85 ml) fairly tightly packed epazote leaves, coarsely chopped**

4 chiles criollos del Istmo or serranos, coarsely chopped

⅔ **cup (170 ml) *zorrapa* (see note p. 426) or *asiento***

1¼ **pounds (about 550 g) textured masa for tamales**

½ **cup (125 ml) melted pork lard**

Salt to taste

THE FILLING

2½ **cups (625 ml) cooked, blended, and lightly fried black beans (see p. 191)**

- Put the water in the blender jar, add the epazote and chiles, and blend well. Add the *zorrapa* and blend to a slightly textured consistency. Add this mixture to the masa with the lard and salt to taste; mix well.

- Put the steamer on to heat.

- Spread one of the cornhusks with a heaped tablespoon of the masa and put a tablespoon of the bean paste down the middle. Fold the husk over to cover the contents completely and proceed with the rest.

- When the water in the steamer is boiling, place the tamales upright, cover, and cook over high heat until the masa separates easily from the husk, about 1 hour.

Tamales de iguana
(Iguana Tamales)

SEÑORA JUANA "CALABAZA," TEHUANTEPEC

Señora Juana, who for some obscure reason inherited her nickname "Calabaza" from her husband's grandfather, who could often be found wandering about the *milpas*, or cornfields, picking up stray pumpkins, is renowned in Tehuantepec for her tamales of black iguana—it is customary to eat the green iguanas baked in the *comizcal* (see Glossary). But, Señora Juana warns: Don't eat iguana if you have an open wound, or it will become inflamed. On the day I had arranged to prepare the tamales with her, the weather was hot and sultry, unrelieved by the almost constant wind that blows fiercely through the Isthmus.

The most laborious part of making these tamales is the preparation of the iguana, which is not recommended for the squeamish. Once you have caught or bought your iguana in the streets outside the main market and killed it, it is necessary to singe it over the flames of a wood fire. The scaly skin can then be easily scraped off. Gutting the iguana is a gory business, followed by cutting off the paws and removing the glands called *bolitas* found at the top part of the legs. It is rinsed in several changes of water with salt before being cooked in salted water. Cooking times can vary with the age and toughness of the iguana and can range from 40 minutes to 2 hours. Once the meat is tender, it is strained—with the cooking water reserved—and cut into small pieces. About 10 cups (2.4 L) of the broth is needed for the recipe.

To prepare the masa, Señora Juana sends the *nixtamal* (see *masa* in Glossary) with *zorrapa* to be ground together at the mill. If this is not possible, then the *zorrapa* can be ground separately with some of the broth and mixed into the prepared masa.

MAKES 50 VERY SUBSTANTIAL TAMALES

Have ready:

A tamale steamer, the top part lined with cornhusks

50 large dried cornhusks, soaked to soften and drained

THE *MOLITO* FOR THE FILLING

4 cups (1 L)—400 g—unhulled pumpkin seeds

1½ pounds (about 670 g) tortilla masa

About 4 cups (1 L) iguana broth

Salt to taste

THE CHILE

2 cups (500 ml) iguana broth

3 large tomatoes, coarsely chopped

1 teaspoon pure *achiote*

10 chiles de árbol, left whole, not soaked

8 guajillo chiles, seeds and veins removed and soaked in warm water for 15 minutes

About 2 cups (500 ml) water

THE MASA

6 pounds (2.8 kg) roughly textured masa for tamales

About 4 cups (1 L) iguana broth

1¾ pounds (800 g) *zorrapa*

1½ pounds (about 670 g) melted pork lard

Salt to taste

PREPARING IGUANA TAMALES: *LEFT*, ADDING LARD TO MASA; *RIGHT*, FORMING TAMALE IN CORNHUSK/DIANA KENNEDY

THE MOLITO

- Toast the pumpkin seeds in an ungreased pan, stirring them constantly to avoid burning.

- Cool and grind dry, in a blender or electric spice grinder, to a fine powder. In a large bowl, mix the seeds with the tortilla masa and 4 cups (1 L) of the iguana broth and strain; there will be quite a lot of debris left in the strainer.

- *To prepare the chiles:* Put 2 cups (500 ml) of the iguana broth in the blender and blend the tomatoes with the *achiote* and chiles de árbol until smooth. Gradually add the guajillos, blending well after each addition. Add this to a casserole through a strainer, pressing hard to extract all the juice and flesh possible. There will be a debris of chile skins in the strainer. Cook over medium heat until it comes to a boil and continue cooking for 5 minutes more.

- Add the *molito* and cook over medium heat, stirring constantly because it will stick and lump readily. Cook until the mixture thickens, about 6 minutes. Cool.

THE MASA

- Put the tamale masa into a large bowl. Put 2 cups (500 ml) of the broth into the blender jar, add the *zorrapa*, and blend smooth. Add to the masa with the lard, the remaining broth, and salt as necessary and mix well to a medium consistency.

- Make a double layer of 2 large cornhusks. First, put a heaped tablespoon of the *molito* (yes, the *molito*) then a small piece of the iguana into the cornhusks. Cover with about ⅔ cup (190 ml) of the masa, finishing off with another heaped tablespoon of the *molito*.

- When the water in the steamer is boiling, lay the tamales down horizontally in overlapping layers in the top section of the steamer and cook until spongy to the touch, about 1½ to 2 hours.

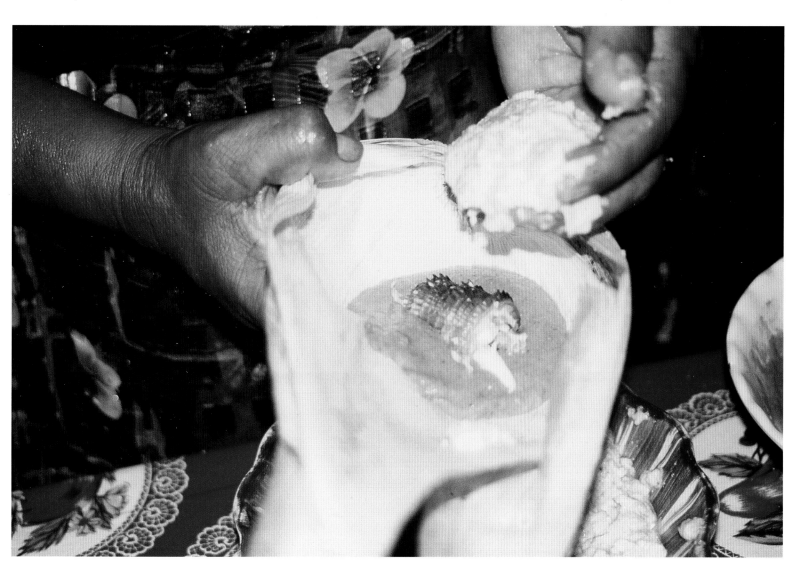

Tamales de camarón o pescado seco
(Tamales with Dried Shrimps or Fish)

TEHUANTEPEC

The same "lost" person in Tehuantepec generously showed me how to make these and the bean tamales on p. 225. Although dried fish is used more often as a filling, dried shrimps are more easily available and, in my opinion, more delicious.

MAKES ABOUT 25 TAMALES ABOUT 4½ INCHES (12 CM) LONG

DRIED AND SEMIDRIED SHRIMPS FROM THE ISTHMUS IN THE OAXACA MARKET/DIANA KENNEDY

Have ready:

25 pieces banana leaf approximately 9 × 7 inches (23 × 18 cm)

A tamale steamer with the top part lined with banana leaves

25 small pieces dried fish, or 75 large dried shrimps, 3 per tamale

THE MASA

2¼ pounds (about 1 kg) textured tamale masa

8 ounces (about 225 g) melted pork lard

1 cup (250 ml) water

8 ounces (about 225 g) *zorrapa* (see note p. 426)

Salt to taste

THE *MOLITO*

MAKES ABOUT 2½ CUPS (625 ML)

1¼ cups (315 ml) unhulled pumpkin seeds

About 2 cups (500 ml) water

9 ounces (250 g) tomatoes, coarsely chopped

1 thick slice white onion

¼ teaspoon pure *achiote* or 1 teaspoon prepared *achiote* paste

3 chiles de árbol, toasted whole

3 tablespoons tortilla masa

1 tablespoon pork lard

Salt to taste

- Rinse the fish or shrimps to eliminate excess salt. Cover with fresh water and leave fish to soak for about 15 minutes and the shrimps about 5 minutes. Remove heads, tails, and legs of shrimps; do not peel. Drain.

- Put the tamale masa into a large bowl with the lard. Put the water in the blender jar, add the *zorrapa*, and blend smooth. Add to the bowl with salt and beat well, either by hand or in an electric mixer, until the masa is well aerated.

- In an ungreased skillet, toast the pumpkin seeds over low flame, stirring to make sure they toast evenly; they will start to jump around, about 10 minutes. Cool, then grind in an electric grinder to a slightly textured powder.

- Put 1 cup (250 ml) of the water into the blender jar; add the tomatoes, onion, *achiote*, chiles, and masa and blend smooth. Melt the lard in a skillet, add the blended mixture, and cook over medium heat for about 3 minutes. Add the ground pumpkin seeds and the second cup of water and continue cooking over medium heat, stirring to prevent sticking, until the *molito* thickens, about 5 minutes. Add salt to taste.

- Put the steamer on to heat and set out the pieces of banana leaves.

- Give the masa a final beating for about 3 minutes. Spread about ¼ cup (65 ml) of the masa over the center of the leaf in a square about 4½ inches (about 12 cm); it should be about ⅛ inch (4 mm) thick. Put a piece of the fish or 3 shrimps on one half of the masa, cover with a heaped tablespoon of the *molito,* and fold the leaf over so that the other half of the masa covers the filling; make a fold with the edges of the leaves to seal in the contents, and fold back the ends to make a "package."

- When the water in the steamer is boiling, lay the tamales flat in the top section in overlapping layers and cook until the masa separates easily from the leaf, about 1–1¼ hours.

Totopos istmeños

Throughout Mexico there is a large variety, in form and size, of *totopos*, crisp tortillas, but they cannot hold a candle to those of the Isthmus. There they are made by hand in rather primitive kitchens (I hope they will forgive me for saying so) in modest homes where several members of the family lend a hand. San Blas, on the outskirts of Tehuantepec, and Santa María Xadani, a short distance from Juchitán, are two areas where they are made on a large scale to be sold in the local market or, wrapped in used brown paper sacks, to be shipped to the City of Oaxaca, to *oaxaqueños* who live in other parts of Mexico, or even to California.

These *totopos* are made in various sizes, the smallest being about 2 inches (5 cm) for *botanas*, graduating to about 8 inches (20 cm). Their main characteristics, apart from their texture and flavor, are the little holes made with either the finger, as shown, or a wooden peg, which prevents the masa from ballooning up and falling off the surface of the *comizcal* as they cook.

Local cooks say that they have to be made of locally grown white corn, which has a thin, hard kernel. The corn is cooked and soaked overnight in a lime solution, as for any *nixtamal*. The following morning, it is taken to the mill to be ground to a very fine (*cueste*) masa.

Some cooks prefer to form their *totopos* by hand, as shown, while others prefer to press them out onto a piece of plastic.

Although the majority of *totopos* are made only of corn, others have a proportion of black bean paste mixed into the masa. There are also those mixed with *panela*, raw sugar, and enriched with *corrozo* (*Elaeis oleifera*; the oily fruit of a palm tree) or with grated coconut.

FORMING, PERFORATING, AND COOKING A *TOTOPO*/DIANA KENNEDY

La Cañada

View of La Cañada in autumn/Diana Kennedy

La Cañada

BY MARCUS WINTER

The region locally known as La Cañada is a valley in the form of a deep canyon in the north-central part of the state between the Oaxaca Valley and the Tehuacán Valley, Puebla. La Cañada served as a corridor and trade route between the Valley of Oaxaca and central Mexico. The Río Grande from the Sierra Zapoteca flows through La Cañada at around 500 meters above sea level. At the town of Quiotepec it joins the Río Salado from Tehuacán, and together they form the Santo Domingo, a major tributary of the Papaloapan. The valley floor of La Cañada is in a rain shadow and may go for years with essentially no rain. The climate and soils are favorable for agriculture, which is practiced today using pumps and canal irrigation. Simple canal irrigation was probably practiced in pre-Hispanic times. Mangos, limes, and, in the past, sugarcane are cash crops. Chicozapotes and other fruits abound. The unique chilhuacle chiles and other vegetables are produced.

Early settlements have been found along the main river in the valley bottom. Later sites are common on the higher slopes, where springs, mountain streams, and wet-season rains provide water. The Cuicatecs are the indigenous group native to La Cañada, and they are separated geographically from the Mixtecs in the highlands to the west and the Mazatecs to the northeast, on the other side of the Río Santo Domingo canyon.

MAP OF LA CAÑADA/SERGIO AGUIRRE

Amarillo de Cuicatlán
(Yellow Mole from Cuicatlán)

SEÑORA JUANA MEJÍA DE HERNÁNDEZ, CUICATLÁN

This simple *amarillo* differs from other recipes of the same name because the yellow chilhuacle adds its very special flavor, color, and bite to the sauce.

It would not be exaggerating to say that this is probably the most exclusive chile in the world, since production is very limited; there are few growers in the area, and it commands a very high price compared with that of other chiles.

MAKES 4–5 PORTIONS

1¼ pounds (about 500 g) pork, ribs and boneless, cut into serving pieces

Salt to taste

2½ ounces (about 65 g)—or 12 large—dried chilhuacles amarillos, seeds removed

2 garlic cloves, peeled and roughly chopped

¼ teaspoon cumin seeds, crushed

2 cloves, crushed

2 allspice, crushed

½ cup (125 ml) tortilla masa

1 medium chayote, peeled, cut into wedges, and parboiled

¼ pound (about 115 g) green beans, trimmed, halved, and parboiled

Reserved vegetable water

2 *yerbasanta* leaves, torn into large pieces

- Put the pork into a pot with salt and 5 cups (1.25 L) water. Cook over medium heat until almost tender. Strain, reserving the broth; the sauce will need about 3 cups (750 ml), so reduce or make up that amount with water.

- Put the chiles into hot water and bring to a simmer. Leave to soak for 10 minutes and strain.

- Put ⅓ cup (85 ml) of the pork broth into the blender; add the garlic and spices and blend smooth. Add 1 cup (250 ml) of the broth and blend the chiles well.

- Transfer the mixture to a wide pan and cook over low heat for a few minutes.

- Put the masa into the blender with 1 cup (250 ml) of the broth and blend smooth.

- Stir into the chile blend and continue stirring as the mixture thickens, making sure it does not form lumps or stick to the bottom of the pan. Cook for 10 minutes.

- Add the meat, the half-cooked vegetables, and the *yerbasanta* with the remaining broth; adjust salt and continue cooking until the pork and vegetables are tender, for about 10–15 minutes more. The sauce should be of medium consistency; if it thickens too much, dilute to taste with the vegetable cooking water.

YELLOW CHILHUACLE PLANT/DIANA KENNEDY

Arroz guisado
(Savory Rice)

MAESTRO GUILLERMO MÉNDEZ CRUZ, CUICATLÁN

This is yet another delicious version of *arroz con pollo*. But, of course, in rural Oaxaca, cooks insist on using a farmyard hen for preference, *una gallina criolla*, that has been running around. They are right; the flavor is far superior to the usual commercial chicken, even the organic ones.

In Cuicatlán, this is an indispensable dish to serve for the Días de Muerto, the first and second of November. The rice should be very moist, not dry.

8 SERVINGS

A large chicken, about 3½ pounds (1.5 kg), cut into serving pieces and including (optional) giblets and feet
1 medium white onion, roughly chopped
1 small head of garlic, cut in halves horizontally
2 quarts (2 L) of water
Salt to taste
1½ cups (375 ml)—or 10½ ounces (300 g)—long-grained unconverted rice
3 tablespoons vegetable oil or melted chicken fat
3 garlic cloves, peeled and roughly chopped
½ small onion, roughly chopped
2 cloves, crushed
3 allspice, crushed
½ inch (1.5 cm) cinnamon stick, crushed
12 ounces (30 g) tomatoes, roughly chopped—about 2 cups
Approximately 3 cups (750 ml) chicken broth
2 chilcosles secos or guajillos, seeds removed, torn into strips
½ tablespoon dried Oaxacan oregano leaves or ¼ tablespoon Mexican oregano

- Put the chicken with giblets and feet (if used) in a large pot with the onion, garlic, water, and salt and cook over medium heat until it is barely tender, slightly undercooked (it will continue cooking in the rice), about 30 minutes.

- Meanwhile, soak the rice in hot water for 5 minutes. Strain, rinse in cold water, and strain again, shaking the strainer well to remove excess water.

- Heat the oil in a heavy casserole, add the rice, and fry, stirring well to fry evenly, until it just begins to change color.

- Put ¼ cup (65 ml) of the chicken broth in the blender. Add the garlic, onion, and spices and blend until almost smooth. Gradually add the tomatoes and blend to a smooth consistency. Add to the rice and fry, stirring and scraping the bottom of the pan to prevent sticking, until the mixture is almost dry, 5–8 minutes.

- Add the chicken pieces, giblets, and feet; 3 cups (750 ml) of the broth; the chiles; and the oregano, with salt to taste. Cover the pan and cook over slow heat until all the liquid has been absorbed and the rice and chicken are tender, about 20 minutes. Set the pan aside, off the heat, for the rice to season about 15 minutes before serving.

- This dish can be reheated but not frozen.

Caldo de orejonas
(Soup of Pitahaya Flowers)

SEÑORA GRACIELA SANTIAGO AÑAS, CUICATLÁN

I have visited Cuicatlán on many occasions over the past fifteen years, entranced by La Cañada, a rift valley, and that particular area that produces those wonderful chilhuacles.

But there are always gastronomic surprises, and this one came more recently one afternoon when by chance I visited the local market much later than usual. There I saw, for the first time on sale, *pitahayas* flower buds (probably *Hylocereus undatus*) about 6 inches (about 15 cm) long. These were a creamy yellow color and, I was told, are made into a *caldo*, or broth. Other bystanders said they should still be *en botón y verdes*, in green buds; but I took a chance and bought them for the cook where I was staying.

The adults shared the fragrant soup with me, but the children turned up their noses and wouldn't eat it.

4–6 PORTIONS

6 pitahaya flower buds, rinsed and drained
5 cups (1.25 L) water
½ medium white onion, cut into small pieces
2 garlic cloves, peeled and finely chopped
1 chile de agua, toasted, peeled, seeds removed, and cut into strips
2 large sprigs epazote
Salt to taste

- Open up the flowers; remove and discard the pistils, which, they say, are bitter; and cut the flowers into rings.

- Put the water into a pot with the onion and garlic and simmer for about 5 minutes. Add the chiles, flowers, epazote, and salt and continue simmering until the flowers are tender, about 15 minutes. Serve in soup bowls with tortillas.

CALDO DE OREJONAS / DIANA KENNEDY

VIEW OF CHILE FIELDS / DIANA KENNEDY

Chilecaldo
(Beef Stew with Fresh Chiles)

It used to be a tradition, but now dying out, in Cuicatlán to celebrate the harvest of the local chiles—most importantly chilhuacles (see photo p. xix)—in October by preparing a meal in the *chileros*, the fields where chiles are planted. Nowadays a *chilecaldo* is more likely to be cooked in the home.

The main ingredient of the dish is meat, beef and pork, but it also includes locally grown seasonal vegetables: pumpkin known as *tamala* and a type of tender bean cooked in its pod called *frijol mayeso*, apart from the chiles themselves, which are added toward the end of the cooking time and lend their brilliant colors—yellow, red, and black—to the stew.

Chilecaldo is served in deep dishes with plenty of broth, accompanied by tortillas made of the local corn and plenty of *mezcal* and beer to wash it all down.

When I was last there, a *chilecaldo* was prepared in the fields for me and twenty-five people, most of whom were harvesting the chiles.

For the few great aficionados who will want to try it, I suggest substituting either dried chilhuacles or poblanos, both green and ripened to red.

9 pounds (about 4 kg) beef on the bone with some fat: short ribs, brisket, and shin, cut into large serving pieces
2 large heads of garlic, halved horizontally
Salt to taste
2¼ pounds (about 1 kg) pork knuckle, cut into small pieces
5½ pounds (2.5 kg) pumpkin, cut into large pieces with rind, but seeds and fleshy substance removed
4½ pounds (about 2 kg) *frijol mayeso* in the pod, or tender lima beans
6½ pounds (3 kg) tomatoes, finely chopped
1 pound (450 g) white onion, roughly chopped
2 large bunches cilantro, coarsely chopped with tender stems
1 large bunch mint, coarsely chopped
10 fresh black chilhuacles, left whole, unpeeled
10 fresh red chilhuacles, left whole, unpeeled
10 fresh yellow chilhuacles, left whole, unpeeled

- Put the beef into a very large pot, cover well with water, add the garlic and salt to taste.

- Cover the pot, and when it comes to a boil, cook over medium heat for 30 minutes.

- Add the pork and continue cooking for a further 30 minutes. Add the pumpkin pieces, and when they are almost tender, approximately 20 minutes, remove and set aside.

- Then add the beans and tomatoes to the meats in the pot and cook for 15 minutes more.

- Finally return the pumpkin to the broth with the herbs and chiles and continue cooking until all the ingredients are tender, about 15 minutes.

Ciruelas en dulce
(Candied Native Plums)

MAESTRO GUILLERMO MÉNDEZ CRUZ,
CUICATLÁN

In one of our long conversations about the regional foods of the Cuicatlán area, Maestro Memo, as everyone calls him, offered me a sweet that looked like dried prunes. They were in fact the native (of Mexico) plums, *ciruelas* (*Spondia mombin*), cooked in sugar and then dried in the sun. In this form, they can last for at least one year, and even improve in flavor.

It is worth making this quantity while you are at it. To the syrup in which they are cooked he adds a bottle of aguardiente, which he then uses to sweeten a punch.

The ideal pan is a stainless preserving pan or, traditionally, an unlined copper *cazo*.

24 cups (6 L) water
2¼ pounds (about 1 kg) sugar
100 firm plums, mature but not soft
4-inch (10 cm) piece cinnamon stick

- Heat the water in a wide, heavy pan, add the sugar, and stir until dissolved.

- Add the fruit and cinnamon and cook over low heat—the water should simmer not boil fast—until the water has evaporated, the syrup thickened, and the fruit acquired a dark color, about 3–4 hours. Strain and spread out on a rack to cool. Put the fruit in the sun to dry for 2 days, turning them over from time to time so they dry evenly.

- Store in a cool, dry place.

Salsa macha de achilitos
(Salsa Macha with Achilitos)

MAESTRO GUILLERMO MÉNDEZ CRUZ, CUICATLÁN

Other places in Mexico have their *salsa macha*, a strong, dominating sauce, usually made with their local very hot chiles. In Cuicatlán, it is made with the small, usually triangular (looks like a miniature chilhuacle) achilito.

At the end of October when the chiles ripen, it is used fresh, mature but still green, in the sauce, but for the rest of the year, it is used dried, when it has acquired a deep orangey-red color.

The sauce, which is better made in a *molcajete*, is served with rice, fried eggs, grilled meats, and *antojitos*.

MAKES ABOUT 1 CUP (250 ML)

½ cup (125 ml) achilitos secos, or substitute costeños
3 garlic cloves, left whole
6 ounces (about 150 g) tomatoes, cooked in water and drained, water reserved
Approximately ⅔ cup (170 ml) of the cooking water
Salt to taste

- Wipe the chiles clean; remove stems, if any, and shake out any loose seeds.

- Toast lightly in an ungreased skillet, turning them around to avoid burning. They should be crisp when cool. Toast the garlic and peel.

- Put ¼ cup (65 ml) of the tomato cooking water into the blender jar with the crumbled chiles and garlic and blend well. Add the tomatoes, unskinned, with salt to taste and blend again to a slightly textured consistency. Dilute with the rest of the water.

Mole Coloradito from Cuicatlán

MAESTRO GUILLERMO MÉNDEZ CRUZ, CUICATLÁN

Maestro Guillermo, a renowned cook of Cuicatlán, makes a concentrated paste of this mole, which, refrigerated, will last at least 6 months in this form.

When ready to prepare the dish, he dilutes the paste with cooked and blended tomatoes and chicken broth.

The sauce is also used for the local enchiladas and empanadas.

MAKES ABOUT 1 POUND 2 OUNCES (ABOUT 500 G) *COLORADITO* PASTE

5 ounces (about 125 g) chilcosles—about 20 chiles—seeds and veins removed and lightly toasted

5 ounces (about 125 g) ancho chiles—about 7 chiles—seeds and veins removed and lightly toasted

¼ teaspoon cumin seeds, crushed

1 inch (2.5 cm) cinnamon stick, crushed

3 cloves, crushed

2 allspice, crushed

½ cup (125 ml) sesame seeds, lightly toasted

Melted pork lard for frying

½ medium white onion, toasted and fried

½ head garlic, toasted, cloves peeled and fried

½ tablespoon dried Oaxacan oregano leaves or ¼ tablespoon Mexican oregano, lightly fried

1 small bunch of dried herbs: thyme, marjoram, and bay leaves, lightly fried

½ bread roll, sliced and fried

2 ounces (about 50 g) Mexican drinking chocolate, broken up into small pieces

2 ounces (about 50 g) sugar, or to taste

Salt to taste

- All of the prepared ingredients are usually sent to the mill to be ground into an almost-dry paste.

- When ready to use, prepare about 10 portions of cooked chicken, strained and broth reserved.

18 ounces (about 500 g) tomatoes, cut into halves

Approximately 2 tablespoons lard

18 ounces (about 500 g) *coloradito* paste

Approximately 4 cups (1 L) chicken broth

- Put the tomatoes into a pan with very little water and cook over medium heat until soft. Transfer to the blender and blend to a purée.

- Heat the lard in a casserole or large pan in which you are going to cook the mole and cook the purée until reduced a little, about 3 minutes. Add the mole paste and continue cooking and stirring to avoid sticking for another 5 minutes. Add 3 cups (750 ml) of the broth and continue cooking until well seasoned, about 20 minutes.

- Add the chicken, adjust salt, and heat through for about 10 minutes more.

- Add the remaining broth if necessary to dilute the mole to a medium consistency.

Enchiladas cuicatecas

Maestro Guillermo Méndez Cruz, Cuicatlán

These enchiladas differ from the more usual ones in that they are made of very large, lightly fried fresh tortillas that are then doubled over in four before being immersed in the mole *coloradito* (see recipe page 243). They are served either alone, topped with *queso fresco*, onion, and parsley, or to accompany a portion of cooked chicken fried with a paste of garlic and oregano (see Chicken in Chile Paste page 155), the whole smothered in shredded lettuce and radishes.

Makes 12 enchiladas

6 ounces (about 180 g) tomatoes
1 tablespoon lard
6 ounces (about 180 g) *coloradito* paste (see page 243)
Approximately 1½ cups (375 ml) chicken broth
Salt to taste
Approximately ½ cup (125 ml) vegetable oil for frying
12 9-inch (22.5 cm) or 16 5-inch (12.5 cm) very thin tortillas

To serve:
9 ounces (250 g) crumbled *queso fresco*
¾ cup (190 ml) finely chopped white onion
Roughly chopped parsley to taste
12 romaine lettuce leaves, shredded
12 radishes, thinly sliced
6 portions cooked and fried chicken (see page 155)

• Put tomatoes into a pan, barely cover with water, and cook gently until soft, about 10 minutes, depending on size. Blend, unskinned, until smooth. Heat the lard in a skillet and fry the purée over high heat until it is reduced a little, about 3 minutes. Add the paste and broth and continue cooking over medium heat until all the flavors are well combined, about 5 minutes. Add salt to taste. The sauce should be of medium consistency so that it will coat the tortillas well.

• In a second skillet, heat the oil and briefly fry the tortillas so that they wilt but do not become crisp; fold them into four and then dip them into the sauce. Serve as explained above.

Pico de gallo cuicateco
(Pico de Gallo from Cuicatlán)

MAESTRO GUILLERMO MÉNDEZ CRUZ, CUICATLÁN

Throughout Mexico there are many versions of *pico de gallo,* but they are all based on chopped raw ingredients, which can vary slightly.

This is how it is prepared in Cuicatlán, where it is sometimes called gazpacho, and served as a *botana* with freshly made tortillas or tostadas.

When the local chiles are fresh at the end of October, small achilitos are used, or sometimes chilhuacles, toasted and peeled. At other times of year, the cooks use chiles de agua brought from the city.

MAKES ABOUT 2 CUPS (500 ML)

10 ounces (300 g) tomatoes, finely chopped

4 small scallions, finely chopped with leaves

4 (or to taste) green achilitos (see above), or substitute finely chopped serranos

⅓ cup (85 ml) firmly packed, finely chopped cilantro

Approximately 3 tablespoons lime juice

Salt to taste

3 tablespoons finely grated *queso añejo*

• Mix all the ingredients together, except the cheese, and leave to season a few minutes before serving. Serve sprinkled with the cheese.

ACHILITO PLANT/DIANA KENNEDY

Rajas de chiles cuicatecos

SEÑORA MARÍA DE JESÚS MATA MORALES, CUICATLÁN

There are no more delicious and colorful chiles than fresh chilhuacles that have ripened from dark green to black, yellow, and red (each color from a different plant, rather than a progression of ripening; see photo p. xviii). Their succulent flesh has a decidedly fruity flavor and is very picante.

Most of the crop in October is destined to be dried and sent to the markets of Oaxaca and Puebla, where they command a high price. But in the harvest season, while mature but still green, they are used skinned and stuffed with a paste of black beans or canned tuna.

They are also prepared in *rajas*, "strips," like the more usual poblano chiles (in fact, for this recipe, you could use poblanos as a substitute). But the height of their deliciousness was even more apparent when an agricultural engineer with ranches in Cuicatlán brought his family to visit me in Michoacán, bearing newly harvested dark green chilhuacles. I let them ripen to their respective colors and then made the *rajas* shown below. The *rajas* can also be served with grilled meats or added to melted cheese or scrambled eggs.

20 mature chilhuacles or poblanos
3 tablespoons vegetable oil
1 very large scallion, sliced with its green stem leaves
6 garlic cloves, finely chopped
2¼ pounds (about 1 kg) tomatoes, unskinned and finely chopped
About ½ cup (125 ml) water
2 large stems of epazote
Salt to taste

- Char/toast the chiles (as for chiles rellenos); remove skin, seeds, and veins and cut into strips about ½ inch (1.25 cm) wide.

- Heat the oil in a skillet and fry the onion and garlic over low heat until translucent. Add the tomatoes and continue frying over high heat until reduced, about 5 minutes.

- Add the chile strips, water, epazote, and salt and continue cooking until well seasoned, about 10 minutes.

Cooked fresh chilhuacles/Diana Kennedy

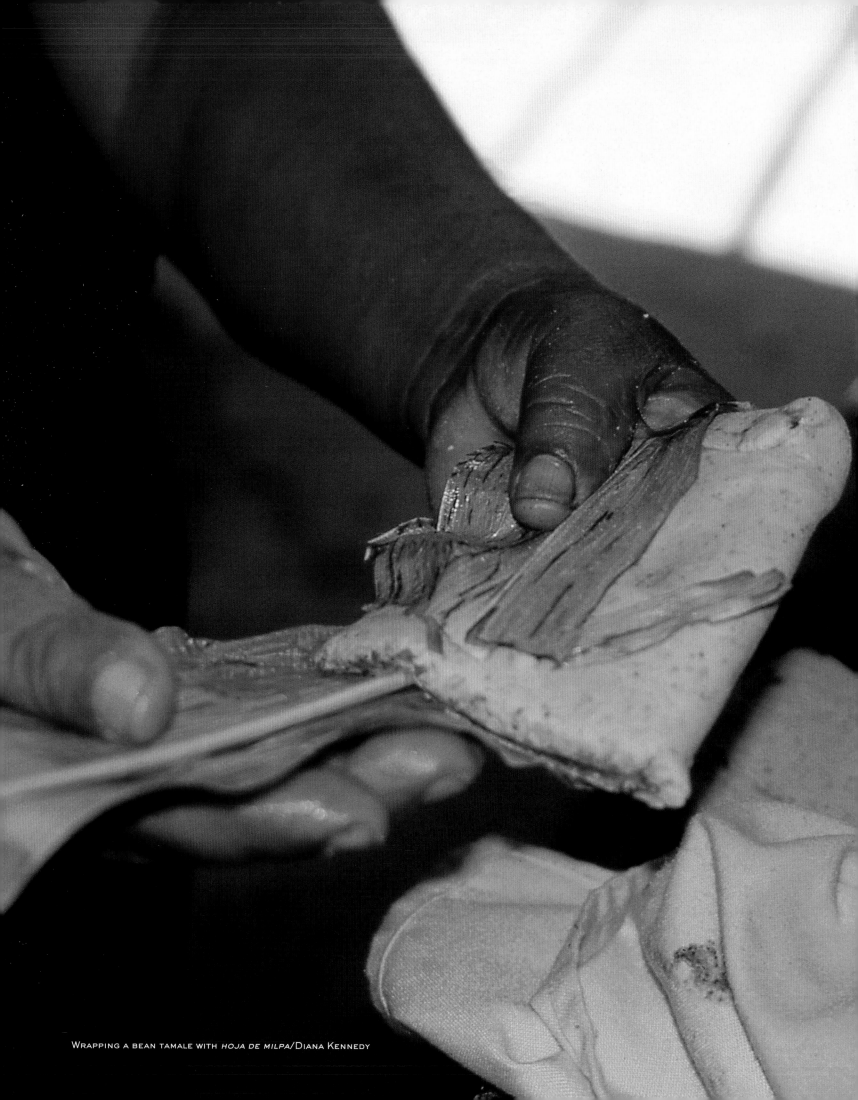

WRAPPING A BEAN TAMALE WITH *HOJA DE MILPA*/DIANA KENNEDY

Tamales de pañuelo
(Handkerchief Tamales)

Tamales formed with masa folded in layers over a paste of beans can be found in several regions of Oaxaca, but the finest are those made in Cuicatlán, where they are called "handkerchief" tamales, and in Huautla de Jiménez in the neighboring Sierra Mazateca. The "*tamales de siete cueros*," "tamales of seven layers," made in La Chinantla Baja, though formed in the same way, are more bulky.

A simple masa, usually without fat of any kind, is spread in a very thin layer over a sheet of plastic or a thin cloth. This is covered with a thin layer of bean paste. With the aid of the plastic or cloth, the masa is folded and smoothed over the beans and cut into portions (about 3 × 5 inches; 8 × 13 cm). They are usually wrapped in *hoja de milpa*, the corn leaf; *totomoxtle*, dried corn-husk; or *hoja de plátano*, banana leaf, and steamed.

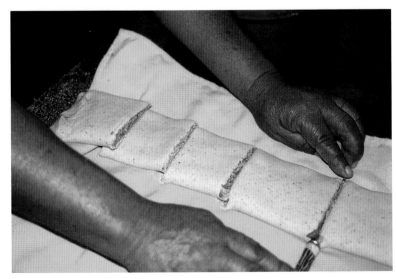

Tepache de cardón
(Tepache and Sauce of Cardon Tuna)

SEÑORA EPIFANIA MEDINA JUÁREZ, CUICATLÁN

Tepache de cardón is a seasonal drink that is prepared in Cuicatlán in May, when, among other tunas, the *cardones* are ripe; the intensely sweet flesh is fermented for the *tepache* and the strained seeds used for a sauce.

The fruit, which is collected with a long hooked pole from a tall organ cactus, is round, about 2½ inches (6.25 cm) in diameter, with a deep reddish skin covered with long spines; it takes a patient expert to remove these by rubbing them with a wooden stick.

The flesh has an intense purplish red color and is dotted with small brownish/black seeds.

To prepare the *tepache*, the fruits are cut open, the flesh scooped out and beaten to a purée. This is diluted with water and cooked for about 20 minutes. When cooled, it is strained to remove the seeds, which are saved for the sauce. The liquid is then left for two days to ferment, which it does readily with its very high natural sugar content.

A rustic pot was formerly used for this, but now, alas, has been displaced by a plastic bucket.

About 4 quarts (about 4 L) of water are used for 6½ pounds (almost 3 kg) of fruit.

Tepache de cardón/Diana Kennedy

Toasting *CARDÓN* SEEDS/DIANA KENNEDY

Salsa de semillas de cardón
(Sauce of Cardon Seeds)

The strained, cooked seeds of the fruit are dried in the sun. Some are used immediately for a sauce, while the rest are saved for future use. These are stored in a cool, dry place; otherwise, they become rancid.

While this is called a sauce, it is in fact a paste used to spread on freshly made tortillas or to season a plate of *frijoles de olla*.

MAKES APPROXIMATELY 1½ CUPS (375 ML)

2 cups (500 ml) cardon seeds (see recipe for *tepache*, p. 250)
16 achilitos or other small hot chiles
3 avocado leaves (see Note on Toxicity, p. 426)
Salt to taste
Approximately ½ cup (125 ml) water

- Toast the seeds over low heat, preferably on a clay comal (they tend to burn on metal), moving them constantly so that they toast evenly, about 3 minutes.

- Toast the chiles and the leaves and crumble them over the seeds. Crush and grind the toasted ingredients with the salt and water, preferably on a metate or in a mortar, until the mixture resembles a slightly textured paste.

MIXTECA ALTA

VIEW OF MIXTECA ALTA/DIANA KENNEDY

Mixteca Alta

By Marcus Winter

The mountainous Mixteca Alta, just west of the Valley of Oaxaca, is formed by numerous small valleys at about 2,000 meters above sea level surrounded by oak and pine forests on the slopes that reach 3,000 meters. The principal inhabitants were and are Mixtecs, with the Triques in the area to the south of Tlaxiaco, the Chocholtecs to the north in the valleys of Tejupan and Coixtlahuaca, and the few remaining Ixtcatecs to the northeast.

Parts of this region, especially in the Nochixtlán Valley, the Alta's most extensive valley, were precocious in pre-Hispanic times. Etlatongo and Yucuita, for example, had major Early and Late Preclassic occupations (1400 BC–AD 250). Huamelupan, Monte Negro, and Yucuita were major early urban centers, followed in the Classic by Yucuñudahui, Cerro Jaltepec, Yatachio, and many others.

The Mixteca Alta is particularly well known for its Late Postclassic (AD 1250–AD 1521) culture, manifested in the important city-state capitals such as Inguiteria in Coixtlahuaca, Pueblo Viejo at Tamazulapan, Yucundaa at Teposcolula, and Yanhuitlán in the present-day town. Other outstanding cultural remains include polychrome ceramics, gold and silver ornaments, and pictorial manuscripts or codices painted on deerskin. In the Late Postclassic, the Mixtecs, under their unifying leader, Lord 8 Deer Tiger Claw, whose life is depicted in various historic codices, invaded and conquered the coastal region and established a capital at Tututepec overlooking the Rio Verde floodplain. In the highlands, alliances were formed between Mixteca and Zapotec royal families. In the Early Colonial period, between AD 1521 and AD 1550, Dominican friars from Spain established religious centers (now ex-conventos) and churches precisely at the main centers of Mixtec and Zapotec popula-

tions, for example, at Achiutla, Coixtlahuaca, Teposcolula, Yanhuitlán, and Cuilapan. The overgrazing by herds of goats and sheep brought from Spain led to deforestation and the erosion of hill slopes, very apparent today in many parts of the Mixteca region.

The Mixteca Alta, with the "nudo mixteco," or Mixtec knot, in the geographic center, spans the continental divide, with rivers, like Río Verde, flowing to the Pacific and others to the Gulf of Mexico. A distinctive form of intensive agriculture, known as "lama-bordo," has been practiced in the Alta since pre-Hispanic times. Terraces are built in arroyos perpendicular to the water course; adjoining slopes are cut back, and with the rainfall, sediments fill in behind the walls, forming flat cultivable surfaces designed to take advantage of the available moisture. Important materials and products from the Mixteca Alta include high-quality chert used to make arrowheads, dart points, and scrapers; cochineal produced by insects on the nopal cactus and used for a red dye shipped to Europe; and pulque produced from the aguamiel, or juice siphoned from the huge agaves.

Contrast of Flavors

Driving from Michoacán, I enter the state of Oaxaca from the state of Puebla, passing first and briefly through the very mountainous Mixteca Baja region and on to the Mixteca Alta.

For the most part, the limestone soil is covered with scrubby vegetation, small palms that are used for weaving hats and baskets, and cacti. The highway continues through a valley where it is difficult to pass by without visiting the magnificent monastery of Yanhuitlán, and a few kilometers off the highway those of Teposcolula and Coixtlahuaca, which bear witness to a very different age when the land was fertile. Much is now sadly eroded, but through the valley from Tamazulapan there are cultivated fields of wheat, corn, pumpkins, and beans, depending on the season of the year. In the higher areas, there are oak and pine forests that shelter many types of mushrooms during the rains.

The basic foodstuffs are those that are grown in the area, and I always marvel at how, by contrast, the most complex of moles, with all its accompaniments, has survived in Tlaxiaco. To be fair, this town was considered, until perhaps the 1950s, the Paris of the Mixteca, which the comparative sophistication of their moles, breads, and pastries demonstrate. And in Tamazulapan, the popular bread is *pan francés*, though it would not be recognizable to a Frenchman today.

The market in Nochixtlán also reveals what is produced in the area: there are large brown tortillas of wheat or wheat mixed with corn, several local chiles (see photo p. xx), simple clay cooking pots and pulque jugs, sieves made of horsehair.

Señor Alfonso García, who until his recent bout with diabetes worked in the Jardín Etnobotánico in the Santo Domingo complex, spoke to me for hours about the foods prepared in his village, San Isidro Yododeñe, not far from Nochixtlán.

Some of the recipes that follow are from there, but we cannot leave aside the intriguing ways that local plants and flowers are used in everyday seasonal food.

Before the male flower at the top of the corn plant, a thin green sheath, opens, it is slit open and the anthers scraped from the creamy-colored strands of the flower. These anthers are mixed with masa to make tortillas—a labor-intensive process using about 300 g to one kilogram of masa. The tortilla acquires a subtle taste of fresh corn.

But who could not be enchanted by the way they prepare the *flores de calabaza*? Only the stringy sepals of the flowers are removed (it is quite erroneous to remove the pistil, which is not bitter). After stripping off the stringy exterior of the stems, each stem is cut into 4 pieces of no longer than 1 inch. They are placed inside the flower, which is then folded over to cover them, making a small secure package. They are then toasted on an ungreased comal for about one minute on each side and eaten immediately with salt, wrapped in a tortilla.

No celebratory meal for Christmas, New Year, the patron saint's day, or a funeral would be complete without a *caldo*, really a soupy stew, of goat or mutton cooked with onion and garlic, flavored with mint, and served with chopped green chiles and *memelas* (thick whole wheat tortillas).

The custom on the day of a wedding is for the godparents of the bride to take her pulque, sweetmeats, and biscuits as well as a live ram with its horns painted red and adorned with bows. For breakfast the next day, *pan de yema* (semisweet yeast bread made with yolks of egg and pulque) is served with hot chocolate or pulque, followed by mutton or lamb in mole *negro*.

When a pozole of mutton is served, it is customary to eat it with a *cucharilla* in place of a spoon. The corn traditionally used for pozole is called *cajete*, deriving its name from the implement used to make a hole for planting the seeds. The grains are wider than those used generally for pozole, and the stalks of the plants are thick and juicy. They are eaten by the children as if they were sugarcane.

The chiles used locally are paraditos and morongos, elsewhere known as perón or manzano, which are either toasted and skinned for a sauce or cut into strips, unskinned, and seasoned with lime juice, salt, and onion.

Atole de trigo y aguamiel (Atole of Wheat and Aguamiel)

Señor Alfonso García Villagómez, San Isidro Yododeñe

The colder climate and thin, limey soil of the high Mixteca lands lend themselves to the cultivation of wheat. It is used in various ways: mixed with a corn masa for making tortillas or *memelas* (thicker type of tortilla); for a local pozole, sweetened with raw sugar and drunk cold; and for this unusual *atole* of wheat mixed with *aguamiel*. It is made during the dry months of the year, from October to April, when the milky-like liquid, *aguamiel*, is extracted from the magueys that abound in the area.

Aficionados of this *atole* can't say enough about its beneficial effects on health in general and particularly its curative effects for kidney stones! It is generally taken for *almuerzo*, accompanied by the local white bread.

FOR 4 TO 5 PORTIONS

6 ounces (150 g) cleaned wheat grains
1½ quarts (about 1½ L) fresh *aguamiel*
2 Mexican bay leaves

• Grind the wheat to a rough texture. Put the *aguamiel* into a clay pot, add the wheat and bay leaves, and cook over slow heat, stirring well to keep the grains evenly dispersed in the liquid. When the mixture begins to thicken and the wheat is soft, continue cooking until the surface appears gelatinous, about 20 minutes. It is then ready to serve.

Wildflowers from Tlaxiaco area/Diana Kennedy

Chiles rellenos en salsa de frutas (Stuffed Chiles in Fruit Sauce)

SEÑORA CLEMENTINA BAÑOS, TAMAZULAPAN

What a surprise it was to be introduced to such an exuberant dish in the rather sober, dry landscape of the Mixteca Alta. These stuffed poblano chiles in their colorful sauce now rival the regional mole as a festive dish for weddings, baptisms, and other important occasions. Señora Clementina said that the origin of this unusual combination of ingredients is unknown.

Traditionally, the chiles rellenos follow a "*sopa*" of rice and are accompanied by refried black beans. The sauce can also be used as a separate dish with pork or chicken.

This filling is sufficient for 12 large poblano chiles, but if you have some left over, you could always fill some onion "shells" (see recipe that follows).

2 pounds (900 g) boneless stewing pork with some fat
1 small white onion, roughly chopped
6 garlic cloves, unpeeled
Salt to taste
2 cloves, crushed
1 inch (2.5 cm) cinnamon stick, crushed
½ tablespoon dried Oaxacan oregano leaves or ¼ tablespoon Mexican oregano
4 tablespoons melted lard or vegetable oil
1 large scallion, finely chopped with leaves
5 garlic cloves, peeled and finely chopped
1¼ pounds (about 500 g) tomatoes, finely chopped
2 apples, peeled and cut into very small cubes
½ pineapple, peeled and cut into very small cubes
20 almonds, skinned and finely chopped
½ cup (125 ml) small raisins
1 small plantain, about 9 ounces (250 g), peeled and cut into very small cubes

- Put the meat into a pan with the onion and garlic, cover with water, and add salt to taste.

- Cook over medium heat until tender, about 40 minutes; strain, reserving the broth. You will need 6 cups (1.5 L), so reduce or make up that amount with water.

- Grind together the cloves, cinnamon, and oregano. Chop the meat finely, mix with the spices, and salt as necessary.

- Heat the lard in a skillet and fry the onion and garlic until translucent. Add the tomatoes and cook over high heat until reduced and thickened, about 10 minutes. Add the meat and continue frying the mixture, stirring and scraping the bottom of the pan from time to time to prevent sticking, about 10 minutes. If necessary, add a little more lard.

- Add the apple, pineapple, almonds, and raisins and continue cooking until the apple is almost soft. Finally add the plantain, and more salt if necessary, and cook until the mixture is well seasoned, about 10 minutes more.

- Set aside and keep warm, ready to stuff the chiles.

CEBOLLAS RELLENAS

(STUFFED ONIONS)

FOR 6 PORTIONS

3¼ pounds (about 1.5 kg) tomatoes, roughly chopped

1 small white onion, roughly chopped

5 garlic cloves, peeled and roughly chopped

2 tablespoons vegetable oil

2 Mexican bay leaves or 1 bay laurel

1 inch (2.5 cm) cinnamon stick

2 whole cloves

½ tablespoon dried Oaxacan oregano leaves or ¼ tablespoon
  Mexican oregano

6 cups (1.5 L) meat broth

2 medium potatoes, peeled, halved horizontally, and sliced

1 apple, peeled and cut into wedges

1 plantain—about 1¼ pounds (about 500 g)—peeled and cut into
  rounds

2 thick slices of pineapple, cut into triangles

⅓ cup (85 ml) raisins

15 pitted olives, halved

2 tablespoons large capers, roughly chopped

1 cup (250 ml) sweet white wine or sherry

1 tablespoon sugar, or to taste

Salt to taste

- Blend together the tomatoes, onion, and garlic. Heat the oil in a
  casserole in which you are going to serve the chiles in their sauce.
  Strain the tomato purée into the oil, add the bay leaves, whole
  spices, and oregano and cook over high heat, stirring to prevent
  sticking, until reduced and well seasoned, about 10 minutes.

- Add 3 cups of the broth, and when it comes to a boil, add the
  potatoes and cook for 8 minutes. Add the fruit and the rest of the
  ingredients and cook for a further 10 minutes over medium heat.
  Add the rest of the broth, adjust the seasoning, and cook for 10
  minutes more.

- Cover the chiles with beaten egg, as for chiles rellenos, and heat
  through in the sauce.

1 large white onion

- Cut a slice off the root end of the onion. Make a vertical cut to the
  depth of 6 layers, taking care it doesn't collapse. Put the onion in
  a small pan, cover with hot water, and add salt to taste. Cover the
  pan and cook over medium heat until it is tender but not too soft,
  about 15 minutes.

- Strain the onion, allow to cool, and separate the layers, leaving only
  the core. Put 1 tablespoon of the filling in each piece and roll to
  cover the filling.

- Proceed to dust with flour, cover with beaten egg, and fry as for
  chiles rellenos.

Chileatole mixteco
(Mixtec Chileatole)

SEÑOR ALFONSO GARCÍA VILLAGÓMEZ, SAN ISIDRO YODODEÑE

Chileatole is generally prepared to take to the cornfield, or *milpa*, to celebrate a good harvest. It is usually a family occasion.

This spicy *atole*, as its name implies, is a meal in itself. While it is often served with a tortilla, which takes the place of a spoon, traditionally the concave flower of the *cucharilla* (*Dasylirion* sp.) is used.

The corn used for this *atole* should be mature but still juicy, like field corn.

5 PORTIONS

6 large ears of fresh corn
2 quarts (2 L) water
3 guajillo chiles, cleaned of seeds and veins
2 chiles de árbol
2 large sprigs epazote
Salt to taste

- Shave the kernels from four of the ears of corn and cut each of the remaining two into 5 slices.

- Put the water to boil in a large pot (preferably earthenware), and when it is bubbling, add both the kernels and slices of corn and cook until tender, about 20 minutes.

- Remove 1½ cups (375 ml) of the kernels, add to the blender, and blend to a fine purée. Return to the pot, pressing down well to extract all the starchy juice.

- Toast the chiles (guajillos and de árbol). Soak the guajillos only in warm water to soften, about 15 minutes. Strain.

- Put 1 cup (250 ml) of the water from the pot in the blender, add the chiles, and blend well. Add to the pot through a strainer. Add the epazote and salt to taste and continue cooking until it has thickened slightly, about 15 minutes more.

BREAD FROM TAMAZULAPAN/DIANA KENNEDY

Chimeco
(Bean Paste)

MAESTRA GUDELIA LÓPEZ JIMÉNEZ, TLAXIACO

According to the *Diccionario de mejicanismos* (although it is now not considered totally reliable), *chimeco* is, or was, used in part of Guerrero to describe someone who has a dirty face: a boy or a charcoal vendor, for example, or even an animal. Maestra Gudelia laughed when I told her this and said it was probably because of its dirty color.

Chimeco is a concentrated dried food to take to the fields or on long journeys. It can either be moistened and spread on tortillas or made into a kind of soup. Either way it is nutritious and delicious.

MAKES 2 CUPS (500 ML)

1 cup (250 ml) black beans
1 cup (250 ml) unhulled pumpkin seeds
4 dried costeño chiles
4 avocado leaves (see Note on Toxicity, p. 426)
Salt to taste
Approximately 1½ cups (375 ml) water

- Pick over, rinse, and dry beans. Using a heavy skillet, spread the beans in not too thick a layer and toast over a fairly low flame, moving them around the whole time so that they toast evenly; but be careful not to burn them, or they will be bitter. (As a test, crush a few of the beans to see if they are crisp right through.) This will take about 20 minutes. Toast the pumpkin seeds, then the whole chiles and the avocado leaves.

- When all the ingredients are completely cool, grind to a fine powder in a hand-cranked or electric grinder. Add salt to taste. In this state, the *chimeco* can be stored in a dry place for several months.

- To use as a paste for tortillas, add just enough cold water to make it spreadable. To be eaten as a meal, dilute with water and heat through, stirring until it thickens.

Pottery vendors, Tlaxiaco market, 1993/Diana Kennedy

Cuitlacoche pasta y mole
(Cuitlacoche Paste and Mole)

SEÑOR ALFONSO GARCÍA VILLAGÓMEZ, SAN ISIDRO YODODEÑE

This is a very unusual way of using *cuitla-coche* in the Mixteca Alta. Traditionally, it is mashed on the metate and cooked to a paste and then eaten either spread on a freshly made tortilla with *queso fresco* or chicken, or diluted to form a mole.

MAKES 2 CUPS (500 ML) PASTE

4 guajillo chiles, seeds and veins removed
Approximately 1 cup (250 ml) water
4 (or to taste) chiles de árbol, toasted
1 large slice white onion, toasted
4 garlic cloves, toasted and peeled
2 cloves, crushed
2 mild black peppercorns, crushed
½ teaspoon dried Oaxacan oregano leaves or ¼ teaspoon Mexican oregano
2 tablespoons melted pork lard or vegetable oil
6 cups (1.5 L) *cuitlacoche*, shaved from cob, coarsely chopped, and blended with about 2 cups (500 ml) water
Salt to taste

- Toast the guajillo chiles lightly, cover with hot water, and soak for 10 minutes.

- Strain. Put ½ cup (125 ml) of the water in the blender jar and add the chiles de árbol, onion, garlic, spices, and oregano and blend until almost smooth. Add the rest of the water and the guajillos and blend, adding more water if necessary, to a smooth sauce.

- Heat the lard in a casserole, add the sauce, and fry for about 3 minutes to reduce and season. Blend the *cuitlacoche* with the water, add to the casserole with salt to taste, and cook over medium heat, stirring and making sure the mixture does not stick to the bottom of the pan, for about 15 minutes. The mixture should be thick and almost dry.

THE MOLE

8–10 PORTIONS

7 ounces (200 g) masa for *atole* (p. 395)
Approximately 6 cups (1.5 L) water
2 cups (500 ml) *cuitlacoche* paste
2 large sprigs epazote
Salt to taste

- Dilute the masa with 2 cups (500 ml) of the water. Put the *cuitlacoche* paste in a casserole over low heat, add the masa through a strainer, and continue cooking, stirring and scraping the bottom of the casserole to prevent sticking. As the mixture thickens, add the water by degrees and continue cooking until it is like any thick mole. Add the epazote and salt to taste, and a little more water if the mole thickens too much.

Empanadas de Tlaxiaco
(Empanadas from Tlaxiaco)

SEÑORA GLORIA SIMANCAS GONZÁLEZ, TLAXIACO

Among the foods served by Señora Gloria for her Sunday morning breakfast are these empanadas filled with a mixture of either ricotta with squash flowers or wild mushrooms or chicken giblets with *casita* (see below).

The filling is stuffed into an uncooked tortilla about 4 inches (10 cm) in diameter and cooked on an ungreased comal. They are eaten alone, not with a sauce.

RICOTTA AND SQUASH FLOWER FILLING

MAKES 2 CUPS (500 ML), SUFFICIENT FOR 6 MEDIUM-SIZED EMPANADAS

1¾ cups (445 ml) drained ricotta
1 cup (250 ml) tightly packed squash flowers, sepals removed and coarsely chopped
4 (or to taste) dried costeño chiles, toasted whole and crumbled
3 tablespoons coarsely chopped epazote leaves
Salt to taste

• Mix all the ingredients together but do not cook.

CHICKEN GIBLET FILLING

MAKES ENOUGH FOR 6 MEDIUM-SIZED EMPANADAS

4 chicken gizzards, cleaned
2 garlic cloves, peeled
Approximately 2 cups (500 ml) water
Salt to taste
4 chicken livers, cleaned
3 tablespoons melted pork lard
⅔ cup (170 ml) very coarsely ground masa, or *nixtamal*, roughly broken up
4 (or to taste) dried costeño chiles, toasted whole and crumbled
1 *yerbasanta* leaf, finely chopped
Salt to taste

• Put the gizzards into a pan with the garlic, add the water with salt to taste, and cook over medium heat until almost cooked, about 20 minutes. Add the livers and cook for 10 minutes more. Strain, reserving the water, and chop into small pieces.

• Heat the lard in a skillet, add the masa, and fry for 3 minutes, stirring to avoid sticking.

• Put ½ cup (125 ml) of the broth into the blender jar, add the chiles, blend smooth, and add to the skillet with the *yerbasanta*. Add 1½ cups (375 ml) of the broth to the pan and cook over medium heat until the masa is cooked and the broth reduced, about 10–15 minutes. Add the meats with salt as necessary and cook for 3 minutes more. The mixture should be fairly thick.

POTTERY IN TAMAZULAPAN MARKET/DIANA KENNEDY

Encaladas

Machucada and Tutuní

SEÑORA GLORIA SIMANCAS GONZÁLEZ, TLAXIACO

Encaladas are a specialty of Tamazulapan; they are like flour tortillas that have been enriched with lard and egg. The top surface is covered with a thin white layer of confectioners' sugar mixed with egg white.

Encaladas are sold in packages in the market in various sizes from about 2½ inches (about 6 cm) to 6 inches (15 cm) in diameter.

Every Sunday morning, Señora Gloria and her husband set up tables in an open-air, but roofed, area at the back of their house for *almuerzo*, that hearty late Mexican breakfast. Everything is cooked right there, and the sights, sounds, and aromas are tantalizing until you are finally served.

On one occasion, Señora Gloria showed me how to make these little masa snacks typical of that area of the Mixteca Alta.

Machucada—the word means "squashed up" or "crushed"—is made with a 6-inch (15 cm) tortilla straight from the comal that is squashed up and bathed with some dark melted lard, doused with a costeño chile sauce (p. 280) or *salsa de ajo* (p. 304), and topped with crumbled cheese. You can order *frijoles de olla*, soupy beans, either black or *bayos*, to accompany the *machucadas*.

Tutuní is the Mixtec word for a ball of screwed-up paper, or *torito*. A 6-inch (15 cm) tortilla is cooked on one side just until the dough comes cleanly away from the surface. It is turned over and cooked briefly on the second side. The dough is still half raw.

The tortilla is crumpled up with some salt, a dried costeño chile, and a *yerbasanta* leaf, both toasted and crumbled. It is then re-formed into an oval shape just over ¼ inch (about 65 mm) thick and cooked again on both sides on the comal. It is eaten just like that.

ENCALADAS, TAMAZULAPAN MARKET/DIANA KENNEDY

Frijoles negros con patas de puerco (Black Beans with Pig's Feet)

SEÑORA CLEMENTINA BAÑOS, TAMAZULAPAN

This simple, earthy dish is typical of the Mixteca Alta: it satisfies the appetite, especially in the colder altitudes, and is economical.

While Señora Clementina cooks the pig's feet with salt only, I use a little onion and garlic to intensify the flavor of the broth. In that area, nopales are boiled in water with "sal blanca" (the mineral salt used in the area), whereas I cook them "*al vapor*," which means stewing them in their own juice. I hope she will forgive me these slight aberrations.

8 SERVINGS

Have 1¼ pounds (about 500 g) black beans, cooked with salt only, in a large pot or casserole

2¼ pounds (about 1 kg) pig's feet, well cleaned, each one cut into 6 pieces

1 small white onion (optional), roughly chopped

½ small head garlic (optional), unpeeled and broken up

Salt to taste

1¼ pounds (abut 500 g) nopales, cleaned and cut into small squares

16 red costeño chiles, stalks removed

2 large sprigs epazote

Salt to taste

To serve: finely chopped white onion

- Put the pig's feet into a large pot with the onion and garlic. Cover well with water, add salt to taste, and cook over medium heat until just tender, not soft, about 1½–2 hours, depending on their quality. Drain and reserve the broth.

- To cook the nopales "*al vapor*": heat 2 tablespoons vegetable oil in a large skillet. Add the nopales, with salt to taste, cover the pan, and cook over medium heat, stirring them from time to time, until the viscous juice has exuded; they will lose their bright green color. Remove the lid and continue cooking, stirring from time to time to avoid sticking, until the juice has been absorbed by the cactus pieces.

- Add the cooked nopales and pig's feet to the pot of beans in their broth.

- Rinse the chiles and tear them into pieces (with the seeds). Add them to the blender with 2 cups (500 ml) of the meat broth and blend well. Add to the pot and continue cooking over medium heat for about 10 minutes. Add the epazote, adjust salt, and continue cooking for about 5 minutes more.

- The dish should be soupy; if it thickens too much, add extra meat broth to the required consistency. Serve in deep bowls, topped with finely chopped white onion.

Mole negro mixteco (Black Mixtec Mole)

SEÑORA DOLORES ROSA CRUZ, TLAXIACO

No festive occasion in this part of the Mixteca Alta would be complete without this mole and all its accompaniments. It is served with a *picadillo* of sheep's offal and a rather complicated "sweet sauce." For a festive meal, the mole is preceded by a "dry soup" called *sopa rellena*.

Señora Dolores is renowned for her mole, which she prepares for banquets and serves among other regional dishes in her small restaurant, Comedor Lolita.

APPROXIMATELY 25 PORTIONS

Have ready:

25 portions of turkey or chicken, cooked—but still a little underdone—in water with onion, garlic, and salt

2¼ pounds (about 1 kg) lard
2¼ pounds (1 kg) ancho chiles, cleaned of seeds and veins, seeds reserved
2 large white onions, cut into thick rings
3 small heads garlic, cloves separated
4¼ pounds (2 kg) plantain, peeled and cut into rounds
1 pineapple, peeled and cut into small pieces
18 ounces (500 g) almonds, unskinned
18 ounces (500 g) shelled pecans
18 ounces (500 g) shelled peanuts
2¼ pounds (1 kg) sesame seeds
18 ounces (500 g) unhulled pumpkin seeds
8 inches (20 cm) cinnamon stick
10 mild black peppercorns
10 cloves
2 tablespoons dried Oaxacan oregano leaves or 1 tablespoon Mexican oregano
l small bunch thyme
4¼ pounds (2 kg) tomatoes, halved
18 ounces (500 g) raisins—about 4 cups (1 L)—loosely packed
1 cup (250 ml) sugar
2¼ pounds (about 1 kg) Oaxacan drinking chocolate
25 serving pieces of turkey or chicken, cooked in water with onion, garlic, and salt, the broth reserved
Salt to taste

• Heat a little of the lard and fry the following ingredients separately, adding the lard by degrees as necessary and straining to drain off excess fat: the chiles until black, onion, garlic, plantain, and pineapple.

• Toast the following ingredients: the chile seeds, almonds, pecans, peanuts, sesame seeds, pumpkin seeds.

• Grind together the fried and toasted ingredients with the spices and herbs, using a minimum of water to make a slightly textured paste. Set aside.

• Put the tomatoes into a pan and simmer with the raisins and sugar, without adding any water, for 15 minutes. Transfer to the blender jar and blend until smooth.

• In the casserole in which you are going to cook the mole, heat 4 ounces (115 g) of the lard and cook the tomato purée with the chocolate over medium heat until the chocolate has melted. Add the ground ingredients, and lard as necessary to avoid sticking, and continue cooking over medium heat, stirring constantly for 20 minutes.

• Add broth to dilute to a medium consistency, then the turkey or chicken pieces and salt to taste, and continue cooking until the meat is cooked through and the fat forms in small pools on the surface of the mole.

SALSA DULCE PARA EL MOLE NEGRO MIXTECO

(SWEET "SAUCE" TO ACCOMPANY BLACK MIXTEC MOLE)

The preparation for this "sauce" should start the day before the cooking. This quantity will serve about 40 portions of no more than about two tablespoons each.

Have ready:

A casserole about 10 inches (25 cm) in diameter and 5 inches (12.5 cm) deep, very well greased with lard

4½ pounds (about 2 kg) tomatoes, sliced in rings
9 ounces (250 g) white onion, sliced in rings
4 ounces (about 125 g) *tomate verde*, sliced in rings
15 large garlic cloves, peeled and halved
50 pitted green olives, left whole
1⅔ cups (420 ml) raisins
2 cups (500 ml) almonds, skinned and left whole
10 cloves, left whole
5 allspice, left whole
2 inches (5 cm) cinnamon stick, broken up into 4 pieces
10 Mexican bay leaves or 5 bay laurel, left whole
5 chiles jalapeños *en escabeche*, left whole
½ cup (125 ml) sugar
Salt to taste

- Put the first seven ingredients in three layers in the casserole and finish off by sprinkling the whole spices, bay leaves, chiles, sugar, and salt over the top. Cover the casserole and set aside in a cool place to season overnight.

- The next day, cook the mixture, tightly covered, over very low heat for about 4 hours.

- The *salsa dulce* should still be moist. Serve hot with the mole.

PICADILLO PARA EL MOLE NEGRO MIXTECO

(PICADILLO FOR BLACK MIXTEC MOLE)

This *picadillo* is served in small portions as part of a festive meal with Mole *negro mixteco*. It is made with the offal of a sheep, weighing about 3 pounds (1.350 kg), or of a goat, weighing 2¼ pounds (1 kg).

3½ ounces (100 g) skinned and finely chopped almonds—rounded ½ cup
3½ ounces (100 g) chopped raisins—about ⅔ cup
3½ ounces (100 g) finely chopped pitted green olives—about 1 cup
2 ounces (about 50 g) chopped large capers—about ⅓ cup
1 medium white onion, finely chopped
1 small head garlic, cloves peeled and finely chopped
9 ounces tomatoes, finely chopped
5 *tomates verdes*, finely chopped
2 cups (500 ml) crumbled semisweet egg bread
5 cloves, crushed
5 mild black peppercorns, crushed
½ teaspoon cumin seeds, crushed
2 teaspoons dried Oaxacan oregano leaves or 1 teaspoon Mexican oregano
Sugar to taste
Salt to taste
20 eggs, separated
18 ounces (500 g) melted pork lard for frying

- Wash the offal in several changes of water, rinse, and drain. Cut the liver into 6 pieces, and slice the heart and lungs. Put the offal into a large pot with salt and plenty of water to cover. Cook over medium heat until tender, about 2 hours, or 45 minutes in the pressure cooker. Strain and cut into small cubes.

- Put the cooked offal into a bowl and add all the raw ingredients (except eggs) and the spices ground with the oregano, sugar, and salt.

- Cover the bowl and set aside in a cool place or refrigerator to season overnight.

- The next day beat the egg whites and salt until stiff but not dry. Add the yolks and beat until well incorporated. Then fold in the seasoned ingredients.

- In a large, deep casserole, heat the lard (yes, you need it all), add the mixture, and cook over low heat, stirring—at first continuously—with a wooden spatula so that the mixture doesn't set into a solid lump.

- This will take about 1 hour. Drain to eliminate the excess fat before serving about 2 tablespoons per portion.

TORREJAS, TLAXIACO/DIANA KENENDY

Pan de muerto

The semisweet yeast rolls of various sizes made for the Day of the Dead, All Saints and All Souls, are encrusted with a face made of *alfeñique*, traditionally made of sugar mixed with almond oil. Each one is supposed to represent the soul of a departed family member or friend.

The faces illustrated here were just a few of the hundreds being made by Señora Clementina Baños when I visited her one year at the end of October.

Pipián de quelites
(Wild Greens in Pumpkin-Seed Sauce)

MAESTRA GUDELIA LÓPEZ JIMÉNEZ, TLAXIACO

Maestra Gudelia, originally from San Juan Achiutla, was a teacher for many years in remote villages and *rancherías* throughout the Mixteca. She has a fund of memories about the foods, both cultivated and wild—greens, roots, herbs, and mushrooms—that were prepared there.

Just the tender leaves and stalks of the greens are used.

8 PORTIONS

1½ pounds (about 750 g) cleaned wild greens: *quelite cenizo*, lambs' quarters, *quintonil*, wild amaranth, *violetas*, mallows, etc.

10 cups (2.5 L) water

2 thick slices white onion

3 unpeeled garlic cloves

Salt to taste

12 ounces (350 g) unhulled pumpkin seeds

10 costeño chiles, left whole

6 guajillo chiles, seeds removed

¼ teaspoon cumin seeds, crushed

½ inch (about 1.5 cm) cinnamon stick, crushed

3 cloves, crushed

4 mild black peppercorns, crushed

1 tablespoon dried Oaxacan oregano leaves or ½ tablespoon Mexican oregano

1 tablespoon lard or vegetable oil

1 large scallion, finely chopped with leaves

2 garlic cloves, peeled and finely chopped

18 ounces (about 500 ml) tomatoes, finely chopped

2 large sprigs epazote

Salt to taste

- Rinse and strain the wild greens. Put the water into a pot with the onion, garlic, and salt and boil for about 2 minutes. Add the *quelites* and cook, covered, over high heat until tender, about 10–15 minutes, depending on how mature they are. Strain and return the cooking water to the pan.

- In a heavy skillet, toast the pumpkin seeds over low heat, stirring them constantly to ensure even toasting, until golden, about 10 minutes. Set aside to cool.

- On an ungreased griddle or skillet, toast the chiles lightly, turning them over so they do not burn, until when cool they crumble, about 5 minutes.

- Grind together, in a metal hand-grinder, blender, or food processor, the pumpkin seeds, chiles, spices, and oregano until they become a textured powder. Put the powder into a bowl and stir in 2 cups (500 ml) of the cooking water. Stir into the water in the pan. Cook over medium heat, stirring to prevent sticking, until the *pipián* begins to thicken a little and season, about 15 minutes.

- Heat the lard or oil in a skillet and fry the onion and garlic until translucent. Add the tomatoes and cook over high flame, stirring to prevent sticking, until reduced, about 5–8 minutes. Add to the *pipián* and cook for 10 minutes more.

- Finally, add the cooked *quelites*, the epazote, and salt as necessary and cook until all the flavors are well combined, about 10 minutes more. The *pipián* should be of a medium consistency; if it thickens too much, add water as necessary.

Early morning, Tlaxiaco market/Diana Kennedy

Pozole de Tlaxiaco (Pozole of Tlaxiaco)

SEÑOR GONZALO CRUZ, TLAXIACO

Saturday is market day, or *día de tianguis*, in Tlaxiaco, where practically everyone who comes to sell, or buy, breakfasts on pozole, either inside the market or at the stands set up around the main plaza.

This type of pozole is different from most other soupy versions: it is not brothy and the corn is cooked until mushy. It is served in deep soup bowls with a piece of pig's head and other meat and topped with a simple mole *amarillo* with the predominating flavor of epazote. It is traditionally eaten with a white bread roll, *semita blanca*, and the usual accompaniments of chopped onion, quartered limes, and dried wild oregano.

The cooks of that area use a locally grown (dried) white corn with a large kernel, larger than that of the *cacahuazintle* generally used elsewhere for pozole.

According to Señor Gonzalo, there have been some changes over the years: cooks did not remove the pedicel, which enables the kernels to "flower" when cooked; they used costeño chiles instead of the guajillos and de árbol of today. Now they often make the pozole with chicken instead of pork.

MAKES ABOUT 8 PORTIONS

1¾ pounds (800 g) dried white corn, cooked with lime, rinsed, skins rubbed off, and pedicels removed
½ pig's head—about 3½ pounds (about 1.5 kg)—cut into four pieces
1¾ pounds (800 g) stewing pork, cut into large cubes
2 very large scallions, quartered
1 head of garlic, halved horizontally
Salt to taste

- Put the corn into a large pot with plenty of water to cover and cook over medium heat until the kernels begin to open up like a "flower" and most of the liquid has been evaporated, about 3 hours.

- Meanwhile, put the meat into another large pot with the scallions, garlic, and salt and cover well with water. Cook over medium heat until the bones can be easily removed from the head pieces, but the meats should be only half cooked, about 1½ hours. Strain the meat, reserving the broth; you should have about 12 cups (3 L)—if not, add water to that amount.

- Carefully remove all the bones and cartilage from the head and cut the meat into large cubes.

- Add the meat and 8 cups (2 L) of the broth to the corn and continue cooking until both are soft and the water has been absorbed, about 1 hour. Adjust salt as necessary.

THE AMARILLO

12 guajillo chiles, cleaned of seeds and veins
4 chiles de árbol, left whole
12 ounces (350 g) tomatoes
4 cups (1 L) of the meat broth
1 large scallion, coarsely chopped with leaves
5 small garlic cloves, peeled and finely chopped
3 tablespoons melted pork lard
Salt to taste
⅓ cup (85 ml) tortilla masa
⅓ cup (85 ml) coarsely chopped epazote leaves

- Put the chiles and tomatoes into a pan, barely cover with water, and cook over medium heat for 10 minutes. Strain.

- Put 1 cup (250 ml) of the meat broth into the blender jar, add the onion and garlic, and blend until smooth. Add 2 more cups (500 ml) of the broth to the jar, add the chiles and tomatoes, and blend to a smooth purée.

- Heat the lard in a casserole, add the purée through a strainer, pressing out well (but there will be some debris of chile skins left in the strainer), and cook over medium heat, stirring to prevent sticking, for 10 minutes. Add salt to taste.

- Put the remaining broth into the blender jar, add the masa, and blend until smooth.

- Stir into the mole and continue stirring to prevent lumping until the sauce begins to thicken (it should be of medium-thick consistency), about 10 minutes. Add the epazote, test for salt, and cook for 10 minutes more.

Sopa rellena

Señora Dolores Rosa Cruz, Tlaxiaco

This *sopa rellena* is served as a *sopa seca* before a festive meal of mole in Tlaxiaco.

In essence, this is a very sophisticated vegetable casserole that is served in very small quantities, but it is hardly worth making this recipe in a smaller quantity.

Señora Dolores cooks the *sopa* on top of the stove over a very low heat, but if not watched carefully, it will stick and burn at the bottom; she would add more tomato, but to avoid this, I suggest baking it very slowly in the oven for about 3½ hours.

An ideal size casserole for this dish is about 10 inches (about 26 cm) in diameter and about 4 inches (about 11 cm) deep.

MAKES 15 VERY SMALL PORTIONS

Melted pork lard or vegetable oil for greasing the dish and frying
18 ounces (500 g) medium *fideo* or spaghetti
3 cups (750 ml) small dried bread cubes
9 ounces potatoes, peeled and cubed—about 1¾ cups—and cooked al dente
9 ounces zucchini, trimmed and cubed—about 2 cups—and cooked al dente
9 ounces green beans, trimmed, quartered, and cooked al dente
7 ounces carrots, scraped and cubed—about 1½ cups—and cooked al dente
¾ cup (190 ml—about 4½ ounces or 125 g) almonds, peeled and slivered
1 cup (250 ml/125 g) raisins
2¼ pounds (1 kg) tomatoes, coarsely chopped
¼ medium white onion, coarsely chopped
3 garlic cloves, peeled and coarsely chopped
2½ tablespoons sugar
Approximately 1½ cups (375 ml) chicken broth
Salt to taste
2 teaspoons powdered cinnamon

- Thickly grease the casserole in which you are going to cook the "*sopa*."

- Heat ½ cup (125 ml) of the lard in a skillet and fry the pasta, turning it over constantly, until golden. Strain and break it up into smaller pieces. Return the excess lard to the pan, fry the bread cubes in it until golden, and strain.

- The prepared ingredients (up to and including the raisins) will now be put into the prepared casserole in three layers: the pasta; the vegetables, almonds, and raisins; and the bread cubes.

- Blend the tomatoes with the onion and garlic. Heat 2 tablespoons of the lard in a skillet and fry the purée with the sugar until reduced, about 8 minutes. Add the broth and continue cooking for 5 minutes more. Add salt to taste. Pour this over and around the edge of the ingredients, making sure that it penetrates the layers, and sprinkle the surface with the cinnamon. Cover the casserole with a cloth and set aside to season overnight in a cool place or in the refrigerator.

- Either cook on top of the stove over very low heat for 3 hours or in the oven, as suggested above. The *sopa* should be soft and moist but not juicy.

Ticondichi

SEÑORA ESTELA MORALES OSORIO, YOLOMÉCATL

One day, when driving to Tlaxiaco, a sign saying "La Única" caught my eye, probably because I was hungry. I was soon eating a very simple but delicious *almendrado*, which led me to talk to the owner and cook, Señora Estela. She is considered an expert on the dishes of that part of the Mixteca Alta that use locally produced and wild ingredients: *ndutenduchi*, black beans cooked with nopales and costeño chiles; *ndutemino*, the inner flesh of thick nopales cooked with dried fish and seasoned with avocado leaf and epazote; and *ticondichi*, the recipe given here.

It is curious that the black beans are cooked with the dried, purple-colored pods of a large bean that grows in the corn-fields, *frijol andador*. The masa balls are also different from those of other regional dishes: they are egg-shaped and seasoned with avocado leaves.

The beans are served in their broth in deep bowls, with the masa balls broken up and a sauce made with costeño chile and *tomate verde*. Even if you don't use the bean pods, *ticondichi* is delicious.

6–8 PORTIONS

16 ounces (450 g) black beans, picked over, rinsed, and drained
8 ounces (225 g) dried bean pods
Salt to taste

TO MAKE 12 MASA BALLS

16 ounces (450 g) tamale masa
2 ounces (about 60 g) softened pork lard
3 dried avocado leaves (see Note on Toxicity, p. 426), toasted and ground
Salt to taste

THE SAUCE

MAKES ABOUT 1½ CUPS (375 ML)

6 dried red costeño chiles
1 garlic clove, peeled
8 ounces (225 g) *tomates verdes*, broiled
Salt to taste

- Put the beans and pods into a large pot with plenty of water to cover, and cook over medium heat until the beans are soft, about 2½ hours, depending on the age of the beans. Add salt to taste.

- Meanwhile, prepare the masa balls. Mix the ingredients together well and divide into 12 parts, each approximately 1½ ounces (about 40 g). Form each one into an egg shape and make a deep hole in the middle. Add to the simmering beans and cook, covered, until the masa is well cooked through, about 20 minutes.

- Serve the beans in deep bowls with plenty of broth and masa balls. Pass the sauce separately.

THE SAUCE

- Lightly toast the chiles on a comal, turning them so they do not burn. Remove the stems and shake the chiles to remove some of the seeds. Crumble them into a *molcajete* or blender, and grind dry with a little salt to a textured consistency. Add the garlic, crush, then add the *tomates verdes* and blend to a textured consistency.

Tortillas de quintonil
(Tortillas of Wild Greens)

INFORMATION: MAESTRA GUDELIA LÓPEZ JIMÉNEZ, TLAXIACO

I must confess that I have reconstructed this recipe after a conversation with Maestra Gudelia, who told me that they were made in her pueblo, San Juan Achiutla, to eke out the corn, especially during the rainy season when wild greens were abundant. And not only were wild greens, *quelites*, used but also diverse seeds and roots.

These tortillas have become a constant in my kitchen, since they are so delicious and nutritious at the same time. Their flavor is best appreciated when served as a *botana* with a fresh cheese and/or a sauce. They reheat well even after two days.

Any softer greens, like spinach, can be used. You will need about 1 pound (450 g). The proportion of greens to masa will vary with the quality of the masa and its malleability.

To make the greens even tastier, once cooked and squeezed, they can be lightly fried with a little chopped onion and garlic.

MAKES 10 TORTILLAS ABOUT 5 INCHES (ABOUT 12 CM) IN DIAMETER

1 cup (250 ml) tortilla masa, as dry as possible
1 cup (250 ml) cooked and strained finely chopped greens (squeezed as dry as possible)
Salt to taste

- Mix the ingredients together well until completely smooth. Divide the mixture into 10 equal parts and roll them into smooth balls; they should be about 1¼ inches (about 3 cm) in diameter. Press out, as for any tortillas, in a tortilla press lined with plastic bags. To ensure that the masa does not stick, open up the press, lift up the top bag, and replace. Turn the bags with dough over; then remove the top bag and cook on an ungreased comal for a few minutes on each side. Keep the tortillas warm in a cloth-lined basket.

Mixteca Baja

Early mornng near Huajuapan de León, Mixteca Baja/Diana Kennedy

Mixteca Baja

By Marcus Winter

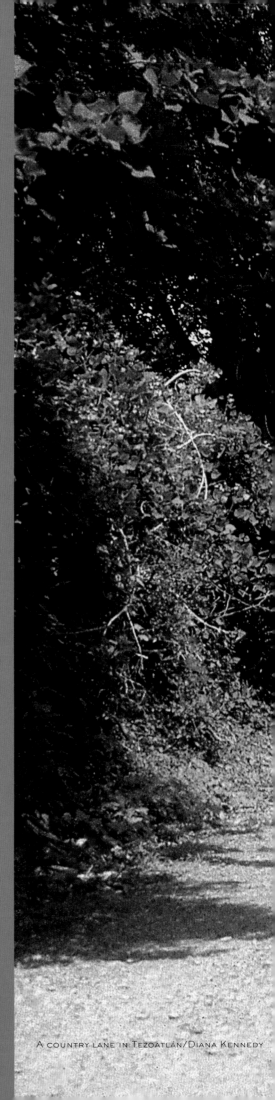

The Mixteca Baja is a mountainous area in western Oaxaca that continues into the neighboring states of Puebla and Guerrero. Like the Mixteca Alta, it is formed by many separate small valleys, although at slightly lower altitudes with valley floors around 1,500 meters above sea level. Also, the Mixteca Baja is hotter and rockier than the Alta, with xerofitic and scrub vegetation at low altitudes. Most of the region is in the upper reaches of the Mixtec-Balsas river system, which drains into the Pacific. Both Mixtec areas share a similar culture, highlighted during the Late Preclassic period (100 BC–AD 250) by early urban centers. However, during the Classic (AD 300–AD 800), they diverged, with the emergence and flourishing in the Baja of the Ñuiñe culture, with its distinctive architecture, writing, ceramics, and religion. Cerro de las Minas in Huajuapan de León is the only site open to the public, though many Ñuiñe-style carved stones are on display in the community museum in San Pedro and San Pablo Tequixtepec. While most of the inhabitants of the Mixteca Baja region are Mixtec speakers, the Amuzgos occupy parts of Oaxaca and Guerrero in the southern Baja near the coast.

PUEBLA

HUAJUAPAN DE LEÓN

TEZOATLÁN

MIXTECA BAJA

GUERRERO

MAP OF MIXTECA BAJA/SERGIO AGUIRRE

A COUNTRY LANE IN TEZOATLÁN/DIANA KENNEDY

Albóndigas de puerco (Pork Meatballs)

SEÑORA ALDEGUNDA CISNEROS DE ANDRADE, TEZOATLÁN

Meatball dishes are always popular in Mexico, and this is no exception in Tezoatlán, where they have an interesting and delicious way of cooking them. They are served there with white rice and tortillas.

6 PORTIONS

THE MEATBALLS

8 cups (about 2 L) chicken, pork, or beef broth
1 pork hock bone, cut into 4 pieces
1 small white onion, coarsely sliced
2 whole garlic cloves
Salt to taste
½ medium white onion, finely chopped
3 garlic cloves, peeled and finely chopped
¼ teaspoon cumin seeds, crushed
3 cloves, crushed
1 large tomato, unskinned and finely chopped
20 mint leaves, finely chopped
Salt to taste
1 pound (450 g) finely ground pork
2 hard-cooked eggs, cut into small pieces

FOR THE BROTH

1 tablespoon lard
2 garlic cloves, peeled and finely chopped
1 small white onion, finely chopped
1 pound (450 g) tomatoes, unpeeled and finely chopped
Salt to taste
⅓ cup (85 ml) fine, soft breadcrumbs

- Put the broth into a pan with the pork bone, onion, garlic, and salt and cook over moderate heat. Grind the second onion and garlic together with the cumin, cloves, tomato, mint, and salt and mix well into the ground meat. Divide the mixture into 18 portions and roll them into smooth, compact balls, inserting a piece of the cooked egg into the center of each one. Add the balls to the broth and cook over moderate heat, moving them around from time to time, for 15 minutes.

- In a separate casserole, heat the lard and fry the garlic and onion until translucent. Blend the tomatoes smooth, add to the pan, and fry the mixture until reduced and seasoned, about 5 minutes. Add the meatballs with 3 cups (750 ml) of the broth in which the meatballs were cooked, adjust salt, and cook over moderate heat for about 10 minutes, adding the breadcrumbs to give more body to the sauce for the last 3 minutes of the cooking time.

Asado de res (Beef Stew)

SEÑORA ALDEGUNDA CISNEROS DE ANDRADE, TEZOATLÁN

This savory stew, despite its name *Asado*, is an everyday dish prepared by Doña Aldegunda for her family. It follows a dish of rice served as a *sopa seca*, accompanied by frijoles and chiles jalapeños *en escabeche*.

4–5 PORTIONS

2 tablespoons vegetable oil
1 medium white onion, thinly sliced
4 garlic cloves, peeled and coarsely chopped
1¾ pounds (about 750 g) beef, cut into 4 or 5 thick pieces
Salt and pepper to taste
2 chiles jalapeños, cut into 4 at the tip
2 Mexican bay leaves
3 cloves, crushed
1 tablespoon dried Oaxacan oregano leaves or 1 heaped teaspoon Mexican oregano
⅓ cup (85 ml) pineapple or fruity mild vinegar (p. 386)
1 pound (450 g) tomatoes, toasted
12 ounces (about 300 g) potatoes, peeled and thinly sliced
6 ounces (180 g) carrots, scraped and cut into thin slices
1 cup (250 ml) water

• Put the oil into a heavy, but not too deep, casserole. Spread the onion and garlic in one layer, top with the meat, and season with salt and pepper. Sprinkle the chiles, herbs, and spices over the top. Cover the pan and cook over low heat for the meat juices to exude, about 5 minutes. Add the vinegar and gently cook again, covered, for about 8 minutes. Add the tomatoes and reduce their juice over high heat for about five minutes. Spread the vegetables over the top of the meat and add the water, with salt as necessary. Cover the casserole and cook over low heat until all the ingredients are very tender, approximately 1 hour.

Barbacoa de Tezoatlán
(A Tezoatlán Barbecue)

My first visit to Tezoatlán in the Mixteca Baja was in the 1970s. The caretaker of a small, but elegant, apartment block where I used to stay with friends in Mexico City and his wife, knowing that I was researching the foods of Mexico, invited me to their pueblo, Tezoatlán, to see the unique local *barbacoa*. I happily accepted and offered to pay for the goat.

One Friday toward the end of October, we set out on what was to be an unforgettable culinary adventure (about which I have written at length in *The Essential Cuisines of Mexico*). Tezoatlán in those days was only accessible by a dirt road—to this day only slightly improved—some 30-odd kilometers off the main road just south of Huajuapan de León. In the light of the full moon, the landscape was eerie and bare except for clusters of small palms, cacti, and thorny scrub. Finally, we crossed a small river with narrow strips of cultivation on either side and drove into the small town, our destination.

We arrived at the home of their relatives just in time to see the preparation of the corn: for tortillas, the *pasta*, and the *lligue*. The *lligue* is akin to a pozole, but the raw dried corn, left to soak overnight, was sent to the mill the following morning just to be roughly broken up, or *martajado*. It was then rinsed three times in between separating the skins from the grains with the hands. Nothing was wasted; the skins were then thrown to the chickens and pigs.

Early the next morning we rode in a truck through the drying cornfields to a larger river about a mile from the village, where the *matancera*—surprisingly, a woman—simply known as "*la señorita*," was sharpening her knives, her gray braids swaying from under a rather battered sombrero. She made short work of sacrificing the

pretty little goat, which weighed about 100 pounds, skinning and cutting it up before washing the intestines and viscera in the swift-flowing river.

Meanwhile, the women were preparing the *lligue*; the grains were divided into two large clay *ollas* filled with water. Guajillo chiles, seeds removed, were blended with whole costeños and added to the pots with the goat's intestines and fat, along with plenty of salt and a bough of avocado leaves that had been singed on the hot stones lining the bottom of the barbecue pit. The men and boys had dug the rectangular pit the day before—it was about 2¼ feet deep and about 3 × 2½ feet in length and width. The bottom was lined with large flat stones that had been heated since the crack of dawn.

The stomach of the animal, which had been well scrubbed, was filled with the blood, liver, kidneys, heart, etc., all chopped up into small cubes and seasoned with onion, garlic, mint, and dried oregano. The opening was tied up and secured with a piece of the intestine around a thick wooden peg. The prized goat's head, destined for the grandmother who was an invalid and couldn't come, was stuffed with a dried corncob to prevent the brains from falling out.

Next came the preparation of the *pasta*, which is an integral part of most Oaxacan barbecues. In Tezoatlán, the corn masa of which it is made takes the form of a flat tamale, either with masa alone or with a layer of black beans in the middle. The *nixtamal* prepared for it is ground to a textured consistency. It is then beaten with lard, salt, and water in which the husks of *tomates verdes* had been cooked (20 *tomate verde* husks cooked for two minutes in ½ cup

Preparing goat for barbecue/Diana Kennedy

of water and strained). Cooks there say it prevents the lard from seeping out of the masa. (In all my years in Mexico, this is the first time I have heard that explanation. Usually it is used as a raising agent instead of baking powder, typically with the addition of *tequesquite*.)

The masa was spread about ¾ inch (about 2 cm) thick onto metal trays thickly lined with *yerbasanta* leaves. The top was covered with more leaves.

When the stones were pronounced hot enough, first the open pots of *lligue* were placed in the pit, and above them, so as to collect the meat juices, an improvised rack made of the peeled strips of *cazahuate* (a native tree, probably *Ipomoea murucoides*, used

because they withstand the heat and do not burn easily. On this was placed the meat wrapped in banana leaves, the stuffed stomach, the head, and, last of all, the trays of *pasta*.

The pit was covered with wet *petates*, "straw mats," and earth so that no heat could escape.

It is usual to leave the *barbacoa* cooking overnight, but time was short and in 6 hours the pit was opened and the meal served: a hearty plateful with meat, a slice of the stomach, and *pasta*, with a bowl of *lligue* served apart. A green sauce was prepared at the last moment: 30 raw *tomates verdes* were ground on the metate with 20 serrano chiles, garlic, and a large bunch of cilantro. Chopped onion was sprinkled on the top before serving.

Chilate de pollo
(Chicken in Chile Costeño Sauce)

SEÑORA ALDEGUNDA CISNEROS DE ANDRADE, TEZOATLÁN

This *chilate* is typical of the lower Mixtec region of Oaxaca. It is a very simple but very tasty way of cooking chicken, to which I have added my touches: cooking the chicken in broth instead of water and using melted chicken fat instead of oil.

6 SERVINGS

6 large serving pieces of chicken
¼ medium white onion, roughly chopped
Chicken broth or water to cover
Salt to taste
15 red or yellow costeño chiles
3 garlic cloves, peeled and roughly chopped
3 tablespoons melted chicken fat or vegetable oil
2 thick slices white onion
10 *tomates verdes*, roughly chopped
⅓ cup (85 ml) tortilla masa
2 large sprigs of epazote
Salt to taste

- Put the chicken and onion into a pan, cover with the broth or water, adding salt if necessary. Cook over medium heat until almost tender, about 25 minutes. Strain the meat and reserve the broth, which should measure about 4 cups (1 L). Reduce over high heat or add water to make up that amount.

- Remove the stalks from the chiles and shake them to remove the loose seeds. Cover with warm water and leave to soak for 10 minutes. Drain and transfer to the blender jar.

- Add the garlic and ½ cup (125 ml) of the broth and blend until smooth.

- Heat the fat or oil in a casserole and fry the onion slices until translucent. Add the sauce and cook over high heat, stirring and scraping the pan to prevent sticking, until the sauce has reduced, about 5 minutes.

- Blend the *tomates verdes* with another ½ cup (125 ml) of the broth and add to the pan. Cook for another 3 minutes. Blend the tortilla masa with ½ cup (125 ml) of the broth and stir into the mixture. As it begins to thicken a little, make sure to stir well because the masa readily sticks to the bottom of the pan. After 5 minutes, add the chicken pieces, epazote, and remaining broth; adjust seasoning and cook until all the flavors have intensified, about 10 minutes.

Chileajo de puerco I
(Pork in Chile-Garlic Sauce I)

SEÑORA JUVENTINA LEYVA, HUAJUAPAN DE LEÓN

This very picante dish is served with *frijoles de olla*, usually *bayos*, or pintos. It is usually made with pork on the bone with some fat: ribs or pieces of the meaty backbone, a favorite in Mexico. Some cooks add cooked potatoes, but this is optional.

6 PORTIONS

2¼ pounds (about 1 k) pork (see above), cut into serving pieces
Salt to taste
3 guajillo chiles, cleaned of seeds and veins
2 ounces (50 g)—or 4 cups loosely packed—red costeño chiles, left whole
¼ teaspoon cumin seeds, crushed
1 tablespoon dried Oaxacan oregano leaves or 1 heaped teaspoon Mexican oregano
2 cloves, crushed
1 garlic clove, peeled and roughly chopped
3–4 tablespoons melted pork lard
9 ounces (250 g) *tomates verdes*, cooked in water and drained
1¼ pounds (about 500 g) tomatoes, cooked in water and drained

- Put the meat, salt, and water to cover in a pan and cook over medium heat until just tender—do not overcook—about 35 minutes. Strain, reserving the broth. You will need about 3 cups (750 ml).

- Lightly toast the chiles guajillos, cover with hot water, and leave to soak for about 15 minutes. Strain.

- Lightly toast the chiles costeños over low heat until they "shine" (explains Señora Juventina) and become brittle when they cool off. Crumble coarsely into the blender.

- Add ½ cup (125 ml) of the broth, the cumin, oregano, cloves, and garlic and blend well.

- Add the guajillos with 1 cup (250 ml) more of the broth and continue blending to a purée.

- Heat the lard in a casserole and fry the meat until lightly browned; add the purée and cook over medium heat, scraping the bottom of the pan from time to time to avoid sticking, until reduced and seasoned, about 10 minutes.

- Blend together the *tomates verdes* and tomatoes until smooth. Add to the pan and cook for a few minutes before adding the remaining broth and salt to taste.

- Continue cooking over medium heat until the sauce thickens slightly and the meat is thoroughly cooked, about 20 minutes.

Chileajo de puerco II (Pork in Chile-Garlic Sauce II)

SEÑORA MICAELA CISNEROS DE SOLANO,[†] TEZOATLÁN

La Señora Micaela used a wild "oregano," known locally as *oreganillo*, that is usually used for pozole or for an herbal remedy (probably for stomach ills).

She served this *chileajo* topped with slices of white onion and accompanied by frijoles.

SERVES ABOUT 6 PORTIONS

2¼ pounds (about 1 kg) stewing pork and ribs, with some fat

Salt to taste

8 guajillo chiles, seeds and veins removed

1 ancho chile, seeds and veins removed

8 costeño chiles (yellow or red), left whole

½ head garlic, toasted, cloves separated and peeled

2 whole cloves, crushed

½ tablespoon Oaxacan oregano leaves or 1 teaspoon Mexican oregano

¼ teaspoon cumin seeds, crushed

3 tablespoons lard

2 medium tomatoes, simmered in water for 10 minutes

12 medium Mexican *tomates verdes*, simmered in water for 10 minutes

- Put the meat in a pan with water to cover and salt to taste. Cook over medium heat until just tender, about 35 minutes. Strain, reserving the broth. You will need 3 cups for the sauce. Reduce or make up to that amount with water.

- Toast the guajillo and ancho chiles briefly, cover them and the untoasted costeños with hot water, and leave to soak for 10 minutes. Strain.

- Put ½ cup (125 ml) of the broth into the blender; add the garlic, cloves, oregano, and cumin and blend smooth. Add another 1 cup of the broth and the chiles, a few at a time, blending well after each addition—add a little more of the broth if necessary to release the blades of the blender—to obtain a smooth purée.

- In a heavy pan in which you are going to cook the *chileajo*, heat the lard and fry the meat lightly. Add the chile sauce and fry over medium heat, stirring and scraping the pan to avoid sticking, for about 5 minutes.

- Put both kinds of tomatoes into the blender and blend well. Stir into the meat/chile mixture and cook for about 5 minutes before adding the remaining broth. Adjust salt and continue cooking until the sauce is well seasoned and of medium consistency.

Dulce de chilacayote
(Fruits in Syrup)

SEÑORA ALDEGUNDA CISNEROS DE ANDRADE, TEZOATLÁN

This is considered a *dulce fino*, an elegant and fitting end to a festive meal, in Tezoatlán in the Mixteca Baja.

The mature *chilacayote* (*Cucurbita ficifolia*), used here when the rind becomes hard, is from a higher altitude, whereas the papayas and pineapples are from tropical areas.

This preparation is labor intensive, but the final result is delicious (and this from a non-sweet-toother).

It is better to make this *dulce* at least one day ahead to allow the flavors to mature.

Stored in a cool, dry place or in the refrigerator, it will last for several days.

APPROXIMATELY 20 PORTIONS

1 small *chilacayote*—about 6½ pounds (about 3 kg)—cut into 6 pieces
2 green (unripe) papayas weighing 2¼ pounds (about 1 kg) each
½ large pineapple
2 quarts water
2 tablespoons powdered lime
4 quarts (4 L) water
2¼ pounds (1 kg) sugar
1 egg white, beaten
6 2-inch (5 cm) lengths cinnamon stick

- Remove the fibrous interior of the *chilacayote* with the seeds and discard (though I think this is a waste, as they are delicious and nutritious if dried and toasted as a snack). Peel off the rind and cut the flesh into triangles about ¾ inch (2 cm) thick.

- Using rubber gloves (to protect your skin from the enzymes), peel the papayas, cut open, and remove the seeds. Cut the flesh into wedges about ½ inch (1.5 cm) thick.

- Peel the pineapple, cut into 1-inch (2.5 cm) slices, and then into triangles.

- Put the 2 quarts of water into a nonreactive pan, add the powdered lime, and stir well. Set aside for 1 hour.

- Transfer the clear water to another nonreactive pan, large enough for all the fruit, discarding the residual lime at the bottom. Add the *chilacayote* and papaya with extra water, if necessary, to cover. Leave to soak for 2 hours, then strain the fruit, rinse, and strain again.

- In a wide, heavy pan that is not too deep, ideally a preserving pan, put the 4 quarts (4 L) of water, the sugar, and the cinnamon and cook over medium heat, stirring until the sugar has dissolved. When it comes to a boil, add the egg white to clarify. Skim. Add the *chilacayote* and papaya and cook over medium heat, stirring from time to time, for 1 hour. Add the pineapple and continue the cooking until the *chilacayote* is transparent and the syrup has been reduced by one-half and is of medium consistency, about 3 hours.

- Remove from heat and set aside until the next day.

Frijoles con yerbasanta
(Beans with Yerbasanta)

SEÑORA ALDEGUNDA CISNEROS DE ANDRADE, TEZOATLÁN

In the Mixteca Baja, this way of cooking beans calls for *frijoles bayos* or *colorados* grown in the area and not the ubiquitous black beans used in many parts of Oaxaca. Pinto beans can be used as a substitute.

Locally, this dish is served as a main course with white rice or to accompany a *carne asada*.

8–10 PORTIONS

1¼ pounds (about 500 g) pinto or other light brown beans, cleaned, rinsed, and strained
Salt to taste
⅓ cup (85 ml) water
12 costeño chiles, toasted and broken up with seeds
3 garlic cloves, roughly chopped
¼ teaspoon cumin seeds, crushed
½ teaspoon dried Mexican oregano leaves
4 tablespoons lard or vegetable oil
2 large *yerbasanta* leaves, fresh or dried

- Put the beans into a large pot, cover well with water, add salt to taste, and cook over medium heat until soft, about 2 hours, depending on age of beans. They should be rather soupy.

- Put the water into the blender jar; add the chiles, garlic, cumin, and oregano and blend until smooth.

- Heat the lard in another pan and fry the chile mixture over high heat until reduced and seasoned, about 3 minutes. Add to the beans and their broth, mashing the beans down a little to absorb the seasoning, about 10 minutes over medium heat.

- Add the *yerbasanta* leaves in small pieces and continue cooking for 3 minutes more. Serve in soup bowls.

Frijoles lavados o martajados ("Washed" or Crushed Beans)

SEÑORA JUVENTINA LEYVA, HUAJUAPAN DE LEÓN

This way of preparing beans is perhaps the most representative, the soul food if you will, of the area around Huajuapan where a variety of beans are grown. However, the preparation is rather laborious!

Frijoles lavados (sounds better in Spanish) are either eaten alone or to accompany *chileajo* (See recipes, pp. 294–295) or adobo. Pinto beans can be substituted.

It is customary to add some *sal blanca*, a mineral salt extracted in a nearby area, or *tequesquite* (see Glossary) to soften the beans.

6 PORTIONS

1 pound *flor de mayo* or pinto beans, picked over, rinsed, and drained
Salt to taste
2 tablespoons melted pork lard
½ medium white onion, finely chopped

- Cover the beans with boiling water, which should come about 3 inches above the surface of the beans. Cook over high heat, skimming off the flotsam on the surface, until the skins of the beans are wrinkled, about 25 minutes. Strain, discarding the water.

- The beans are now crushed to loosen the skins (though traditionally this is done on a metate with two grindings, it is more practical to use the food processor). Process intermittently with the plastic blade until the skins have been severed and loosened.

- Patiently remove as many of the skins as possible, leaving the beans a very light color.

- Put 4 quarts (4 L) of fresh water to boil with the salt, add the beans, and cook over medium heat until they are soft to the point of falling apart, approximately 1 hour.

- Meanwhile, heat the lard in a small skillet and fry the onion until golden; add to the beans a few minutes before serving. The mixture should be smooth and resemble a loose paste.

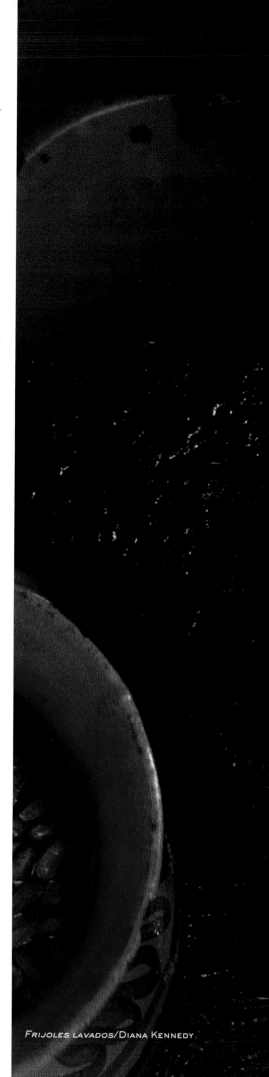

FRIJOLES LAVADOS/DIANA KENNEDY

Guaximole de chivo
(Goat in a Guaje Sauce)

SEÑORA JUVENTINA LEYVA, HUAJUAPAN DE LEÓN

This is a very picante regional dish using barbecued goat or sometimes mutton.

The sauce, or mole, is made with red costeño chiles and the pungent seeds, *guajes* (they look like small, flat lime beans), from pods of a native tree, a variety of *Leucaena esculenta*. (In other areas of Puebla, a similar dish is known as *guaxmole* or *guasmole*.)

It is served in bowls, accompanied by corn tortillas.

For the very adventurous few, *guajes* are often to be found fresh in Mexican markets in the United States.

6 PORTIONS

1 ounce (25 g)—or 2 cups—dried costeño chiles
¾ cup (195 ml) water
2 tablespoons melted pork lard or vegetable oil
Salt to taste
13 ounces (375 g) Mexican *tomates verdes*, roughly chopped, about 15 medium
4 cups (1 L) water
½ cup (125 ml) water
⅓ cup (85 ml) *guaje* seeds
2 pounds (900 g) barbecued goat or mutton
1 small bunch cilantro
1 dried avocado leaf (see Note on Toxicity, p. 426), toasted
Salt to taste

- Rinse the whole chiles. Put them into the blender with the ¾ cup (195 ml) of water and blend to a smooth sauce.

- Heat the lard in a casserole, add the sauce with salt to taste, and fry over medium heat for 5 minutes. Add the raw tomatoes to the casserole and cook, still over medium heat, for 8 minutes. Add the 4 cups (1 L) water and continue cooking for another 8 minutes.

- Meanwhile, put the ½ cup (125 ml) of water into the blender jar, add the *guajes*, and blend well. Add to the pan with the meat, cilantro, avocado leaf, and salt and cook over medium heat for 10 minutes. The sauce should be of medium consistency.

Mole verde de codillo
(Pork Knuckles in Mole Verde)

SEÑORA MICAELA CISNEROS DE SOLANO,[†] TEZOATLÁN

Thick slices of pork knuckle are cooked in this very fragrant mole verde, which was given to me many years ago by the late Señora Micaela. In many of the more rustic dishes like this mole, it is customary to use *carne de hueso*, meat with a good proportion of bone, along with a little boneless pork. Naturally, you can substitute chicken for the pork, but it won't be as tasty.

This mole verde is an everyday dish in Tezoatlán served with black beans.

6 SERVINGS

2½ pounds (just over 1 kg) pork (see above) with some fat, cut into serving pieces
Just over 1 pound (500 g) stewing pork, cut into 2-inch (5 cm) cubes
Salt to taste
3½ ounces (100 g)—about ½ cup—hulled raw pumpkin seeds
6 ounces (about 180 g)—about ¾ cup—*tomates verdes*
6–8 (or to taste) fresh chiles serranos
1 cup (250 ml) roughly chopped scallion leaves
3–4 tablespoons melted lard or vegetable oil
1 cup (250 ml) roughly chopped radish leaves
½ cup (125 ml) roughly chopped epazote leaves
1 cup (250 ml) roughly chopped cilantro
2 cups (500 ml) roughly chopped romaine lettuce
4 *yerbasanta* leaves, main vein removed, roughly chopped
Salt to taste

- Place the meats in a large pot. Cover liberally with water, add salt to taste, and cook over medium heat until almost tender, about 45 minutes. Strain and measure the broth. You will need about 7 cups (1.750 L); reduce or make up that amount with water.

- Put the seeds into an ungreased skillet and toast over medium heat, stirring them from time to time so that they toast evenly. They should just begin to swell and pop around but not brown. Set aside to cool completely, then grind to a fine texture—preferably in an electric coffee/spice grinder. Put into a bowl, add about ½ cup (125 ml) of the meat broth, and stir until smooth.

- Put 1 cup (250 ml) of the meat broth into the blender and gradually add the *tomates verdes*, the serranos, and the scallion leaves, blending well after each addition, until almost smooth.

- Heat the lard or oil in the casserole or pan in which you are going to cook the mole, add the seed paste, and fry, stirring constantly to avoid sticking, for about 3 minutes. Add the blended ingredients and the meats and continue cooking for about 8 minutes more.

- Put 1 cup (250 ml) more of the broth into the blender and add the rest of the ingredients a little at a time, blending well after each addition and only adding a little more broth if necessary to loosen the blender blades. Blend as smoothly as possible then add to the pan, pressing the greens through a strainer to extract as much liquid as possible. Continue cooking over medium heat, stirring from time to time, adding salt as necessary, for about 10 minutes more. The mole should be of medium consistency.

El presente
(The Christening Present)

Some acquaintances of mine from Tezoatlán were invited by a family in the small, rather isolated village of Yucuquimi to be the godparents to their newborn child. They agreed, but knowing the customs of the village, took a case of beer for the parents and baskets of fruit for the children who would be present at the meal served after the mass. When it was time to go, the godparents were ceremoniously given the traditional *presente*, the gift of a turkey and tortillas in a tall basket, called *chiquihuite*, lined with an embroidered cloth. In the base were a dozen very large tortillas, one side spread with mole. A turkey that had been cooked in water, with salt only, had also been coated with mole, then wrapped in several layers of plain tortillas and placed in the basket. A bowl containing the remaining mole completed the offering. The recipients took the *presente* home to reheat—by slowly frying—and share with the rest of their family. The basket, cloth, and bowl were to be returned the next day.

I went to Yucuquimi soon after this occasion and saw the preparation of this very unusual *presente*. The ingredients for the mole sold there are brought in from Huajuapan de León, about two hours over a loose gravel road, and those, combined with the cost of a local turkey, amounted to about 60 dollars, which must represent an enormous sacrifice to the family who normally lives on less than a minimum income in this bare, scrubby countryside.

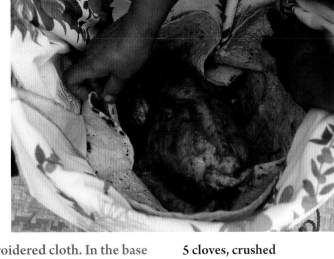

FOR A TURKEY ABOUT 6½ POUNDS (ABOUT 3 KG) COOKED IN WATER AND SALT, THE BROTH—ABOUT 6 CUPS (1.5 L)—RESERVED FOR THE MOLE

1 ounce (25 g) red costeño chiles, lightly toasted whole

4 ounces (about 125 g) mulato chiles, cleaned of seeds and veins and lightly toasted

4 ounces (about 125 g) pasilla (Mexican, not Oaxacan) chiles, cleaned of veins and seeds and lightly toasted

15 almonds, toasted and crushed

½ cup (125 ml) sesame seeds, toasted

½ cup (125 ml) raisins

1 inch (2.5 cm) cinnamon stick, crushed

5 cloves, crushed

1 small head garlic, toasted and peeled

8 ounces (about 250 g) tomatoes, cooked in a little water and drained

8 ounces (about 250 g) *tomates verdes*, cooked in a little water and drained

Approximately 6 cups (1.5 L) turkey broth

½ cup (125 ml) melted pork lard or vegetable oil

1 medium white onion, sliced

• Cover the chiles with warm water and leave to soak 10 minutes. Drain and blend with 1½ cups (375 ml) of the turkey broth. Transfer to a bowl.

• Put another 1½ cups of the broth into the blender jar and first blend the almonds, sesame seeds, raisins, spices, and garlic until almost smooth. Then add the tomatoes and *tomates verdes* and blend to a thick, slightly textured sauce. Cook over a low heat for about 20 minutes.

Salsa de ajo
(Garlic Sauce)

SEÑORAS ROSA AND OTILIA SANDOVAL,
CHICAHUAXTLA

I was given this recipe with a warning from the cooks that it is absolutely necessary to use the *miltomates* grown in the area, which are greenish purple or almost white in color.

They have a very special taste. However, this is not possible for anyone not living there, so use what is available.

It is used like any table sauce, but not cooked.

MAKES 1 CUP (250 ML)

1 small head garlic
6 ounces (about 150 g) *tomates verdes* (see above), husks removed
5 red costeño chiles
Salt to taste
½ cup (125 ml) water

• Heat a comal or skillet over low heat. Add the whole head of garlic and the tomatoes and cook, turning them from time to time so that they toast evenly.

• Toast the whole chiles until crisp, and crumble them (yes, with seeds) into a blender or *molcajete*.

• Separate the garlic cloves, peel, and add with salt to the blender. Grind to a paste. Gradually add the tomatoes, blending well after each addition, then dilute with the water to a textured, medium consistency.

Salsa de guajes
(Guaje Sauce)

SEÑORA ROSA CRUZ, CHICAHUAXTLA

Guajes are the seeds of a pod-bearing tree native to Mexico, *Leucaena esculenta*. The very strong-tasting seeds are eaten alone raw, crushed for an uncooked sauce, or cooked in sauces like *guaximole* (p. 300). They are also dried and toasted as a snack.

The seeds, which resemble small, thin lima beans, should be used when tender. Once matured, they become hard and have an even stronger flavor.

This sauce is eaten with tortillas.

MAKES 1½ CUPS (375 ML)

1 cup (250 ml) *guajes*
1 garlic clove, toasted and peeled
2 serrano chiles, toasted whole
9 ounces (250 g) tomatoes, toasted
Salt to taste
¼ cup (65 ml) finely chopped white onion
⅓ cup (85 ml) roughly chopped cilantro

• The day before, put the *guajes* to soak in water overnight.

• The next day, strain the *guajes* and crush them to a paste, preferably in a *molcajete*, or mortar. Add the garlic and chiles, and when these are reduced to a paste, gradually add the tomatoes. Add salt to taste and blend together to a slightly textured sauce. Mix in the onion and cilantro and serve.

Sopa de calabaza
(Pumpkin Soup)

SEÑORA ALDEGUNDA CISNEROS DE ANDRADE, TEZOATLÁN

Señora Aldegunda makes this simple but delicious soup with a tender pumpkin called *tamalayota* (also used for tamales in the Sierra Sur, among other uses).

If a tender pumpkin is not available, then use a mature yellow or green squash.

I hope my expert friend Aldegunda will forgive me for adding my touch; when finishing, I take out about 1 cup of the cooked squash, blend it, and return it to the pot to give a little more body to the soup.

It is always best to make a soup of this kind an hour or so ahead to allow the flavors to intensify.

If you are using a pumpkin of, say, 2¼ pounds (about 1 kg), after peeling and removing the inside flesh and seeds, you will probably end up with about 1½ pounds (about 700 g).

The soup is served sprinkled with a fresh cheese and accompanied by chopped onion and green chiles with lime quarters.

MAKES 6 SERVINGS

9 cups (2.25 L) water
1 thick slice white onion
2 garlic cloves
Salt to taste
1½ pounds (about 700 g) mature squash or tender pumpkin, cut into ½-inch (about 1.5 cm) cubes
1 tablespoon vegetable oil
⅓ medium white onion, finely chopped
2 garlic cloves, peeled and finely chopped
½ pound (about 200 g) tomatoes, finely chopped
2 large stalks epazote

- Put the water into a large pot with the slice of onion, garlic cloves, and salt; bring to a boil and cook for 5 minutes. Lower the heat to medium, add the pumpkin, and cook until almost tender, about 10 minutes. Remove onion and garlic and discard.

- Heat the oil in a skillet and fry the second onion and garlic until translucent. Add the tomatoes and continue frying until reduced, about 5 minutes.

- Blend a few pieces of the pumpkin with a little of the broth and return to the pan. Add the blended mixture, with salt as necessary. Add the epazote and cook over low heat for about 10 minutes. Set aside to season for at least ½ hour before serving.

Tetelas

SEÑOR AMADO RAMÍREZ LEYVA, HUAJUAPAN DE LEÓN

These flattish, triangular *tetelas* represent yet another way of combining corn masa and black beans. They are served the minute they come off the comal, with cream, crumbled cheese, and a sauce. (Confusingly, they are called *memelas* in the market of Acatlán, in the neighboring state of Puebla.)

MAKES 12 *TETELAS*

2 cups (500 ml)—or 18 ounces (500 g)—tortilla masa
1½ cups (375 ml) black bean paste (p. 40)

• Divide the masa in 12 parts and roll each one into a ball about 1½ inches (about 4 cm) in diameter. Cover with a damp cloth while you form the *tetelas*.

• Using a tortilla press lined with 2 pieces of plastic, press one of the balls out to a disk 6 inches (15 cm) in diameter. Lift up the top piece of plastic just to make sure the masa does not stick to it. Replace, turn the whole thing over, and remove the second piece of plastic. Spread a layer of the bean paste over the surface of the masa, leaving the edges free. Then, assisted by the plastic, fold the masa over to form a long triangle.

• Heat an ungreased comal over medium heat and cook the *tetela* until lightly browned on both sides, about 4 minutes each side. Proceed with the rest of the *tetelas* and serve immediately.

Drying *totopo de tuétano*/Diana Kennedy

Totopos de tuétano
(Marrow-Fat Totopos)

SEÑORA FILIBERTA AGUILAR MARTÍNEZ, TEZOATLÁN

These *totopos* were served in a little restaurant—one of the very few—in Tezoatlán.

They were so crisp and delicious I had to find out how to make them. Señora Filiberta is now, I think, the only person making them to sell, and she learned from her mother thirty years ago.

For the aficionados, and there are always some, who will want to make these from scratch, buy 4 pieces of marrow bone about 2 inches (5 cm) each. Put them into a heavy skillet with ½ cup (125 ml) of water, cover the pan, and cook over low heat until all the water has evaporated and the marrow fat is soft and melting, about 30 minutes.

Now, since it isn't always possible to get enough marrow bones from the local butcher, she uses rendered beef fat or pork lard instead.

The corn for the *nixtamal* is locally grown white corn (she says the hybrid corn won't produce the right texture), and it is cooked a little longer than is usual for tortilla masa.

This large *totopo* is cooked over very low heat until dried, not crisp, otherwise it would break in transit. To obtain this texture, she puts a flat stone on the comal so the *totopo* is tilted, but when served, it is toasted crisp.

For those who want to make them, I suggest starting with a small quantity and making them no larger than 5 inches (about 12 cm) in diameter.

MAKES 8 TOTOPOS

3 tablespoons melted marrow fat or pork lard
1¼ cups (315 ml) tortilla masa
Salt to taste

- Mix all the ingredients together into a smooth but manageable dough. Divide the dough into 8 parts and roll each into a smooth ball. Using a tortilla press lined with plastic wrap, press one of the balls out to a circle 5 inches (12.5 cm) in diameter. Remove top plastic to loosen, and replace; turn the whole thing over and remove the top plastic.

- Carefully place the tortilla onto the comal and cook over very low heat, turning the *totopo* from time to time so that it does not burn but will dry out. Place a flat stone on the comal to hold up the *totopo* on one side to help the drying process—it should take about 10 minutes.

VIEW OF THE SIERRA JUÁREZ/DIANA KENNEDY

Sierra Juárez and Mixe Region

By Marcus Winter

The Sierra Juárez—or Sierra Norte—includes the mountains north of the Valley of Oaxaca inhabited by Zapotecs. The same mountain range continues to the east, where it is inhabited by Mixes, and it then drops off and borders the Isthmian lowlands.

While the higher, colder areas have pine forests, the area is relatively dry to the north, though some pockets occur at lower elevations and have abundant rainfall and lush vegetation. The Papaloapan drainage begins immediately north of the Valley of Oaxaca, in the Río Grande Valley of Guelatao and Ixtlán.

The Mixe region spans the continental divide; some rivers flow to the Gulf of Mexico and others to the Gulf of Tehuantepec. Climate and ecological zones vary widely from high, cold country in places in the west, such as Totontepec and Zacatepec, to temperate and hot areas in the east, such as San José el Paraíso and San Juan Guichicovi.

VERACRUZ

IXTLÁN

SIERRA JUÁREZ / REGIÓN MIXE

BENITO JUÁREZ

CD. OAXACA

MAP OF SIERRA JUÁREZ AND MIXE REGION/ SERGIO AGUIRRE

Benito Juárez

Benito Juárez is one of a group of villages in Sierra Juárez that constitute *"los pueblos mancomunados,"* villages that have banded together to form a zone of ecotourism.

They are situated at high altitudes, mostly surrounded by well-managed forests of pine and oak. One of their main crops in winter is potatoes of good quality and flavor. It is no wonder, therefore, that they are used in many traditional ways, as well as those that have been invented in fairly recent years.

A few years ago, I was invited to Benito Juárez by the authorities to try their dishes as well as the unique *atole colorado*. For a *botana*, I was offered very small potatoes cooked in their skins, accompanied by a sauce of chile de onza (see recipe p. 327). I was then taken to visit many of the cooks who had prepared some of the following dishes for me to try.

Amarillo de papa
(Potato in Yellow Mole)

Señora Irma Hernández Hernández, Benito Juárez

This *amarillo* is undoubtedly unique to the area. The sauce is not smooth, as the potatoes give it an interesting, slightly lumpy quality. Señora Irma crushes the potato on the metate, but a rolling pin will do the job.

Serve just with tortillas.

MAKES 8 PORTIONS

3 pounds (about 1.3 kg) beef with bone, short ribs cut into serving pieces
2 large *yerbasanta* leaves, center rib removed, torn into pieces
Salt to taste
3½ pounds (about 1.5 kg) potatoes, peeled and cut into cubes about 1 inch
Salt to taste
5 guajillo chiles, seeds and veins removed
¼ teaspoon cumin seeds, crushed
1 black peppercorn, crushed
1 clove, crushed
1 tablespoon Oaxacan oregano leaves or ½ tablespoon Mexican oregano
6 garlic cloves, toasted and peeled

- Put the meat and *yerbasanta* leaves into a large pot. Cover well with water, add salt, and cook over medium heat until just tender, about 40 minutes. Strain, reserving the broth. You will need about 8 cups (2 L) broth, so reduce or make up that amount with water.

- Meanwhile, put the potatoes to cook in water with salt until soft. Strain.

- Crush the potatoes until you have a somewhat textured consistency. Dilute with 5 cups (1.25 L) of the beef broth and mix until it resembles a somewhat lumpy "slurry."

- On an ungreased comal, toast the chiles until they are brittle, taking care not to burn them. Crumble them into the blender. Add the spices, oregano, and garlic and blend well with 1 cup (250 ml) of the broth; add to the meat with another cup of the broth and cook over low heat for about 10 minutes. Add the potato mixture and continue cooking over low heat, stirring and scraping the bottom of the pan to avoid sticking. The consistency should resemble that of a thinnish gruel. If it is too thick, add the remaining broth.

- Adjust salt and continue cooking over low heat for 20 minutes more.

Coloradito de papas (Potatoes in Coloradito)

SEÑORA IRMA HERNÁNDEZ HERNÁNDEZ, BENITO JUÁREZ

This *coloradito* is typical of the Benito Juárez area, where potatoes are harvested in large quantities. It is served as the main meal of the day with white rice and soupy black beans.

The flavor of the mole is enriched if chicken broth is used instead of water. It is a matter of individual taste if the potatoes are peeled or not.

MAKES 5–6 PORTIONS

4 cups (1 L) water or chicken broth
Salt to taste
2¼ pounds (about 1 kg) of waxy potatoes, cut into 1-inch (2.5 cm) cubes
5 guajillo chiles, seeds and veins removed
2 mild black peppercorns, crushed
2 cloves, crushed
¼ teaspoon cumin seeds, crushed
½ inch (1.5 cm) cinnamon stick, crushed
1 tablespoon dried Oaxacan oregano leaves or 1 heaped teaspoon Mexican oregano
5 garlic cloves, toasted and peeled
3 tablespoons vegetable oil
1 pound (450 g) tomatoes
Salt to taste

- Put the water or broth into a pan with salt, bring to a boil, add the potatoes, and cook over medium heat until almost tender, about 12 minutes. Strain, reserving the cooking water. You will need at least 3 cups (750 ml).

- Toast the chiles lightly, cover with water, and leave to soak for 15 minutes. Strain.

- Put the spices and oregano into the blender and grind to a powder. Add 1½ cups (375 ml) of the broth, the garlic, and chiles and blend to a smooth purée, adding more liquid if necessary to release the blades of the blender.

- Heat the oil in a casserole and add the sauce through a strainer, pressing down hard to extract all the flesh possible; there will be debris from the chile skins in the strainer. Fry, stirring to prevent sticking, for about 10 minutes.

- Meanwhile barely cover the tomatoes with water and cook over medium heat until soft but not falling apart, about 15 minutes, depending on size. Strain, put into the blender jar, and blend smooth. Add this purée to the pan and cook for 10 minutes over medium heat. Add the potatoes, the remaining water, and salt as necessary and cook about 15 minutes more.

- The *coloradito* should have a medium consistency; if not, add a little more water.

Memelas de papa
(Potato Memelas)

Señora Elvia Mecinas, Benito Juárez

One of the chief crops grown in this area of the Sierra Norte is potatoes, so it is not surprising to find a number of recipes that have been created around them. These *memelas* (a word that usually refers to thick tortillas, often oval in shape) are no exception. They are delicious served hot from the comal with a sauce of chile de onza (p. 327).

Each cook will use a slightly different proportion of corn masa to potatoes, but once mixed, the masa should be used or "*se pone feo*," "it will become ugly," as Señora Elvia says. There is a trick, however: The potatoes should be cooked, but not mashed, the day before using so that they don't become so gummy.

Señora Mecinas makes her *memelas* large and thin, which requires a larger than normal tortilla press.

Makes about 10 6-inch (15 cm) memelas

12 ounces (350 g) floury potatoes, cut into large pieces, unpeeled
Salt to taste
10½ ounces (300 g)—approximately 1¼ cups or 315 ml—tortilla masa as dry as possible
Salt to taste

• Put sufficient water into a pot to cover the potatoes, add salt, and bring to a boil. Add the potatoes and cook until tender but not falling apart. Strain, cool a little, and peel. Set aside in the refrigerator overnight.

• Using a food processor (traditionally, a metate), mix the potatoes with the masa, adding salt to taste, to a smooth dough. Divide the dough into 10 parts and roll each into a smooth ball about 1¾ inch (about 4.5 cm) in diameter.

• Warm the comal or griddle over medium heat. Line the tortilla press with soft thin plastic—the dough will stick if it is thicker. Press one of the balls out to a diameter of about 6 inches (about 15 cm). Remove the top plastic, simply to loosen it, and replace.

• Turn the whole over, then remove the (now) top plastic. Moisten your hands with water and very gently, as it is rather fragile, transfer the dough to the comal. If the masa is uncontrollable and keeps breaking, add a little more tortilla masa.

• Cook the *memela* for a few minutes over medium heat until it is slightly browned on the underside, about 2 minutes; turn it over and cook on the second side a few minutes more then back on the first side for 1 minute—it might just puff up!

• Cover with a cloth or towel, as for any freshly made tortillas, and eat as soon as possible. They can be reheated, of course, but I don't recommend freezing.

Taquitos de papa (Potato Tacos)

SEÑORA IRMA HERNÁNDEZ HERNÁNDEZ, BENITO JUÁREZ

These delicious little tacos vary in that they are made with uncooked masa, which is then fried. The frying is slower than usual to ensure that the raw masa is cooked through.

Although most cooks have resorted to vegetable oil for frying, lard will give extra flavor and a better texture to the masa.

The tacos must be served without delay, topped with shredded lettuce and a red or green sauce.

THE FILLING

MAKES 2 CUPS (500 ML), SUFFICIENT FOR 12 TAQUITOS

1¼ pounds (about 500 g) potatoes, cut into small cubes, unpeeled
Salt to taste
2 guajillo chiles, cleaned of seeds and veins
4 garlic cloves, toasted and peeled
Lard or vegetable oil for frying
1¼ pounds (about 500 g) tortilla masa

- Put the potato cubes into a pan, cover with water, add salt, and cook until soft. Drain, reserving a little of the water, and put into a bowl.

- Meanwhile, toast the chiles lightly on a comal. Cover with hot water and leave to soak for about 15 minutes. Drain. Put ⅓ cup (85 ml) of the potato water in the blender. Tear the chiles into pieces and add, with the garlic, to the blender. Blend as smoothly as possible, then add into the potatoes through a strainer, pressing down hard to extract as much as possible of the chile. Mix thoroughly and divide the mixture into 12 balls.

- Heat the lard. Making one at a time in quick succession, press out the masa in a tortilla press, both plates lined with a plastic bag. Lift up the top bag, just to loosen the dough, and replace; turn the bags over and lift up the top bag. Put a portion of the potato filling along one side of the dough, near the edge, and roll up, aided by the bottom bag, into a fairly tight roll, covering the filling completely. Fry the *taquito* without delay, turning it over in the fat until evenly golden. Drain and serve immediately.

Pata amarilla wild mushrooms, Tlaxiaco, Mixteca Alta/Diana Kennedy

Amarillo de hongos
(Mushrooms in Yellow Mole)

EUSEBIO LÓPEZ, LA ESPERANZA

Many species of edible wild mushrooms grow in this and many parts of the Sierra Juárez, which is essentially part of the Chinantla Alta. Eusebio says that the most popular ones for this simple *amarillo* and tamales are: *orejas de duende, hiel de ardilla, hongos de chile, hongos grasos, hongos de niebla,* and *de jonete,* but, he advises, you should never mix them.

Naturally, cooking time will have to be adjusted for the smaller, juicier mushrooms, which should be cooked whole, and the more substantial, larger ones that should be cut into pieces and cooked until tender but not soft.

MAKES 4–5 PORTIONS

3 guajillo chiles, veins and seeds removed
Approximately 2 cups (500 ml) water
½ medium white onion
3 garlic cloves, peeled and finely chopped
Salt to taste
1¼ pounds (about 500 g) wild mushrooms (see note above)
½ cup (125 ml) tortilla masa
2 *yerbasanta* leaves, torn into pieces

• Toast the guajillos lightly on a comal, cover with hot water, and leave to soak for about 15 minutes. Strain.

• Bring the water to boil in a pan with the onion, garlic, and salt and simmer for about 5 minutes. Add the mushrooms and cook over medium heat until tender, about 10 to 20 minutes, depending on quality (see above). Strain.

• Put 1½ cups (375 ml) of the cooking water into the blender, add the chiles, and blend as smoothly as possible. Add the masa and blend again, adding more of the cooking water, if necessary, to obtain a very smooth consistency. Place the mixture in a pan with the mushrooms and cook over medium heat, stirring well because the mixture tends to stick to the bottom of the pan. After 5 minutes, add the torn-up *yerbasanta* leaves and continue cooking over low heat until well seasoned, about 10 minutes. Add more of the cooking liquid if you do not like a thick sauce. Serve with tortillas.

INGREDIENTS FOR THE FOAM OF *ATOLE COLORADO*/DIANA KENNEDY

Atole colorado
(Red Atole)

SEÑORA ELVIA MECINAS, BENITO JUÁREZ

Señora Elvia welcomed me to her home in Benito Juárez with a bowl of hot *atole*, topped with a colorful, and surprising, crown of red, bubbly foam—surely the most glamorous of all Mexican *atoles*.

Atole rojo is prepared not only as a way of welcoming strangers but for special occasions: religious ceremonies or for weddings and baptisms.

The basic *atole* is made in the traditional way with a masa made of corn cooked without lime, *tiziahual* or *nezahual*. The foam, or *espuma*, is made with a powder, or *pinole*, of toasted corn or wheat, cacao beans, cinnamon stick, and *achiote*.

Señora Mecinas prepared the *pinole* for me by toasting each ingredient on a clay comal thinly coated with a wash of lime, or *cal*, over a charcoal brazier. First she toasted the wheat grains; then the cacao beans separately over a very low heat, moving them around constantly until they sounded brittle; and finally the cinnamon.

When the cacao beans had cooled, their brittle coating was easily peeled off (this is often used ground with coffee beans).

Traditionally, these ingredients are crushed and ground on a metate, but nowadays, more often than not, a metal hand-cranked grinder is used. This process had to be repeated four times, with the help of members of the family, before the ingredients had been reduced to a fine powder. But there was a moment of concern: the *achiote* had not lent sufficient color to the powder. We all looked and tasted it. It seemed as though raw sugar had been added to the ground *achiote* (it is rare to find pure, unadulterated *achiote* paste). But she had used the same batch before, so it must have been "*el mal de ojo*" (the evil eye). There were too many people and too much activity around the kitchen. She added more *achiote*, and the color was then right.

Nobody could say exactly when they began to serve *atole* with this red foam in the village. Señora Elvia remembers that her grandmother used to make it using yellow corn, which, undisputedly, is more nutritious, but she herself found it easier and more effective to use wheat.

The *pinole* is usually made in fairly large quantities, because it can be kept for several months and is always available for some unforeseen emergency.

FOR ABOUT 80 PEOPLE

About 9 pounds (4 kg) wheat grains, toasted
About 2¼ pounds (1 kg) cacao beans, toasted and peeled
Scant 2 ounces (about 55 g) cinnamon stick, lightly toasted and crushed
Scant 2 ounces (about 55 g) *achiote*, crumbled
Sugar to taste

- *To prepare the foam:* Using a clay bowl, dissolve the powder by stirring it in by hand (a clean, greaseless one) in enough cold water to obtain a thin, smooth liquid.

- Leave this to soak for one hour. Then add sugar to taste and begin beating the mixture in a clay bowl called an *apastle* with a *molinillo* (as shown in the photograph) until a red foam with large bubbles forms on the surface. This is then scooped up with an oval *jonate* and placed on top of an individual serving of *atole*.

- 1 cup (250 ml) of the *pinole* is sufficient for 10 servings.

BEATING FOAM FOR *ATOLE COLORADO*/ DIANA KENNEDY

Calabacitas con huevo (Green Squash with Egg)

SEÑORA PETRONILA GUTIÉRREZ DE MORALES, ON THE WAY TO IXTLÁN

The tender green squash used in Oaxaca called *huichi* (see photo opposite) imparts its delicate flavor to the eggs in this dish and to the *caldo* of the recipe that follows.

Serve with a sauce of chile pasilla (see p. 56) or chile de onza (see p. 327).

Makes 4 portions

1 cup (125 ml) water
2 tablespoons finely chopped onion
1 garlic clove, peeled and finely chopped
Salt to taste
12 ounces (about 340 g) *huichi* squash, trimmed and cut into small cubes
Leaves of 2 large sprigs epazote, roughly chopped
4 large eggs, lightly beaten with salt

• Put the water, onion, garlic, and salt into a shallow pan and simmer for a few minutes.

• Add the squash and epazote leaves and cook over medium to low heat until squash is tender and the water has been absorbed, about 8 minutes. Stir in the eggs and continue stirring until the eggs are set.

Calabacitas en caldo (Green Squash in Broth)

SEÑORA PETRONILA GUTIÉRREZ DE MORALES, ON THE WAY TO IXTLÁN

Typically this dish is made from very tender green pumpkins, *calabaza huichi*, but it can also be prepared with squash or chayote vines.

It is generally served for *almuerzo* or for the main meal with tortillas, accompanied by a sauce of chile de onza (p. 327) or of chile pasilla (p. 56).

I suggest letting this dish sit for about ½ hour before serving to allow the rather delicate flavor to intensify before adding the eggs.

4 portions

4 cups (1 L) water
½ small white onion, finely chopped
2 peeled garlic cloves, finely chopped
Salt to taste
1¼ pounds (about 550 g) green squash, rinsed, trimmed, and cut into small cubes
OR
6 chayote or squash vines, stringy outsides removed, cut into small lengths
2 large sprigs epazote
4 large eggs

• Put the water into a pan with the onion, garlic, and salt. Boil for 3 minutes. Add the vegetables and epazote and cook over low heat until tender, about 10 minutes.

• (See note above before adding the eggs.) Break one of the eggs onto a small plate and slide it into the simmering broth. Proceed with the rest of the eggs, cover the pan, and poach until set, about 5 minutes.

Calabacitas huichi/Diana Kennedy

Chichilo de chícharos
(Chichilo with Peas)

SEÑORA ELVIA MECINAS, BENITO JUÁREZ

When the fresh peas cultivated around Benito Juárez are harvested, Señora Elvia cooks them in this *chichilo* and uses the same sauce for wild mushrooms in the rainy season.

It is served for the main meal of the day just with tortillas.

4–6 PORTIONS

4½ cups (1.25 L) water
Salt to taste
3⅓ cups (835 ml) shelled fresh peas
1 *yerbasanta* leaf, torn into large pieces
6 guajillo chiles, seeds and veins removed
2 dried tortillas
5 garlic cloves, toasted and peeled
¼ teaspoon cumin seeds, crushed
1 tablespoon dried Oaxacan oregano leaves or 1 heaped teaspoon Mexican oregano
1½ cups (375 ml) cooked and strained *tomates verdes*
3 tablespoons vegetable oil
⅓ cup (85 ml) tortilla masa

- Put water and salt into a pan and bring to a boil. Add the peas and the *yerbasanta* and cook until they are just tender, not soft, about 8 minutes. Strain and reserve the cooking water; it should measure about 4 cups (1 L). If not, add more water to complete.

- Toast the chiles well on a comal or in a skillet, rinse, strain, and put into hot water to soak for 15 minutes. Strain.

- Toast the tortillas until black, cover with cold water, soak for 5 minutes, and strain.

- Put ½ cup (125 ml) of the cooking water into the blender jar; add the garlic, cumin, and oregano and blend smooth. Gradually add the *tomates verdes* and the tortillas and blend again until smooth, only adding more water if necessary to release the blades of the blender.

- Heat the oil in a casserole, add the blended ingredients, and fry over fairly high heat, stirring to prevent sticking, for 5 minutes. Add another cup of the cooking water to the blender jar and blend the chiles until smooth. Add them to the pan through a strainer, pressing down hard to extract all the flesh; there will be debris from the chile skins in the strainer. Continue cooking and stirring over medium heat until the flavors have concentrated, about 10 minutes.

- Put yet another cup of cooking water into the blender jar with the masa and blend until smooth. Add to the pan and cook until the sauce thickens a little, about 3 minutes.

- Add the peas and *yerbasanta* with the remaining water and salt as necessary, and cook for about 10 minutes more. The *chichilo* should be of medium consistency; if it thickens too much, add a little more extra water.

Chintesle

This *chintesle* is totally different in flavor to the more commonly known one prepared in the Mixe or the Valley. Of course, the texture is better, or more authentic, when the ingredients are ground on the metate, but here is a more practical method that still tries to obtain a texture as near as possible to the original.

Chintesle is really a paste, which was often carried on journeys and used for spreading on a *tlayuda*.

Makes about ½ cup (125 ml)

20 red chiles de onza
6 black peppercorns, crushed
6 whole cloves, crushed
¼ teaspoon cumin seeds, crushed
Coarse salt to taste
1 small white onion, cut into 8 pieces and toasted
1 small head garlic, toasted, cloves separated and peeled
About ¼ cup (65 ml) water

- Toast the chiles until brittle, taking care not to let them burn. Crumble them into the blender and blend them dry with the spices and salt to a fine texture. Add the onion and garlic alternately with water sufficient only to loosen the blades of the blender.

Frijoles negros con ejotes y memelas
(Black Beans with Green Beans and Memelas)

SEÑORA PETRONILA GUTIÉRREZ DE MORALES, ON THE WAY TO IXTLÁN

This is yet another substantial and delicious way of preparing beans that constitutes a complete meal in many communities in the area of Ixtlán in the Sierra Juárez; it is served with a picante sauce of either fresh or dried chiles.

The original recipe calls for *ejotes serranos*, large fresh beans, for which green beans or tender fava beans can be substituted, although they will take much less time to cook.

Cooking time for the black beans varies considerably, so I suggest you add the green or fava beans at the same time as the *memelas*.

The *memelas* here are thick ovals of tortilla masa covered with avocado leaves.

8 PORTIONS, APPROXIMATELY

16 ounces (450 g) black beans, picked over, rinsed, and drained
½ medium white onion, coarsely chopped
½ small head of garlic, halved horizontally, unpeeled
Salt to taste
12 cups (3 L) water
2 large sprigs epazote
16 ounces (450 g) *serrano* beans, shelled; or tender fava beans, shelled; or green beans, trimmed and cut into 3 pieces

THE *MEMELAS*

16 ounces (450 g) tortilla or tamale masa
2 ounces (60 g) melted pork lard
Salt to taste
32 fresh avocado leaves (see Note on Toxicity, p. 426)

- Put the black beans into a large pot with the onion, garlic, salt, and the 12 cups (3 L) of water and cook, covered, over medium heat until tender but not too soft; there should be plenty of broth. Add the fresh beans, epazote, and the *memelas,* spread in two layers over the surface of the beans. Cover and continue cooking over fairly low heat until the masa is completely cooked through, approximately 25 minutes.

- To make the *memelas*: Mix the masa with the lard and salt, and when well combined, divide into 20 pieces. Roll the pieces of dough into bobbin shapes; flatten a little to an oval about ½ inch (1.25 cm) thick, pressing an avocado leaf onto each side.

Pozontle

Salsa de chile de onza (Chile de Onza Sauce)

SEÑORA ELVIA MECINAS, BENITO JUÁREZ

The traditional festive drink in and around Yalalag is called *po-zontle*. It is an *atole* topped with foam, the active ingredient being a climbing plant, *cocolmécatl* (*Smilax* sp.; see photo p. 149). Although it is generally brought from where it grows wild in a more tropical climate, I have seen it cultivated in *macetas* (pots) in Yalalag, but on a very small scale.

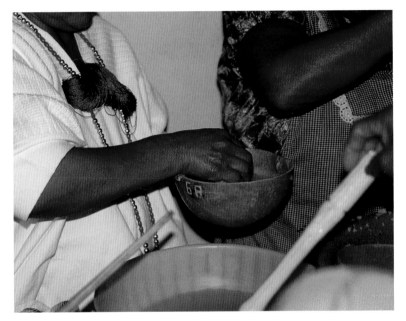

Chiles de onza, both red and yellow, are grown in the Sierra Norte and the Sierra Mixe. They are mostly used dried. They resemble chiles costeños and can easily be mistaken for them in appearance but not in flavor.

This is a rustic, uncooked table sauce served with the potatoes grown in the Sierra Norte or with bean tamales or fried tacos.

MAKES 1¼ CUPS (235 ML)

10 red chiles de onza
4 garlic cloves, toasted and peeled
Salt to taste
9 ounces (250 g) *miltomates* (*tomates verdes*), halved and cooked in a little water
Approximately ½ cup (125 ml) water

- Put the whole chiles to toast on a comal or in a skillet over low heat, turning them over to avoid burning, until crisp. Remove stalks and crumble them into a *molcajete* or blender. Grind them together with the garlic and salt and then add the *miltomates* a little at a time, grinding well after each addition. Dilute with the water to a medium consistency.

Tepejilotes (Palm Buds)

TEPEJILOTES GUISADOS CON HUEVO

(TEPEJILOTES COOKED WITH EGGS)

Tepejilotes are the long, pointed buds that grow out of the trunk of the palm *Chamaedorea tepejilote* (Ramírez and Alcocer) that grows in high tropical forests. (Buds of other similar species are used too.) They are collected in January and February and sold in bundles in the local markets in the Sierra Norte and in the roadside stands in Tuxtepec.

The edible flowers, which consist of up to 25 cream-colored, crisp notched strands, are tightly wrapped in several layers of tough dark green leaves. It is advisable to cook them within 4 or 5 days of harvesting, because after that time they become bitter.

One method of preparing them, toasted, is to make a slit up through the leaves but, without peeling, place the whole sheath either on a hot comal or on a grill over a wood fire. Within about 5 minutes, the flowers emerge from the leaves. Or they can be peeled and boiled in water for about 20 minutes. Whichever way they are cooked, they retain their crisp texture; the taste is slightly bittersweet.

Once cooked, *tepejilotes* are eaten in several ways: plainly with salt and lime juice, with eggs (recipe follows), added to an *amarillo*, in frijoles, or seasoned for a salad. Twelve *tepejilotes* cooked and cut into pieces yield about 2½ cups (675 ml).

In the Tuxtepec markets, they sell another type of palm bud, shorter and fatter with a rough hairy brown skin, called *espinosos*. Along the coast there is yet another called *soyamiche* (*Cryosophila nana*).

Prepared like this, *tepejilotes* are eaten for *almuerzo* with soupy black beans or in tacos.

MAKES 2 OR 3 PORTIONS

2 tablespoons vegetable oil
3 tablespoons finely chopped onion
1–2 serrano chiles, finely chopped
Salt to taste
½ cup (125 ml) finely chopped tomatoes
½ cup (125 ml) cooked and chopped *tepejilotes*
2 large eggs, lightly beaten with salt

- Heat the oil in a skillet. Add the onion, chiles, and salt and fry until onion is translucent. Add the tomatoes and continue cooking over medium heat until juice has evaporated, about 3 minutes. Add the *tepejilotes* and cook for 2 minutes more.

- (At this stage they can be used for a taco filling.)

- Stir in the eggs and cook until set, about 3 minutes more.

Making yellow corn tortillas, Yalalag/Diana Kenned

Torta de berros
(Watercress Torta)

SEÑORA ELVIA MECINAS, BENITO JUÁREZ

Watercress is cultivated in the streams around Benito Juárez, not only for use by the villagers but also to sell in the Oaxaca market.

This torta is served either for *almuerzo*, a hearty breakfast, or for the main meal of the day with a tomato and dried chile sauce (p. 327).

The ideal skillet for this recipe is 10 inches (about 26 cm) in diameter and 2 inches (5 cm) deep.

4–6 PORTIONS

3 cups (750 ml) tightly packed watercress, washed and drained
3 tablespoons vegetable oil
½ medium white onion, finely chopped
9 ounces (250 g) tomatoes, finely chopped, unpeeled
Salt to taste
6 large eggs

- Remove the thick stems from the watercress and chop coarsely.

- Heat the oil in the skillet, add the onion, and cook until translucent, about 2 minutes.

- Add the tomatoes and salt and cook over fairly high heat until reduced to a sauce, about 4 minutes.

- Beat the eggs until foamy, with salt to taste; stir in the watercress and add to the pan.

- Cover the pan and cook over low heat until the eggs are set, about 6 minutes. Carefully turn the *torta* over and cook for a few minutes more. Serve immediately with the chile sauce and tortillas.

Cazuela, Yalalag/Diana Kennedy

SIERRA MAZATECA

VIEW OF SIERRA MAZATECA/DIANA KENNEDY

Sierra Mazateca

By Marcus Winter

The Mazateca region includes the mountains and piedmont immediately to the northwest of La Chinantla. It is similar to the Chinantla area in geological and ecological terms, and includes communities in climatic zones ranking from cold, high country to hot, wet lowlands. Mountain slopes are within the Papaloapan and Gulf Coast drainage area, though the highlands have few rivers, owing to the limestone karst formations perforated by sinkholes and caverns that quickly absorb surface water. Some of the world's deepest caves are found near Huautla de Jiménez and on the Cerro Rabón plateau. Pre-Hispanic Mazatecs used the mouths and passages of these caves for burying their dead and carrying out related ceremonies. Coffee is grown in the medium altitudes, similar to those of the eastern Sierra Mixe and the Sierra Sur. The mountains in the western Mazateca, in the extreme northwest of Oaxaca, form part of a range oriented northwest–southeast in the states of Puebla and Veracruz. The portion in Oaxaca near the Puebla border is inhabited by Nahuatl speakers.

PUEBLA

VERACRUZ

HUAUTLA

SIERRA MAZATECA

MAP OF SIERRA MAZATECA/SERGIO AGUIRRE

Of Rites and Banquets

The Sierra Mazateca rises steeply out of La Cañada like a rugged escarpment in the south through semidesert and pine forests before it descends to the north and east toward Veracruz through majestic tropical landscapes. The Sierra is appropriately described in Mexico as "*muy accidentada*," that is, ruggedly mountainous with deep ravines, sadly deforested and eroded.

Perhaps this destruction is not surprising, given that as late as 1997 a manual of the agricultural, ritual, and festival calendar of the area instructed that during Chan Ntjao (January 21 through February 9): "Start preparing the land for planting, which consists of felling trees, cutting and burning the undergrowth and stubble; all the timber must be dry."

The Mazatec culture is centered around Huautla de Jiménez, which, until about fifteen years ago, could only be reached from Flores Magón in La Cañada by dirt roads carved out of the mountainsides along deep ravines and across countless streams that become torrents as soon as the rains begin. That track is now a paved but narrow highway that still has to be negotiated with precaution.

I first got to know the Sierra and Huautla in March 1999, when I was invited to join a group of ethnobotanists organized by Alejandro de Ávila, the director of the spectacularly beautiful Jardín Etnobotánico in the Santo Domingo Monastery complex in the City of Oaxaca.

We arrived in late afternoon for a *comida* organized by the late Señor Renato García and cooked by his wife, Blanca, assisted by other family members. It was a truly memorable occasion, featuring a series of traditional dishes using the local produce with herbs and wild greens gathered in the hills around. It was February, when the *tepejilotes* (*Chamaedora tepejilote*; see p. 328) and *tempesquistles* (*Bumelia laetevirens*; known popularly as the Mexican olive because of its similar appearance in form and color) were in season. The dishes included a *pilte* (wrapped like a tamale) of chicken (see recipe p. 340), eggs in *pipián* (recipe p. 345), *tesmole* and empanadas of wild (dried) mushrooms, *ayocote* beans with *tempesquistles* (recipe p. 342), *chicharrón en tesmole*, cooked wild greens—*hierbamora*, *quintonil*, *chapulquelite* (*Cleome serrulata*)—pickled *tepejilotes* (see recipe p. 352), and a very picante sauce of chiltepes fried with garlic (recipe p. 349). Before going to the market the next day, we were served an abundant breakfast of bean tamales and eggs cooked in *yerbasanta*, accompanied by *atole* to drink.

The weekly market day, or *tianguis*, in the Sierras is always a revelation, and here was no exception, with produce and collected ingredients brought in from the surrounding areas and sold, often on the ground, along the streets. There was *achiote* as loose seeds, in their husks, and ground into a paste with salt. There were small piles of chile chiltepe seeds for the *pipián*, bunches of *platanillo* (*Canna indica*), *hojas de pozole* (*Calathea lutea*), and *guazmole* (called *cherimole* elsewhere; *Renealmia* sp.) leaves—all for wrapping different types of tamales or *piltes*.

There were baskets of *guazmole* fruits (see p. 343) that sold out rapidly; local whole and ground coffee beans; ugly orangey-

colored *zapotes* (see photo below) vulgarly called *caca de niño*, "little boys' stools"; rustic earthenware pots from San Lucas (see photo p. 337); and the longest-handled spoons you can find anywhere in Mexico to stir huge pots of food.

The late Señor Renato left as a legacy notes and recipes on the rituals of the Mazatecs and the food that accompanied those rites.

1. THE CEREMONY OF PREPARING AND PURIFYING THE BRIDE ON HER WEDDING DAY—*LA CEREMONIA DE LA PURIFICACIÓN DE LA NOVIA, COMO PREPARACIÓN PARA SU BODA*

In the bride's home, *atole agrio* is served to the godmother of the bridegroom and the godmother of the *velación* who have come to wash the head, arms, and feet of the bride, accompanied by an orchestra playing "La flor de naranjo" (*Naxo loxa*), "Orange Blossom." Then the civil and religious ceremonies proceed.

2. THE CEREMONY TO OBSERVE THE MOURNING OF A DEAD RELATIVE, WHICH LASTS FOR FORTY DAYS—*LA CEREMONIA PARA OBSERVAR EL LUTO, QUE SE GUARDA POR 40 DÍAS*

On the tenth, twentieth, and fortieth days after the funeral, families, friends, and neighbors gather to pray in front of the altar set up in the family's house. (I was there.)

They sit silently around the room on chairs. *Atole agrio* is served, followed by a *tesmole* of chicken and later tamales of light-colored beans—because they say it is not appropriate to use black for a mourning occasion.

3. A MEAL IN THE CORNFIELD—*COMIDA EN LA MILPA (KJIEN KJON)*

When a meal is served in the center of a cornfield—to bring luck for a good harvest—the ritual foods served are: tamales of soured masa, turkey in *tesmole*, and a big tamale with a whole *totol* whose bones are buried in the field. Extreme care is taken that no particle of food falls to the ground, for that would mean something fatal would happen.

Those taking part have to abstain from sex for four days.

4. THE PROSCRIBED DRINK FOR *MAYORDOMÍAS* IS *TEPACHE* MADE OF SUGARCANE WITH PINOLE (A POWDER OF TOASTED DRIED CORN), AND FOR THE CEREMONY OF THE MUSHROOMS: HONEY.

During Holy Week, when the *mayordomos* serve food to the twelve Apostles, *tesmole de pollo* and bean tamales are the order of the day.

ZAPOTE, HUAUTLA MARKET/DIANA KENNEDY

Atole agrio
(Soured Atole)

SEÑORA BLANCA FLORES, HUAUTLA DE JIMÉNEZ

In the Sierra Mazateca, no wedding feast is complete without serving this *atole* of soured masa. It is also prepared for funerals and to observe the tenth, twentieth, and fortieth days after the funeral. It is particularly nutritious, since the *atole* is topped with *ayocote* beans and a *pipián* of ground sesame and chile seeds.

On a recent visit, Señora Blanca was preparing the *atole* for four hundred guests who were to attend the forty days' remembrance after her husband's death. (He, Renato García, has left an invaluable written account and calendar of the Mazateca customs and rituals as well as many of the local recipes.)

Señora Blanca had already soaked 55 pounds (about 25 kg) of local dried white corn in an earthenware pot for four days, which by then had begun to sour. With the help of her sisters and friends, the corn had been rinsed (uncooked) and ground at the mill to a very fine masa. It had then been left from one day to another to continue the souring process.

On the morning of the ceremony, the masa was diluted with water and strained, ready to be cooked for the *atole*. The *ayocote* beans were cooked separately, only seasoned with salt, until they were soft but not disintegrating. They were to be served at room temperature in small portions on top of the *atole*.

For the *pipián*, about 6½ pounds (3 kg) of sesame seeds had been toasted and ground with about 5½ pounds (2.5 kg) of

chiltepe seeds and a little water to a soft paste. It was diluted with water and then thickened with a small quantity of tortilla masa.

Each guest was served a bowl of the *atole* topped with some of the beans and *pipián*.

On another occasion, I joined one of these funeral ceremonies. Chairs had been set around three sides of a large room; on the fourth, a simple altar had been set up with a large photograph of the deceased. Not one word was spoken as the bowls of *atole* were passed around. The next day, flat bean tamales would be served.

I was welcomed into the kitchen, where preparation had begun. The unsalted masa had been spread out in an even film (yes, that thin) over a large square of cloth. This was covered with an equally thin coating of bean paste—surprisingly of light-colored, not the usual black local, beans, which I was told were not suitable for a *luto*. Aided by the cloth, the layers were folded over and flattened at intervals of about 2½ inches (about 6 cm); the layered mixture was then cut into rectangular pieces.

The tamales were wrapped in *hoja de milpa*, the leaf of the corn plant, not the cornhusk, and piled high in a huge *cazuela* and steamed over a wood fire for several hours.

(For very special occasions, I was told these tamales are wrapped in *álamo* leaves, but obviously not the usual poplars.)

*Chile canario en pilte/*Diana Kennedy

Chile canario en pilte
(Canario Chiles Cooked in Yerbasanta)

SEÑORA BLANCA DE GARCÍA, HUAUTLA DE JIMÉNEZ

Cooking in *pilte* is akin to cooking tamales, in this case, wrapping ingredients in banana leaves and steaming them.

This *pilte* is only for those who love their food extremely hot, since the chile canario—known in other parts of Mexico as perón or manzano and in other parts of Latin America as rocoto—can rival the habanero chile in ferocity.

4 PORTIONS

12 chiles canarios, wiped clean
2 very large scallions, cut into thin slices with green leaves
Salt to taste
4 pieces of banana leaf 16 inches square (about 40 cm), wilted
12 large *yerbasanta* leaves
4 long ties made from the veins of banana leaves or pieces of string

• Prepare a steamer, lining the top section with banana leaves, and put over low heat.

• Remove the stalks, if any, of the chiles. Cut them in halves lengthwise and scrape out the seeds and mix with the scallions and salt.

• Spread out the banana leaves and cover each piece with 2 or 3 *yerbasanta* leaves. Divide the chile mixture between them, then fold the leaves over the filling to form a rectangular package. Tie firmly.

• Place them in the steamer, cover tightly, and cook over high heat for about 30 minutes.

POLLO EN PILTE

(MAZATEC CHICKEN)

SEÑORA BLANCA DE GARCÍA, HUAUTLA DE JIMÉNEZ

The word *pilte* refers to foods cooked wrapped in banana or other large leaves.

Here the chicken was first wrapped in *yerbasanta* then in *platanillo* (*Canna indica*).

When practical, it is always better to season the chicken several hours ahead or overnight. This *pilte* is eaten with corn tortillas only.

4 PORTIONS

Have ready:

8 large leaves of *platanillo* or pieces of banana leaf

8 large *yerbasanta* leaves

4 pieces of string to tie the packages

A steamer with water in the bottom section with small coins and the top lined with more of the leaves

6 guajillo chiles, cleaned of veins and seeds

20 chiltepes, or other small very hot chile like chiltepín, lightly toasted

¼ medium white onion, roughly chopped

3 garlic cloves, peeled and roughly sliced

8 ounces (225 g) tomatoes, broiled

Salt to taste

4 large serving pieces of chicken, with skin and bone

- Put the guajillos in a small pan, cover with water, and simmer them for about 5 minutes; leave to soak for a further 10 minutes. Strain.

- Put ¾ cup water (190 ml) in the blender; add the chiltepes, onion, garlic, and tomatoes and blend. Lastly, add the guajillos and blend well to a smooth purée. Pass through a strainer to remove any stray bit of tough chile skin. Add salt to taste. Pour the purée over the chicken pieces and leave to season several hours or overnight.

- Put the steamer over medium heat.

- For each *pilte*, place two pieces of the *platanillo* in the form of a cross. Place two *yerbasanta* leaves in the center. Place a piece of the chicken, with plenty of the sauce, on the leaves and wrap and tie into a tight package so that the sauce does not ooze out. Cook over medium heat until the chicken is tender and well seasoned, 1–1½ hours.

Chayocamote en tesmole (Chayote Root in Tesmole)

HUAUTLA DE JIMÉNEZ

The bulbous roots of the chayote vine are used in many parts of Mexico and often called *chinchayote*. This is a very simple way of cooking *chayocamote*, as it is known in the Sierra Mazateca, but meat can be added to make the dish more substantial. This *tesmole* is soupy and served in bowls, with bean tamales instead of tortillas.

4 PORTIONS

1 chayote root about 1¾ pounds (500 g)
5 cups (1.25 L) water
2 avocado leaves (preferably *criollo*, which have more flavor; see Note on Toxicity, p. 426)
Salt to taste
12 dried chiltepes, or substitute 6 chiles de árbol
1 teaspoon pure *achiote* or 2 teaspoons of prepared *achiote* paste
⅓ cup (85 ml) tortilla masa

- Peel the chayote root and cut into 8 pieces. Put into a pan; add the water, avocado leaves, and salt and cook over medium heat until just soft, about 20 minutes.

- Put the chiles in a pan with water just to cover and cook over medium heat until soft, about 10 minutes. Drain and put into the blender jar with 1 cup (250 ml) of the chayote cooking water and blend with the *achiote* and masa until smooth. Add to the pan and cook over low heat, stirring from time to time to prevent sticking, until the *tesmole* begins to thicken a little, about 15 minutes.

Chilecaldo mazateco (Beef in Light Chile Sauce)

SEÑORA JUDITH FLORES, HUAUTLA DE JIMÉNEZ

The *chilecaldo* prepared in the Sierra Mazateca is completely different from that prepared in Cuicatlán. It is always served for *mayordomías* and often for weddings as well. The *chilecaldo* is served in deep plates, with bean tamales or just tortillas.

FOR 5–6 SERVINGS:

3½ pounds (about 1.5 kg) beef with bone and some fat: shins, ribs, and brisket
1 medium white onion, roughly chopped
1 small head garlic, cut in half horizontally
Salt to taste
¼ cup (about 65 ml) chiltepes
Scant 1 teaspoon pure *achiote*
1 large or 2 small chayotes, peeled and cut into cubes
1 medium cabbage, cut into 6 pieces
6 large sprigs cilantro *de monte* (see photo p. 69)
Salt to taste

- Put the beef into a large pot with the onion, garlic, and salt and cook, covered, over medium heat until the meat is almost tender, about 1½ hours.

- In a small pan, cover the chiles with water and simmer for about 5 minutes. Leave them to soak for a further 10 minutes; strain and transfer to the blender. Add the *achiote* and blend with about 1 cup (250 ml) water until smooth. Strain the mixture into the pot, pressing down well to extract as much as possible.

- Add the vegetables and cilantro to the pot and cook over medium heat until tender, adding more salt as necessary, about 30 minutes.

Frijol ayocote con tempesquistles (Ayocote Beans with Tempesquistles)

Señores Renato[†] and Blanca García, Huautla de Jiménez

This is a seasonal dish when the *tempesquistles* (*Bumelia laetevirens*) are collected from January to March. *Tempesquistles* have been called the Mexican olive. They do, in fact, resemble small olives in shape and color and grow on quite large indigenous trees in the area of Tehuacán, in the state of Puebla, and in parts of the Sierra Mazateca. They have a pronounced perfumed flavor and a seed that resembles a soft husk.

Tempesquistles take about 1½ hours to cook; they exude a sticky substance that local cooks say will adhere to a dried cornhusk if it is put into the cooking water.

They also say it must be cooked in an earthenware *olla*.

Ayocotes are like large kidney beans of varied earth tones in color. They grow wild but are also cultivated; their red flowers are also cooked and eaten in various forms.

This dish is eaten with tortillas and constitutes the main meal of the day.

8-10 PORTIONS

Approximately 5½ quarts (5.5 L) water
2¼ pounds (about 1 kg) dried *ayocotes*, picked over, rinsed, and drained
Salt to taste
2½ pounds (about 1 kg) *tempesquistles*, rinsed and drained
2 dried cornhusks
3 medium tomatoes
35 chiltepes or 15 chiles de árbol
5 guajillo chiles, seeds and veins removed
5 garlic cloves, peeled and coarsely chopped
2 thick slices white onion
3 tablespoons vegetable oil
2 large sprigs epazote
Salt to taste

- Put 3 quarts of the water into a large pot, add the *ayocotes* with salt to taste, and cook over medium heat until tender, 3–4 hours, depending on the age of the beans.

- Put the *tempesquistles* into another pot and cover with 2 quarts (2 L) of the water, add the cornhusks, and cook over medium heat until tender, approximately 1½ hours.

- Strain, rinse in a change of water, and remove the papery seed.

- Put 2 cups (500 ml) of water into a small pan. Add the tomatoes and chiles and cook until soft, about 8 minutes. Transfer to the blender jar with 3 of the garlic cloves and 1 slice of the onion and blend until almost smooth.

- Heat the oil in a small skillet, fry the remaining garlic and onion until dark brown, and remove. Add the sauce through a strainer, pressing the debris down well, and fry over fairly high flame for about 5 minutes. Add this to the pot of beans with the epazote and *tempesquistles*. Add salt to taste and cook for 15 minutes—it should be quite soupy. Add a little more water if it is too thick.

Guazmole

Señora Blanca Flores Vda. de García, Huautla de Jiménez

Guazmole is one of the most extraordinary dishes made with the fruit of a tropical plant (*Renealmia* sp.). The fruits are brought up from a lower altitude and sold in the Huautla market.

A slightly different dish is called *cherimole* in La Esperanza in the Sierra Juárez, where the plant grows wild, and *guilimole* in another part of La Chinantla (also used below Cuetzalan where Puebla and Veracruz meet).

The fruit is small and oval in shape. When ripe, it is a brilliant red, which darkens to a deep wine color as it matures. The flesh inside is a brilliant orange dotted with small round black seeds (see photo below).

These dishes can only be described as very concentrated, roughly textured slippery sauces with a pronounced fruity flavor—very much an acquired taste—but considered highly nutritious. The leaf of the plant is used for wrapping bean tamales in many areas of La Chinantla and lends its fruity flavor to the masa.

Guazmole is served as the main dish in a local meal with tortillas only.

To prepare *guazmole*, the fruits are cut open and the flesh is scraped out of the tough, almost shell-like casing. It is diluted with water, and using your hands, the strands of the flesh are separated, the small seed removed and put into a strainer to extract any extra flesh adhering to them. Local cooks know that the flesh *pica las manos*—"So what if it does," says Señora Blanca, "it's not that bad!"

The flesh is put to cook over a low flame with a little salt, a torn-up leaf of *yerbasanta*, half a chile cera, and 10 chiltepes that have been simmered, ground, and strained into the sauce. The *guazmole* is then cooked very slowly for about 20 minutes until it thickens and all the flavors are concentrated.

Eggs cooked in wood ash/Diana Kennedy

Huevos cocidos en ceniza (Eggs Cooked in Wood Ash)

HUAUTLA DE JIMÉNEZ

This rustic way of cooking eggs is, of course, best done on a clay griddle coated with a lime wash and over a wood fire. Only possible for the hardened aficionados!

These eggs have a distinctive flavor, but the slightly gritty texture is not to everyone's taste. But it is healthy! In Huautla, they are served with a sauce of chiltepes, but a chile de árbol sauce would be a good substitute.

1 PORTION

Approximately ¼ cup (65 ml) finely sifted ash
2 large eggs
Salt to taste

- Heat the griddle or skillet with a thin layer of the ash in the center. Break the eggs onto the ash and cook over low heat until set underneath, about 5 minutes. Turn the eggs over carefully and cook on the second side until set to taste, about 3 minutes.

Huevos en pipián (Eggs in Pipián)

SEÑORA BLANCA FLORES VDA. DE GARCÍA, HUAUTLA DE JIMÉNEZ

This egg dish is served either for breakfast or the main meal, with tortillas.

MAKES 3 SERVINGS

2 tablespoons vegetable oil or lard
1¼ cups (about 315 ml) *Pipián mazateco* (see p. 348)
Approximately 1½ cups (375 ml) water
6 eggs, cooked until firm
2 large sprigs epazote
Salt to taste

- In a small casserole or skillet, heat the oil and fry the *pipián* for about 2 minutes, stirring to avoid sticking. Add the water and cook over medium heat until it begins to thicken a little, for about 3 minutes.

- Add the whole eggs and epazote, adjust salt, and cook slowly until well seasoned, about 7 minutes.

Huevos en yerbasanta (Eggs Wrapped in Yerbasanta)

HUAUTLA DE JIMÉNEZ

For those who like the strong anisey flavor of *yerbasanta*, or *hierbasanta,* as it is known in Oaxaca, eggs prepared this way are delicious, especially when cooked on a clay comal over a wood fire. There they are accompanied by a sauce of chiltepes (p. 349).

Make sure that the eggs are securely wrapped in the leaves so that they do not ooze out onto the comal.

1 PORTION

2 eggs
Salt to taste
2 very tender *yerbasanta* leaves, veins removed, torn up into small pieces
3–4 thicker whole *yerbasanta* leaves

• Heat the comal or a skillet over medium heat. Beat the eggs with the salt and mix in the tender leaves. Place the whole leaves flat in several layers and pour the eggs in the center. Fold the leaves so that they cover the eggs completely, and cook for 5 minutes.

• Turn the "package" over and cook until the eggs are set, about 5 minutes more.

• Eat with the toasted leaves in which they were cooked.

Huevos zapateros (Shoemaker's Eggs)

SEÑORA BLANCA DE GARCÍA,
HUAUTLA DE JIMÉNEZ

These eggs, with the Mazatec name of Chao Ndiajón, are poached in a very spicy tomato broth. They are usually served for *almuerzo* in a bowl, accompanied by corn tortillas. Chiles de árbol can be substituted for the chiltepes.

2 PORTIONS

1½ cups (375 ml) water
Salt to taste
10 chiltepes or 5 chiles de árbol, left whole
8 ounces (225 g) tomatoes—about 2 medium
1 large sprig epazote
4 large eggs

• Heat the salted water in a small casserole, add the chiles and tomatoes, and cook until soft, about 10 minutes. Remove with a slotted spoon, blend smooth (traditionally ground on a metate), and return the purée to the cooking water. Add the epazote and carefully break the eggs into the broth. Cover the casserole and cook on low heat until the eggs are set.

Pipián mazateco
(Pipián from the Sierra Mazateca)

Señora Blanca Flores de García, Huautla de Jiménez

In the Huautla market, you will see vendors selling small piles of seed, which are chiltepe seeds. They are to be toasted with sesame seeds and ground for *pipián*.

This regional *pipián* is mainly used as a topping for *atole agrio* (see p. 337) but is also served as a meal with hard-cooked eggs (see p. 345) or as a snack spread on tortillas.

When the *pipián* is prepared in small quantities, it is ground at home on the metate, but larger quantities are sent to the local mill.

I suggest toasting and, when cooled, grinding first the chile seeds and then the sesame separately and in small quantities, in an electric coffee/spice grinder.

APPROXIMATELY 1½ CUPS (375 ML) PASTE

1 cup (250 ml) chile seeds
1 cup (250 ml) sesame seeds
Salt to taste
Water as necessary

- In an ungreased skillet, toast the chile seeds, stirring so that they toast evenly to a light brown. Cool. Toast the sesame seeds to a deep gold color and cool.

- Grind both ingredients separately with salt and mix together with just enough water to make a cohesive paste.

Salsa de arriero
(Mule-Driver's Sauce)

This is more of a paste than a sauce; one could say it is a "portable" sauce like *chintestle*, originally made to be taken on a journey by a mule driver, as its name implies, to eat with a tortilla or on top of beans. Since there is no water, the chiles are best crushed and ground in a *molcajete* or mortar. It is very picante.

MAKES APPROXIMATELY ¾ CUP (ABOUT 195 ML)

2 tablespoons vegetable oil
1 cup (250 ml) chiltepes
1 garlic clove
Salt to taste

- Heat the oil in a small skillet and fry the chiles until crisp and the garlic until well browned.
- Grind all together with the salt, adding only a drop or so of water if necessary.

Salsa de chiltepes
(Chiltepe Sauce)

SEÑORA BLANCA DE GARCÍA,
HUAUTLA DE JIMÉNEZ

The small dried chiltepes and the fresh canarios (manzanos) are the local chiles most used in the cooking of the Sierra Mazateca, with guajillos brought in from the markets in Puebla.

This sauce should be thick and potent; Señora Blanca assures me it is better made with the chiles cultivated around Ayautla. It is served with frijoles, eggs, or tortillas and *queso*.

MAKES ABOUT 1 CUP (250 ML)

1 garlic clove, peeled
1 cup (250 ml) chiltepes (or substitute 8 chiles de árbol), toasted whole until crisp
⅔ cup (170 ml) water
Salt to taste

- Crush the garlic in a *molcajete* and add the chiles, a few at a time, alternately with the water. Add salt to taste.
- Take care because the chiles burn easily. Grind together, without water, to a textured paste.

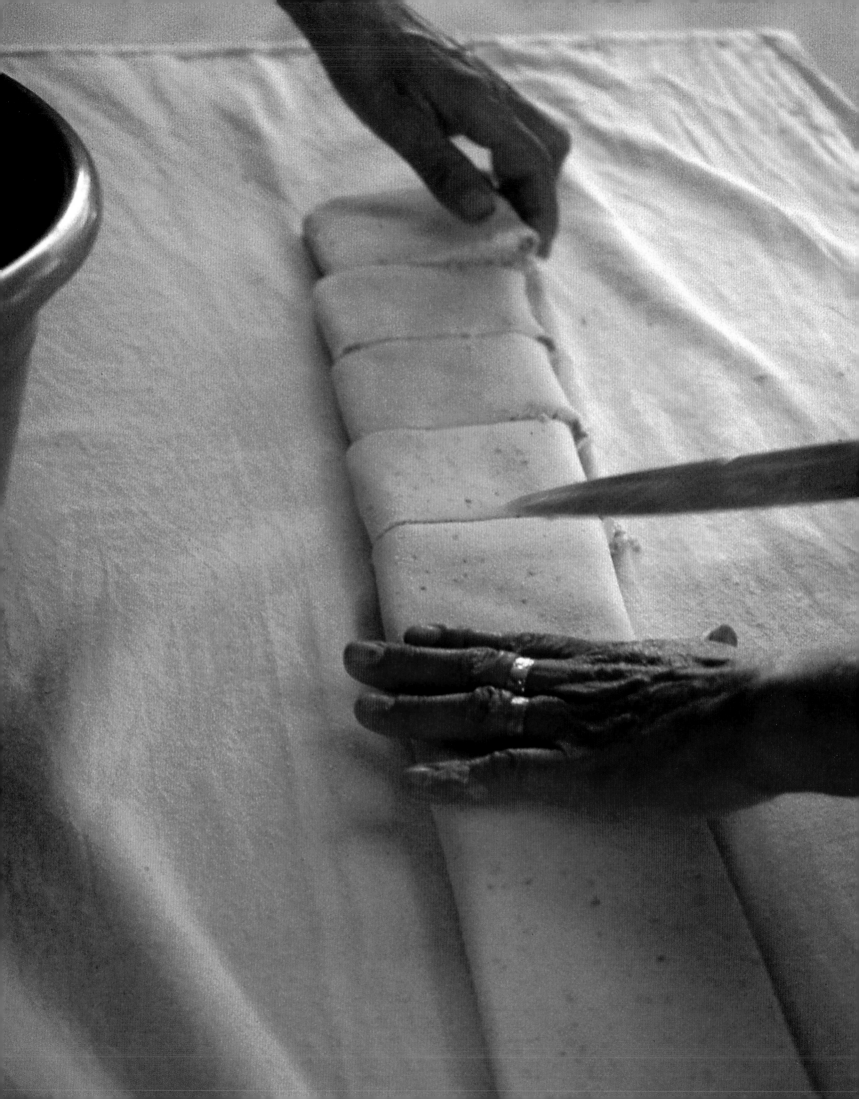

Salsa de tomate con cilantro grueso
(Tomato Sauce with Wild "Cilantro")

The wild or "thick" cilantro is a climbing plant with heart-shaped, fleshy leaves that grows in tropical areas, probably *Piper pseudo-alpino* (see photo p. 355). It has many local names, including *tequelite* in the Sierra Norte de Puebla.

Cilantro grueso is cooked with soupy beans or in meat broths.

Makes 1½ cups (375 ml)

10 ounces (about 300 g) tomatoes
1 chile canario, seeded
1 garlic clove, peeled and finely chopped
6 leaves of *cilantro grueso*, finely chopped, or substitute cilantro
Salt to taste
Finely chopped white onion

- Put the tomatoes and chile into a small pan with water to barely cover and cook over medium heat until both are soft, about 10 minutes.

- Put the garlic, the leaves, and salt into the blender with one of the tomatoes and blend until smooth. Strain the chile and the rest of the tomatoes, add to the blender jar, and blend again, adding some of the cooking water to make a slightly textured sauce of medium consistency.

- Serve with chopped onion on top.

Tepejilotes mazatecos (Mazatecan Tepejilotes)

SEÑORA BLANCA FLORES VDA. DE GARCÍA, HUAUTLA DE JIMÉNEZ

A description of *tepejilotes* is to be found in the Sierra Juárez–Mixe Region section (p. 329), but to describe them briefly, they are inflorescent buds of a palm (*Chamaedorea tepejilote*). They are served like a *botana*.

MAKES 2½ CUPS (625 ML)

12 *tepejilotes*
½ medium white onion, finely chopped
1 chile canario, seeds removed, cut into thin strips
About ½ cup lime juice
Salt to taste

- Cut the base off the *tepejilotes* and make a slit in the tough leaves to release the flower, which is composed of tightly knit strands. Cut the flower into small lengths. Put them into a small pot, cover with boiling water, add salt, and cook over high heat until tender.

- Strain and put into a nonreactive container, mix in the rest of the ingredients, and leave to season for about one hour before using. The dish will keep several days in the refrigerator.

Tesmole de pollo (Ndá se Xo'nda)

SEÑORA BLANCA FLORES VDA. DE GARCÍA, HUAUTLA DE JIMÉNEZ

This is a simple everyday dish in Huautla but also occasionally prepared for some ritual meals. It is considered to be a "cold" dish because of the *yerbasanta* that grows wild in the mountains. They say "*. . . de ahí trae la frialdad,*" or "it brings the cold with it."

The sauce of the *tesmole* is served in a deep plate, but the *yerbasanta* is removed, squeezed into a ball, and served apart. Then a piece of chicken is added. The dish has a lot of flavor because it is cooked with a free-range local chicken.

There is also a local saying that when the masa is added, it must be stirred constantly with a Yá Tobi stick. No other stick should be used because it will spoil the dish: "*Se le echa la masa en la olla moviéndola constantemente con un palo de Yá Tobi. No cualquier palo se usa, porque descompone la comida.*"

MAKES 6 SERVINGS

1 large chicken, cut into 6 portions
Salt to taste
7 cups (1.750 L) water
30 chiltepes, left whole
2 guajillo chiles, seeds removed, or ¼ teaspoon *achiote*
6 *yerbasanta* leaves, tough rib removed, torn into large pieces
1 cup (250 ml)—about 8 ounces—tortilla masa

- Put the chicken pieces to cook with salt in 6 cups (1.5 L) of the water in a pot over medium heat.

- Meanwhile, leave the chiles to soak in hot water for 15 minutes and then strain.

- Put the remaining 1 cup (250 ml) of water into the blender, add the chiles, and blend well. Add to the pot through a strainer with the *yerbasanta* leaves.

- After the chicken has been cooking for about 20 minutes, remove from the broth. Stir 1 cup of the broth into the masa and mix until smooth. Stir into the broth and keep stirring to avoid lumping until the broth starts to thicken a little. Put the chicken back into the pot and cook until the meat is tender, about 20 minutes more.

- The sauce should be of medium consistency.

OLLAS IN SAN LUCAS/DIANA KENNEDY

TACOS OF *POCHICUILES* WITH PULQUE/DIANA KENNEDY

Tesmole de res
(Ndá se Yao Nraja)

SEÑOR RENATO GARCÍA DORANTE,[†]
HUAUTLA DE JIMÉNEZ

The *tesmole* is served in deep bowls with tortillas.

MAKES 6 PORTIONS

3½ pounds (about 1.5 kg) beef with bone and some fat: short ribs and brisket, cut into
    serving pieces
Salt to taste
30 chiltepes, left whole
3 guajillo chiles, seeds removed
4 avocado leaves (see Note on Toxicity, p. 426), fresh or dried, toasted
1 cup (250 ml) tortilla masa

• Put the meat to cook, preferably in a clay pot, with 8 cups (2 L) water and salt for about 30
    minutes.

• Cover the chiles with hot water and simmer for 5 minutes. Drain and blend with ½ cup
    (125 ml) of the meat broth as smooth as possible. Add the purée to the meat through a
    strainer, pressing down to extract as much as possible.

• Add the avocado leaves.

• In a bowl, dilute the masa with 1 cup of the broth, stirring well to a smooth consistency.

• Gradually add to the pot and stir well to
    make sure lumps do not form. Adjust salt.

• Continue cooking over low heat until the
    meat is tender, about another 30 minutes.

TESMOLE DE TASAJO
(NDÁ SE YAO JTÉ NRA)

If *tasajo* is used for a *tesmole*, chiltepes are
used, but a small piece of pure *achiote* is
used instead of the guajillo chiles.

SIERRA SUR

View of the Sierra Sur/Diana Kennedy

Sierra Sur

By Marcus Winter

The Sierra Sur, a mountainous area to the south and southeast of the Valley of Oaxaca, extends toward the coast. The higher areas have pine and oak forests, while the lower areas are warmer and favorable for cultivation of coffee and fruit. The inhabitants are Zapotecs and Chatinos. Typical of the area is mottled white and black granite bedrock that was used in pre-Hispanic times for carved monuments as well as for metates (grinding stones) and manos (mullers, pestles). The mountain slopes of the Sierra Sur are cut by many rivers that flow in nearly parallel courses to the Pacific Ocean.

MAP OF SIERRA SUR/SERGIO AGUIRRE

Adobo de pollo o de carne de res (Chile-seasoned Chicken or Beef)

SEÑORA LUCHA LUZ MENDOZA CUEVAS, JUQUILA

If you are making this adobo with beef, you don't need an expensive cut of meat; any type of stewing beef will work, but with a little fat.

The dish is served topped with sliced onions that have been wilted in lime juice and, of course, with corn tortillas.

6 PORTIONS

6 large portions chicken or 3 pounds (about 3 kg) stewing beef, cut into 12 portions
¼ cup (65 ml) sea salt
¼ cup (65 ml) mild vinegar
2 large ancho chiles, veins and seeds removed
4 (or to taste) red costeño chiles, left whole
10 guajillo chiles, veins and seeds removed
1 pound (450 g) tomatoes, roughly chopped
2 whole cloves, crushed
2 mild peppercorns, crushed
⅛ teaspoon cumin seeds, crushed
1 tablespoon dried Oaxacan oregano leaves or 1½ teaspoons Mexican oregano
4 garlic cloves, roughly chopped
Approximately 1 cup (250 ml) water
3 tablespoons lard or vegetable oil
1–2 cups (250–500 ml) water
4 Mexican bay leaves or 2 bay laurel leaves
1¼ pounds (about 1 kg) very small potatoes, unpeeled
Salt to taste

To serve:
3 medium white onions, cut into half-moons and seasoned with lime juice and salt

- Put the meat into a nonreactive bowl and barely cover with water. Add the salt and vinegar and leave to soak for about one hour. Strain.

- Meanwhile, soak the chiles in warm water until rehydrated, about 15 minutes; strain, leaving the guajillos apart.

- Blend a few of the tomatoes together with the spices and garlic until smooth.

- Gradually add the rest of the tomatoes with the anchos and costeños, adding a little water only if necessary to reduce to a purée. Transfer to a bowl. Put 1 cup of water into the blender and blend the guajillos as smoothly as possible. Add to the other blended ingredients through a fine strainer, pressing hard to extract as much juice as possible from the very tough pieces of skin. Mix together well.

- Heat the lard or oil in a pot in which you are going to cook the adobo, and fry the chicken or meat until golden. Add the blended ingredients and continue frying over medium heat, scraping the bottom of the pan to prevent sticking, for about 5 minutes. Add the bay leaves, potatoes, and water—1 cup for chicken, 2 cups for beef—adjust salt and cook, covered, over low heat until meats are tender and well seasoned, approximately 1 hour for the chicken and up to 2 hours for the beef, depending on quality. It may be necessary to add a little more water for the beef. The sauce should be of medium consistency.

Local breads/Diana Kennedy

Atole de cacahuate
(Peanut Atole)

SEÑORA CLOTILDE CALLEJA, SOLA DE VEGA

A driver who passed through Sola de Vega, in the Sierra Sur, on his frequent trips with visitors to the sanctuary of Juquila, told me about this *atole*. The next time I was driving back from the coast via that route, I stopped on the highway at the modest little Comedor Myra that he had recommended and, after trying the *atole*, asked the owner, Señora Clotilde, for her recipe. It is nutritious and delicious, especially if you like peanuts.

MAKES ABOUT 1½ QUARTS (6 CUPS OR 1.5 L)

8 ounces (250 g) skinned peanuts
1 3-inch (8 cm) piece (or to taste) cinnamon stick, broken up
Approximately 1½ quarts (6 cups or 1.5 L) water
9 ounces (250 g) masa for *atole* (see p. 395)
Piloncillo or brown sugar to taste

- Toast the peanuts (traditionally on a clay comal) slowly, turning them over from time to time, to a golden brown. Set aside to cool. Grind the peanuts (traditionally, this is done on a metate) with the cinnamon and about ½ cup (125 ml) water to a smooth paste.

- Although this can be done in a food processor or heavy blender, I suggest roughly chopping and then grinding the toasted peanuts in a coffee/spice grinder first.

- Put 4 cups (1 L) of the water to heat in a heavy pot or earthenware *olla*. Mix the masa together with the peanut paste and dilute with about 1 cup (250 ml) of the water.

- Add this mixture to the hot water in the pot, pressing it through a strainer; cook over low heat, pressing out any lumps and scraping the bottom of the pan to prevent sticking, until the *atole* begins to thicken. Add the rest of the water and *piloncillo* and continue cooking and stirring for 10 minutes. If the *atole* thickens too much, add water as necessary. If it becomes lumpy, throw it back into the blender.

Empanadas de Sola de Vega (Empanadas of Sola de Vega)

Señora Elodia Quiroz, Sola de Vega

It is traditional in Sola de Vega to serve these wickedly rich empanadas for breakfast on special occasions, weddings, and baptisms. They are filled with the same *picadillo* used for chiles de agua or pasillas de Oaxaca and served topped with sliced onion, parsley, and crumbled cheese. They are also sometimes heated through briefly in a tomato sauce, which of course, softens the pastry a little.

MAKES ABOUT 20 4½-INCH (11 CM) EMPANADAS

Have ready:
About 4 cups (1 L) *picadillo* (p. 190)

18 ounces (roughly 4½ cups) all-purpose flour
4 yolks of large eggs
5½ ounces (150 g) pork lard—about ¾ cup (195 ml)
2 teaspoons sea salt
Approximately ½ cup (125 ml) cold water
Flour for dusting
Melted pork lard for frying

- Mix together flour, yolks, lard, and salt. Gradually add the water, working the dough until all the ingredients are well incorporated and the dough is smooth. Put the dough into a plastic bag and let it rest at room temperature for at least one hour.

- Divide the dough into 20 pieces and roll each one into a smooth ball. Take one of the balls and roll it out into a circle of approximately 5½ inches (about 14 cm). Put 2 tablespoons of the *picadillo* on one side of the dough and fold the other side over to cover it. Pinch the edges together (moisten if necessary) as though you were finishing off a piecrust.

- Heat the lard in a skillet at least 1½ inches (3.75 cm) deep. Dust the empanada lightly with flour just before putting it into the skillet, and fry on both sides until the dough is cooked through and turns a deep golden color, about 2 minutes on each side. Drain on paper towels before serving.

Frijol ancho negro en pipián
(Black Beans in Pipián)

FAMILIA ZABALETA, JUQUILA

I saw large, broad black beans about the size of *ayocotes* being sold in the Juquila market. When I inquired how they were used, the Zabaleta family, who sold them in their store nearby, came to the rescue and gave me this recipe. The beans are grown in the surrounding countryside and brought into town by the growers, half dried and still in their pods.

They are cooked and eaten with their pods, which give a delicate flavor to the *pipián*.

It is impossible to eat this dish delicately, since the stringy sides of the pod are tough and inedible. (It is not impossible for the growing number of home gardeners to leave the pods on their beans.) This *pipián* is served as a main dish with tortillas.

Local cooks bring these beans to a boil and then discard the water before replenishing it for the final cooking.

8 ounces (225 g) large dried or half-dried beans, with their pods wherever possible
Salt to taste
6 ounces (about 180 g) unhulled pumpkin seeds
4 guajillo chiles, seeds and veins removed
3 mild black peppercorns, crushed
1 tablespoon Oaxacan oregano leaves or ½ tablespoon Mexican oregano
3 garlic cloves, peeled and chopped
1 sprig *pitiona* (or substitute marjoram)

- Cover the beans with water in a large pot. Bring to a boil and strain, discarding the water.

- Cover the beans with fresh water, add salt to taste, and cook over medium heat until just tender, about 3 hours.

- In an ungreased pan, toast the seeds until golden, moving them constantly to avoid burning. When they are cool, grind to a fine texture either dry in an electric coffee/spice grinder or in the blender with 2 cups (500 ml) water. If ground dry, mix with 2 cups of water to a smooth consistency. Pass through a fine strainer, pressing down hard to extract as much of the seeds as possible. Set aside.

- Toast the chiles lightly, cover with water, and leave to soak and rehydrate for 10 minutes.

- Drain, add 1 cup of water to the blender, and blend the chiles to a smooth consistency.

- Add to the cooked beans through a strainer (the guajillo skins are usually very tough).

- Put 1 cup of the bean broth into the blender; add the peppercorns, oregano, and garlic and blend smooth. Add this, together with the seeds and the *pitiona,* to the beans; adjust salt and cook over medium heat, stirring from time to time to avoid sticking, for about 20 minutes.

- Serve in deep bowls.

Flores de guachepil
(Guachepil Flowers)

I came across piles of these small yellow flowers one January in the Puerto Escondido market, where they were called *guachepil*. I was told that they were brought down from the sierras rising above the coast, but nobody could tell me what sort of plant they came from. Driving the following year to Sola de Vega, I saw the scraggy trees (*Diphysa robinioides*) covered with these yellow flowers. (I have also seen them used in Huejutla in Hidalgo State.)

The *guachepil* flowers have a faint perfume even when cooked, but unfortunately they lose their color. They are then prepared, either with scrambled eggs, in fritters or *tortitas,* or fried with tomatoes and fresh chile tusta. They are generally eaten for *almuerzo* with tortillas.

3–4 PORTIONS

2 cups (500 ml) *guachepil* flowers
Salt to taste
2 tablespoons vegetable oil
2 tablespoons finely chopped onion
2–3 (or to taste) fresh tusta chiles (or substitute serranos)
3 medium tomatoes, finely chopped
4 eggs, lightly beaten with salt

- Remove the tough little stems of the flowers, rinse in cold water, and strain. Put sufficient water to cover the flowers into a pan with salt to taste. Bring to a boil, add the flowers, and cook until tender, about 5 minutes. Strain.

- Heat the oil in a skillet, add the onion and chiles, and fry until the onion is translucent, about 3 minutes. Add the tomatoes and cook until reduced, about 4 minutes. Add the flowers and continue cooking until all the ingredients are well incorporated, about 5 minutes. Stir in the eggs and keep stirring until they are set.

Mole chatino con puerco
(Chatino Mole with Pork)

SEÑORITA FRANCISCA PÉREZ, SANTA CRUZ ZENZONTEPEC

This mole from the Sierra Sur is not as well known as the other moles of Oaxaca.

It is exceptional in that it includes a variety of nuts and sesame seeds, all of which, except the almonds, are grown in the area. It is very picante.

A tomato cooked in the broth is unusual, but it is only there for flavor.

Pork or chicken can be cooked, or a mixture of the two, in this mole. It is served with white rice.

The amount of lard may seem exorbitant, but it is necessary to prevent the ingredients from sticking to the pan; it can be skimmed off at the end of the cooking.

APPROXIMATELY 10 PORTIONS

THE MEAT

3½ pounds (about 1.5 kg) pork rib chops, with some fat, about ¾ inch (2 cm) thick
1 large tomato, thickly sliced
1 small white onion, coarsely chopped
½ small head of garlic, unpeeled
Salt to taste

THE MOLE

26 (approximately 140 g) guajillo chiles, cleaned of seeds and veins and lightly toasted
25 (½ ounce or 15 g) chiles de árbol, toasted whole
4½ ounces (125 g) unhulled pumpkin seeds, toasted and crushed
4½ ounces (125 g) shelled peanuts, toasted and crushed
2 ounces (about 60 g) unskinned almonds, toasted and crushed
2 ounces (about 60 g) *nuez criollo* (or substitute pecans), toasted and crushed
2 ounces (about 60 g) sesame seeds, toasted
2 tablespoons dried Oaxacan oregano leaves or 1 tablespoon Mexican oregano
¼ teaspoon thyme leaves
4 allspice, crushed
2 cloves, crushed
¼ teaspoon cumin seeds
1 small white onion, sliced and toasted
½ small head garlic, toasted, cloves separated and peeled
½ cup (125 ml) melted pork lard
12 ounces (350 g) tomatoes, toasted (more if the mole is too picante)
Salt to taste

• Put water (sufficient to cover the meat) into a large pot with the sliced tomato, onion, garlic, and salt and cook for about 5 minutes. Lower heat to medium, add the meat, and cook until almost tender, about 40 minutes. Strain, reserving the broth; you will need 10 cups (2.5 L) for the mole. Add water if necessary to make up this amount.

• For the best flavor, grind all the prepared ingredients to a slightly textured paste, without adding water, in a hand-cranked metal grinder or food processor. If not possible, then use the blender, adding the smallest quantity of meat broth possible without burning out the blender motor.

• Heat the lard in a heavy-bottomed casserole, add the paste, and fry over a fairly low flame, stirring constantly and scraping the bottom of the pan to prevent sticking, for 10 minutes.

• Blend the tomatoes and add to the casserole, stirring until well incorporated. Add the remaining broth and continue cooking until the mole begins to thicken. Add the meat with salt to taste and cook over medium heat until tender, about 15 minutes more.

• Skim off excess fat. The mole should be of a medium consistency.

Mole negro de Nopala
(Black Mole of Nopala)

Señora Tomasa Sánchez Rojas, Nopala

This black mole is very similar to that made around Pinotepa, but it is rather more stringent in flavor, owing to the amount of dried herbs—particularly the *almoraduz*—which are cultivated higher up in the Sierra Sur near Miahuatlán.

Since the *almoraduz* is not available (except in some markets of Oaxaca), I have increased the quantity of the other two herbs.

Meat: Either chicken, turkey, or pork is cooked and added with its broth to the prepared mole.

MAKES ENOUGH MOLE FOR 12 PORTIONS

8 ounces (about 250 g) guajillo chiles
10 costeño chiles, dried
Approximately 3 cups (750 ml) water
1 small head of garlic, toasted, cloves separated and peeled
1 medium white onion, cut into quarters and toasted
1½ tablespoons dried thyme leaves
1½ tablespoons dried marjoram leaves
2 peppercorns, crushed
1-inch (2.5 cm) piece cinnamon stick, broken up
5 whole cloves, crushed
1 small corn tortilla, charred black and broken up
4 tablespoons lard or vegetable oil
2¼ pounds (about 1 kg) tomatoes, toasted
Salt to taste
½ cup (125 ml) soft breadcrumbs

- Remove the seeds from the guajillos and costeños, reserving those of the guajillos.

- Toast the chiles in an ungreased skillet until black; cover with cold water and set aside to soak for about 25 minutes. In the same pan, toast the reserved seeds until black (open the windows and have Kleenex and a glass of water at hand), rinse briefly in cold water, and strain. Strain the chiles, add to the blender jar with 2 cups of the water, and blend to a smooth consistency. Strain to remove any tough pieces of skin remaining.

- Add another 1 cup of the water to the blender jar; add the chile seeds, garlic, onion, herbs, and spices and blend well. Then add the tortilla pieces and blend again well, adding a little more water if necessary.

- Heat the lard in a large pan in which you are going to cook the mole, add the (first) blended ingredients and cook over fairly high heat, scraping the bottom of the pan to prevent sticking, for about 5 minutes. Then add the blended chiles and continue frying over medium heat until well seasoned, about 15 minutes.

- Blend the tomatoes (with skins), add to the pan with salt to taste, and cook over medium heat for a further 10 minutes. The mole should have a fairly thick consistency.

- At this stage the mole can be stored for a few days in the refrigerator or freezer.

- When ready to use, heat the mole until bubbling, dilute with about 4 cups of the meat broth, and when it returns to a boil, add the meat and heat through over medium heat for about 15 minutes.

Pan de yema y pulque
(Bread Made of Egg Yolks and Pulque)

SEÑORA MARTHA ÁLVAREZ, JUQUILA

Every afternoon around four o'clock, a large basket of these breads straight from the oven is taken from Señora Martha's house to be sold in the central plaza of Juquila.

There are so many types of *pan de huevo*, sweet breads made with egg yolks, in Oaxaca, but these are, to me, the most interesting and delicious. But, of course, you have to have pulque as a leavener and not blink an eyelid at the thought of 20 egg yolks.

Señora Martha was taught by her mother-in-law, who had spent thirty years making these small round breads with a deliciously rich crust in her wood-fired oven.

The pulque should be specifically for bread making: that is to say, half from the day before and the other half fresh that day.

Baking time and temperature in a wood-fired oven is, of course, very different, so I will give the time for a domestic oven for those who can obtain pulque and can't resist making them.

25 SMALL BREADS ABOUT 3 INCHES (7–8 CM) IN DIAMETER

2¼ pounds (about 1 kg) all-purpose (not bread) flour
7 ounces (200 g) pork lard
1½ cups (250 g) sugar
20 egg yolks
Approximately ¾ cup (about 150 ml) pulque mixed with ⅓ cup (85 ml) sugar

- Put the flour in a circle on a wooden surface. Make a well in the middle; add the lard, sugar, and egg yolks; and mix well together. Gradually work in the flour with the pulque until all ingredients are well integrated. Knead until the dough is smooth and elastic. Form into a round cushion shape, cover with plastic wrap, and leave in a warm place (about 75°F [24°C]) for 14 hours. The dough will be spongy but not inflated like other yeast doughs.

- Divide the dough into 25 portions and roll each one into a smooth ball. Place on a well-floured board or tray, cover, and set aside for about 4 hours.

- Heat oven to 375°F (190°C), slash the tops, and bake breads until they are firm to the touch and a rich brown color (see photo).

Local pan de yema/Diana Kennedy

ANIMAL BREADS/DIANA KENNEDY

Pastel chatino
(Tamale of Chicken Giblets)

Señora María de la Luz Mendoza, Juquila

This is without doubt the most spectacular of all tamales, and delicious to boot.

It is prepared on festive occasions as a *botana*. It was also a way of using up the giblets left over from chicken used for the main dish of mole or whatever.

Although the recipe comes from Señora Mendoza, Señora Malena Solana is its great proponent, and it was she who taught me how to make it.

Although the "*pastel*" can be made even larger, this recipe for one almost 14 inches (35 cm) in diameter is more manageable and fits into a standard-sized aluminum commercial steamer. Originally, of course, it was probably cooked in an earthenware *cazuela*.

Although chicken giblets are used, any meats or vegetables could be substituted.

MAKES ABOUT 25–30 PORTIONS AS A *BOTANA*

START THE DAY BEFORE

Have ready:

A piece of cloth about 25½ inches (65 cm) square to wrap the tamale
    for cooking

10 pieces of banana leaf 47 inches (120 cm) long plus extras for
    lining the steamer

6 pieces of string 47 inches (abut 120 cm) long

15–18 large *yerbasanta* leaves

2 circular pieces of plastic 14 inches (35 cm) in diameter

THE MEAT TO PREPARE THE DAY BEFORE

3½ pounds (1.5 kg) chicken livers and gizzards

⅓ cup (85 ml) fresh lime juice

THE MOLE TO PREPARE THE DAY BEFORE

40 (about 250 g) guajillo chiles, seeds and veins removed

10 dried red costeño chiles, seeds removed

1 medium white onion, coarsely chopped

Cloves of 1 small garlic head, peeled and coarsely chopped

Salt to taste

½ teaspoon cumin seeds, crushed

20 mild black peppercorns, crushed

THE MASA

4 pounds (1.75 kg) textured tamale masa

3 rounded cups (about 700 g) pork lard

Salt to taste

About 1⅓ cups (335 ml) of the chile mixture

THE MEAT

- Wash the giblets well in several changes of water, removing any discolored parts of the livers. Cut into medium-sized pieces. Cover with fresh water, add the lime juice, and leave to soak for 1 hour. Strain.

THE MOLE

- Rinse the chiles, strain, cover with 3 cups (750 ml) hot water, and soak for 20 minutes.

- Strain chiles and reserve the water. Put 2 cups (500 ml) of the water into the blender jar, add the chiles with the onion and garlic, and blend as smooth as possible. Strain into a bowl and add salt to taste.

- Put another ½ cup (125 ml) of the water into the blender jar, add the spices, and blend smooth. Add to the chile purée. Mix ALL BUT 1⅓ cups (335 ml) of the chile mixture into the giblets. It must be juicy, so add a little more of the water if necessary. Refrigerate overnight.

THE MASA

- Beat the masa with the lard and salt. Add the reserved chile purée and continue beating until a ball of the masa floats on the surface of a glass of water. Although this was done by hand, the masa can be beaten in an electric mixer. Divide into three portions.

- Spread the cloth out flat onto a board or tray. Wilt the banana leaves and place them crosswise over the cloth. Place the *yerbasanta* leaves, overlapping, to form a circular layer 39½ inches (1 m) in diameter. (The leaves have to cover the *pastel* completely.)

- Start the heat under the steamer.

- Sprinkle water over one of the pieces of plastic. Spread one-third of the masa evenly over it; it will be just over ½ inch (about 1.5 cm) thick. Turn it onto the layer of *yerbasanta*. Spread half of the giblet mixture evenly over this. Repeat with another third of the masa, add the remaining giblets, and cover with the remaining masa.

- Fold the *yerbasanta* leaves over the top layer of masa until it is completely covered.

- Then fold over the banana leaves to form a round package. Cover with the cloth and tie the corners into a knot on top. Tie the package firmly, but not too tightly, with the string and carefully place in the top of the hot steamer. Cook over fairly high heat until the masa is firm to the touch, about 2½ to 3 hours. Let the *pastel* rest for about 15 minutes to allow the masa to set a little before serving.

Pastel de pollo ("Pastel" of Chicken)

Señora Elodia Quiroz, Sola de Vega

This *pastel* is prepared for very special occasions: weddings, baptisms, and *mayordomías*. Traditionally, it is cooked in a clay *cazuela* over a charcoal fire.

And that was how Señora Elodia cooked it for me.

This is a very substantial and rich dish that is served alone.

Since the *nixtamal* is cooked and soaked for a very short time, it is necessary to use more lime than is generally necessary.

MAKES 20 PORTIONS

START THE DAY BEFORE

Have ready:

A large *cazuela* or casserole, liberally greased with lard

THE MASA

2¼ pounds (about 1 kg) dried yellow corn

2 heaped tablespoons powdered lime

2¼ cups (565 ml) melted pork lard

3 saffron threads, blended in a little broth

25 cooked egg yolks, crumbled

2 tablespoons sugar

Salt to taste

THE FILLING

3¼ pounds (about 1.5 kg) stewing pork, cut into 1-inch (2.5 cm) cubes

1 large white onion, coarsely chopped

1 garlic head, halved horizontally

Salt to taste

1 large chicken, cut into 8 pieces

3¼ pounds (about 1.5 kg) tomatoes, finely chopped

1 small head garlic, cloves peeled and finely chopped

¾ cup (195 ml) peeled and chopped almonds

1 cup (250 ml) raisins

1 small bunch parsley, thick stalks removed, roughly chopped

5 mild black peppercorns, crushed

5 cloves, crushed

1 inch (2.5 cm) cinnamon stick, crushed

1 tablespoon dried Oaxacan oregano leaves, crushed, or 1½ teaspoons Mexican oregano

Salt to taste

½ cup (125 ml) sugar

About 1 cup (250 ml) meat broth

Cooked whites of 25 eggs, quartered

THE MASA

- Put water, sufficient to well cover the corn, into a nonreactive pot and bring to a simmer. Stir in the lime and corn kernels and cook over medium heat until you can scrape the skin off the corn easily, about 10 minutes. Set aside to cool and, as soon as possible, strain and wash in several changes of water, rubbing the kernels to loosen as much of the skins as possible. Crush the corn roughly in a mill or a food processor; it is not ground to a normal masa for tamales.

- Beat the prepared corn with the lard, saffron, yolks, sugar, and salt.

THE FILLING

- Put the pork into a large pot with the onion, garlic, salt, and water to cover. Bring to a boil and cook over medium heat for about 20 minutes. Add the chicken pieces and continue cooking until the meats are almost cooked, about another 30 minutes. Strain, reserving the broth.

- Cut the meat into very small cubes. Add the tomatoes, garlic, almonds, raisins, parsley, spices, oregano, salt, and sugar and mix well. Moisten with 1½ cups (375 ml) of the meat broth, finally stirring in the egg whites, taking care not to break them up.

TO MAKE THE PASTEL

- Take two-thirds of the masa and spread it evenly over the interior of the casserole—it should be about ¾ inch (about 2 cm) thick. Fill with the meat mixture and cover smoothly and evenly with the rest of the dough. Spread the surface with a thin coating of lard and cover securely with two layers of banana leaf. Cook either traditionally, as mentioned above, or in a very low oven for about 7 hours.

PALO DE CHILE/DIANA KENNEDY

Huichimil beans/Diana Kennedy

Torta de huevo con masa (Egg-and-Masa "Omelet")

SEÑORA TOMASA SÁNCHEZ, NOPALA

Presumably, this was a way to extend eggs for a numerous family, but eaten with a sauce, it makes for a very tasty breakfast.

Señora Tomasa ground the salt and chile together in a *molcajete* and cooked the *torta*, without oil, on an unglazed clay comal. I have adapted this slightly and suggest cooking with a little lard or oil in a 10-inch (25 cm) cast-iron skillet. I also like to add some finely chopped onion.

FOR 2 PORTIONS

1 fresh chile costeño or serrano, finely chopped
1 tablespoon finely chopped white onion (optional)
Salt to taste
⅔ cup (170 ml) tortilla masa
About 4 tablespoons water
2 large eggs, lightly beaten
1 *yerbasanta* leaf, stalk and main vein removed, finely shredded
1 tablespoon melted lard or vegetable oil

• Mix the chile, onion (if used), salt, and masa together with the water.

• Add the egg and *yerbasanta* and combine well.

• Heat the lard or oil in a 10-inch (25 cm) skillet. Add the mixture and cook over low heat until it begins to brown slightly underneath. Turn the *torta* over and cook on the second side—for a total of about 8 minutes. Serve immediately.

Huichimiles con res (Beans with Dried Beef)

It was one Saturday in January, and Juquila was in a festive mood for their patron saint's day. The Indians from villages around the area were selling in the central plaza herbs and produce from their smallholdings, among them yellow ochre–colored beans still in their dried pods, or *huichimiles*. These beans, cooked in their pods with semidried beef, are one of the most popular dishes of the area. Because of their rather strong taste, it is customary there to first bring the beans to a boil in water and strain before cooking. This water is then discarded.

On the upper floor of the market, you can find the meat stands draped with the thinly cut dried flank steak specifically for this dish.

The cooked bean pods are juicy and flavorful but stringy, and eating them is a rather messy business! This meal is served in deep bowls, with corn tortillas.

1 pound (450 g) *huichimil* beans in their pods or mature peas in their pods
1¼ pound (about 550 g) flank steak, thinly cut, dried, and cut into serving pieces
2 very large scallions, roughly chopped with leaves
½ small head garlic, cut horizontally
Salt to taste
4 quarts (4 L) water
10 dried red costeño chiles
6 cloves, crushed
6 mild black peppercorns, crushed
½ tablespoon dried Oaxacan oregano leaves or ¼ tablespoon Mexican oregano
1 small bunch mint
1 small bunch cilantro

• Put the beans and their pods into a large pot, cover with boiling water, and cook for 5 minutes. Strain and cover with 3 quarts fresh water. Add the meat, onions, garlic, and salt (but remember, the meat may be salty) and cook over medium heat until both beans and meat are just tender, about 2½ hours, adding more water if necessary.

• Meanwhile, toast the whole chiles lightly, cover with water, and leave to soak for 10 minutes. Drain and put into the blender jar with the cloves, peppercorns, oregano, and 1 cup (250 ml) of the cooking water. Blend smooth and add to the pot.

• When the meat and beans are tender, add the bunches of herbs and cook for a further 10 minutes.

THE CENTRAL VALLEYS

CENTRAL VALLEY AGRICULTURE/MICHAEL CALDERWOOD

The Central Valleys

By Marcus Winter

The Valley of Oaxaca, situated in the center of the state, is the largest flat area in the Mesoamerican highlands between the state of Puebla and central Guatemala. The climate is temperate, and the valley floor, at an elevation of 1,500 meters above sea level, has extensive areas of arable alluvial soil. The alluvium is bordered by low foothills covered with guajes, mesquites, and cacti such as nopal, pitahaya, and maguey. The limits of the valley are marked by the higher piedmont and mountains with oak and pine forests.

The valley has three branches: the Etla Valley to the northwest, the Tlacolula Valley to the east, and the Zaachila-Zimatlán Valley to the south. Even farther south and sometimes included in the same Central Valley area, or Valle Grande, are the valleys of Ocotlán, Ejutla, and Miahuatlán, all part of the highland valley Zapotec region. Outside the Central Valleys to the south is the area of Ocotepec, Guilá, and Chichicapan, which are sometimes considered part of the same region.

The Central Valleys are the cradle and heart of Zapotec language and culture. Remains of squash and corn dating back to 8000 BC and 4300 BC, respectively, are among the oldest evidence for plant cultivation in Mesoamerica. Implements for preparing plant foods (metates and manos, or grinding stones and mullers) also attest to early agriculture in Oaxaca.

Permanent village settlements appear in the Valley by around 1500 BC, and between 1200 BC and 900 BC the Valley Zapotecs interacted with the Olmecs of the Gulf Coast. At this time, cylindrical ceramic vessels, possibly used for drinking cacao beverage, appear in the Valley of Oaxaca and the Mixteca Alta. Centuries later, at approximately 600 BC, the comal was invented, evidently by Zapotecs living near the center of the Valley. Use of the comal means that maize was consumed in the form of tortillas; this may be a unique contribution by the Valley Zapotecs to Mesoamerican culture. Slightly later, small ceramic molcajetes (called Suchilquitongo bowls by archaeologists for the first examples recognized) appear widely in the Valley, where they were used to grind chiles and prepare sauces.

Monte Albán, Oaxaca's first city, was founded approximately 500 years BC on a cluster of hills in the center of the Valley, where it flourished for about 1,300 years. Monte Albán, together with numerous other well-known archaeological sites, such as San José Mogote, Dainzú, Lambityeco, Mitla, Yagul, and Zaachila, attest to the complexity and grandeur of the pre-Hispanic Zapotecs.

ETLA   o
CD. DE OAXACA
LOS VALLES
TEOTITLÁN DEL VALLE
OCOTLÁN
EJUTLA

MAP OF THE CENTRAL VALLEYS/SERGIO AGUIRRE

VIEW OF CENTRAL VALLEY/DIANA KENNEDY

Ejutla Area

/Diana Kennedy

Coloradito de pollo
(Coloradito with Chicken)

SEÑORITA SOLEDAD DÍAZ, CIUDAD DE OAXACA

Coloradito is one of the several moles typical of the cooking of the Valley of Oaxaca.

Traditionally, the ingredients were toasted then ground on the metate. Nowadays, the ingredients are prepared and taken to be ground dry at the nearest commercial *molino*.

Failing those options, the prepared ingredients can either by ground dry in a hand-cranked metal grinder at home or blended with broth in the blender. This latter method is the one given here.

ABOUT 10 PORTIONS

1 large scallion, cut into 4 pieces with leaves
½ small head garlic, cut in half horizontally
Salt to taste
10 large serving pieces of chicken (or pork)
8 ancho chiles, seeds and veins removed
18 guajillo chiles, seeds and veins removed
⅓ cup (85 ml) sesame seeds
1 small head garlic
1 medium white onion, cut into 4 pieces
¼ teaspoon dried thyme leaves
¼ teaspoon dried marjoram leaves
4 cloves, crushed
4 mild black peppercorns, crushed
1-inch piece cinnamon stick, crushed
Melted pork lard for frying
¾ cup (190 ml) roughly chopped pecans
Rounded ½ cup (about 300 ml) unskinned almonds
6 small rounds dry, semisweet bread (semisweet Oaxacan *pan de huevo*)
½ cup (125 ml) raisins
1½ pounds (675 g) tomatoes
2 ounces (about 50 g) Oaxacan drinking chocolate, broken up
Sugar and salt to taste

- In a large pot, put water to boil (enough to cover the chicken pieces); add the onion, garlic, and salt and cook for a few minutes. Lower heat, add the chicken pieces, and cook over medium heat until almost tender. Strain, reserving the broth; you will need 5–6 cups (1.25–1.5 L). Add water if necessary to make up this amount.

- Put a comal or skillet over low heat and toast the chiles lightly until they just begin to change color. Rinse in cold water, strain, then cover with warm water and leave to soak and soften, about 15 minutes. Strain.

- In an ungreased pan, toast the sesame seeds until golden—take care because they burn easily. When cool, grind finely in a *molcajete* or electric grinder.

- On the comal, toast the garlic and onion until partially cooked and slightly browned.

- Separate the garlic cloves, peel, and put into blender jar with ¾ cup (190 ml) of the chicken broth. Add the onion, the herbs, the spices, and the ground sesame and blend, adding more broth if necessary, to a fairly smooth paste.

- Heat 3 tablespoons of lard in a heavy casserole in which you are going to cook the mole. Add the paste and fry over medium heat, scraping the bottom of the pan to prevent sticking, about 3 minutes. Remove from heat.

- Put 1 cup (250 ml) of the broth into the blender and first blend the ancho chiles. Add to the casserole. Repeat this process with the guajillos but adding the sauce through a strainer, pressing down hard to extract as much juice and flesh as possible. There will be some tough skin debris left in the strainer. Remove casserole from heat.

- Put a little more lard into a small skillet and fry separately, and then crush, the pecans, the almonds, and the bread; then fry the raisins, adding a little more lard as necessary.

- Shake these ingredients in a strainer to drain off excess fat and put into the blender; blend with another 1 cup of the broth. Add to the casserole and cook the mixture over medium heat, stirring to prevent sticking, for about 20 minutes.

- Meanwhile, put the tomatoes into a pan, barely cover with water, and cook until soft, about 10 minutes. Blend smooth and add to the mole with the chocolate, sugar, and salt as necessary and cook over medium heat for 15 minutes. Add the chicken pieces and heat through for about 10 minutes more.

Enchiladas de mole/Michael Calderwood

Enchiladas de bautizo
(Enchiladas for a Christening)

SEÑORITA SOLEDAD DÍAZ, CIUDAD DE OAXACA

Señorita Soledad gave me this and other recipes from her late grandmother, Señora Paula Ríos, a native of Ejutla.

These delicious enchiladas, served with white rice, used to be the traditional dish served at baptisms, but times have changed and other dishes have taken precedence.

The tortillas are covered with a *coloradito* and filled with a rich *picadillo*, usually made on those occasions with three different meats: chicken, pork, and beef.

12 ENCHILADAS

Pork lard or vegetable oil for frying
12 6-inch (15 cm) tortillas
Approximately 3 cups (750 ml) mole *coloradito* (p. 243), heated
Approximately 4 cups (1 L) *picadillo* (p. 28), heated

To garnish:
1 cup (250 ml) crumbled *queso fresco*
1 medium white onion, halved and cut thinly into half-moons
1 cup (250 ml) coarsely chopped flat-leaved parsley

Have ready:
1 or 2 ovenproof dishes, about 2 inches (5 cm) deep, into which the enchiladas will just fit in one layer

- Heat a little of the lard or oil in a skillet and fry the tortillas, one by one, on both sides, only adding small quantities of oil as necessary.

- Drain on paper towels and pass through the mole so that the tortilla is well coated.

- Fill the enchilada liberally with the *picadillo*, roll up, and place on the serving dish.

- Decorate with the cheese, onion, and parsley and serve.

Pipián de frijol negro
(Black Bean Pipián)

INFORMATION: SEÑORITA SOLEDAD DÍAZ AND SEÑORA PAULA RÍOS, EJUTLA

This extraordinary *pipián*, a combination of black beans, pumpkin seeds, and the fragrant herb *chepiche* (*Porophyllum tagetoides*), is considered a meal in itself, but it is sometimes accompanied by *tasajo* or other grilled meats.

Traditionally, the local taviche chiles are used, but an acceptable substitute would be catarino or cascabel chiles (although not Oaxacan chiles).

4–6 PORTIONS

8 ounces (about 250 g) black beans, picked over and rinsed
½ small white onion, coarsely chopped
6 small garlic cloves, unpeeled
Salt to taste
4 ounces (about 125 g) unhulled pumpkin seeds, toasted
1½ cups (375 ml) water
7 ounces (200 g) tomatoes, coarsely chopped
3 small garlic cloves, peeled and coarsely chopped
1 small bunch *chepiche*, about 3 heaped tablespoons leaves
3 dried taviche chiles, lightly toasted and broken into pieces
1 small ball of tortilla masa—2 ounces (about 60 g)
2 large sprigs epazote
Salt to taste

• Put the beans into a large pot with the onion, garlic, salt, and water to well cover.

• Cook over medium heat until almost tender, about 2 hours, depending on the age of the beans. They should be very soupy, with about 6 cups (1.5 L) of broth. If not, add water up to that amount.

• Meanwhile, grind the pumpkin seeds to a very fine texture. Transfer to a bowl and mix well with the water. Strain the mixture, pressing out well—there will be quite a bit of debris left in the strainer. Set aside.

• Blend together the tomatoes, garlic, *chepiche*, and chiles; add to the beans and cook over medium heat for 10 minutes. Mix the masa with 1 cup (250 ml) of the bean broth and add to the pan with the pumpkin seeds, epazote, and salt to taste and continue cooking the *pipián* until it is well seasoned, stirring to avoid sticking, about 15 minutes. The broth will thicken a little.

Salchichas de res
(Beef Sausages)

Señor Miguel Angel Hernández Corroso, Ejutla

A favorite snack in Ejutla is a "tostada" topped with beef sausage. In fact, it consists of two crunchy tortillas, one spread with a paste of black beans, the other with avocado mixed with a green sauce. Sandwiched in between, skinned and crumbled, is the beef sausage, with pickled chiles with their juice; shredded cabbage; and a mixture of tomato, onion, and radishes seasoned with cilantro, lime juice, and salt—a very satisfying mixture, with all its textures and flavors, but very messy to eat!

The important element in this, of course, is the smoked beef sausage unique to Ejutla.

Señor Miguel Ángel and his son generously showed me how his family has made these sausages almost daily for more than fifty years. They are sold, freshly made, in the market stand of his wife, Señora Ana.

The sausages, skinned and halved horizontally, are also served as a *botana*. They are seasoned with a chile pasilla sauce, the plate decorated with vegetables and radishes.

The sausages are smoked in a specially constructed type of oven. It is, in effect, a rectangular brick construction 50 inches high, the top covered with a grill. Attached to one side is a hinged flat sheet of metal that acts as a cover to retain the heat. Only about five thick logs burning slowly are necessary for the smoking process (see photos here and next page).

MAKES 20 SAUSAGES JUST LESS THAN 3 INCHES (7 CM) LONG

Have ready:
3 pieces of well-cleaned, narrow pork casing, each about 39 inches (98 cm) long and tied securely with a knot at one end
20 small lengths of string for tying

2¼ pounds (1 kg) tender beef, cleaned of fat and cut into cubes
Approximately 1 cup (250 ml) pulque-and-fruit vinegar (see recipe p. 386)
24 small garlic cloves, peeled and roughly chopped
1 heaped tablespoon mixed herbs: dried leaves of thyme, marjoram, and *almoraduz* (see Glossary)
1 tablespoon dried Oaxacan oregano leaves or 1 heaped teaspoon Mexican oregano
Salt to taste

- Grind the meat as finely as possible and put into a glass bowl.

- Put the vinegar into the blender jar; add the garlic, herbs, and salt and blend until smooth. Add to the meat and mix well. Set aside to season for ½ hour.

- Start heating the oven/grill. Stuff the meat into the casings, either by hand with a funnel or by using the stuffing attachment to a electric mixer. Twist and tie into 3-inch (7.5 cm) lengths, securing the ends tightly. Place the lengths of stuffed casings onto the grill, cover with the lid, and smoke for ½ hour. Then change from one side to the other and smoke for a further ½ hour. By this time, the sausages should have acquired a dark brown tone and a slightly wrinkled surface.

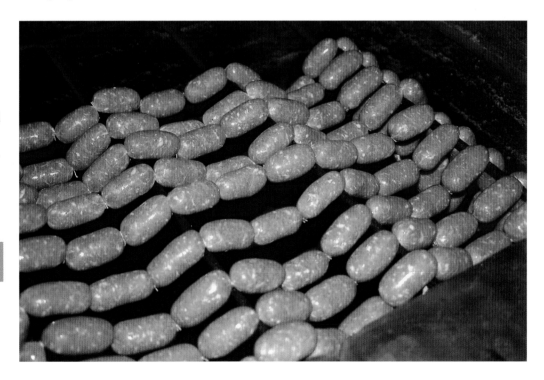

SALSA PARA SALCHICHAS DE RES

(SAUCE FOR BEEF SAUSAGES)

SEÑORA FELISA SORROZA, EJUTLA

Although this sauce is made specially for the local beef sausages, it is also used as a condiment for other *antojitos* in Ejutla.

The sauce is very thin and smooth. Stored in the refrigerator, it will last for months.

MAKES ABOUT 4 CUPS (1 L)

20 medium-sized Oaxacan pasilla chiles
Approximately 4 cups (1 L) fruit vinegar or fruity commercial vinegar
1 small head garlic, cloves separated, peeled, and chopped
5 cloves, crushed
5 mild black peppercorns, crushed
4 inches (about 10 cm) cinnamon stick, crushed
1 tablespoon dried Oaxacan oregano leaves or 1 heaped teaspoon Mexican oregano
Salt to taste

• Remove the stalks from the chiles and wipe them clean with a damp cloth.

• Put them whole into a nonreactive bowl, cover with the vinegar, and soak until soft, about 25 minutes. Tear them up and put into the blender jar with the vinegar in which they were soaking. Add the rest of the ingredients and blend until smooth. Strain and store in glass jars in the refrigerator.

VINAGRE DE PULQUE Y FRUTAS

(PULQUE-AND-FRUIT VINEGAR)

SEÑORA FELISA SORROZA, EJUTLA

Señora Felisa makes a large quantity of this delicious vinegar in a big plastic drum, although originally it was fermented in earthenware barrels. She uses very small, sweet pineapples and apples that have not been grown or sprayed with chemicals. She makes about 100 quarts at a time, and for that she uses:

12 quarts (12 L) pulque
13 pounds (about 6 kg) *panela* (round cakes of raw sugar)
5 very small pineapples, each cut into 6 pieces with the rough skin
20 ripe plantains, cut open, unskinned
15 very small, sweet apples, halves unpeeled
Water to cover

• She puts all the ingredients into the drum with water to cover well. She covers it with just a cloth and, after five days, stirs it all up. It is then left to ferment in a cool place for about 40 days. Then it is strained through a filter and bottled. The vinegar is completely clear and has a light orange color.

SMOKING BEEF SAUSAGES/DIANA KENNEDY

CANELA (CINNAMON STICKS) WITH PILONCILLOS (RAW SUGAR CONES) AND PANELA (RAW SUGAR CAKES)/JORGE LÓPEZ

Etla Area

Making *quesillos*/Michael Calderwood

Tamales de puerco y calabacitas
(Pork and Squash Tamales)

Señora Emilia Arroyo, Etla

In Oaxaca, a delicately flavored squash called *huichi* is grown throughout the year (see photo p. 323). However, you can substitute zucchini for this recipe. The masa is enriched with either *asiento* or *viuces* (see Glossary) but crumbled *chicharrón* and lard could be used as a substitute.

Makes about 30 tamales

Have ready:
A tamale steamer
About 40 cornhusks, soaked to soften and shaken dry

THE FILLING

1¼ pounds (about 500 g) pork ribs, cut into small pieces
½ medium white onion, roughly chopped
½ small head garlic, unpeeled
Salt to taste
1¼ pounds (about 500 g) green squash, trimmed and cut into narrow strips
¼ cup (65 ml) roughly chopped epazote leaves
1¾ pounds (about 750 g) tomatoes, toasted
2 serrano chiles, toasted
About 2 tablespoons lard
½ medium white onion, finely chopped
4 garlic cloves, finely chopped
Salt to taste

THE MASA

2¼ pounds (about 1 kg) tamale masa
5 ounces (140 g) *asiento* or *chicharrón*, finely crumbled
8 ounces (225 g) *viuces* or *chicharrón*, finely crumbled
5 ounces (140 g) lard
Salt to taste
About 1 cup (250 ml) pork broth

- Put the meat, onion, and garlic into a pan with water to cover and salt to taste. Cook over medium heat until the meat is half cooked, about 25 minutes.

- Strain and reserve the broth. You will need about 3 cups (750 ml).

- Return the broth to the pan and bring to a boil; add the squash and cook for 3 minutes only. Strain, set aside to cool, and then mix with the epazote.

- Blend together the tomatoes and chiles.

- Put the meat into a skillet and fry lightly in its own fat, adding a little lard if necessary. Add the onion and garlic and fry until translucent. Add the blended tomatoes and continue frying until the sauce is reduced a little, about 5 minutes.

- Adjust salt.

- Mix the masa with the *asiento*, *viuces*, and lard, adding salt to taste. Add a little of the broth if it is too dry. It should have a moist but not loose consistency.

- Put the steamer to heat.

- Spread 2 scant tablespoons of the masa thinly inside a cornhusk, add a few strips of the squash and a piece of the meat with sauce, and fold the husk so that the masa covers the filling. When all the tamales are assembled, place them vertically in the top part of the steamer and cook until the masa separates easily from the husk, about 1 hour.

Squash Flower tamales/Diana Kennedy

Tamales de flor de calabaza y puerco (Squash Flower and Pork Tamales)

SEÑORA MARGARITA PÉREZ SANTIAGO, SAN GABRIEL ETLA

Señora Margarita, who gave me the recipe for these tamales, wraps them in 2 cornhusks so that they resemble, in her words, "a small ear of (fresh) corn." Although it's not traditional, these tamales can also be filled with a black bean paste and are almost equally delicious.

Señora Margarita uses a small, narrow, very hot chile that she grows in a pot in her patio; it grows with its pointed end upward, hence its name "paradito." It can be substituted by a chile de árbol or any small hot chile ripened to red.

MAKES ABOUT 40 TAMALES

Have ready:
A tamale steamer, lined with dried cornhusks
80–90 dried cornhusks, rinsed and shaken dry

2 pounds (about 900 g) pork ribs, cut into 1½-inch (3.75 cm) pieces, with bone
1 medium white onion, cut into quarters
1 small head garlic, unpeeled, cut in half horizontally
Salt to taste

THE MASA

12 ounces (about 350 g) lard
2¼ pounds (about 1 kg) very textured masa for tamales
Salt to taste
About 1 cup (250 ml) pork broth
3 chiles verdes paraditos or jalapeños, roughly chopped
8 garlic cloves, roughly chopped
1 small bunch epazote, leaves and small stems roughly chopped
1 small bunch flat-leaved parsley, roughly chopped
3 large *yerbasanta* leaves, stems and main veins removed, roughly chopped
12 ounces (about 350 g) green squash, trimmed and cut into small cubes
Salt to taste
20 squash flowers, the bulbous bases halved and petals roughly chopped

- Put the meat, onion, and garlic into a pan; cover with water, add salt, and cook over medium heat until the meat is just tender, but not too soft. Strain, reserving the broth; you will need about 1½ cups (375 ml). Remove bone and shred the meat, but not too finely.

- Using an electric mixer, put the lard in the mixer bowl and beat until fluffy. Gradually add the masa and salt, beating well after each addition. The mixture needs to be rather dry.

- Put ¾ cup (190 ml) of the pork broth in the blender; add the chiles, garlic, and herbs and blend smooth, adding a little more broth if necessary. Stir the mixture with the squash into the masa. Adjust salt.

- Put the tamale steamer on to heat.

- Spread a heaped tablespoon of the masa in one of the husks, fill with a little of the shredded pork and a few of the chopped squash flowers. Fold husk over as for any tamale, cover with a second husk, and form into a cylinder shape.

- When the water in the steamer is boiling, add the tamales vertically in the top section. Cover and steam until the masa separates easily from the husk, about 1 hour.

Tamales de trigo con frijol y poleo
(Flour Tamales with Black Beans and Poleo)

SEÑORA MARGARITA PÉREZ SANTIAGO, SAN GABRIEL ETLA

These tamales were probably invented to use the flour that was produced for decades by the imposing, now-defunct mill in San Gabriel Etla. They are eaten alone as a bread, with a cup of coffee.

Flour tortillas sweetened with *piloncillo* are also made there; they are eaten with fresh cheese.

The herb *poleo* (see Glossary, or *hierba del borracho*, used in these tamales has a minty flavor. While it is often cooked with beans, it is more commonly used in an herbal tea.

The local cooks in Etla usually take their black beans, cooked and strained, to the mill to be ground to a loose paste with the chiles, *poleo*, and some of the bean broth.

Senora Margarita insists that they should be cooked over a wood fire.

MAKES 52 TAMALES

FORMING FLOUR TAMALES/DIANA KENNEDY

Have ready:

A tamale steamer, with the top section lined with cornhusks

About 104 dried cornhusks, with the cupped ends intact, soaked and spun dry

THE BEAN PASTE

18 ounces (500 g) black beans, cooked with salt, broth reserved
½ cup (125 ml) tightly packed *poleo* leaves, rinsed and strained
3 local chiles paraditos or brujas, ripened to red, coarsely chopped
Salt to taste

THE MASA

1¾ pounds (800 g) flour
Salt to taste
About 2 cups (500 ml) cold water

- Strain the beans, reserving the broth. Blend with the *poleo* leaves, the chiles, and about 1½ cups (375 ml) of the broth. (Although in Etla this is taken to the mill to be ground, it can be done in a food processor, although not quite as well.) Add salt as necessary.

- To make the masa, put the flour and salt into a large bowl and stir in the water, a little at a time, mixing well to form a smooth, flexible dough, about 7 minutes. (Experienced cooks here divide the dough into pieces that, miraculously, are all the same size.)

- Form the dough into a roll and cut into 13 pieces; roll each piece into a smooth ball and cover with a damp cloth to prevent drying out. With a thin dowel, roll the ball of dough into a circle—it will be almost paper thin (don't worry if it is irregular). Cut the circle into 4 equal pieces. Roll out the rest of the balls.

- *To form the tamales:* Lay a piece of the dough flat inside the cup of the husk, spread a layer of the bean paste over the surface of the dough, then double one of the points of the dough over to cover the paste, and cover that surface with the paste.

- Continue doubling over the other points, and each time spread paste over the next clean surface. Cover firmly with a second cornhusk and then fold back the pointed ends of the husks.

- Put the steamer to heat; when the water is boiling, place the tamales overlapping in the top section. Cover and cook over high heat for 50 minutes. The masa will be rather chewy when cooked.

EMPOLEADAS

SEÑORA MARGARITA PÉREZ SANTIAGO,
SAN GABRIEL ETLA

Empoleadas are made with any bean paste left over from the tamales and eaten either for *almuerzo* or *comida* to accompany eggs cooked on the comal or a piece of *tasajo*.

Freshly made hot tortillas are dipped into the diluted bean paste to cover well, folded into four, just like *enfrijoladas*, and topped with onions wilted in lime juice (see p. 359) and *queso fresco*.

Hueyapam Area

Cuanesle (Maize Cooked with Wood Ash)

Señora Paula Santiago Ruiz de Méndez, San Andrés Hueyapam

The most traditional of cooks in the Valley of Oaxaca will prepare *cuanesle*, a type of masa, to thicken moles or for some types of tamales. The preparation of the corn differs from that of masa for tortillas in that the corn is cooked with wood ash instead of lime. Señora Paula insists it must be made with local corn.

Makes almost 2 pounds (about 850 g) masa

1¼ pounds (about 500 g) white corn
3 cups (750 ml) wood ash
3 cups (750 ml) water

- Doña Paula rinsed the corn and removed the chaff, then strained it.

- In an earthenware pot, she mixed the ash with the water and heated until well incorporated. Then she added the corn over low heat, stirring constantly to make sure the thick mixture did not stick to the pot. It cooked for about 35 minutes; the grains acquired a dark color.

- She then rubbed the corn to remove the skins in various changes of water. Then she let it soak for about 15 minutes and rinsed it twice more in a perforated clay pot that acted as a strainer. Although she prefers to grind it herself until smooth on the metate (photo p. 21), it can also be taken to the local mill to be ground to a very fine masa.

MAÍZ PARA ATOLE

(CORN COOKED FOR ATOLE)

White (dried) corn is traditionally cooked for *atole* with minor exceptions, and it is cooked without *cal* (lime) or other ingredients. It has various local names, but in Hueyapam it is called *tlaxiahual*.

Of course, there are slight differences in the way cooks prepare theirs. For example, Abigail Mendoza (pp. 420–421) only cooks the corn for 5 minutes and leaves it to soak all night. She refers to it as *naciahual*.

About 1 pound (500 g) dried white corn

- First clean the corn of all impurities, then rinse and strain. Put the corn into (preferably) a clay pot, or *olla*, with water to come about 2 inches (5 cm) above the surface of the corn. Cook over medium heat for 20 minutes—the corn should only be half cooked. It can either be left to soak overnight and then strained, or strained when cool, then sent to the mill to be ground to a completely smooth masa.

- *To make the* atole*:* Dilute the masa with cold water—about 5 cups (1.25 ml)—and strain through cheesecloth into the pot in which you are going to cook the *atole*. (Señora Paula strains hers through a cloth, straining out the residue, or *chilcuastli*, which is given to the pigs or chickens.) It is then cooked over a low heat, stirring and scraping the bottom of pot, because as the mixture thickens it easily sticks and forms lumps. It will take about 15 minutes to cook. The *atole* can then be diluted again to the thickness required either with water or milk. Depending on the type of *atole*, cinnamon sticks, raw sugar, or chocolate can be added as it cooks. As the *atole* stands, it will thicken again.

Frijoles blancos guisados (Stewed White Beans)

Señora Paula Santiago Ruiz de Méndez, Hueyapam

A typical meal during Lent would consist of this dish of small white beans, often served with some dried fish fried in a batter.

Señora Paula, among other cooks, will first cook and strain the beans, throwing the water away—a pity, because a lot of the flavor is lost, so I have omitted that step in this recipe.

6 PORTIONS

12 ounces (350 g) small white beans, picked over and rinsed
1 small white onion, coarsely chopped
½ small head garlic, halved horizontally, unpeeled
Salt to taste
2 cloves, crushed
2 allspice, crushed
1 teaspoon dried Oaxacan oregano leaves or ½ teaspoon Mexican oregano
2 tablespoons vegetable oil
½ medium white onion, thinly sliced
3 garlic cloves, peeled and thinly sliced
6 ounces (165 g) tomatoes, thinly sliced
3 large sprigs flat-leaved parsley, roughly chopped
Salt to taste

- Put the beans into a large pot with the onion, garlic, and salt to taste. Cover well with water and cook, covered, over medium flame until they are tender but not too soft, about 2½ hours, depending on the age of the beans. They should be very brothy.

- Grind together the spices and oregano.

- Heat the oil in a casserole and fry the onion and garlic, with the spices, until translucent.

- Add the tomatoes and continue cooking until the mixture has reduced and seasoned, about 5 minutes. Add 1 cup (250 ml) of the beans and mash well to thicken the mixture a little. Add the beans with their broth and the parsley and cook, uncovered, over low heat until all the flavors have blended, about 25 minutes. Adjust the salt.

Tejate vendor in Tlacolula market/Diana Kennedy

Tejate

Visitors to the central market of Oaxaca are always fascinated to see, and try for the first time, a beige-colored foamy drink being dispensed from a large green-glazed *cazuela*.

The women beating this *tejate* to a froth and serving it in gourds will most likely be from San Andrés Hueyapam, a village situated a few kilometers from the City of Oaxaca, where it has been prepared for centuries. *Tejate* is an indigenous drink that not only quenches the thirst but provides calories in a most intriguing form. Naturally, through the years, I am sure it has undergone several changes: the addition of commercial white sugar, for instance, and, in this recipe, the addition of peanuts, frowned on by other cooks.

Some years ago, Señora Irene prepared some *tejate* for me at her home in Hueyapam. Her father had collected the fragrant white flowers called *rositas de cacao* from a large tree (*Quararibea funebris*) in front of the house; the flowers had been dried for the *tejate*.

Preparing this drink is a laborious process that begins with the preparation of the corn; this has to be a native white corn, *maíz criollo*, with a thin, almost round kernel.

First, she put wood ash in a pot with water to cook for about 15 minutes; this water was then strained through a fine-mesh plastic bag. One kilogram (about 2¼ pounds) of the dried corn was added to the water and cooked for 15 minutes. When cool, it was rinsed and rubbed between the hands to loosen the papery skins; this process had to be repeated several times until the corn was completely clean. It was then taken to the mill and ground to a very smooth dough. But that was not good enough for Señora Irene; she pressed it out on the metate to make sure it was completely smooth and then spread it out to cool off completely.

She then toasted on the comal, briefly and separately: a handful of the dried flowers; the shelled peanuts; and 10 *pixtles*, the large oval, shiny brown seeds of the mamey fruit (other cooks will use *coquito de aceite*, the fruit of a palm), which had been soaking in water for ½ hour. Finally, the cacao beans were toasted until the skin was brittle and could be peeled off. This also took about ½ hour.

Then the grinding on the metate began: first the *pixtles*, with the cacao and flowers, and after they had been reduced to a smooth paste, she added the corn masa and the peanuts.

For the final preparation of the *tejate*, a ball of this paste was beaten with water in a gourd, sugar was added, and within only a minute, a rich foam formed on the surface; the *tejate* was ready to serve.

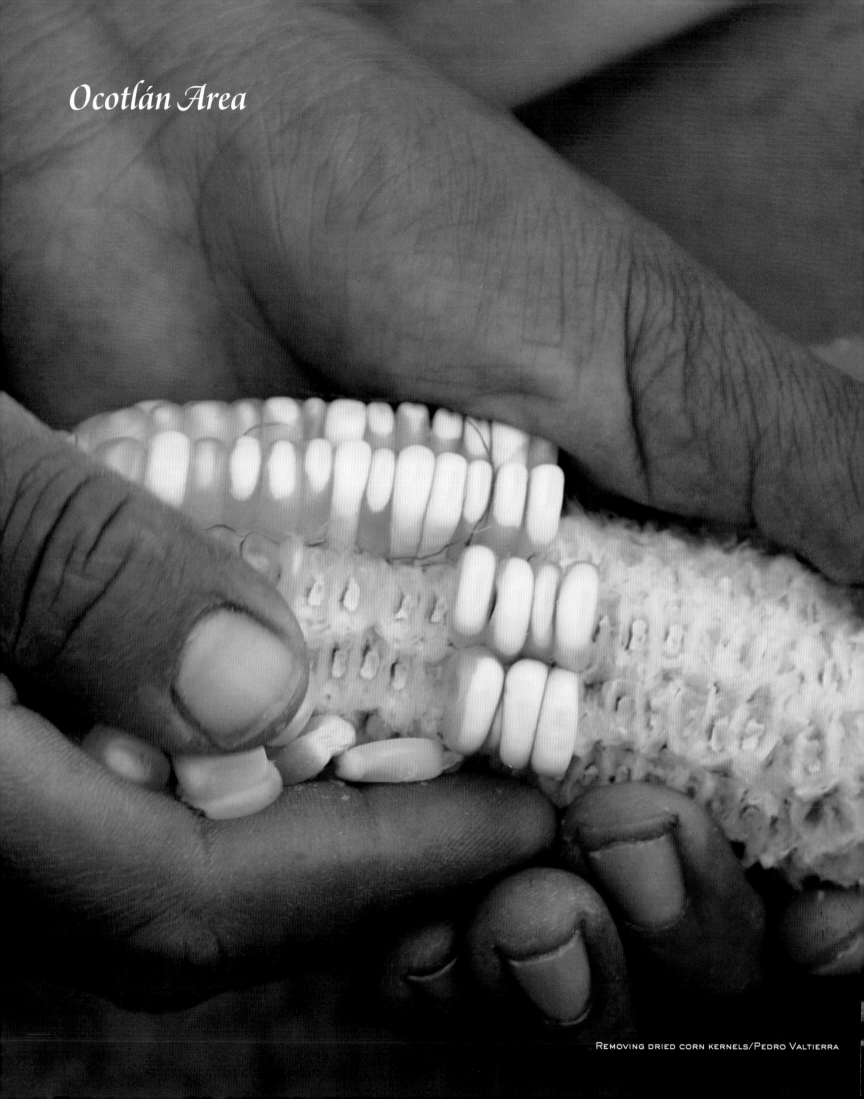

Ocotlán Area

Chichilo negro de Ocotlán
(Black Chichilo from Ocotlán)

SEÑORA GUILLERMINA SÁNCHEZ VDA. DE MORALES, OCOTLÁN

Señora Guillermina, sister-in-law to the famed artist Rodolfo Morales, is a renowned cook in Ocotlán, especially for this *chichilo*. It was a favorite of Maestro Morales, as were her tamales of black mole. The predominant flavor, apart from the chiles, is that of an aromatic herb, *hierba de conejo* (*Tridax coronopiifolia*), used in Oaxacan food, for which, alas, there is no substitute.

The *chichilo* is served in deep plates with sliced onion and limes.

10 PORTIONS

THE MEAT AND VEGETABLES

1 medium white onion, roughly chopped

1 small head garlic, cut in half horizontally

4½ pounds (about 2 kg) beef, with bone, cut into serving pieces: brisket, short ribs, etc.

Salt to taste

12 ounces (340 g) green beans, trimmed and each cut into two pieces

1 chayote about 12 ounces (340 g), cut into 10 wedges, with seed

1 pound (450 g) small potatoes, or large ones, peeled and cut into small pieces

1 cup (250 ml) cooked and skinned chickpeas

THE MOLE

2 medium tomatoes, toasted

4 *tomates verdes,* cut into quarters raw

2 whole peppercorns, crushed

¾-inch (about 2 cm) piece cinnamon stick, broken up

2 whole cloves, crushed

¼ teaspoon cumin seeds, crushed

6 black chilhuacles, cleaned of veins and seeds

3 mulato chiles, cleaned of veins and seeds

3 guajillo chiles, cleaned of veins and seeds

About 4 tablespoons lard

1 cup (250 ml) tortilla masa

5 avocado leaves (see Note on Toxicity, p. 426), toasted crisp

1 large bunch *hierba de conejo* (optional)

Salt to taste

- Put 3 quarts (3 L) water into a large pot, add the onion and garlic, and cook for 5 minutes.

- Add the meat, with salt to taste, and cook over medium heat until just tender, not soft, about 1¼ hours, depending on the cut used. Add the vegetables and chickpeas and continue cooking for about 20 minutes more. Strain and reserve the broth, which should yield about 10 cups (2.5 L); if not, reduce or add water to that amount.

- Toast the chiles, pressing them out on the comal or griddle with a spatula until they are almost charred. Put the chiles into a bowl, cover with warm water, and leave to soften—about 15 minutes. Strain.

- Put 1 cup (250 ml) of the broth in the blender; add the tomatoes, *tomates verdes,* and spices and blend well. Add a second cup of the broth and blend the chiles, a little at a time, blending well after each addition, until smooth.

- Heat the lard in a large pot in which you are going to cook the *chichilo* and fry the chile mixture, stirring and scraping the bottom of the pan to avoid sticking, over fairly high heat until reduced and seasoned, about 10 minutes.

- Put 2 cups (500 ml) of the broth into the blender, add the masa, and mix until smooth.

- Add this little by little to the chile mixture, stirring continuously to avoid lumping or sticking to the pan, which it readily does. Add the whole avocado leaves and *hierba de conejo* with the remaining broth and cook over medium heat until bubbling for about 15 minutes.

- Add the meat and vegetables, adjust seasoning, and continue cooking over medium heat until all is well seasoned and pools of fat form on the surface, about 15–20 minutes.

Empanadas de San Antonino
(Empanadas of San Antonino)

SEÑORA GUILLERMINA SÁNCHEZ VDA. DE MORALES, OCOTLÁN

These large, orange-colored empanadas filled with chicken and *amarillo*, heavily seasoned with cilantro, are, it is said, originally from San Antonino. Along the main street outside the market of Ocotlán, the making of these delicious empanadas by several local women is now a daily sight. They are traditionally cooked on a clay comal coated with a lime wash over a charcoal-fired brazier. If enough lard has been used, the orangey color of the mole will seep through the masa and make the empanada even more delicious. They are served with chopped onion and lime juice, with a radish or two to bite on.

It is best to use this quantity of lard because, apart from the flavor it imparts, it prevents the empanada from drying out when reheated.

> **MAKES 24 EMPANADAS APPROXIMATELY 8 INCHES (20 CM) LONG**
> **(YOU CAN, OF COURSE, MAKE SMALLER ONES.)**

Have ready:

A large tortilla press at least 9 inches (22.5 cm) in diameter

5½ pounds (2.5 kg) tortilla masa

THE CHICKEN

4 cups (1 L) water or chicken broth

1 very large scallion, coarsely chopped with leaves

3 garlic cloves, peeled

Salt to taste

3 chicken breasts, with bone and skin—approximately 2¾ pounds (1.35 kg)

- Put the water or broth, with the onion, garlic, and salt, into a pan and cook for about 5 minutes. Add the chicken and cook over low heat until just tender, about 25 minutes.
- Set aside to cool in the broth. There should be 5 cups (1.2 L) broth for the mole.
- Strain, reserving the broth. Remove the bones and shred the meat not too finely, with skin, if desired, for flavor. Season with salt to taste.

THE YELLOW MOLE

MAKES 8 CUPS (2 L)

4 ancho chiles, seeds and veins removed

12 guajillo chiles, seeds and veins removed

5 cups (1.25 L) chicken broth (see above)

1 medium tomato, toasted

2 garlic cloves, toasted whole and peeled

2 mild black peppercorns, crushed

2 cloves, crushed

¼ teaspoon cumin seeds, crushed

12 ounces (350 g) tortilla masa—about 1⅓ cups (about 335 ml)

16 ounces (450 g) melted pork lard—about 2 cups (500 ml)

3 tightly packed cups coarsely chopped cilantro

Salt to taste

- Lightly toast the chiles on a warm comal or in a skillet, rinse in cold water, strain, and soak—anchos and guajillos separately—in hot water until soft, about 10–15 minutes. Strain.
- Put ½ cup (125 ml) of the broth in the blender jar. Add the tomato, garlic, and spices and blend well. Add the ancho chiles with another cup of the broth and blend until smooth. Transfer to a casserole. Add 1 cup (250 ml) of the broth to the blender and blend the guajillos, a few at a time, to a smooth purée. Add this to the casserole through a strainer, pressing down well. There will be some debris of chile skins left in the strainer.
- Put the masa into the blender jar with 2 cups (500 ml) of the broth and blend until smooth. Add to the casserole with the melted lard, cilantro, and salt to taste. (The mole is not cooked.)

MAKING THE EMPANADAS

- Divide the tortilla masa into 24 pieces and form each one into a smooth ball of about 2 inches (5 cm) in diameter. Cover with a damp cloth while you form and cook the empanadas.
- Roll one of the balls of masa into a cylinder about 6 inches (15 cm) long. Line the tortilla press with plastic and press dough out to a very thin oval shape.
- Spread ⅓ cup (85 ml) of the mole over the center of the dough, leaving an edge of about 1 inch (2.5 cm) free. Sprinkle liberally with more cilantro, add some of the chicken, and, aided by the plastic, fold the masa over to cover the filling. Press the edges together to seal, and cook on an ungreased comal over medium heat for about 10 minutes on each side.

Guetabaches
(Steamed Masa-and-Yerbasanta Tortillas)

SEÑORA GUDELIA LÓPEZ DE RUIZ, SANTIAGO APÓSTOL

This very unusual and little-known tortilla is unique to the area around Ocotlán.

Señora Gudelia's daughter, Ana Bertha, a judge, taught me how to make them.

Guetabaches are made when there are fresh corn leaves (not husks) available for wrapping. Traditionally, they are served to accompany a mole in a festive meal.

Any leftovers are reheated for supper or breakfast, spread with a bean paste or eaten with a chile sauce.

Originally *guetabaches* were steamed in an earthenware *cazuela* set on an organic rack—reeds rolled into a type of nest, which held the tortillas above the level of the water—and, of course, cooked over a wood fire.

> **MAKES 14 TORTILLAS ABOUT 6½ INCHES (ABOUT 17 CM) IN DIAMETER**

Have ready:

About 50–56 long, fresh corn leaves

A steamer at least 8 inches (29 cm) in diameter and a rack to hold the tortillas above the water

8 *yerbasanta* leaves, stems and main vein removed

3¼ pounds (about 1.5 kg) tortilla masa

Salt to taste

- Put the steamer to heat. Tear or cut the *yerbasanta* leaves into small squares and mix them, along with salt to taste, into the masa until they are evenly dispersed. Divide the masa into 14 pieces and roll each one into a smooth ball a little over 2 inches (5 cm) in diameter.

- Using a tortilla press lined with plastic, press one of the balls out to a circle about 6½ inches (17 cm) in diameter. Remove the top plastic just to loosen, and replace. Turn the whole thing over and remove the (now) top plastic. Cover the exposed surface of the dough with the zigzagging doubled-over corn leaves to form a support for the tortilla, then remove the second plastic and cover the other side. Proceed with the rest, placing them one on top of the other on the steamer rack. Cover the steamer with a tightly fitting lid and steam until the masa is cooked, about 30 minutes.

- Serve immediately in their wrapping.

Teotitlán Area

Teotitlán del Valle

Teotitlán del Valle is a Zapotec weaving village situated 23 kilometers to the east of the City of Oaxaca. The inhabitants there have faithfully preserved their traditions despite the great changes that have occurred during the last few decades in the capital city not far away and influences brought back by those who have emigrated to the United States in search of work.

Like the life in all traditional villages, the year is punctuated by religious festivals, *mayordomías*, and *fandangos* to celebrate weddings. These occasions require communal efforts to produce ritual meals on a very large scale to respect the interchange of social responsibilities, or Guelaguetza; in the case of a *fandango de boda*—a five-day wedding celebration—there are responsibilities and reciprocities to be met between families or future families or neighbors who have helped in the preparation of the meals.

Without a doubt, one of the most distinguished protagonists in this field is Señorita Abigail Mendoza. She is the eldest daughter of a large family whose late father was very much respected, having been the *mayordomo* in celebrating La Imagen de la Preciosa

Sangre de Cristo on various occasions. Owing to her mother's ill health, she was obliged to assume the responsibility at a youthful age of organizing the preparations of the ritual foods indispensable for these occasions. Taught and guided by her maternal grandmother and an aunt, she quickly learned the delicate and precise preparation of *cacao blanco*, for example (p. 412), and by the age of twenty, she, helped by her "galaxy" of younger sisters, was capable of organizing these laborious events with a precision that many accomplished banquet chefs, even CEOs, of today would respect and even envy.

Several years ago, I was invited to attend a family *fandango* celebrating the marriage of one of Abigail's brothers. It was a memorable experience, and I still marvel today at the enormous communal effort involved, with the woman working so hard for such long hours for five consecutive days with such good humor and patience. But I learned that it served as a social get-together for exchanging news and gossip, particularly among the younger women and girls; as a large group of them were grinding cacao, kneeling in front of their metates, I heard giggles and discreet laughter ebbing and flowing over them like waves.

Agua del pastor
(Shepherd's Water)

Señorita Abigail Mendoza, Teotitlán del Valle

Until a few years ago, when the women of the Zapotec village of Teotitlán went down to the river to wash clothes or the campesinos to work in the fields, they would take with them their food for the day: a refreshing but nutritious *agua del pastor*. The water and ingredients are carried separately and the meal prepared just before serving in one large communal *cazuela*, or several smaller ones, that are also shared, each person using a *tlayuda* to scoop up the mixture.

A piece of grilled *tasajo* is often eaten with it.

For 6–8 portions

3 quarts (3 L) cold water

Juice of 4 limes

2 large scallions, finely chopped with leaves

2 chiles de agua, toasted, skinned, and seeds removed, cut into strips

4 large Oaxacan pasilla chiles, lightly toasted (in ash) and seeds removed, torn into small pieces

1 large bunch cilantro, roughly chopped

4 hard-cooked eggs, cut into small pieces

Salt to taste

• Add all the prepared ingredients to the water with salt to taste.

Edible bean flowers/Diana Kennedy

Chapulines

Although *chapulines* are consumed in rural communities in many parts of Mexico, and have been throughout the ages, today one immediately thinks of Oaxaca, where *chapulines* (*Sphenarium magnum*) are sold in large quantities throughout the year in the markets of the Central Valley. They are at their best during the early part of the rainy season, starting around June 24, when they are small and feed on alfalfa. Later on in the season they become slightly bitter when they begin to eat the plant that gives a yellow flower known as *acahual*.

When the *chapulines* are very small, they have to be separated, *expurgados* (Abigail's word), as they are usually collected along with smaller, sometimes bitter-tasting insects—a very exacting job that requires good eyesight! At this stage, they are cooked for about three minutes in boiling water and left intact. When they are much larger, *patones*, they have to be cooked for about 5 minutes and their long legs removed.

Chapulines are seasoned with a *mojo*, a mixture of garlic, lime juice, and salt crushed together in a *molcajete* or *chilmolera*, and just before serving they are fried crisp in a little oil and either put into tacos or served as part of a *botana oaxaqueña* (photo p. 54), accompanied by a *salsa de chile pasilla* (see p. 55) or guacamole.

Apart from being delicious, *chapulines* are nutritious, containing a high proportion of proteins and amino acids.

The demand for *chapulines* has grown to such an extent that they are now commercially bred in the state of Puebla the year round, but aficionados say they do not have the same flavor.

Chintesle

Señorita Abigail Mendoza, Teotitlán del Valle

Chintesle is a type of savory paste to spread on a *tlayuda* or be eaten with *tasajo*, a hard-cooked egg, or fresh cheese. It is an indispensable food for taking on picnics, pilgrimages, or any journey for that matter.

Maintaining their traditional cooking methods, Señorita Abigail and her sisters always "*calentar*"—as they would say, whereas in this case it is to lightly toast—the chiles and head of garlic in the hot, but not red, ashes of the cooking fire. First, they grind the whole chiles on the metate, but put them aside while they grind the toasted leaves with the garlic, then the shrimps with a little water. Lastly, the chiles are added and all ground together once more with a little more water, as Señorita Abigail said, to "*lavar el metate*" or "clean the metate," to make a smooth, spreadable paste.

Chintesle will last for months even without refrigeration. It can also be diluted with water and eaten as a sauce.

MAKES ABOUT 1 CUP (250 ML)

4 ounces (115 g) small, whole dried shrimps, black eyes removed
5 Oaxacan pasilla chiles, lightly toasted whole
5 *yerbasanta* leaves, toasted
1 small head garlic, toasted, cloves separated and peeled
Approximately ⅓ cup (85 ml) water

- In an ungreased skillet, toast the dried shrimps, stirring them from time to time so they toast evenly, but taking care not to let them burn, about 7 minutes, depending on size and dryness.

- If you have no intention of grinding on a metate, use a blender or food processor. First, blend the shrimps to a textured powder. Gradually add the chiles and leaves and, finally, the garlic with the water. If the blades of the machine are seizing up, then add a little more water. In that case, the mixture will have to be dried in the sun or in a slow oven.

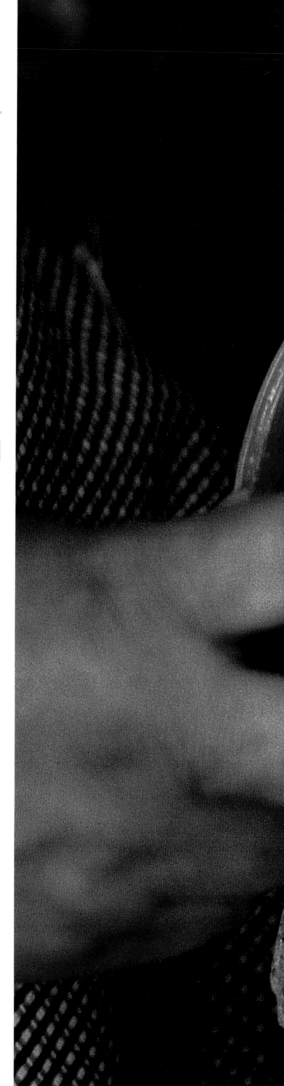

GRINDING CHILE PASILLA SAUCE IN A *CHIRMOLERA*/JORGE LÓPEZ

Chocolate Atole

SEÑORITA ABIGAIL MENDOZA, TEOTITLÁN DEL VALLE

Teotitlán del Valle is a Zapotec village in the Valley of Oaxaca, about 23 kilometers from the capital of the state, where many of the men and women are extraordinarily gifted weavers. There the inhabitants hold on steadfastly to the ancient traditions of their religious festivities and culinary heritage, and no festival of whatever nature would be complete without serving chocolate *atole*, a white *atole* topped with a very pale, coffee-colored foam, to the guests. If, on arriving at a home, you are first offered a bowl of hot chocolate accompanied by a *bizcocho* (a round semisweet bread with an inflated, hollow surface sprinkled with red sugar), it is a sure sign that you will be offered *chocolate atole* later on.

The basic *atole* is made, as usual, with a masa of corn cooked without lime, *tiziahual*, but the foam is produced by diluting and beating a paste made of a sophisticated mixture of toasted cacao beans ground with *cacao blanco* (white cacao), corn or wheat, and cinnamon.

But white cacao! The genuine ingredient—there are many fake copies—undergoes a rather prolonged and laborious process delegated to one of the very few specialists in the village. To begin with, the cacao must be of the finest quality Pataxle from Chiapas, which has a lightish brown color in its raw state. The beans are put into a large clay pot, covered with water, and left to soak for one week.

Meanwhile, if one doesn't already exist, those in charge of the work dig a pit approximately 2 m (6½ ft.) long, 1.5 m (5 ft.) wide, and about 1.5 m (5 ft.) deep—large enough to hold 100 kilos (220 lbs.) of cacao beans. The beans are placed in the pit and covered with water, with a layer of sand to keep any insects out, and finally with a *petate* (a woven mat). The contents are inspected daily and more water added if necessary.

After one month, the cacao is washed (they say that it "*huele muy feo*," "smells bad") and again covered up; this process is repeated six times. By this time, it should be white and not have a bad odor; it will have been reduced to half the original quantity.

The paste for the foam is made at least 2 days before it is to be used so that it will dry out sufficiently; but most families always have some on hand ready for an unexpected occasion.

Since this recipe is for the record only, I will give it in its original weights:

BEATING CACAO FOR FOAM FOR CHOCOLATE *ATOLE*/DIANA KENNEDY

250 g cacao beans
125 g white cacao
300 g wheat, whole grains
15 g cinnamon bark

- The cacao beans are toasted (traditionally on a clay comal) until the outer skin is brittle enough to remove. After cleaning the comal, the wheat is toasted until browned and brittle. It is then ground to a flour on a metate.

- The toasted and peeled cacao is then ground with the cinnamon on a metate (one strictly reserved for cacao) over the low heat of a wood fire.

- The white cacao is then peeled and ground on another metate, without heat, because, Abigail warns, it is greasy and if the natural oil exudes, the cacao will not produce the required foam. Then all the ingredients are ground together over a low heat until, after four *pasados*, or grindings, on the metate, a cohesive paste is formed.

- It is then divided into equal pieces, which are rolled into balls to be dried in the sun.

- When the occasion arises to prepare this festive drink, depending on the number of guests, a number of the balls are broken up and dissolved in water in a scrupulously clean *cazuela* (traces of sugar or fats in particular will impede the volume of foam).

- Then the beating begins with a wooden *molinillo*. Then comes the test of dexterity, when a woman's prestige is at stake. The experts will soon achieve a thick layer of foam on the liquid. This is scooped off with a *jícara*, sweetened with sugar, and floated on top of a bowl, or gourd, of hot *atole*. The unfortunate woman who does not manage to get a good head of foam, however hard she tries, is said to have had either unclean utensils or been affected by "*mal de ojo*"—perhaps a child or visitor has come near precipitously, hot and flurried—so a remedy has to be found. A pregnant woman is brought in to beat and bring life back into the foam.

Conejo en amarillo
(Rabbit in Yellow Mole)

SEÑOR ALEJANDRO RUIZ, LA RAYA DE ZIMATLÁN

Señor Alejandro gave me his mother's recipe for preparing a rabbit in this mole and for cooking in the same sauce the tiny wild mushrooms, *nanacates*, that appear in the rainy season along the riverbanks near the village.

Pitiona (*Lantana involucrata*) is a rather pungent herb used in a few recipes in the Central Valleys of Oaxaca mostly and on the coast, where it is called *candó*. I suggest substituting sage leaves or oregano.

The *amarillo* is served with chiles de agua in lime juice (recipe p. 25) and tortillas.

ABOUT 6 PORTIONS

3 pounds (about 1.5 kg) rabbit, cleaned and cut into 8 serving pieces
2 quarts (2 L) water
Salt to taste
3 Mexican bay leaves or 1½ bay laurel
4 mild black peppercorns
1 small white onion, roughly chopped
½ small head of garlic
2 sprigs *pitiona* (see Glossary)

THE SAUCE

6 guajillo chiles, cleaned of seeds and veins
2 garlic cloves, toasted and peeled
½ medium white onion, cut into thirds and toasted
4 peppercorns, crushed
2 cloves, crushed
3 tablespoons lard
2¼ pounds (about 1 kg) tomatoes, toasted
8 ounces (about 200 g) tortilla masa
2 sprigs *pitiona*

- Put enough water to cover the meat into a pan; add salt, the bay leaves, pepper, onion, garlic, and *pitiona* and cook over medium heat for about 5 minutes. Add the rabbit and cook over low heat until tender, about 45 minutes, depending on the age of the animal. Strain, reserving the broth. You will need about 4 cups (1 L). Reduce or add water up to that amount.

- Briefly toast the chiles, cover with hot water, and leave to soak for 10 minutes. Strain and set aside.

- Put ½ cup (125 ml) of the rabbit broth in the blender; add the garlic, onion, and spices and blend well. Heat the lard in a casserole, add the blended ingredients, and fry over high heat for about 2 minutes. Blend the tomatoes and add to the pan and cook over high heat for about 5 minutes.

- Put the chiles in the blender with 1 cup (250 ml) of the rabbit broth and blend to a purée. Add to the pan through a strainer, pressing down well—there will be some pieces of guajillo skin left in the strainer—and cook, stirring and scraping the bottom of the pan to prevent sticking, for about 10 minutes.

- Put 1 cup (250 ml) of the broth into the blender. Add the masa and mix until smooth.

- Add to the pan, stirring to avoid lumps forming. When the sauce begins to thicken, add the meat and the remaining broth and continue cooking for about 30 minutes.

- The sauce should be of medium consistency. Add the *pitiona* 5 minutes before serving.

HONGOS EN AMARILLO

(WILD MUSHROOMS IN YELLOW MOLE)
SEÑOR ALEJANDRO RUIZ, LA RAYA DE ZIMATLÁN

If small wild mushrooms are not available, use cultivated ones, cutting them into small pieces.

2 tablespoons melted pork lard
4 tablespoons finely chopped onion
4 garlic cloves, peeled and finely chopped
2¼ pounds (about 1 kg) cleaned mushrooms (see note above)
Salt to taste
4 *yerbasanta* leaves, stalks and main vein removed, cut into strips

- Heat the lard in a large skillet and fry the onion and garlic until translucent.

- Add the mushrooms, with salt to taste, until the juice has been absorbed and they just begin to brown. Transfer to the mole and cook over medium heat for about 15 minutes, adding the *yerbasanta* about 5 minutes before serving.

CALABACITAS CRIOLLOS AND FLOWERS/DIANA KENNEDY

Frijoles negros con hierba de conejo (Black Beans with Hierba de Conejo)

SEÑORITA ABIGAIL MENDOZA, TEOTITLÁN DEL VALLE

This "rabbit" herb (*Tridax coronopiifolia*), with its long, narrow serrated leaves that are rough to the touch, gives a delicate but distinctive flavor to the beans. Señorita Abigail adds a whole bunch because the stems in themselves have a lot of flavor. It is interesting that she also adds 6 sprigs of *piojito* (*Galinsoga parviflora*), a much more delicate herb that grows wild and has almost the same flavor. (*Note:* It is impossible to give a substitute for the herbs, but even without them, this method of cooking black beans is delicious.)

When served with masa balls, *chochoyotes*, and watercress, this dish makes a substantial and healthy meal (even with the fat of the masa balls).

4–5 PORTIONS

8 ounces (about 250 g) black beans, picked over, rinsed, and strained
1 very large scallion, cut into 4 with leaves
½ small head of garlic, halved horizontally, unpeeled
Salt to taste
1 small bunch of *hierba de conejo*
6 sprigs *piojito*
12 *chochoyotes* (see recipe p. 29)

To serve:
2 cups (500 ml) coarsely chopped watercress
Approximately ½ cup (125 ml) finely chopped white onion
Strips of chile de agua in lime juice (recipe p. 25)

- Put the beans into a large pot with the onion, garlic, and salt. Cover well with water and cook over medium flame for 1 hour. Add the herbs and continue cooking until the beans are soft but still very brothy, about 1½ hours, depending on the age of the beans.

- Discard the stalks of the *hierba de conejo*.

- While the beans are still on high simmer, add the *chochoyotes* and cook over medium heat until they float to the surface and the masa is cooked through, about 15 minutes.

- Serve the beans with plenty of broth, a few of the *chochoyotes*, and topped with the watercress, passing the onion and chiles separately.

Higaditos de fandango

SEÑORITA ABIGAIL MENDOZA, TEOTITLÁN DEL VALLE

Abigail's brother was getting married, and it was to be *fandango*, a four-day celebration in their home in Teotitlán. I was invited and was able to see at firsthand the preparation of this festive breakfast for five hundred people, including guests and helpers.

When I arrived, the women in charge of preparing the *higaditos* were taking it in turns to stir the egg and meat mixture in huge vats with long wooden paddles. (I have also seen the same dish made many times by Abigail on a smaller scale for a class, but it still involved using 30 eggs!)

There are, of course, very specific instructions for, and folklore around, their preparation.

For example, the meat and the eggs have to be from *gallinas criollas*, locally raised hens. And the eggs have to be beaten until they make a slapping sound and hang in thick strands from the knife; they must never be foamy. Traditionally, they would use two sticks of reed to beat them instead of a knife.

When cooking the *higaditos*, if the egg mixture will not set and looks curdled, somebody has caused *mal de ojo*, given it the evil eye, by arriving on the scene hot and in a hurry. There are several remedies to be applied: burning two reeds in the fire behind the pot, and if that doesn't work, putting the *tejolote*, or pestle, of the *molcajete* in the pot, or adding a chile. But if all else fails, they search for a pregnant woman to stir the mixture a couple of times until it finally reaches the right consistency.

The *higaditos* are served in bowls, with a dried chile sauce and *tlayudas*.

10-12 PORTIONS

1 large chicken (preferably a hen), cut into pieces, with feet and giblets
8 garlic cloves, peeled and coarsely chopped
1 heaped teaspoon cumin seeds
⅓ cup (85 ml) water
1 large scallion (*cebolla de rabo*), coarsely chopped with leaves
15 eggs
Salt to taste
4 medium tomatoes, cut into 4 sections, seeds removed

- Put the chicken, with giblets and feet, into a pot with water to cover well and cook (without salt) until tender, about 35 minutes. Strain, reserving the broth. You will need about 8 cups (2 L); if not, add water to make that amount.

- When the chicken is cool enough to handle, remove the bones and break up the meat (do not shred) with the skin. You will only need half the meat, so reserve the other half for some enchiladas or tacos.

- Crush the garlic together with the cumin and dilute with the ⅓ cup (85 ml) water.

- Add ¼ of this mixture with the onion to the broth and boil over medium heat for 5 minutes.

- In a large bowl, beat the eggs with the salt until thick ribbons form (see note above), stir in the meat with the rest of the garlic-cumin mixture, and add to the broth. Continue cooking over medium heat, and as the eggs cook, press the curds together with a perforated spoon until you have a compact mass of eggs and meat and the broth is completely clear, about 20 minutes. About 3 minutes before it reaches this point, add the tomatoes and cook briefly; they should not become too soft or fall apart.

- Serve the *higaditos* in bowls, each with 2 pieces of tomato, and the chile sauce apart.

Memelas en pasta de semilla de calabaza (Memelas in Pumpkin-Seed Paste)

SEÑORITA ABIGAIL MENDOZA, TEOTITLÁN DEL VALLE

These *memelas* in a diluted pumpkin-seed paste are prepared as a main meal during Lent. They are served with *queso fresco* or hard-cooked eggs and strips of chile de agua and often with a plate of toasted dried shrimps to accompany them. At other times of the year, they are eaten with a piece of grilled *tasajo*.

The *memelas*, made of tortilla masa, are thin and oval in shape: about 2 inches (5 cm) wide and 3 inches (about 8 cm) long. They are cooked on a comal and immediately immersed in the sauce (diluted paste). It is customary to serve the *memelas* not on a plate, but on top of a large tortilla or *tlayuda*, which is then rolled up to eat like a taco.

Señorita Abigail always toasts the pumpkin seeds on a clay griddle covered with a coating of lime. She moves them around constantly, with either a dried cornhusk or a halved *jícara*, so that they toast evenly. The seeds are then ground to a paste on the metate. It is hard work because the paste has to be ground on the metate as many as ten times to obtain a smooth texture. (When trying the recipe, I naturally used another method. Even just putting them into the food processor doesn't do it.)

MAKES ABOUT 2 CUPS (500 ML) SAUCE FOR 6 *MEMELAS*

1 cup (250 ml) unhulled pumpkin seeds—3½ ounces (100 g)
4 avocado leaves (see Note on Toxicity, p. 426), toasted
1 chile de árbol, toasted whole
Approximately 1½ cups (375 ml) water
Salt to taste

- Put the seeds into a skillet over a very low flame and keep moving them around so that they toast evenly. The husks should be lightly browned, after about 13 minutes. Set aside to cool and then grind to a powder (I find it best to first grind in the blender and then in the electric spice grinder). Toward the end of the grinding, add and grind the avocado leaves and chile. Transfer to a bowl and add ¼ cup (65 ml) water and mix to a paste, adding salt to taste.

- When ready to use, dilute with the remaining water. Dip the *memelas* into the sauce, which should cover them thickly, and serve them either alone or in the traditional way.

Mole zapoteco
(Zapotec Mole)

SEÑORITA ABIGAIL MENDOZA, TEOTITLÁN DEL VALLE

This mole, under the puzzling name of *mole de Castilla,* has for years been the most important dish served for weddings and *mayordomías* in the Zapotec villages around Teotitlán. But now the *grande dame* of Zapotec cooking has decided it should be called *mole zapoteco.*

Señorita Abigail says that the herbs should be fresh to obtain just the right flavor, and that the chiles should be prepared the day before. The bread used to thicken the sauce at the end, *pan de mole,* is specially made for this mole in Tlacolula. It is not sweet. One roll yields about 1 cup (250 ml) crumbs.

The mole is served with the meat and tortillas: *blandas* or *tlayudas.* Of course, the flavor will be much better if the turkey and chickens are *criollos,* or locally raised.

ABOUT 10 PORTIONS

1 turkey or 2 chickens, cut into serving pieces
Salt to taste
9 ounces (250 g) guajillo chiles—about 35–40 (depending on how dry they are)
4½ ounces (125 g) ancho chiles—about 7
4 small heads garlic
10 allspice, crushed
10 cloves, crushed
1 teaspoon crushed cumin seeds
⅓ cup (about 5 g) fresh *orégano criollo* leaves (or substitute marjoram)
½ cup (about 5 g) fresh thyme leaves
10 cups (2.5 L) toasted breadcrumbs (see note above), coarsely crumbled

- Put the pieces of turkey or chicken in a large pot, cover with water, add salt, and cook over low heat until the meat is tender—about 40 minutes for the chicken and 55 minutes for the turkey, depending on quality. Strain, reserving the broth; you will need about 12 cups (3 L) for the mole. Add water, if necessary, to make up that amount.

- *This step can be done the day before*: Remove seeds and veins from the chiles, reserving the seeds. Heat a comal over low heat and toast the chiles, turning them so they toast evenly, until they are *dorados*, golden, being careful not to let them burn. Rinse, strain, and then soak in fresh water for about 5 minutes. Strain again. In a skillet, also over low heat, toast the chile seeds, moving them around to toast evenly, to a golden color, no darker. Cover with water, leave to soak for 5 minutes, then strain.

- Toast the heads of garlic on the comal (or, better still, traditionally in hot ashes). Separate the cloves and peel. (Again traditionally, the ingredients would be ground with very little water on the metate or sent to the *molino*. However, without these options, use the blender.)

- Put ½ cup (125 ml) of the broth into the blender jar and add first the spices and seeds and blend well. Add another ½ (125 ml) cup broth with the garlic and herbs and blend again until almost smooth. Gradually add the chiles with 1 more cup (250 ml) of the broth and blend to a soft, slightly textured paste.

- Add this to a casserole with the remaining broth and cook over medium heat for 20 minutes. Add meat and salt to taste and cook a further 10 minutes. Then stir in the breadcrumbs about ½ cup (125 ml) at a time so that they are absorbed before you add the next lot. Reserve the remaining bread. (You may not need to add the whole quantity.) Cook for about 5 minutes more. The mole should not be thick, but rather of medium consistency.

Abigail Mendoza cutting cactus/Diana Kennedy

Nopal grueso en caldillo
(Thick Nopal Served in Its Broth)

SEÑORITA ABIGAIL MENDOZA, TEOTITLÁN DEL VALLE

There is a belief in the Zapotec village of Teotitlán that if you cut this big, fat nopal on a cloudy morning, or if you are jealous of someone, the nopal will turn out to be very acidy.

This nopal is called *de Castilla*, *gruesa*, or *de toro*, among other names. It is used in many parts of Oaxaca. In the Mixteca and the Sierra Sur, it is cooked by grilling, *asando*, over a hot fire, but in Teotitlán, it is boiled and served like a soup with chopped onion, a sauce of chile pasilla, and *tlayudas*. For a more substantial meal, it is accompanied by a piece of grilled beef liver *tasajo*.

Abigail added another interesting note: Years ago it was customary to prepare for this *caldillo* large, oval *memelas* about 12 inches (30 cm) long and 4 inches (10 cm) wide and about ½ inch (about 1.5 cm) thick. They were made of a very different *nixtamal*: The dried corn was left to soak in a lime solution for one hour only. Without the usual washing to remove the skins, it was then ground on the metate, through three *pasados*, to a roughly textured masa. The *memelas* were formed and cooked on a comal in the usual way and then left to dry out around the edge of the comal, as is done for drying *tlayudas*. They were then broken into pieces, which were used to sop up the *caldillo*.

After cutting three large *pencas* (fleshy "leaves") and scraping off the thorns with a machete, a thin slice was cut off around the periphery. Then Señorita Abigail cut the *pencas* into pieces and rinsed them in cold water. A large earthenware pot filled with water was put over the fire and the nopal was added with 12 avocado leaves and two large sprigs of epazote. Once the water had come to a boil, salt was added and the nopal cooked until the inner flesh was soft; this took about 25 minutes.

Two pieces of the nopal were served with their broth in deep dishes, but before attempting to eat them, Señorita Abigail mashed the pieces down to loosen the inside flesh from the tough outer skin. It is customary to do this with a *tejumate*, half of a small, hollowed-out gourd. And not to waste one scrap, Abigail and her mother, who was with us, chewed and sucked on the tough skin as well.

ABIGAIL MENDOZA PREPARING CACTUS FOR SOUP/
DIANA KENNEDY

YOUNG WOMEN SIFTING CORN FOR *FANDANGO*/
DIANA KENNEDY

Salsa de chile seco (Dried-Chile Sauce)

This is a very thin and completely smooth sauce that is ground in Teotitlán on the metate.

Although chile chontal is called for, costeños rojos can be substituted.

10 chiles secos
2 garlic cloves, peeled and coarsely chopped
Salt to taste
Approximately 1 cup (250 ml) water

- Toast the whole chiles very lightly and grind together with the garlic and salt, adding the water to make a very thin consistency.

DIANA KENNEDY BY BREAD OVEN AT QUINTA/PEDRO VALTIERRA

About Diana Kennedy and the Contributors

PULLING DIANA KENNEDY'S CAMIONETA OUT OF A DITCH NEAR OAXACA COAST/DIANA KENNEDY

MUD-COVERED TRUCK WITH TRAVEL COMPANIONS MAESTRA GLORIA AND DRIVER FELIPE IN THE SIERRA ABOVE CUICATLÁN/DIANA KENNEDY

PHOTOGRAPHING TAMAL TUXTEPAC/ CONCEPCIÓN GUADALUPE GARZA

TAKING A SIESTA IN THE ISTHMUS HEAT

DIANA SOUTHWOOD KENNEDY arrived in Mexico in 1957. She is widely considered the foremost researcher, teacher, and writer on the regional foods of Mexico and has written eight books on the subject. She has been bestowed the highest honor given to foreigners by the Mexican government, the Order of the Aztec Eagle, for her work of disseminating Mexican culture through its foods. She has also received numerous awards from other gastronomic institutions and was decorated with an MBE by Queen Elizabeth for her work of strengthening cultural relations between Mexico and the United Kingdom. For the past thirty years, her studies have been centered around her ecological house in the state of Michoacán.

AMADO RAMÍREZ LEYVA, born in the Mixteca Baja region of Oaxaca, is the founder of the Proyecto "Itanoni Flor de Maíz." He is a pioneer in the recognition and identification of native races of corn and their development. He is the promoter of their traditional uses as a way to conserve their diversity.

FRAY EUGENIO MARTÍN TORRES TORRES, born in the City of Guanajuato, is a Dominican friar and a historian of the mining and evangelization by his order in Oaxaca. Since 1997, he has been doing pastoral work with indigenous groups in Oaxaca, especially among the Mixes, Trijes, Chatinos, and Zapotecs. Since 2005, he has been the director of the Dominican Institute for Historical Research and a professor at the Autonomous University of Querétaro.

MARCUS WINTER has worked for more than thirty-five years as an archaeologist in the Oaxaca office of the Mexican National Institute of Anthropology and History. He has directed excavations in various regions of the state, including Monte Albán and Macuilxóchitl in the Valley of Oaxaca, Huamelulpan and Yucuita in the Mixteca Alta, Cerro de las Minas in the Mixteca Baja, and most recently at several sites in the Isthmus of Tehuantepec.

Notes to the Cook

These brief notes should just be considered a guide to certain aspects of the ingredients and techniques of Oaxaca. However, since this is not a book of basics that gives instructions about how to make tortilla masa, etc., I recommend you consult my book *From My Mexican Kitchen: Techniques and Ingredients* (see bibliography).

ASADO: See TOAST.

ASIENTO and ZORRAPA (described on pp. 428 and 430, respectively): These two ingredients are both used to enrich the masa for some tamales, but *asiento* is also used for *chochoyotes*, or to spread on tortillas. *Asiento* is usually available in Mexican markets in areas where there is a concentration of Oaxacan immigrants—California in particular. *Asiento* can be duplicated by melting lard with crispy crumbs of *chicharrón* until it acquires a dark color. For *zorrapa*, use the melted lard but with crispy pieces of pure fat.

AVOCADO LEAVES: One of the intriguing flavors of black beans in Oaxacan cooking is lent by the leaves of the native, or *criollo*, avocado trees. These can often be found dried, either broken up in packages or powdered, in Mexican food markets.

Note on Toxicity: Care should be taken when substituting other varieties, according to the following note on their toxicity, which has been published in my other books. The toxicity reports relate to a study done in 1984 at the University of California at Davis, which showed that dairy goats suffered some toxic effects from ingesting very large amounts of avocado leaves (the toxic agent remains unknown). The crucial point according to Dr. Arthur L. Craigmill, toxicology specialist at Davis and one of the authors of the study, is that the toxic effects were traced to the Guatemalan avocado (*Persea americana*). When the goats were fed Mexican avocados (*Persea drymifolia*), a different variety, there were no problems.

The Hass avocado, the best-tasting one grown in America, is a hybrid of indeterminate origin, though its DNA tests positive for a Guatemalan ancestor—hence the suspicions. No one has ever tested the Hass leaves for toxicity, but it seems unlikely that the small amounts used in cooking would cause any problems in any case. When in doubt, choose based on taste, and that leads you to the aromatic Mexican leaves.

CHILES: There are many chiles, both fresh and dried, unique to Oaxaca. Substitutes are generally given for the fresh chiles. The most

important dried chiles: pasilla de Oaxaca (or chile Mixe), costeños, and chilhuacles can be obtained from The Chile Guy (www.thechileguy .com); also try www.mymexicanpantry.com or www.mesamexican-foods.com/market. *Method*: Larger dried chiles used in the moles are generally toasted, rinsed, strained, and then soaked in fresh water until reconstituted. The smaller dried chiles used for uncooked (table) sauces served as condiments are usually toasted crisp, with seeds, and ground without soaking.

CINNAMON STICK: Make sure you use the soft, layered cinnamon "bark." It is the dried, rolled bark of a tree, Ceylon cinnamon (*Cinnamomum verum*). The darker-colored, harder stick sold as cinnamon is *Cassia*, not cinnamon at all. It has a different flavor and is practically impossible to grind. Take care when buying because it is invariably mislabeled, especially when packed commercially in glass containers or jars.

GARLIC: Traditionally, the heads of garlic are small, and recipes often call for them to be toasted (*asado*) whole. The cloves are then separated and peeled. For broths, the heads are cut into halves horizontally and added unpeeled.

MASA: This is the word used in Mexico generally to denote a smooth dough of finely ground (dried) corn that has been very briefly cooked and left to soak in a solution of lime (Calcium oxide); it is used for tortillas, *tlayudas*, *memelas*, and some types of tamales. A more coarsely ground masa is used for other types of tamales. Then there is *tlaxiahual*, a masa made by substituting the lime for a large quantity of wood ash; it is used for yet another type of tamale and for thickening moles. Masa used for making *atoles* is made of (dried) corn that has been briefly cooked in water alone. It is then ground and strained and cooked for the *atole*.

OREGANO: You will notice that the quantities given for Oaxacan oregano is for leaves only and is double the amounts given for the more ubiquitous Mexican oregano. The reason for this is that the "oregano" mostly used in the cooking of central Oaxaca is a dried marjoram that is sold in bunches with all the stems and is much lighter in flavor.

PORK LARD: Many recent studies on lard have totally vindicated it, so unless dietary or religious reasons prohibit it, it should be used where indicated. Of course, I don't mean the white solid stuff sold in many supermarkets, but the real thing. It can be found in Mexican and other ethnic markets: Italian, Hungarian, etc. But if not readily available, it is easy to make, and instructions are given in all my books (see *From My Mexican Kitchen: Techniques and Ingredients*).

TOAST: In Oaxaca (and generally throughout Mexico), there is a method of cooking a number of ingredients—tomatoes, *tomates verdes*, onion pieces, whole heads or unpeeled garlic cloves—referred to as *asado* (see photo p. 98 showing a clay comal coated with a paste of lime, the typical tool used for this process). These ingredients are placed on an ungreased comal over medium heat and turned until the surface is browned, even slightly charred, and the flesh quite soft. In the case of

dried chiles, *asado* means that they are toasted slowly to a point that, when cooled, they are crisp. The word "toast" is used throughout for *asado*.

TOMATOES: In most areas of Oaxaca, ordinary red tomatoes are called *tomates rojos*. When cooked for sauces, they are either *toasted* (see description above) or boiled. The latter method is different from that of most other parts of Mexico. The tomatoes are halved and stewed in the minimum of water. The same method is used for cooking *tomates verdes* (tomatillos in the United States; in Mexico, tomatillos are very small *tomates verdes*), which in Oaxaca, are also called *tomate de milpa*, *miltomate*, *tomate milpero*, or *tomate de cáscara*.

Asando tomatoes/Diana Kennedy

Glossary

Note: Descriptions of lesser-known ingredients are generally given in the text of the recipes in which they appear.

ACHIOTE (*Bixa orellana*). The seed of the annatto tree has a red coating that is used as a dye and flavoring for many dishes throughout southern Mexico (see photo p. 143). In Oaxaca, it is prepared in a paste alone (see photo p. 187) and not with the added condiments used in the seasoning's paste, *recados*, of Yucatán.

AHUATE. Small, almost invisible thorns that cover some plants, for example, nopales.

ALMUERZO. Generally refers to a late, substantial breakfast, like a brunch.

AMARILLO. Generally refers to a mole that is either yellow or a deep orange color, depending on the chile with which it is prepared, which can vary regionally (see photo p. 8).

ANTOJITO. A *botana,* or snack, generally based on a corn dough called masa.

ASADURA. Offal, generally of pork, beef, or goat.

ASIENTO. The residual "crumbs" in dark-colored lard left at the bottom of the vat in which *chicharrón* (sheets of crisp-fried pork rind) has been fried.

ATOLE. The most important indigenous nutritional drink of Mexico dating back to pre-Hispanic times. It is a gruel of corn masa traditionally prepared with dried corn that has been barely cooked, without lime, and ground to a fine masa. It is served hot or cold, sweetened or seasoned, with a variety of ingredients, depending on the local custom.

AYOCOTE. A large bean with a silvery-grayish skin used in the Oaxaca Valley, where it is called *frijolón*. The red flower is also eaten.

BLANDAS. The name given in Oaxaca for large, soft corn tortillas.

BOTANA OAXAQUEÑA. A snack to pick at with drinks; differs from an *antojito*, which is (usually) made of masa.

CALABAZAS. Pumpkins; two of the most commonly used pumpkins are *tamala* and *huichi*. They are used in stews, for tamales, or in desserts. The seeds are used in *pipián* sauces or toasted for snacks. The vines are used for a soup.

CARDON. The small, round fruit of a cactus (*Opuntia streptacantha*).

Its deep-red-colored flesh is studded with small black seeds. The fruits are eaten raw, or the flesh is fermented for *tepache* (p. 250) and the seeds used to make a sauce (p. 253).

CEBOLLÍN/ES, CEBOLLINA (*Allium schoenoprasum*). A small wild onion with chivelike leaves (see photo p. 121).

CHAPULQUELITE (*Cleome serrulata*). A wild plant (see photo p. 335) also cultivated as a *quelite* and eaten in the Sierra Mazateca and Sierra Juárez.

CHICAL. The name given to a gourd (see photo p. 99) in the Papaloapan area used to keep tortillas hot.

CHICHILO. A type of mole for which chile seeds and tortillas are burned black (see photo p.19).

CHINTESLE. A type of paste used to spread on tortillas and especially to take on picnics or journeys.

CHIRMOLERA or CHILMOLERA. A clay bowl for grinding ingredients for raw sauces (see photo p. 411). The surface inside is deeply scored.

CHOCHOYOTE. A small masa dumpling (see photo p. 29). It is round in shape with a depression in the center to ensure even cooking of the dough. It is often enriched with *asiento* (see above) or lard and added to soups, beans, and some moles.

COCOLMÉCATL. A climbing tropical plant (*Smilax* sp.; see photos pp. 113 and 149) mainly used as a catalyst to create foam for the topping of *atoles* in the Chinantla and Yalalag areas. Also used as a *quelite* to fill empanadas.

COMIZCAL. A tall clay oven (photo p. 191) made in a round, globular shape. It is secured firmly over a small fire pit in the ground or a specially constructed concrete counter. As with the Indian tandoor, the cooking is done on the sides of the *comizcal* that have been heated by a fire in the bottom. *Totopos* or even fish are cooked on the sides of the oven, and tamales are piled inside over the hot embers (photo p. 222).

CUANESLE. Masa made of corn cooked with ash; used to thicken moles and for certain types of tamales.

CUCHARILLA (*Dasylirion* sp.). The creamy white base of the long, narrow serrated leaf of a succulent used mostly as a decoration for religious festivals but also as an eating implement in the Mixteca Alta.

CUETLA. A large black caterpillar eaten in the Sierra Mazateca and Sierra Mixe, among other areas.

ELOTE. Fresh, tender corn.

GUAJES (*Leucaena* spp.). Pods of trees whose seeds are eaten as a snack or ground for a stew in the Mixteca Baja.

GUAZMOLE or GUAXMOLE. Name given to different dishes, depending on the region. In the Sierra Mazateca, it is made from the fruit of *Renealmia* sp. (same as *cherimole* elsewhere; see photo p. 343); in the Mixteca Baja, it refers to a stew made with *guajes*.

HOJA DE MILPA. Long, thin leaves of the corn plant used mainly to wrap tamales (see photo p. 148).

MAÍZ NUEVO. Mature corn in the first stages of the (field-) drying process.

MASA. A dough of *nixtamal*, dried corn cooked in a lime solution and ground either to a smooth consistency for tortillas or to a textured consistency for tamales.

MASA CUESTE. Masa ground as finely as possible for tortillas, *blandas*, and *tlayudas*.

MASA MARTAJADA. Masa ground to a rough texture for some tamales or *tlaxiahual*.

MAYORDOMÍA. A ritual feast arranged by a *mayordomo* or *mayordoma* to celebrate the patron saint of the local church.

MEMELA. A thick tortilla of masa, often oval in shape.

MILTOMATE or TOMATE DE CÁSCARA. See TOMATE VERDE (tomatillo in United States).

MOJO. A seasoning of Cuban origin found in the Papaloapan area of Oaxaca; a mixture usually made of garlic crushed with lime juice and salt.

MOLCAJETE and TEJOLOTE. Volcanic rock mortar and pestle used to crush spices, chiles, and other ingredients and especially to prepare raw sauces (see photo p. 159).

PANELA. Round or rectangular cakes of unrefined sugar (see photo p. 258; called *piloncillo* when conical in form.

PICADILLO. A chopped-meat filling for chiles rellenos, empanadas, and enchiladas.

PILTE. The name given to food wrapped and cooked in *yerbasanta* leaves.

PIXTLE. Oleaginous pit of the mamey (*Pouteria sapota*) fruit, used by some cooks to make *tejate* (see p. 127).

POCHICUIL. Large caterpillar eaten in the Sierra Mazateca (see photo p. 354).

POZOLE. Soup/stew usually made with pork and based on large white corn kernels.

POZOLE LEAF (*Calathea lutea*). A broad, shiny leaf the underside of which is covered with a whitish waxy film that renders it waterproof. The leaf is used for wrapping tamales, and other cooked or raw foods (see photo p. 115).

QUELITES. Edible wild greens, now often cultivated.

QUESILLO. Better known as *queso de Oaxaca*, this is a cheese made of a mixture of fresh and slightly acidic milk. The curds are cooked and stretched into skeins, which are then rolled into balls of different sizes (see photo p. 388).

QUINTONIL (*Amaranthus* spp.). A popular *quelite*, or wild green.

ROSITA DE CACAO. A small white flower of a tree (*Quararibea funebre*) that is used dried for *tejate*.

SICUA. A natural fiber used for tying tamales, for instance.

TASAJO. Very thin, wide strips of beef, salted and semidried.

TEJATE. An indigenous frothy drink with pre-Hispanic roots, served cold (see p. 399).

TENATE. A type of basket, traditionally made of a palm that grows wild in the Mixteca, that is used for storing tortillas or other foods.

TEPACHE. A fermented drink made from fruits or sugarcane.

TEQUESQUITE. A natural mineral salt (*sexquicarbonato de soda y cloruro*) used since pre-Hispanic times. It is used diluted in water as a raising agent for tamale masa and to soften beans, etc. Found abundantly in the dried lakebeds of Mexico's central plateau.

TESMOLE. Name given to rather soupy dishes in the Sierra Mazateca.

TLAXIAHUAL. Masa made of corn that has not been cooked with lime; used for *atoles* and some types of tamales.

TLAYUDA or CLAYUDA. Large corn tortilla that is semidried, almost leathery.

TOMATE CRIOLLO. A native tomato that is mostly harvested in the dry months, particularly, but not exclusively, in the Isthmus. It is formed like a "beefsteak" tomato, pleated at the top. It is thin-skinned and very juicy (see photo p. 201).

TOMATE ROJO. Name used in some parts of Oaxaca for the ordinary red tomato.

TOMATE VERDE. A small green tomato (; called tomatillo in the United States.

TOTOL. Native turkey.

TOTOMOXTLE. Dried cornhusk.

TOTOPO. A crisp tortilla dotted with holes and cooked in a *comizcal*; a specialty of the Isthmus (see p. 231). They are made in various sizes, the smallest used for a *botana*.

VELA. A celebration with pagan roots to honor the saints of a local church.

VIUCES or BIUCES. Small pieces of crisp-fried pork offal.

YUCA (*Manihot esculenta* var.). A starchy root cooked as a vegetable; also used grated fresh for making tortillas and tamales in La Chinantla. Known as manioc or cassava in other parts of the world, where it is also used to make tapioca and starch. (See full details on p. 101 and photo p. 100.)

ZORRAPA. Crisp, browned crumbs of fat cut from the front skin of the pig. Used in the Isthmus (like *asiento* is used in central Oaxaca) to enrich masa for tamales and other *antojitos*.

CULINARY HERBS USED IN OAXACAN FOOD

ALMORADUZ. A highly aromatic herb, a type of marjoram, used dried in the dishes of the Sierra Sur.

BILIJÁN. A plant of the ginger family whose broad leaf is used to wrap tamales in the eastern coastal area of Oaxaca.

CANDÓ (*Lippia germinata*). The local name in the eastern coastal area of Oaxaca for *pitiona*, a rather pungent herb. Sprigs are used in soups and stews in the coastal area.

CILANTRO (*Coriandrum sativum*). Fresh sprigs are used in many areas of the state to season soups/broths, stews, and sauces. The small round green seeds are used for sauces in the Papaloapan/Chinantla area of Oaxaca.

CULANTRO or CILANTRO GRUESO (*Eryngium foetidum*). One name among others for the long serrated leaf used fresh to season soups/broths and some stews.

EPAZOTE (*Teloxys ambrosioides*). Large sprigs are used for black beans, in soups/broths and stews, with mushrooms, and in quesadillas.

HIERBABUENA or YERBABUENA (*Mentha spicata* and var.). Large mint sprigs used in soups/broths and stews.

HIERBA DE CONEJO (*Tridax coronapiifolia*). An aromatic herb with small, narrow abrasive leaves with a delicate flavor used in bunches to season black beans and, rarely, in a *mole verde*.

HIERBAMORA (*Solanum nigrum*). The tender shoots of this nightshade are used as a potherb in La Chinantla Baja and the lower areas of the Sierra Mixe.

LAUREL (*Litsea glaucescens*). These bay leaves, as they are called in Mexico, are from a tall shrub, or small tree. They are used fresh or dried, whole or crumbled, in many ways: soups, stews, *picadillos*, etc. It has a more delicate flavor than the bay laurel with which it is often confused.

MEJORANA (*Marjorana hortensis*). Marjoram; used fresh or dried to season numerous stews, moles, *picadillos*, and other dishes.

MOSTE (*Clerodendron ligustrinum*). A large shrub with small white flowers and tough shiny leaves used fresh; the latter readily burn. They are used to season dishes of the Papaloapan area of Oaxaca.

OREGANO (*O. majorana* and var.). The most commonly used "oregano" in Oaxaca is dried marjoram. It is sold, and sometimes used, with all the stems. The crumbled dried leaves are used prolifically in many Oaxacan dishes: soups, stews, moles, sauces, and particularly as a seasoning with crushed garlic. There are types of *Lippia* growing wild, for example, in the Mixteca, that are called oregano and used for seasoning *menudo*. In La Chinantla Alta, there is yet another plant with a larger triangular leaf, also a *Lippia*, that is used fresh.

OREGANO GRUESO (*Plectranthus amboinicus*). Also known as *oregano extranjero*, among other names, this herb is used fresh for soups/broths and rice dishes.

PEREJIL (*Petroselinum neapolitanum*). This flat-leaved parsley is used in numerous dishes: soups/broths, stews, rice, etc., and is often used as a garnish.

PETIOLE. This is not an herb but a botanical term for the leaf-bearing bract of a plant as distinguished from the main stem.

PIOJITO (*Galinsoga parviflora*). A small wild herb used fresh with rice or in *sopa de guías*.

PITIONA (*Lippia germinata*). A pungent herb also known as *candó* on the coast; used fresh or dried, the small sprigs are used to season a few soups and stews.

POLEO (*Satureja oaxacana*). Also sometimes called *hierba de borracho*, this herb is used fresh or dried mainly with black beans or for an infusion for stomach ills or a hangover, hence its name.

TOMILLO (*Thymus vulgaris*). Thyme; used fresh or dried in countless dishes, among them soups, stews, moles, and *picadillos*.

YERBASANTA, HIERBASANTA, HOJA SANTA (*Piper auritum*). Large aromatic leaves with an anise flavor, used fresh either whole or blended for moles and soups, with eggs, or for wrapping tamales.

Bibliography

Bravo Hollis, Helia, and R. Hernando Sánchez-Mejorada. *Las cactáceas de México.* Vol. 3. Mexico City: UNAM, 1991.

Campos Villanueva, Álvaro, Luis Arriaga Cortés, Patricia Dávila Aranda, Abisai García Mendoza, Jerónimo Reyes Santiago, Griselda Toriz Acosta, Leticia Torres Colín, and Rafael Torres Colín. *Plantas y flores de Oaxaca.* Cuadernos 18, Instituto de Biología. Mexico City: UNAM, 1992.

Casas, Alejandro, Juan Luis Viveros, and Javier Caballero. *Etnobotánica mixteca.* Mexico City: Instituto Nacional Indigenista, CONACULTA, 1994.

Cook, Carmen, and Don Leonard. *Costumbres mortuorias de los indios huaves.* N.p.: Sociedad Alemana Mexicanista, 1949.

Guzmán de Vásquez Colmenares, Ana María. *Tradiciones gastronómicas oaxaqueñas.* City of Oaxaca: N.p., 1982.

Kennedy, Diana. *From My Mexican Kitchen: Techniques and Ingredients.* New York: Clarkson Potter, 2003.

López Hernández, Eusebio. *Recetas chinantecas.* Published privately, 1990.

Musálem López, Amira. *Colores, olores y sabores festivos de Juchitán, Oaxaca.* Mexico City: CONACULTA, 2002.

Rupp, Jaime. "Metáforas y proverbios chinantecos." *Tlalocan, Revista de Fuentes para el Conocimiento de las Culturas Indígenas de México* 9 (1982): 257–299.

Signorini, Ítalo. *Los huaves de San Mateo del Mar.* Mexico City: Instituto Nacional Indigenista and CONACULTA, 1979.

Tapia García, Fermín. *Recetas de platillos vegetarianos de los amuzgos.* Centro de Investigaciones y Estudios Superiores en Antropología Social (CIESAS), November 29, 2002.

Velásquez de León, Josefina. *Cocina oaxaqueña.* Mexico City: Academia de Cocina Velázquez de León, ca. 1950.

Weitlaner, Robert J., and Carlos Antonio Castro. *Usila (Morada de Colibríes).* Mexico City: Museo Nacional de Antropología, 1973.

Winter, Marcus. *Oaxaca: The Archaeological Record.* Mexico City: Minutiae Mexicana, 1989.

Ysunza Ogazón, Alberto, Silvia Diez Urdanivia, and Laurencia López Núñez. *Manual para la utilización de plantas comestibles de la Sierra Juárez de Oaxaca.* 3rd ed. Mexico City: Instituto Nacional de Nutrición Salvador Zubirán, 1998.

Index

HELPER LEAVING *FANDANGO*/DIANA KENNEDY